Instructional Leadership
Concepts, Issues, and Controversies

WILLIAM GREENFIELD
Louisiana State University

Allyn and Bacon, Inc.
Boston London Sydney Toronto

To my kids
Geoffrey, Amelia, Ara, and Monica

and

to all the teachers and school
leaders who have worked so hard
to make schools better for them,
and for children throughout our country

Copyright © 1987 by Allyn and Bacon, Inc.,
7 Wells Avenue, Newton, Massachusetts 02159

Library of Congress Cataloging-in-Publication Data

Instructional leadership.

 Bibliography: p.
 1. School management and organization—United States.
 2. School supervision—United States. I. Greenfield,
William, 1944 –   .
LB2805.I445   1987   371.2'00973   86-22308
ISBN 0-205-10297-2

Printed in the United States of America

10 9 8 7 6 5 4 3 2 1 91 90 89 88 87 86

Contents

Foreword

Doing science in any field involves the periodic assessment of progress that has been made in expanding its knowledge base. Periodic assessment also characterizes advances in practice in the established professions. Our understanding of the nature of leadership and its links to school success has increased tremendously during the last fifteen years. The road ahead to further understanding remains admittedly long. But further progress requires the clearing of the deck, so to speak, the consolidation of findings, the assessment of issues, and the careful weighing of the worth and use of what is known to date. *Instructional Leadership: Concepts, Issues, and Controversies* admirably serves this stock-taking purpose. Its editor, William Greenfield, and contributing authors provide a clear and concise analysis of what is known, of the issues which undergird this knowledge, and of the problems in translating this knowledge into practice. They take the book's subtitle, "Concepts, Issues, and Controversies," seriously by resisting the providing of neat and tidy answers to the complex problem of school leadership.

The research on school effectiveness and teaching effectiveness and their links to successful leadership are a case in point. Though this body of knowledge and accompanying prescriptions for practice are treated respectfully, they are not revered and this stance is an important earmark of scientific progress. No matter how refined a model becomes or how precisely it is translated into practice, the model cannot enlarge the basic premise upon which it rests. This is the Law of Conservation of Information well understood in the more established sciences but often forgotten by those of us who toil in more fledgling fields such as school leadership.

If this book serves no other purpose but to remind us of the Law of Conservation of Information, its worth is justified. The contributors view school leadership from a number of perspectives, including management, human relations, political, and cultural. Each perspective brings forward a set of basic premises that guide how leadership is viewed, researched, linked to school effectiveness, and shaped in the form of practice prescriptions. Models of leadership are much like windows and walls, to borrow a phrase from Dan Fogelberg. As windows, they help expand our view of things, resolve issues that we face, provide us with answers, and give us that surer footing we need in order to function as researchers and practicing school administrators. But as walls, these same models serve to box us in, to blind us to other views of reality, other understandings, other alternatives. Thus whether we are referring to the "School Effectiveness Model," views of schooling aligned with the concept of "Loose-Coupling," or those that provide a more "cultural" perspective, our vision is both increased and decreased at the same time.

The windows and walls problem in school leadership can be illustrated by the following example. Not only did I read the manuscript of this book before it was placed into final form, but I had access as well to the initial prospectus and to reviews of the book in progress. I was struck by what different reviewers considered to be of most worth among the selections in the book and by those selections with which they had difficulty. One reviewer, for example, cited a special affinity for chapters that provided a tighter, linear, more certain view of the issues and surer prescriptions for practice but had difficulty with chapters that relied on case studies, cultural and loose-coupling concepts. "Beware of authors' biases that affect accuracy," the reviewer cautioned. He complained that two of the chapters were questionable because the authors were "unresolved regarding effective schools research and its applicability to the principalship." A second reviewer found these same chapters to be "fascinating" and commented about one of them as follows: "Puts a new perspective on all the work that has appeared before it, and his article is in my view a keystone to understanding the effective schools research." Each of the reviewers brought to the review task a different mindscape of the nature of teaching and leadership and a different understanding of how schools and other organizations operate. This mindscape, like windows and walls, helped provide a sense of rationality and order to the review task, but also blinded the reviewer to alternative perspectives. Unless one gets beyond his or her windows and walls and is able to understand the limits posed by the Law of Conservation of Information, the contents of this book will be viewed as little more than an academic debate—with winners and losers being chosen on the basis of the reader's existing mindscape of how the world of schooling works.

Part of the problem, I think, is that most of us are conditioned to view educational administration as if it were an applied science. Within applied science, practice is enhanced by scientific knowledge on the one hand and by knowledge that emerges from one's experience as an administrator and understanding of the particular context for practice on the other. Knowledge in applied science is created through theorizing and discipline-oriented research. This knowledge is then used to build and field test models of practice through which universal prescriptions and treatments are to be generated. These are, in turn, communicated to professionals for their use in practice. The professional searches the context in which she or he works, carefully diagnosing and characterizing contingencies and situations according to predetermined and standardized protocols. Practices gleaned from research are then matched systematically to these problems.

Applied science, however, frames our thinking too narrowly by projecting an imagery of tight alignment between the worlds of theory and research and the world of practice. Applied science conceptions of school leadership, for example, require practice conditions of reliability, predictability, and stability in order for them to be useful. Patterns of school practice, however, are characterized by a great deal of uncertainty, instability, complexity, and variety. Value conflicts and uniquenesses are accepted aspects of educational settings. For these reasons professional knowledge construed as applied science is mismatched to the changing characteristics and situations of practice.

An alternative to viewing school leadership as applied science is the metaphor reflective practice. Reflective practice is based on the reality that professional knowledge is different from scientific. Professional knowledge is *created in use* as professionals face ill-defined, unique, and changing problems and decide on courses of action. Scientific studies, theoretical statements, and models of practice remain important, but their purpose is to explain phenomena, not to prescribe practices. Professionals rely heavily on informed intuition as they create knowledge in use. Intuition is informed by theoretical knowledge on the one hand and by interacting with the context of practice on the other. Knowing is the action itself, and reflective professionals become students of their practice. They research the context and experiment with different courses of action. Reflection is more than a cognitive process. One's conceptions, values, and beliefs come to play in this process as well. These factors help to shape if not sharpen intuition and comprise an important ingredient in reflective practice. This concept of reflective practice and reflection in action is discussed specifically and tacitly in a number of chapters that comprise this book, and embedded in this concept are clues to transcending our windows and walls.

The point is that one cannot run a school effectively by simply "applying" theories and models of research. But one cannot run a school effectively without using theory and research either.

What does all this say about the book at hand? In reflective practice, theories and models of organization, management, leadership, climate, politics, school effectiveness, supervision, and teaching are not considered to be "theories" that predict and explain or categorize and prescribe, but to be *metaphors* from which school leaders construct their own unique accounts of changing situations. Those who read through the chapters of this book in search of answers will wind up being confused and unhappy, for the answers conflict. This fate will be shared by those who are unable to transcend their windows and walls of leadership and school success. But readers who are seeking understandings from which their own intuitions might become more informed and professional judgments more reasoned will find here a rich reservoir of insights. From this latter stance, this book represents the best thinking presently available on the topic of school leadership and its implications for practice.

Thomas J. Sergiovanni
Lillian Radford Professor of
Education and Administration
Trinity University
San Antonio, Texas

Preface

One of the major purposes of this book is to challenge prevailing conceptions about the nature of school leadership and management. Another is to introduce readers to the complex interplay of factors that shape and constrain the work of teachers and those who lead and manage schools. The perspectives offered are diverse, broad in scope, and frequently conflicting. The contributions represent the thinking of some of the best scholars in the field, and it is anticipated that school administrators, teachers, researchers, and educational policy makers alike will find the various perspectives represented both unsettling and stimulating. The book will have served its purpose well to the extent that the ideas of the contributors provoke useful initiatives at the level of practice and move researchers to pursue new and fruitful avenues of inquiry.

Developing effective schools and facilitating successful instructional leadership by school principals and others is one of the most difficult and challenging problems facing school administrators. The need to understand more about effective schools and the work of school leaders will grow as educational administrators and policy makers at the local, state, and national levels grapple with alternative development strategies, emergent technologies, and increasing demands by legislators and others to reform schools and make them more productive. Schools must adapt and change to meet these challenges, and school administrators will be looked to by teachers and members of the school community to initiate and implement more effective instructional and organizational practices.

Much of the research and reform literature of the past decade has focused on school effectiveness and has emphasized the importance of the principal's role in leading instruction and in making schools more effective. While the casual reader would be correct in concluding that the school principal is a critical actor in the process of school improvement, it is also clear that many of the factors that affect what occurs in schools are beyond the influence of the principal, and that instructional leadership is but one dimension of the principal's role.

Urging school principals to provide instructional leadership is a popular prescription for reforming schools and making them more effective. Instructional leadership is a particularly attractive ideal because it fits neatly with the tenor of the times, the ethos of the profession, and the historical roots of the principalship—the principal teacher. It offers an image of the principalship that has considerable appeal both for principals and for those who would have them assume more resposibility for leading schools and improving instruction. However, the concept itself is ambiguous and does not adequately reflect the actual character of much of the work that a school principal must do. It fails to capture many other important dimensions of the principal's role, and it suggests a view of the principalship that is out of touch with the reality of schools as complex and contextually embedded organizations. These comments are offered not to diminish or undermine the importance of instructional leadership in schools. Rather, the point is that neither the role of the principal nor the process of making schools more effective are simple; both encompass much more than is revealed in popular conceptions of the ideal of instructional leadership.

While other concerns might have been addressed, the focus in this volume is to offer a critical perspective on some of the issues associated with instructional leadership, and to emphasize the complex interplay between the character of schools as work settings, the orientations of principals and teachers toward their work, and the challenges of leading and improving schools as we approach the twenty-first century. The book is divided into four parts: 1. Images of Leadership in Effective Schools, 2. Leading and Managing Schools, 3. School Cultures and Contexts, and 4. Professional Development Practices and Policies. The objective in Part 1 is to examine alternative images of school leadership and administration and to comment broadly on the antecedents and consquences of instructional leadership and efforts to improve schools. The intention in Part 2 is to examine factors shaping instructional leadership from the district perspective and to offer two examples of instructional leadership at the school level. The two-fold objective in Part 3 is to flesh out the interplay between elements of school culture, context, and instructional leadership and to provide illustrations of these phenomena at the school level. Part 4 concludes the book by sketching out some of the broader implications of the foregoing issues as they bear upon efforts related to the supervision and evaluation of teachers and the professional development of teachers and school administrators.

The perspectives of the contributors to this volume are diverse, and conflicting points of view are represented. This is as it should be—criticism and controversy are essential both to the growth of knowledge and to the improvement of practice. It is expected that readers, too, will differ in their viewpoints on these matters, and it is hoped that they will be challenged to reflect critically on their ideas about the nature of leadership in schools and about the roles of teachers and principals in improving schools; to consider how they might contribute to this dialogue and to efforts by educators at all levels to understand schools, and to make them more satisfying and productive places for teachers and children to work and learn.

William Greenfield
Louisiana State University

Contributors

C. M. Achilles is Professor of Educational Leadership and Coordinator of Field Services in the Bureau of Educational Research and Service at the University of Tennessee. He also is the Executive Secretary of Public Schools for Cooperative Research, a school study council comprising twenty districts in Tennessee. He completed his Doctor of Education at the University of Rochester and has served in public and private schools, the U.S. Office of Education, and the research staff at the University of California, Berkeley. He is interested in the humanities as a component of administrative preparation, and has worked closely with the National Diffusion Network and various Labs and Centers and Race/Sex Desegregation Assistance Centers since 1968. He has written widely, and among his publications are "An Analysis of Influencing-Gaining Behaviors of Principals in Schools of Varying Levels of Instructional Effectiveness," *Educational Administration Quarterly* (1986) and "Confidence-Building Strategies in the Public Schools," *Planning and Changing* (1985), with N. Lintz and W. Wayson.

Bruce G. Barnett is Project Director/Associate Program Director in the Instructional Management Program at the Far West Regional Laboratory for Educational Research and Development. He completed the Doctor of Philosophy at the University of California, Santa Barbara, in 1980, and served previously on the faculties of the California Lutheran College, the Mt. Carmel School in Santa Barbara, and All Souls School in Alhambra, CA. He has been responsible for research and development activities related to improving teaching and administrative practices, and his current work focuses on the leadership role of the principal. Among his publications are

"Peer-Assisted Leadership: Using Research to Improve Practice," *The Urban Review* (1985); "Subordinate Teacher Power in School Organizations," *Sociology of Education* (1984); and "Reflection in Action: A Stimulus for Professional Growth," *Thrust for Educational Leadership* (1985).

Roland S. Barth is Director of The Principals' Center and is a Senior Lecturer in Education at Harvard University. He directed the Study on the Harvard Graduate School of Education and Schools (1979–1980) and was awarded a John Simon Guggenheim Fellowship in 1977–1978. He has served as a consultant to more than thirty schools and state departments of education, and over twenty-five colleges and universities, and has made presentations to numerous professional associations and educational agencies. Among his publications are his book, *Run School Run* (1980); "The Principalship: Views from Within and Without," with Terrence Deal, in *The Effective Principal: A Research Summary* (1982); and "How to Ensure an Effective Principalship," *The National Elementary Principal* (1980).

Tom Bird is Project Director of the Far West Educational Research and Development Laboratory's study of the implementation of the California Mentor Teacher Program. He previously served as Program Associate (1975–1984) and Managing Director (1978–1984) of the Center for Action Research, Inc. and has conducted numerous studies and technical assistance activities related to the prevention of juvenile delinquency and to improving youth development services provided by local community agencies. Among his publications and professional presentations are "School Organization and the Professional Structure of Teaching" (1985), prepared for the California Commission on the Teaching Profession, with Judith Little; "School Organization and the Rewards of Teaching" (1984), prepared for the Education Commission of the States; and "Mutual Adaption and Mutual Accomplishment: Images of Change in a Field Experiment, " in *Teachers College Record* (1984).

Arthur Blumberg is Professor of Education in the Division of Administrative and Adult Studies at Syracuse University. He received his Doctor of Education from Teachers College, Columbia University, and previously served on the faculties of Temple University and Springfield College. The social psychology of organizations is his area of specialization, and he has focused particularly on the character of schools as adult work-settings and the nature of the work lives of people who hold leadership positions in schools. He has authored or co-authored numerous articles and several books, including *Supervisors and Teachers: A Private Cold War* (1974); *The Effective Principal* (1986) with William Greenfield; and *The School Superintendent: Living with Conflict* (1985).

Martin Burlingame is University Professor of Educational Leadership in the School of Educational Administration and Research at the University of Tulsa. He completed his Doctor of Philosophy at the University of Chicago and served on the faculties of the University of Illinois at Urbana-Champaign and the University of New Mexico; he also served for two years as a Senior Associate with the National Institute of Education. He teaches about local, state, and federal educational politics and policy, has served as a consultant to numerous school districts and state educational agencies, and has held a number of administrative and advisory positions in professional organizations. Among his publications are *Educational Governance and Administration* (1980) , co-authored with Thomas Sergiovanni, Fred Combs, and Paul Thurston, and "Theory into Practice: Educational Administration," in *Leadership and Organizational Culture* (1984), edited by Thomas Sergiovanni and John Corbally.

John C. Daresh is Assistant Professor in the Department of Educational Policy and Leadership, at Ohio State University. He received his Doctor of Philosophy from the University of Wisconsin at Madison, (1978), served as a project coordinator with the Wisconsin Research and Development Center (1978–1981), and served four years as a member of the Department of Educational Leadership at the University of Cincinnati (1981–1985). He has taught in several high schools and continues to work closely with local schools and professional associations. He is interested in adult learning and its implications for the continuing professional development of teachers and administrators, and he has written numerous technical reports, books, and journal publications, including "Instructional Teams" in *Instructional Leadership Handbook* (1984), edited by J.E. Keefe and J.M. Jenkins, and "Adult Learning and Individual Differences: Keys to More Effective Staff Development," *Contemporary Education* (1985).

Terrence E. Deal is Professor of Education, George Peabody College of Vanderbilt University and teaches about symbolism and processes in organization. He has held faculty appointments at Harvard University and Stanford University, and he consults internationally with both business and nonprofit organizations. His research on the role of myth, ritual and ceremony, and symbols in organizational settings led to the publication of *Corporate Cultures* (1983), co-authored with Allan Kennedy, and his most recent book is *Modern Approaches to Understanding and Managing Organizations* (1984), co-authored with Lee Bolman. In addition to seven books, he has written numerous articles and papers about educational change and effective schools, including "The Symbolism of Effective Schools," *Elementary School Journal* (1985) and "National Commissions: Blueprints for Remodeling," *Education and Urban Society* (1985).

David C. Dwyer is Director of Research in Education, Apple, Inc., and he served previously as Project Director of the Instructional Management Program and Teachers' Knowledge Net in Science at the Far West Laboratory for Educational Research and Development. He taught secondary science for 10 years and has participated in several major studies of change and innovation in American education. Dr. Dwyer received his Doctor of Philosophy from Washington University in 1981, and during the past four years has directed a large-scale field study of instructional leadership by school principals. Among his publications are "The Search for Instructional Leadership: Routines and Subtleties in the Principal's Role," *Educational Leadership* (1984) and "Contextual Antecedents of Instructional Leadership," *Urban Review* (forthcoming).

Chad D. Ellett is Associate Professor of Educational Administration and Coordinator of Research for the College of Education at Louisiana State University. He completed his Doctor of Philosophy at the University of Georgia in 1974 and served on the faculties of the University of Georgia, Georgia Southwestern College, and Tidelands Community School. His specializations are educational psychology, measurement, and research, and he has worked closely with state agencies and local school districts in developing and implementing large-scale teacher performance appraisal systems. Among his publications are "Triangulation of Selected Research on Principal Effectiveness," *Effective School Administration* (forthcoming), edited by John J. Lane and Herbert J. Walberg and "Assessing Minimum Competencies of Beginning Teachers: Instrumentation, Measurement Issues, and Legal Concerns," *Evaluation of Teaching: The Formative Process* (1985).

William Greenfield is Associate Professor of Education at Louisiana State University. He completed the Doctor of Philosophy at the University of New Mexico in 1973 and has served on the education faculties at Kent State University (1980–1983) and Syracuse University (1973–1980). He teaches and studies the principalship and the processes of leadership development and school improvement and has worked closely with school districts and numerous professional associations. Among his publications are *The Effective Principal* (1986) with Arthur Blumberg; "The Moral Socialization of Educators: Informal Role Learning Outcomes," *Educational Administration Quarterly* (1985); and "Career Dynamics of Educators: Research and Policy Issues," *Educational Administration Quarterly* (1983).

Philip Hallinger is Director of the Westchester Principals' Center. Former positions include responsibilities as an Assistant Professor of Administrative and Instructional Leadership at St. Johns University, Associate Director of the School Effectiveness Program, Santa Clara County Office of Education, CA (1981–1983), and Assistant to the Superintendent and High School Vice-Principal, Milpitas School District, CA (1978–1981). He also has served as a special education teacher and administrator (1972–1979) and as a consultant to the Carnegie Foundation for the Advancement of Teaching (1980–1981). Dr. Hallinger received his Doctor of Philosophy from Stanford University in 1983 and has written extensively on instructional leadership and school effectiveness. Among his publications are "The Superintendent as Instructional Leader: Findings from Effective School Districts," *Journal of Educational Administration* (1986) and "Assessing the Instructional Management Behavior of Principals," *Elementary School Journal* (1986).

Ginny V. Lee is Assistant Research Scientist in the Instructional Management Program at the Far West Laboratory for Educational Research and Development and is a doctoral candidate in Sociology of Education at Stanford University. She previously served as a Research Assistant at the Stanford University Institute for Research on Educational Finance and Governance (1979–1980), and as Chair of the English Department at Santa Paula Union High School, CA (1972–1978). Among her publications are "The Instructional Management Role of the Principal," *Educational Administration Quarterly* (1982) with Steve Bossert, David Dwyer, and Brian Rowan; seven case studies of instructional leadership (with David Dwyer, Bruce Barnett, Niki Filby, and Brian Rowan); and *The Principals' Instructional Management Academy: First Year and Beyond* (1984) with Bruce Barnett and F. Mueller.

Judith Warren Little is a Senior Program Director at the Far West Laboratory for Educational Research and Development and previously served as a Program Associate with the Center for Action Research, Inc. (1975–1983). She received her Doctor of Philosophy in Sociology at the University of Colorado, Boulder, in 1978 and has directed field-based research studies of instructional leadership at the secondary school level and of the role of the school principal in fostering work-place norms conducive to professional development. She has served as a consultant to numerous professional associations and national state educational agencies including the California Commission on the Teaching Profession (1984–1985), the National Association of Independent Schools, and state departments of education and legislative committees in California, Arizona, Florida, Illinois, and Colorado. Among her publications are "Seductive Images and Organizational Realities in Professional Development," *Teachers College Record* (1984) and "Teachers as Professional Colleagues" in *Educators' Handbook: Research into Practice* (1986), edited by Virginia Koehler.

Douglas E. Mitchell is Professor and Associate Dean of the School of Education, University of California at Riverside and previously served on the faculty of the Claremont Graduate School (1970–1972). He completed his Doctor of Philosophy in Political Science at the Claremont Graduate School in 1973. He teaches in the area of social theory and educational policy analysis and has conducted numerous research studies and consultations for federal and state agencies, local school districts, and private corporations. He has written extensively and among his publications are "Labor Relations and Teacher Policy" with C.T. Kerchner in *Handbook of Teaching and Policy* (1983), edited by Lee Schulman and Gary Sykes; "Educational Policy Analysis: The State of the Art," *Educational Administrative Quarterly* (1984); and "What Is the Incentive to Teach," *Politics of Education Bulletin* (1984), with F.I. Ortiz and T.K. Mitchell.

Joseph Murphy is Associate Professor in the Department of Administration, Higher and Continuing Education at the University of Illinois, Champaign-Urbana. He previously served as Executive Assistant to the Chief Deputy Superintendent of Public Instruction, CA (1983–1984) and Vice-Principal and School Improvement Manager, Milpitas Unified School District, CA (1979–1982). He has held other teaching and administrative positions, and his areas of specialization are school improvement and educational finance. He has written widely and included among his publications are "Pitfalls to Avoid in Applying School Effectiveness Research to School Improvement Efforts," *Education* (1986); "Effective High Schools: What Are the Common Characteristics?" *NASSP Bulletin* (1985), with P. Hallinger; and "Problems with Research on Educational Leadership: Issues to Be Addressed," *Educational Evaluation and Policy Analysis* (1983), with P. Hallinger.

Kent D. Peterson is Assistant Professor of Education in the George Peabody College for Teachers and is Director of the Principals' Institute at Vanderbilt University. He received his Doctor of Philosophy degree from the University of Chicago in 1983 and served previously as a teacher in Philadelphia and as a lecturer at the University of Pennsylvania. While at the University of Chicago, he was co-editor of *The Administrator's Notebook* (1978–1979) and research project coordinator (1980–1981) in a study of elementary principals. Amond his publications are "The Principal's Tasks," *The Administrator's Notebook* (1978); "Mechanisims of Administrative Control over Managers in Educational Organizations," *Administrative Science Quarterly* (1984); and "Obstacles to Learning From Experience in Principal Training," *Urban Review* (1986).

Diana G. Pounder is Assistant Professor of Educational Administration at Louisiana State University. She completed the Doctor of Philosophy at the University of Wisconsin at Madison in 1984 and previously served as Principal (1980–1982) and Guidance Counselor (1975–1980) of Trumansburg Middle School, N.Y., and as a math teacher with the Fairfax County Public Schools, VA (1973–1975), and the Little Rock Public Schools, AR (1972). She is a member of the Editorial Board of the *Educational Administration Quarterly*, and her teaching and research specializations include personnel, law, and research methods. Among her publications and professional presentations are "Salient Factors Affecting Decision Making in Simulated Teacher Selection Interviews," *Journal of Educational Equity and Leadership* (1985), with I.P. Young and "The Effect of Candidate Age and Type of Screening Information on Teacher Selection Ratings," presented at the American Educational Research Association Annual Meeting in March, 1986.

Louis M. Smith is Professor of Education at Washington University, and his areas of teaching include educational psychology, anthropology and education, and field methods in studying organizations. He received his Doctor of Philosophy from the University of Minnesota and has written extensively about classroom social structure and teacher leader behavior. Among more than eighty publications are *The Complexities of an Urban Classroom* (1968) with W. Geoffrey; "Effective Teaching: A Qualitative Inquiry in Aesthetic Education," *Anthropology and Education Quarterly* (1977); *Federal Policy in Action: A Case Study of An Urban Education Project* (1980) with D. Dwyer; and "Reconstruing Educational Innovation," *Teachers College Record* (1984) with J.P. Pruity, D.C. Dwyer, and P.F. Kleive. His longitudinal study of Kensington Elementary

School stands as one of the most complete and revealing studies of schooling and educational innovation in America.

Robert K. Wimpelberg is Assistant Professor of Educational Administration at the University of New Orleans and is on the Board of Directors of the Principals' Center in New Orleans. He completed his Doctor of Philosophy at the University of Chicago in 1981 and served on the Tulane University faculty for four years. He formerly served as Coordinator of Research with the Educational Finance and Productivity Center at the University of Chicago (1978–1980), as Staff Associate with the Midwest Administration Center (1975–1978), and as a teacher with the Human Development Training Institute (1970–1975) and the Lindbergh Public School District, MO (1968–1972). Among his publications are "The Business of Principals' Inservice," *Theory Into Practice* (1986); "Reviewing the Critiques of Reform Commissions," *Politics of Education Bulletin* (1985); and "Teacher Education in Private Colleges and Universities: Uniformity and Diversity," *Journal of Teacher Education* (1984), with N.J. Nystrom and J.A. King.

PART ONE

Images of Leadership
in Effective Schools

Instructional leadership is a compelling image, deeply rooted in American education. Strong building-level leadership focused on instruction is invariably pointed to by education reformists as one of the key contributors to school effectiveness. Similarly, studies of effective schools generally conclude that strong instructional leadership is a central element associated with school effectiveness. However, despite these claims by education reformists and researchers, the connection between leadership and school effectiveness is not clear, and more important, the concept of instructional leadership provides school administrators and policymakers with few useful insights about the actual nature of leadership in schools.

The chapters in Part One represent varied points of view about school leaders and effective schools. Three very different images of leadership are discussed by Martin Burlingame in Chapter One. His examination of the various assumptions about school leadership that are embedded in the research and writing about effective schools leads him to several conclusions: that the conceptions of leadership represented in the literature are quite diverse and incompatible with one another; that the prevailing conceptions fail to consider the importance of cultural and contextual differences between schools; and that acts of "practical closure" may be one of the most important features about the nature of leadership in schools. Chapter Two, by Charles Achilles, offers an example of "how" administrators in one school district implemented the five correlates undergirding much of the discussion and research about effective schools. The image of leading and improving schools revealed in Chapter Two dominates much of the current literature, and this description of "how" school principals were able to make their schools more effective demonstrates support for that view of instructional leadership.

The traditional images of administrative work as art or science are questioned in Chapter Three. Arthur Blumberg discusses the nature of schools and the work of school leaders, and suggests that a "craft" metaphor may be more revealing of the actual character of administrative work in schools. He argues that, if this idea were to be taken seriously by educators, schools and the nature of the work of teachers and school leaders would change dramatically, and for the better. Part One concludes with a discussion of the concept of "vision," an idea that conveys the possibility of excellence, as in the phrase "visionary leaders." William Greenfield describes the fuller meaning of that image, developing a framework to help us understand socialization for leadership and what the implications are for those who seek to improve schools and to lead well.

While educators and school reformists generally embrace the importance of instructional leadership as a vehicle for school improvement, our understanding of leadership in schools rests upon a shaky empirical foundation. Even though efforts to improve schools must and will proceed despite uncertainties about the nature of leadership in schools, researchers bear a special responsibility to be wary of their preconceived notions about schools and about leadership in schools. The chapters in Part One urge researchers to adopt a more critical and analytical perspective as they seek to understand leadership in schools, and point to the importance of tempering the general conceptions we have about the nature of leadership with more specific insights grounded in the day-to-day reality of schools as work settings.

1

Images of Leadership in Effective Schools Literature

MARTIN BURLINGAME

Much like the storms that frequently sweep the rugged and beautiful coast of Oregon each winter, the effective schools movement seems to have developed very quickly, to have unleashed its fury on the educational shoreline, and now to be waning. In that sense the effective schools movement parallels other efforts to reform schools. An easy set of examples can be drawn from the late 1950s through the 1970s when the federal and many state governments sought to improve local public schools. The roll call of those efforts—National Defense Education Act (NDEA), Elementary and Secondary School Act (ESEA), Management By Objectives (MBO), Planning Programming Budgeting System (PPBS)—still rings in our ears.

Today much of that same reformist energy has been harnessed by what has been called the effective schools movement. Simply, the effective schools proponents have argued that the academic performance of all students can be improved if schools would develop certain clear goals, if particular instructional technologies were used to achieve these goals, and if educational participants (principals, teachers, and students) would adopt a businesslike approach. A businesslike approach seems to mean a serious and conscious effort to attend school, to not waste time, and to be attentive to the educational aims of the moment.

But there are already signs that support for effective schools is flagging. The moral fervor of its advocates will soon be turned against teachers and administrators who fail to achieve or who opposed NDEA, ESEA, MBO, PPBS, and now oppose effective schools. For the supporters of effective schools, educators will once again be found lacking in moral fiber or intellectual talent or both. Those who seek to improve the schools will once again be on the prowl for the next slogan that promises an instant remedy.

Much could and should be learned from the past failures of reform movements and the impending failure of effective schools. Strategies are abundant. The history of these failures can be chronicled. What factors in the historical moment assisted the development of and hindered the fulfillment of reforms in schools? Effective schools could be compared to other reforms. In what ways is the effective schools movement similar to and different from PPBS, for example? Effective schools might be examined as a political strategy. What groups in our society and in education saw effective schools as providing them advantages and what groups saw effective schools as producing disadvantages? In this chapter I wish to look at one small lesson: the not-so-happy consequences of the mystique of strong administrative leadership.

There is something of great value to be learned from the abiding faith the effective schools proponents have in the importance of administrative leadership. The general belief of many in the effective schools movement seems to be that without strong administrative leadership schools will not be effective. Nonetheless, I shall argue that a close reading of the literature produced to support the claims of effective school proponents consists of three very different and incompatible images of what constitutes leadership. The first section of this chapter briefly describes these three images and argues that these images are found in two different sources: reviews of research literature and case studies. This first section concludes by discussing the importance of context and practical closure in leadership. The second section explores two important consequences of the stress on administrative leadership: leadership schizophrenia and the debate over slogans. The summary suggests that leadership in schools consists of acts of practical closure. These acts are influenced by the context, the debate over slogans, and the sense of attractiveness held by a particular administrator.

CONTRASTING IMAGES OF LEADERSHIP

There are three distinct images of leadership to be found in the literature of the effective schools movement. This section examines each of these views in turn, and then discusses some problems connected with these images.

Leadership One

The growing cottage industry of reviews of effective schools research and writings—by early 1985 there were at least fifteen such reviews—draws a portrait of the leader that shall be designated Leadership One. Leadership One presents the leader—nearly always the school principal—as the key figure in effective schools. Leadership One stresses two qualities or properties of the leader. First, the leader is supremely rational. That is, the leader has the intellectual abilities to ascertain appropriate goals for the school, to review possible alternatives, to weigh consequences, and to select appropriate solutions. Second, the leader is supremely pragmatic. If a particular solution does not seem to be working, the leader is wise enough to complete another rational cycle and to propose another option consistent with the overall goal. For example, one reviewer of effective schools literature writes: "The goals of change are strongly focused and clearly defined, but multiple strategies are encouraged ... " (Mackenzie, 1983, p. 11). These two qualities mean that leadership is top-down; followers—such as teachers or students—have little role in defining goals, in weighing alternatives, or in selecting consequences.

The most popular goal for effective schools is raising standardized achievement test scores. The most frequent alternatives selected for producing improved scores are providing a stable and orderly school environment and raising the academic expectations that teachers hold for their students.

Leadership Two

In contrast to the reviews of literature, there exist several good case studies of effective schools (for example, Lightfoot, 1983; also see Lieberman and Miller, 1984). The image of leadership that can be gleaned from these studies is one highlighting the cultural nature of leadership. Leaders act in ways and talk about goals that represent the normal ways of doing and aspiring in that particular community. Leaders are rational and pragmatic; the meanings of rationality and of pragmatism are given by the context of the community. For example, and to use for the moment popular stereotypes of regional cultures, in a suburban northeastern bedroom community the leader of the school (the principal) behaves in ways similar to a business executive while in a rural southwestern small town the principal may behave like a trail boss. The typical inner-city principal is a "bad dude" while in a rural southern community the elementary principal may be a "mammy." Principals who seek to lead do so in ways that maintain the community's understandings of what constitutes proper leadership behavior and proper school goals.

Leadership Two suggests that leadership is constrained in important ways by the cultural context. In contrast to Leadership One, which posits some universal leadership characteristics such as rationality and pragmatism, Leadership Two finds that these traits are operationally defined in different communities in different ways. A business executive principal might flounder in a southern elementary school just as a rural southern mammy principal would not do well in a suburban northeastern bedroom community.

A close inspection of the goals and alternatives would suggest that the cultural context deeply influences their meaning and their selection. Raising test scores, for example, may be seen in a southwestern community as raising the overall average of the class (the arithmetic mean). In a southern community, raising the test scores may mean raising the test scores of each individual child by more points than the standard error of the test. Equally, in some communities leadership is seen culturally as top-down; in others, bottom-up. The trail boss urges students to hitch up their wagons and laces ("paddles") them if need be; the business executive stresses the need to become a member in good standing of a corporate team. The reproduction of each of these cultural communities, in sum, inhibits any universalistic statements about the characteristics of leadership or the content of schooling.

Leadership Three

Leadership Three confounds the issue further. A few case studies find the leader effective only if a consensus has been created by the group. The critical factor is the faculty; the principal may lead to the extent the faculty permits. This image, one found among politicians and those who like to talk of bottom-up leadership, receives scant attention in the literature reviews of research on and writings about effective schools. Typically reviewers suggest that "there is a good deal of uncertainty about the role of informal leadership within the school" (Mackenzie, p. 11).

Few studies carefully document the role of the faculty, or for that matter the role of the superintendent, the central office, the assistant principals, or the community, in the development of effective schools. The extreme emphasis on the principal as the leader has led to a one-dimensional view of the school. In nearly all discussions of the leadership of effective schools, Leadership Three has been ignored; teachers are nonentities.

Some Problems

Three problems created by these multiple images of leadership are worthy of immediate consideration. First, many of the reviews of literature begin with powerful preconceptions of what constitutes leadership; evidence is drawn to support these views instead of being used to create an understanding of the nature of leadership in schools. Second, these preconceptions are biased toward a top-down view of leadership. Third, there are persistent instances of the fallacy of hasty generalizations and of the fallacy of ignoring the context in the reviews. The case studies do not fall prey to these flaws. The fallacy of ignoring the context suggests, importantly, that educational goals may be "open."

First, Leadership One seems as much influenced by the preconceptions of the reviewers as by the research and writing (Rowan, 1984). Some of these preconceptions include the flow of influence from the principal down to the teacher and the benign relation between the school and the classroom. These preconceptions fit neatly with the preconceptions of those who argue for effective teaching. Namely, the authority figure is never challenged in the situation, or, if challenged, has the perfect right to persist without attending to the complaint of the subordinate. Equally, the environment does not intrude on the authority figure. The principal is able to isolate the school from all but benevolent effects from the community just as the teacher is able to control the intrusion of others into the classroom.

Second, these preconceptions fit a long-standing pattern in American education. As described by Callahan (1962), Tyack (1974), and Tyack and Hansot (1982), American educators have been victims of the quest for "one best system" of schooling. This quest has led most educators to an overestimation of the capabilities of planners to devise the best way to teach, to an arrogance about the abilities of other than professionals to understand what constitutes the proper methods and goals of education, and to a deep distrust of the rough-and-tumble of the public arena.

Third, the model that many reviewers carried in their heads, one that has a long history in education, led them to two major fallacies. First, they were hasty in their generalizations (Block, 1983; Rowan, Bossert, and Dwyer, 1983; Rowan, 1984). There are significant problems with the scientific rigor of many of the studies. Moreover, a number of the qualitative case studies contained mixed information on the virtues of administrative leadership, on the goal of raising test scores, and on the means of stability and raised expectations (Lightfoot, 1983).

While the fallacy of hasty generalization is a perennial and well-recognized problem in educational research, the fallacy of ignoring the context is just as perennial if not as well acknowledged. A close reading of the case studies suggests a powerful link between the community and the school. This link influences the goals of the school, the style of leadership, and the means available to "good" teachers. Principals do not adhere to some universal principles about leading schools; they behave in ways that are comfortable to that community if they expect to stay in their roles. Only after they have built up a good deal of goodwill are they able to deviate from the expected; as Durkheim noted: "Chiefs ... can produce new things and even, in certain measure, deny collective usages" (1933, p. 195).

Ignoring the context means missing all the tacit meanings that come to be attached to universal terms such as "raising test scores," "creating stable environments," and "raising teacher expectations for student achievement." These are just not the same things in Community A as they are in Community B. To act *as if* these are universal terms with constant and unchanging meanings is to make an error of the same magnitude as believing that there is a common and unchanging meaning for "open education," "middle school," "junior high school," or "teacher in-service training." The cultural matrices that bind school to community give very general guidelines for the meaning of educational terms; they are about as specific as the guidelines most of us use to declare that an object qualifies as a "chair." To argue that there is some invariant meaning for an educational term that is used to promote reform in many different contexts is to commit the fallacy of ignoring the context.

Ignoring the context occurs when we act *as if* educational goals are all precisely specified and closed. It seems much wiser to consider many educational goals as open. As a goal, for instance, "raising test scores" is "open"; that is, it is an ideal that can never be realized because many legitimate, but differing conceptions of its nature exist (Kerr, 1976; also see Gallie, 1955–56). We can think of several different but perfectly acceptable meanings of raising test scores, e.g., for my child only; for children of a certain sex, race, creed, or color; for all children in the school by one point; for children who are predicted to do poorly by some test, and so on. It is the particular context that provides some "practical closure" to the discussion (Care, 1973). While it is possible to debate the meaning endlessly because the concept is open, we choose to close the concept momentarily. The closure selected by one community sets it apart from another community who made another choice.

By ignoring the context those who have reviewed the writings about effective schools have accepted an implicit top-down model, persisted in a limited historical view of education, and created a caricature of school leadership. By ignoring Leadership Two and Three both the cultural context and the role of others in the school besides principals have been systematically omitted; this is no mere slight.

SOME CONSEQUENCES

Two major consequences that follow from blind acceptance of Leadership One are confusion over the roles of leadership and followership and confusion over the nature of debate in education about slogans. The growing, and often confused, discussion of whether leadership should be either top-down or bottom-up is a good example both of the confusion about leadership and followership and of the import of understanding the logic of slogans in educational discussions.

For the typical school principal the confusion over the images of leadership produces the classic double bind. On the one hand, the optimistically skewed reviews of literature that produce Leadership One tell administrators they must lead by defining goals, creating stability, and raising expectations. Leadership One claims that leadership is very important; without leadership schools will not be effective. Principals are told how other truly successful administrators do their work using some universal kit including all-purpose and all-powerful universal diagnostic and prescriptive tools. On the other hand, the moment that principals seek to follow these universal diagnostic and prescriptive remedies in their particular schools, somebody objects. Teachers see these remedies as limiting their professional prerogatives in their classrooms; parents holler that the principal is violating the normal way of doing things in the community; students want the good old days. The practical closure that had defined the major expectations and the daily behaviors of the schools is now reopened.

The cultural constraints of the particular situation are invoked by participants to limit the universal solutions the principal seeks to impose. Depending on the particular cultural context, some students want creativity and freedom in doing assignments; in other settings students want prescribed and determinate assignments. In some settings parents demand homework; in others they want little. Principals are now in the double bind; they are told to behave one way and then punished for behaving that way.

The result is leadership schizophrenia. Principals seek some psychological refuge from the clash of expectations, some psychological haven from this clash of universal and particular. The solutions of these cross-pressured administrators are simple: either they develop a style that suggests that as principals they are doing something very important when in fact nothing is happening or else they become pointlessly busy.

In the first case, principals become organizationally pathologic: they talk one way and act another. Principals talk as if they were universal leaders using the general findings of effective schools literature reviews to guide their behaviors. But they ignore the opposition that arises quickly to these diagnoses and prescriptions; different understandings of goals are ignored because teachers can simply close their classroom doors or parents can stay away from school. Stability and expectations are just as easily overlooked if a few cases are evident and easily noted. For instance, the good test results of last year's standardized battery can be pointed out while the slippage this year can either be overlooked or rationalized.

Because they are taught endlessly that the universal solution is the best, because they have few opportunities to consider the ways of capitalizing on the specific cultural images of the community, because they are quickly defeated in attempts to clarify goals, raise expectations, and provide stability—all these factors lead principals to speak a public vocabulary of aggressive leadership while privately behaving on the basis of learned timidity. The administrator becomes the flim-flam man promising instant happiness to everybody and then ducking around corners as the truth hurts.

Other principals follow a second route. They become pointlessly busy. These administrators see their role as keeping the hallways clean, as chasing the neighborhood dog out of the building, and seeing that all teachers sign in and out on time. They abdicate any interest in education to the faculty and the community. They are the maintenance personnel of the building, making certain that everything is running smoothly even though they know not where or why it is running. They have been snake-bitten once too often ever to try to lead again.

What is less clear, and of equal importance, is that the confusion over the images of leadership of the effective schools movement creates serious confusion over followership. Leadership One requires docile followers who are impressed by the rationality of the principal, awed by the stability provided, and easy converts to the doctrine of raising expectations. Leadership Two depends upon followers who are good locals; they know what that particular community believes about how a leader is supposed to behave, how a follower is to act, what constitutes a legitimate order, and how far authority can be challenged. Leadership Three requires that the leader be a follower; the principal depends upon teachers who work to create professional schools based on their consensus of what constitutes best practice.

The remedy for both the confusion over leadership and followership seems obvious. We must approach the schools—as we seek to understand how they operate—in ways that do not completely predetermine what we look for and see. Such efforts require, among other things, that we spend a good deal of time working in the school site, that we see how leadership and followership occurs, that we inspect the overt and covert influences of the community, and that we be ever sensitive to the models and biases we bring to the scene. Too much of Leadership One, for instance, is "legislated leading"—if I may borrow (and corrupt) a phrase from Arthur Wise. Too much of Leadership Two ignores the abilities of local leaders to introduce cosmopolitan reforms. Too much of Leadership Three fits the romantic myth of the professional. Those who study the schools must not only be aware of what they bring to that task but also of how these distortions may create confusion, trouble, and, in extreme cases, havoc for leaders and followers in schools. Further, we need to understand the various types of leadership and followership that might exist in a particular site, to compare leadership and followership in multiple sites, and to remain ever sensitive to the specific, and often competing, cultural images of particular locales. Finally, we may wish to reassert the importance of middle-range theories.

However, this remedy acts on the assumption that the argument about leadership is a scientific argument. Others have presented the case that arguments about educational theories, such as leadership of effective schools, may *not* be scientific arguments at all. What we may in fact be participating in is a debate about a slogan system, not a scientific theory. This is an important line of reasoning that deserves consideration.

Komisar and McClellan (1961) argue that educational philosophies or theories are slogan systems. That is, educational philosophies or theories contain both prescriptive and descriptive statements. Slogan systems are thus systematically ambiguous; users of the systems know that a statement can be read in more than one way, i.e., descriptively or prescriptively. (They are, to use Kerr's language, "open.") Interpreting what a slogan system means is both a deliberate and an arbitrary act. At times, both advocates and opponents may know how a sentence in the system is to be used; they will be able to agree mutually to the criteria for that decision. But other sentences may be read in ways that are debatable; advocates seek to legislate the use of some sentences. For example, advocates of Leadership One may be arguing that school principals ought to establish clear goals for the school (prescriptive), not that they in fact do (descriptive).

Over time some slogan systems come to receive a standard interpretation. Both advocates and opponents seem to agree about the meaning of the system. But Komisar and McClellan note that: "Much of the accepted activity of educational debate and discussion is to establish and disestablish standard interpretations of certain slogans" (p. 203). This specific type of debate and discussion is marked by two characteristics. First, in the effort to establish or disestablish a slogan system we are unable to deduce any specific statement about or recommendations for practice. There is not a close linkage between the system and specific activities as there generally is in scientific theories. Second, the chief test of the slogan system's longevity is its attractiveness to educators. Opponents are won over by making the standard interpretation more attractive; advocates are held fast by attractiveness. For instance, Komisar and McClellan point out that those interested in practice will display the eminently practical nature of the slogan while those interested in theory will point to its elegant theoretical solutions. The advocates of a slogan are deeply interested in how they package their product so that it captures the market.

Debates about slogan systems thus differ significantly from scientific discussions or our usual rational arguments. Several of these important differences, and some of the negative and positive consequences of such differences, will now be considered.

First, if we seek to define terms, debates involving slogans will incorporate different uses, and possibly meanings, of the same term. A term in a slogan system such as "effective" can be used not only to describe a set of conditions but also to prescribe a set of conditions that ought to exist. The conditions that are encompassed by the term "effective" may also shift from situation to situation. Both the use of the term and its meaning within the slogan system are systematically ambiguous. Neither of these conditions is acceptable in scientific or rational debates.

Second, because the use shifts, we are unable to show how the slogan system term is to be applied in situations. We are unable to indicate any clear and persistent patterns of behavior associated with the slogan system term. This means, of course, that the slogan system itself can not be tied to any patterns of behavior. At one time the system suggests certain behaviors are described and prescribed by the system; a moment later these behaviors and prescriptions may change. Clearly these shifts are unacceptable in scientific debate and rational discussion.

Third, while in general the extent and quality of information increases in periods of conflict (Bower, 1965), there may be little need to increase information in slogan system discussions. In rational and scientific disputes contestants seek more and better information. This means, in turn, that few events are ignored, few interests overlooked, few potential insights left unattended. Dispute helps maintain intellectual vitality; there is clearly an educative function in conflict. But in slogan system arguments information is of peripheral use. The criterion for deciding is not the preponderance of evidence; it is the attractiveness of the slogan system. Information may or may not make the slogan system more attractive; more and better information may in fact be a hindrance in some slogan system discussions.

Fourth, there is no test to see if what a slogan system proposes is actually in place. In contrast to rational and scientific debates, slogan systems are so inexact that we can never tell if a system has been implemented. Thus, within any large school district, for example, we can find various versions of a slogan system. While a district school board may mandate that all schools be led in such a way that they become effective, what that means in terms of specific behaviors at the school sites is unclear. What one principal calls effective another may see as neutral or not effective. The range of activities encompassed by the slogan system is heterogeneous, to say the least.

Finally, in contrast to disputes of a scientific or rationalistic nature, disputes over educational slogans can be endless. In terms of the details of the argument participants have no standard to decide when a point has been won or lost. The dispute can wander from one point to another in a rather aimless fashion. Equally, participants have no way of knowing when the entire dispute has been won or lost. The discussion can simply meander around, circling back on itself in intricate patterns.

Such endless disputes may have both negative and positive consequences. On the negative side, endless disputes over educational slogans can become simplistic. Bennett (1975) has argued that the more complex the political dispute, the simpler the public display. This same logic seems to apply to educational disputes. The efforts to untangle the complex world of the school often lead to simplifications. The simplifications, first, gloss ambiguities in situations; they reduce the complexity to a simple and often misleading model. The simplifications, second, highlight commonalities and deemphasize differences. Bennett writes: *"successful public definitions tend to conceal the points of political conflict in favor of abstract principles of political resolution"* (p. 38). Disputes over slogans can mask in simplifications the very world they seek to explain and prescribe.

There are two positive consequences of such endless disputes. First, disputes about slogans may lead to a feeling that dogmatism ("My answer is right and all others are wrong"), skepticism ("All answers are equally true—or false"), and eclecticism ("Each meaning gives a partial view so the more meanings the better") are all inappropriate (Garver, 1978, p. 168). Endless disputes over time temper the participants. The rejection of each of these isms—dogmatism, skepticism, and eclecticism—not only heightens the intellectual standards of the dispute but also forces consideration of what pluralism means. Participants over time are denied easy ways; they must come to grips with the fact that others honestly disagree with them. These conflictual circumstances have to be endured; they become the source of an important lesson about educational pluralism.

Second, the endless competition makes (nearly) impossible the (permanent) ascendancy of any single slogan. If any educational slogan system is to hold the paramount role for any length of time, it must sacrifice ideological purity to win adherents. Each slogan thus incorporates some elements of other views to win adherents and gain a numeric majority. Each particular slogan system becomes more catholic over time; constant competition preserves flexibility. The possibilities of such flexible slogans enhancing societal survival are increased because an inflexible slogan can become too refined in a special direction, too fixed to a specific environment, and too specified

in terms of detailed operations (Kaplan and Manners, 1973, p. 52).
Endless disputes over slogans serve an adaptive function.

The pluralistic and adaptive functions of slogan disputes do not
necessarily always go hand in hand. Pluralism suggests increased in-
tellective activity to clarify the nature and meaning of competing slogan systems; adaptiveness suggests increased political activity to gain
adherents. What is of import in both activities is the role that endless
debate plays by enriching the opportunities for the entire field of education. On the more dreary side, education can be seen as the home
of instant traditions (Colson, 1974), ill-begotten reputations, schisms,
orthodoxies, and repetitive sales pitches. On the happier side, education
argues for a historical perspective on efforts to improve, appreciation
of the opportunities that abound, a sense of the joy of discovery, and
a taste for the sweet agony of intellectual discovery.

In sum, we might want to think about disputes over slogans as
political beauty contests. They are political because the contestants
are seeking to gain the support of others; they are beauty contests
because the chief means of gaining adherents is attractiveness. Unlike
traditional political disputes where the outcome is some authoritative
allocation of values in which some are advantaged and some disad-
vantaged, debates over slogans suggest strict limits on the uses of power
and authority to promote concerted action in education (Hartnett and
Naish, 1976). The contestants wish to carry the day but the use of
legislated rules rarely is strong enough to overcome the advocates of
some slogan system; opponents are to be won over ("converted") to a
particular standard interpretation of a slogan. Imagine, if you will, the
time and energy necessary to travel to every elementary school in the
U.S. to insure that each and every principal behaved over time in ways
that made each and every elementary school "effective." Political decisions of an authoritative nature are courts of last resort, but nonetheless easily circumvented. Contests are resolved by the voluntary
acceptance of the slogan; attractiveness carries the day.

SUMMARY

The reviews of research and writing about effective schools must be
examined with great care. Most reviews argue for the importance of
administrative leadership, but more frequently than not the preconceptions of the reviewer and not the evidence in the research and
writings dictate the findings. Most of the case studies present very
different pictures; they suggest the importance of the cultural context
and the important role played by others in the setting.

In contrast to the supporters of Leadership One, the case studies
suggest that leadership in schools involves a good deal of practical

closure. That is, the open nature of educational goals means that in a particular setting the actors may decide for the moment to accept a particular meaning *as if* it were the correct meaning. The process of creating that practical closure may well be one of the definitive acts of leadership. Such acts of practical closure are undoubtedly influenced by the particular community context, by the particular nature of the debate over slogans, and by the particular sense of attractiveness possessed by the contestants in the situation. In contrast to Leadership One, the sensitivity to context, to debate, and to attractiveness admits to important roles for the followers and creative roles for the leader. Followers are important because as discussants trying to understand the nature of the context, the contest of slogans, and the criterion or criteria of attractiveness, they can enrich the discussion. Equally, leaders must seek not only to understand and reward the many participants but also must generate enough enthusiasm and interest to create conditions that lead to practical closure. These sorts of activities are best guided by the tacit understandings of the context; they are badly handled if some universal solution is imposed.

Those who live along the Oregon coast have a rich and robust vocabulary for describing the differences among the many winter storms. In contrast to visitors from states such as Illinois, the natives make many subtle distinctions about winds, surf, and tides. If it is a wise course for those who must endure storms to understand them in careful ways, we in education should not be far behind. Unfortunately, our quest for the universal too often stands in the way. Unlike the coast of Oregon, our winter storms of educational reform do not seem always to produce a beautiful landscape. In fact, the flotsam and jetsam of most educational reforms look more like the pollution of the Chicago River than the beauty of Boiler Bay.

REFERENCES

Bennett, W.L. (1975). Political scenarios and the nature of politics. *Philosophy and Rhetoric, 8,* 23–42.

Block, A.W., ed. (1983). *Effective schools: A summary of the research.* Arlington, Va.: Educational Research Service.

Bower, J. (1965). The role of conflict in economic decision-making groups: Some empirical results. *Quarterly Journal of Economics, 79,* 539–77.

Callahan, R.E. (1962). *Education and the cult of efficiency.* Chicago: University of Chicago Press.

Care, N.S. (1973). On fixing social concepts. *Ethics, 84,* 10–21.

Colson, E. (1974). *Tradition and contract.* Chicago: Aldine.

Durkheim, E. (1933). *The division of labor in society.* Translated by G. Simpson. Glencoe, Ill.: Free Press.

Gallie, W.B. (1955–56). Essentially contested concepts. *Proceedings of the Aristotelian Society, n. s., 56,* 167–98.

Garver, E. (1978). Rhetoric and essentially contested arguments. *Philosophy and Rhetoric, 11*, 156–72.

Hartnett, A., and Naish, M. (1976). Some issues arising from the readings. In *Theory and the practice of education*, edited by A. Harnett and M. Naish, vol. 1, pp. 73–121. Theory, values and the classroom teacher. London: Heinemann Educational Books.

Kaplan, D., and Manners, R.A. (1973). *Culture theory*. Englewood Cliffs, N.J.: Prentice-Hall.

Kerr, D. H. (1976). *Educational policy*. New York: David McKay.

Komisar, B.P. and McClellan, J.E. (1961). The logic of slogans. In *Language and concepts in education*, edited by B.O. Smith, and R.H. Ennis, pp. 195–215. Chicago: Rand McNally.

Lieberman, A., and Miller, L. (1984). *Teachers, their world, and their work*. Alexandria, Va.: Association for Supervision and Curriculum Development.

Lightfoot, S. (1983). *The good high school*. New York: Basic Books.

Mackenzie, D.E. (1983). Research on school improvement: An appraisal of some recent trends. *Educational Researcher, 12*, 5–17.

Rowan, B. (1984). Shamanistic rituals in effective schools. *Issues in education, 2*, 76–87.

Rowan, B.; Bossert, S.; Dwyer, D. (1983). Research on effective schools: A cautionary note. *Educational Researcher, 12*, 24–31.

Tyack, D.B. (1974). *The one best system*. Cambridge, Mass.: Harvard University Press.

Tyack, D.B., and Hansot, E. (1982). *Managers of virtue*. New York: Basic Books.

2

A Vision
of Better Schools

C. M. ACHILLES

Lear: Yet you see how this world goes.

Gloucester: I see it feelingly.

King Lear. Act IV, Scene VI, lines 148–150.

INTRODUCTION

Education is a vast enterprise. It is constantly a topic of discussion and debate; occasionally it is even featured in the public and political spotlight. There is, it seems, no dearth of critics and reformers. Few would disagree that schools are expected to teach each generation the basic building blocks of civilization—reading, writing, arithmetic. Consensus diminishes on other goals for schools. We may talk of altruistic goals for schools, of educating for citizenship or use of leisure time, but we measure and compare schools by the performance of their students on tests of mastery of a few subjects. Some youngsters score higher than others on school tests; youngsters identified as ethnic minorities or those from lower socioeconomic status (SES) groups are overrepresented in the lower-scoring groups.

This patterned difference seems inimical to the American dream of equality. There is a constant quest for better schools—for schools where all youngsters achieve reasonable proficiency in certain basic skills. The search for better schools is part of an ideal, a dream, a vision. One operational step in this vision is the instructionally effective school. In these schools youngsters of lower social classes and ethnic minorities are not overrepresented among those receiving lower test scores, and they are not readily identifiable as members of a group by patterns of test scores.

Vision, the ability to see feelingly, helps us in the quest for better schools. Colton (1985) describes vision as that "which establishes goals or objectives for individual and group action, which defines not what we are but rather what we *seek to be or do*" (p. 33, emphasis in original). Colton notes some influential people from recent history who had vision and worked to achieve the vision. Martin Luther King, Jr.'s vision was a dream; John F. Kennedy's vision led to dramatic new social programs; one of Thomas Jefferson's visions led to improved education ("if a nation wishes to be ignorant and free, in a state of civilization, it expects what never was and never will be"); Ronald Edmonds's (1979, p. 22) vision was of schools that were effective in educating the urban poor ("How many effective schools would you have to see to be persuaded of the educability of poor children?"). These and other influential people pursued lofty visions. Vision is important for better schools—and not just better schools for particular groups, such as Edmonds's urban poor, but for each pupil. How do we get there?

The "craft knowledge" or conventional wisdom of school administration tells us, "As is the principal, so is the school." Edmonds noted that "there are some bad schools with good principals, but there are no good schools with bad principals" (Mazzarella, 1985, p. 1).

The blending of these two themes—vision and building-level leadership—gives meaning to the search for better schools. Principals are key elements in the move toward better schools. Their three-fold task is difficult. They must know *why* we need education and good schools. They must know *what* is needed to improve schools. They must know *how* to administer the schools to achieve the desired results. As a starting point, principals must envision better schools, articulate this vision to others, and orchestrate consensus on the vision. The vision is a criterion to gauge successes. Vision can make dreamers of us all. It lets us "see feelingly."

POTENTIAL CONTRIBUTIONS OF THE EFFECTIVE SCHOOLS "MOVEMENT"

The concept popularly called "effective schools" has emerged as a major element of the vision of better schools. The idea of effective schools began to grow when observant and inquiring educators noticed that some schools apparently served their pupils better than other schools did. Although it seemed true that ethnic minority and low SES youngsters scored lower on school tests than other pupils, nevertheless in some schools the typically low-scoring groups did very well on the same tests. Scores of pupils in these schools were so much higher that the schools were easily identified statistically as "outliers"—they fell well outside the expected range. Why? What was going on in these schools? What similarities or common elements were shared by these outlier schools? Why couldn't pupils in other schools experience the same achievement and success as pupils in the outlier schools? Here, then, is the heart of the vision—schools where poor children and children of ethnic groups are not identifiable based upon their school test results.

Vision may help with the "why" and the "what" questions, but it seldom tells us "how." The "how" problem remains widely prevalent in much of the effective schools work.

Articles on effective schools identify the need for strong building-level leadership. The current literature repeatedly advises as to *what* principals should do to build effective schools, but little attention is given to *how* effective principals go about being effective. Note Donmoyer's comment:

> Recent studies of schools almost invariably identify the principal's leadership as a significant factor in a school's success. Unfortunately these studies provide only limited insight into *how* principals contribute to their schools' achievements. (Donmoyer, 1985, p. 31, emphasis in original).

Although there is considerable room for improvement and sophistication in the research and evaluation dimensions of the effective schools movement, the findings of effective schools studies make sense. They square with the "craft knowledge" of schooling. Even if effective schooling studies don't yet live up to rigorous scientific standards, they feel right. They offer opportunities to "see feelingly" into questions of school improvement. Effective school concepts and practices offer some useful tools to repair schooling's dented image.

EFFECTIVE SCHOOLS IN PERSPECTIVE

Slowly, after the publication of the results of a study of reading achievement by Weber (1971), and much more rapidly with the publication of works by others, such as Edmonds (1979), Brookover, et al. (1979), Rutter, et al. (1979), there issued forth information on effective schools. Early effective schools work—the first generation of studies—sought out schools that seemed to do better than expected on certain schooling criteria. That is, the researchers first identified and then analyzed "good" schools. The study of "good" schools was a significant departure from prior adherence to the "medical model" where researchers considered the pathology of schools that were not "well." Now, instead of studying schools with high dropout rates to find out what was wrong, educators began to analyze schools with few dropouts to discover what was right in those schools. The effective schools' work is based on a positive and optimistic outlook.

Generally speaking, advocates note that effective schools tend to have: strong and positive building-level leadership; an emphasis on teaching the basic skills; a climate or an environment for learning that is orderly and safe but not repressive; a sense of positive expectations for achievement on the part of everyone in the school; and an interest in using data derived from assessment of student progress to help guide the instructional program. Ronald Edmonds greatly standardized the effective schools' work and focused the domain of inquiry. Since Edmonds's (1979) description of the "correlates" of effective schools, researchers have worked to refine and expand them. Thus, although emphasizing Edmonds's correlates, later researchers identified other attendant variables such as community involvement, support from the central office, stability of staff, resources directed at achieving school goals, and staff development efforts. The five correlates, however, have remained central to the effective schools movement. A brief statement about each correlate will help provide insight into how effective schools ideas can help improve education. (Numerous authors discuss the correlates and other supporting variables. Expanded explanations can be found in such sources as Brookover, et al., 1979, 1982; Clark, et al., 1984; Mackenzie, 1983; Purkey and Smith, 1983; and others.)

1. The school leader exercises *strong administrative leadership* and keeps the school moving ahead in the effective schools mode. The principal encourages staff attention to key elements of effective schools and exerts instructional leadership in many ways. (Details of this cor relate appear in Figure 2.2, p. 27.) The leader *demonstrates* some important characteristics. The leader is a believer, is dedicated to quality education, and is committed to school improvement.

2. A *climate* that is safe and orderly without being rigid and repressive provides the learning environment in an effective school. Although instruction and learning are the primary emphases, factors affecting instruction such as discipline, rules, and the physical facilities are important. Expectations of behavior or codes of conduct are developed and reviewed periodically. Motivational devices (slogans, buttons, songs) stress the positive. Respect and pride permeate the building. Esprit and mutual respect between and among staff and students are evident. A sense of community may be displayed through informal coffees, potluck meals, and social activities. Buildings and grounds are neat due to efforts of school and community groups. The school functions as a unit rather than as cliques or groups.

3. High and positive *expectations* are held for students and staff. School personnel establish national norms as the outcome of teaching and learning efforts. Success is seen as attainable by each student and the staff; teachers believe that each student can master basic objectives. Staff development includes work on expectations and the impact of expectations on pupils. Students *Here Are Learning.*

4. Teachers and all school staff *emphasize the basic skills* that will be tested. Teachers agree on the skills to be taught and mastered; they develop and use common lists of skills for the grade levels. The schedule is adjusted to facilitate teaching and learning: blocks of time, major subjects early in the day, etc. Faculty meetings are instruction-oriented, and some staff development emphasizes time-on-task strategies. Several models for remedial or accelerated programs may be observed (not just the usual pull-out program). Interruptions are minimized and the integrity of instructional time is preserved. Academic motivational devices such as writing contests are employed. The *things of school* reinforce the idea that the school is a place where pupils *learn.* Study *Hard And Learn.*

5. Teachers use *regular and continuous assessment* to structure instructional strategies for each pupil. Staff develop or adopt tests for the skills to be learned. Homework policies are enforced; work is checked. Administrators monitor teacher planning and work and help teachers develop lessons that are aligned with the curricular objectives that will be tested. Staff members view declining test scores as a school, not a pupil, problem. Performance is assessed by both standardized and criterion-referenced tests.

Much of the literature on effective schools suggests that implementing these five correlates will increase student test scores and enable schools to reach or exceed comparison norms for student achievement in basic skill areas. While the effective schools literature is not without its critics, and some of their views will be discussed later in the chapter, the next section turns to an example of one district's effort to implement the correlates.

PUTTING EFFECTIVE SCHOOLS IDEAS TO WORK: ONE EXAMPLE

Schools in a midwestern city faced mandatory court-ordered desegregation. Yet, some schools in Area I of that city had little possibility of successful desegregation due to geographic and demographic factors. Although some Area I schools were desegregated, other inner-city schools remained all minority. Pupils in these schools reflected characteristics often associated with inner-city schools: low school achievement, low motivation for school success, and inconsistent family support for schooling. Teachers and school personnel generally were not enthusiastic about student chances of success on school-related activities.

The Area I superintendent was confronted with the problem of poor schools and poor achievement. This area superintendent envisioned that Area I schools should be the best possible schools for the youngsters whether they were desegregated or not. He believed that schools must accept responsibility for educating each child and stop rationalizing that children couldn't learn due to environmental factors such as home and family backgrounds. In the Fall, 1979 the area superintendent attended the meeting of the National Alliance of Black School Educators in Detroit. There he heard Ronald Edmonds discuss "effective schools." Edmonds's descriptions fit the Area I problem exactly.

The solution to the problem was nebulous until the area superintendent heard Edmonds speak. After a period of reflection the area superintendent met with representatives of the Danforth Foundation to seek initial support for an effective schools approach in Area I. The plan had two basic goals. After three years youngsters in project schools would perform at or above national norms on the district's standardized testing program. A second goal was that the project should build a model to guide the implementation and the subsequent replication of successful project ideas. This fortuitous foresight precipitated 1) implementation of the project based on change theory and 2) documentation of the implementation of a major change.

After the vision came the plan. The "why" questions seemed obvious. Why can't inner-city youngsters from generally poor and often broken homes who have met with nothing but failure in the schools have quality education? Why shouldn't they perform well in schools? Why can't inner-city schools do a good job of educating the youth who come to them?

The "what" question initially was, "What can we do to provide successful school outcomes for pupils?" The "what" question was solved when the vision of the best possible schools for all Area I youngsters met with Edmonds's enthusiasm about effective schools. The Area I personnel believed that if the five correlates were *found* in effective schools, then effective schools could be *created* if the correlates could be planted and nurtured in schools previously considered ineffective. The approach of emphasizing the correlates and transplanting them as a means of creating effective schools is the "second generation" of the effective schools movement. It offers additional opportunities for evaluating the results of effective schools efforts and it grapples mightily with the "how" question.

The "how" question culminated in written plans or proposals to the Danforth Foundation and to other groups, such as the Mid-West Race Desegregation Assistance Center and the state. The goal that youngsters would perform at or above the national norm seemed ambitious when only 11 percent of the grades in the project's first four schools were at the norm when the project began, and in some grades nearly half of the pupils scored in the lowest quartile on the city's standardized testing program (the California Achievement Tests, or CAT).

The project, called SHAL (from the first letter of the original four schools), began in late 1980. The first steps provided for readiness activity and the phasing in of additional schools over several years. The general time line was:

11/80–9/81 "Readiness" (This included such things as establishing councils and task forces, visits to other exemplary schools, and orientation activities.)

2/81 Initiation of community meetings and orientation.

9/81 Implementation of SHAL activities in classrooms (four schools).

9/82–8/83 Second year of operation (four original schools) and twelve new schools in their first year of activity.

9/82–8/84 Third year of SHAL activities (the first four schools were in their third year; the next twelve in their second year; and three more schools were added).

Prior to implementation the principals of the first four schools received additional training; they read about and visited effective schools. Before working with students and teachers in their own buildings, they were becoming committed to the vision. This is important. They had to share in the vision so that they would understand the goals for effective change and have the enthusiasm to transmit the vision to faculty, students, and community.

The Area I office provided impetus and strong support for the project. A structure to support the change, including committees and processes for implementing the change, was established. Programs of public information and in-service training were initiated. There was commitment to try the project for several years and to try to maintain stability in administration and teaching personnel in the project schools.

Some Area I instructional supervisors worked directly with schools on implementing the correlates of effective schools. In-service included instruction on direct teaching methods, improving school climate, developing reward systems in the schools, illustrating ways that teacher expectations can influence student achievement (using the Teacher Expectation/Student Achievement model), and other schooling and teaching concerns.

Teacher committees worked to align instructional objectives and content with the objectives of the standardized testing program. Groups brainstormed ways to improve the positive elements of schools: expanded reward systems; scheduled basic subjects early in the day when pupils and staff are rested; developed slogans, logos, and buttons to increase morale; promoted academic "competitions" such as math olympics; emphasized attention to academic rituals such as graduations from grade to grade; and used many symbols, such as prominent displays of school goals and progress in achieving the goals, to focus attention on excellence.

The unit of change was the building. The principal was in charge. Content from effective schools projects became the core of school-based in-service. Principals accepted and worked at the instructional leadership role (See Figure 2.2, p. 27). School staffs developed a collegial approach to such concerns as cooperative planning, academic "competitions," cohesion and esprit through songs and slogans which often built upon the SHAL motif (Study Hard And Learn; Students Here Are Learning), instruction-oriented faculty meetings, and innovative approaches to problem solving. In one school two teachers who assumed lunchroom duty for the whole year soon knew each student and developed a "system." Lunchroom problems diminished dramatically. Principals adjusted school schedules to support instruction. They increased the amount of time they spent observing teachers and working on instructional issues. Student work was prominently displayed in classrooms, hallways, the principal's office, and in trophy cases. Reward systems encouraged students in many ways. There were rewards for academics, attendance, improvement, neat rooms, best cafeteria behavior—rewards were everywhere. Positively worded lists of expected behaviors were visible throughout classrooms and schools (as opposed to negative lists of prohibited behaviors). Positive approaches are proactive and they indicate agreement on goals. Negative approaches are reactive and defensive. In SHAL there were only a few rules agreed upon by all and a few essential goals that were clearly identified. The key was multiple methods and strategies used to achieve limited and focused goals.

Project outcomes were measured most directly by pupil scores on standardized tests. Project processes were tracked by use of a replication model developed for the project. The model, based on a synthesis of concepts from change theory, included four stages described as: 1) orientation and assessment, 2) planning and program design, 3) implementation, and 4) institutionalization and renewal. The change process stages provided one axis for a matrix that included Edmonds's correlates (i.e., instructional leadership, basic skills, climate, expectations, assessment of pupil progress) on the other axis. This matrix is shown in Figure 2.1.

Researchers reviewed the effective schools literature to derive descriptions of each of the correlates. Behavioral descriptors indicating how each of the correlates would look in practice were entered into the top line of the matrix (Level 3, Institutionalization). These descriptors became guidelines focusing the vision, or the goals to be achieved. When these goals were achieved, the schools would, in appearance at least, resemble effective schools. Steps taken to achieve the goals were described and entered into the matrix, thus providing a generalized road map of "how" to become effective. Each "level" relates approximately to one year of project effort (Achilles, Young, and High, 1985). The test of success, of course, would be attainment of the goal for pupil achievement.

Information in Figure 2.2 defines in a general way one important correlate of an effective school, the element of instructional leadership, as it evolved in Project SHAL. These characteristics and behavioral descriptors of effort at each level are very similar to other lists of effective schools variables (e.g., Mackenzie, 1983; Kirst, 1983; Purkey and Smith, 1983; Purkey and Degen, 1985).

Project SHAL was a large-scale innovation. At the outset attention was given to key elements: readiness, establishment of the demonstration in four schools, measured phase-in of other schools, central office support, a structure, community awareness and involvement, pre-project training, planned and continuing in-service, and evaluation. Some activities were large-group in nature but most work was school-based. The implementation was monitored to explain the process so that good things could be replicated later. A field test of the implementation model occurred in Spring, 1984.

Several assumptions were either explicit or implicit in the project and in the field test. These assumptions or propositions included:

1. Amount of time in SHAL would be important in the degree or amount of implementation. (It takes time for substantial change.)
2. Implementation of the important elements (correlates) would not be the same (or "even") among schools, even those in SHAL for the same number of years.
3. It was important to study the degree or amount of implementation for several reasons.
   a. Pupil outcomes (if positive) should not be attributed to SHAL if implementation was weak (or not evident);
   b. Pupil outcomes (if weak or negative) should not be attributed to SHAL if implementation was weak (or not evident).

Change Process Stages	Instructional Leadership	Basic Skills	Climate	The Five Correlates — Expectations	Assess Pupil Progress
					Pupil Achievement: Goal = At or above the national norm.
Institutionalization and Renewal Level 3		Level 3 was completed in advance of project initiation with sample descriptors derived from the literature explaining major characteristics of each correlate as observed in effective schools.			
Implementation (Moving Ahead) Level 2		Level 2 was completed with sample descriptors observed in the second year of project implementation.			
Planning and Program Design (Getting Started) Level 1	See Figure 2.2 for details of this correlate.	Level 1 was completed with sample descriptors observed in the first year of project implementation.			
Orientation and Assessment (Foundation)		District makes a commitment. (Sample steps). Strong support. Develop a proposal. Establish structure: Task forces and committees. School and community readiness and receptivity. Pre-assessment and visits to similar projects. Plan evaluation and collect baseline data.			

FIGURE 2.1 Basic Framework of SHAL Replication Model (Achilles, et al., 1983, 1985). The model, predicated on change theory, provides a way to track SHAL's incremental growth as the correlates become more fully implemented over time.

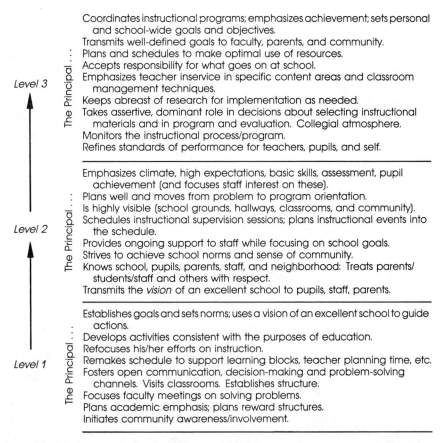

Level 3 — The Principal . . .

Coordinates instructional programs; emphasizes achievement; sets personal and school-wide goals and objectives.
Transmits well-defined goals to faculty, parents, and community.
Plans and schedules to make optimal use of resources.
Accepts responsibility for what goes on at school.
Emphasizes teacher inservice in specific content areas and classroom management techniques.
Keeps abreast of research for implementation as needed.
Takes assertive, dominant role in decisions about selecting instructional materials and in program and evaluation. Collegial atmosphere.
Monitors the instructional process/program.
Refines standards of performance for teachers, pupils, and self.

Level 2 — The Principal . . .

Emphasizes climate, high expectations, basic skills, assessment, pupil achievement (and focuses staff interest on these).
Plans well and moves from problem to program orientation.
Is highly visible (school grounds, hallways, classrooms, and community).
Schedules instructional supervision sessions; plans instructional events into the schedule.
Provides ongoing support to staff while focusing on school goals.
Strives to achieve school norms and sense of community.
Knows school, pupils, parents, staff, and neighborhood: Treats parents/students/staff and others with respect.
Transmits the *vision* of an excellent school to pupils, staff, parents.

Level 1 — The Principal . . .

Establishes goals and sets norms; uses a vision of an excellent school to guide actions.
Develops activities consistent with the purposes of education.
Refocuses his/her efforts on instruction.
Remakes schedule to support learning blocks, teacher planning time, etc.
Fosters open communication, decision-making and problem-solving channels. Visits classrooms. Establishes structure.
Focuses faculty meetings on solving problems.
Plans academic emphasis; plans reward structures.
Initiates community awareness/involvement.

FIGURE 2.2   General Structure of Evolving Instructioal Leadership Activities in an Effective Schools Implementation. Read up the figure. These descriptors "flesh out" the Instructional Leadership column of Figure 2.1. There is similar detail for other columns.

  c. Results of this field test could help SHAL schools redirect their energies or efforts to areas where implementation seemed weak.
  d. The amount and fidelity of implementation would influence pupil performance. (Schools that implemented SHAL elements—correlates—better and longer would show higher pupil outcome scores on CAT Total Reading and Total Math).

(Achilles and Young, 1985, pp. 1–7 passim)

The regular district testing program (CAT) was one basis for evaluating Project SHAL. Special testings were avoided for two primary reasons: (1) special testing takes time and money, and (2) one SHAL goal dealt with pupil achievement relative to national and city norms. The replication model provided a way to "track" project progress and guard against nonimplementation (Charters and Jones, 1973; Hall and

Loucks, 1977). Additional evaluation steps included observations by outside evaluators, interviews, questionnaires, and unobtrusive measures such as teacher and pupil attendance, and community support. Periodic reports of project progress were developed (e.g., Achilles, et al., 1983, 1985); the district also conducted internal assessments.

The SHAL results were generally positive and supported each of the assumptions. In that sense, SHAL was successful. Especially in the first four schools, students performed far better than expected on standardized tests. The school climate was more positive after SHAL implementation than before. There was improved community involvement and interest in schools and in education. The project was manageable; it focused mostly on the five "correlates" and on pupil scores on standardized tests.

Figure 2.3 summarizes results of the gains in pupil performance on the CAT. Not only was there a gain in the percent of grades at or above the norm, but there was a substantial decrease in the percent of pupils scoring in the lowest quartile on the tests. Notice, for example, that Group I (schools in SHAL for three years) moved from 11 percent of grades performing at or above grade level in 1981 to 72 percent by 1984. Eighty-nine percent of the grades showed an increase in grade equivalents and 83 percent of grades tested showed a reduction in the percent of pupils scoring in the lowest quartile (Spring testing, 1981 and 1984). The same magnitude of gains was not present in comparison groups. The best results overall were achieved by schools that were in the project the longest. Schools newer to the project were following in paths similar to those traveled by schools in the project a year or two longer, suggesting that the implementation process could be generalized. By focusing attention on a few goals the project was able to show success.

There also were problems. The second implementation group consisting of twelve schools did not initially do as well as the first and third groups, which were smaller in size (see Figure 2.3). Part of this certainly was the expected variance of a larger group, but there may have been other reasons. The supervisory support staff became spread too thin. Additional Area I personnel were not available to work with teachers and administrators in the additional twelve schools. The original supervisory staff now had sixteen schools to assist. The twelve new schools could not get the intense, personalized service that the first four schools enjoyed. Major change takes effort and personalized attention. The SHAL experience reinforces this precept.

SOME CRITICISMS OF EFFECTIVE SCHOOLS' WORK

Project SHAL, as one example of the application of effective schools' work, seems to have brought about considerable change and success.

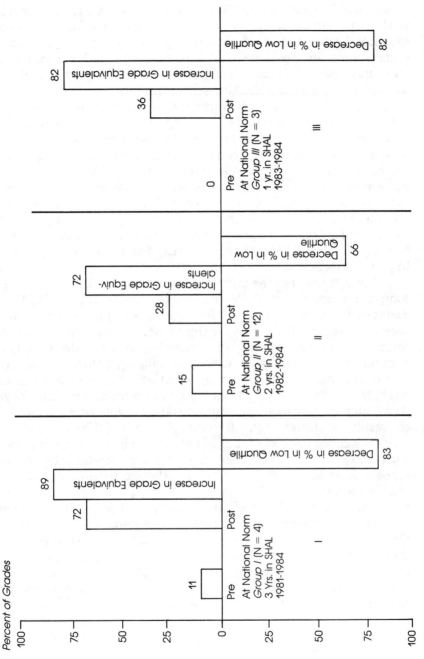

FIGURE 2.3 Comparison of CAT Results by Implementation Groups: Percent at or Above National Norm (Pre/Post), Percent Increase in Grade Equivalents and Percent Decrease in Pupils in Lowest Quartile by Year in Project SHAL. (Achilles, et al., 1985, p. 24).

Project SHAL exemplifies the "second generation" of effective schools' work. Rather than seeking to identify and describe effective schools, the second generation is trying to transplant and implement effective schools ideas, an approach which allows for expanded methods of inquiry and analysis. Nevertheless, there are several important and critical concerns about the effective schools movement.

As it should be, some effective schools ideas are not universally accepted, and others should be accepted with certain reservations. Researchers who know and respect the "scientific method" are uneasy that few if any effective schools studies have met the standards and rigor required to approach asserting cause-and-effect relationships. At best, effective schools' work has been correlational; indeed, much has been case study, and ex post facto field research within quasi-experimental design. Nevertheless, continuing positive results and consistent replications of prior findings are beginning to lend credence to a considerable body of information that, if properly applied, can help improve schools.

Although much of the criticism seems to be a call for more rigor, some is for care in using effective schools results. Cuban (1983), for example, labels his concern a "friendly but cautionary note." Since most effective schools results are from inner-city elementary schools, there is real need to be careful in transferring results. Different schools have different cultures, and the ways of building a climate conducive to learning will differ from setting to setting. What is constant is the need for a positive learning environment. Rowan, Bossert, and Dwyer (1983) suggest more rigor and improved design before we accept blindly the results of effective schools' work. Rowan (1984), noting methodological weaknesses and a burgeoning, cultlike belief in their mystical and curative powers, has likened unquestioning acceptance of effective schools ideas to shamanism. Sirotnik (1985) calls this movement a "bandwagon in search of a tune."

Most effective schools efforts are narrow in focus, usually using student improvement on standardized or criterion-referenced tests as the major goal. These narrow goals are fairly easy to measure. However, there are those who would argue that the most important outcomes of education can not be measured by simple tests. Additionally, if pupils do well and move above the norm (a goal of effective schools), the norm will soon be adjusted upward so that half again fall below the norm. That's the definition of a normal distribution. How will effective schools efforts measure up when the norms are raised? This is yet to be seen.

Insightful school administrators will establish academic goals for their schools based on standardized test results. Contemporaneously they may establish "social goals" to encompass less quantifiable but equally important things such as education for citizenship, use of leisure time, and affective dimensions of schooling. By separating the academic goals (seen by some as the raison d'être of schools) from selected social goals which are difficult to measure, educators will gain more precision at both levels. This process of separating school goals should improve our reporting to parents, to legislatures, and to the general public.

Some have been concerned about the case study approach in effective schools' work and the use of powerful success stories and anecdotes to convey progress (Rowan, 1984; Sirotnik, 1985). This may be a shortcoming in the strict research sense, but the use of stories and anecdotes helps flesh out the effective schools approach and avoids reducing results to numbers. Recent years have brought more attention to the use of success stories. The success story—true or apocryphal— is part of the language of effective schools' work. (School people love to share success stories!) In fact, success stories are important in building and conveying the "culture" of outstanding enterprises. Peters and Waterman (1982) found legend, myth, and success stories in "America's Best-Run Companies":

> As we worked on research of our excellent companies, we were struck by the dominant use of *story, slogan* and legend as people tried to explain the characteristics of their own great institution. All the companies we interviewed ... were quite simply rich tapestries of *anecdote, myth* and *fairy tale.* (p. 75. Emphasis added).

> Values are not usually transmitted ... through formal written procedures. They are more often diffused by softer means: specifically the stories, myths, legends and metaphors. ... And so, as it turns out, the excellent companies are unashamed collectors and tellers of stories, of legends and myths in support of their basic beliefs. (p. 282)

In their analytic article, "Using Bureaucratic and Cultural Linkages to Improve Instruction: The Principal's Contribution," Firestone and Wilson (1985) emphasize the importance of "The Story" in developing an organization's culture. They explain the principal's role in building the culture by being a communicator of that culture. As the values and beliefs of the culture are important, so are the stories transporting them. "Three symbol systems communicate the contents of an organization's culture: stories, icons and rituals" (p. 15). Success stories must include the important anecdotes that convey what the organization is about. For effective schools, that basic organizational goal is success in improving the achievement of pupils on specified criteria.

To the degree that effective schools efforts *are useful, and are not dishonestly employed*, they should be used as rallying points for school improvement. Some effective schools methodology does warrant criticism, and the results should be used with caution. But the effective schools' work has brought to principals some important assistance at a time when schools are harshly under fire. If nothing else, this work gives principals direction in terms of school functions and activities. Principals, for example, can synthesize effective schools ideas and develop building-level in-service programs to focus on improved learner outcomes.

At a time when numerous national studies and commission reports have been decrying education's faults and foibles, the effective schools ideas provide rays of optimism and hope and offer promise for school improvement. The first generation of studies has served its purpose by explaining *what* constitutes an effective school within a clearly defined framework. An effective school includes all or most of Edmonds's (1979) "correlates," an array of other attendant variables, and pupils who achieve well—even above what would usually be predicted for them. Answers to the "what" question have specified variables amenable to further study (climate or expectations, for example). Answers to the "what" question provide descriptive data and lead logically to the "how" question. Once educators ascertain what constitutes an effective school, they are interested in finding out *how* to become effective.

LESSONS LEARNED FROM SHAL AND EFFECTIVE SCHOOLS EFFORTS

The SHAL experiences identified the following *positive* factors supporting implementation of the five central correlates of effective schools. These are illuminative of "how" schools succeed in efforts to become more effective:

1. Vision and commitment by the school principal and the superintendent;
2. A sound plan based on theory and research guides the effort;
3. Efforts to seek external resources and to reallocate internal resources are undertaken;
4. Strong administrative support exists at upper levels in the district;
5. School staffs are stable and norms of collegiality are fostered;
6. Limited goals are set and pursued by many methods;
7. Goals are clear and there are high expectations for success;
8. A structure for support and coordination of effort exists at the school and district level;
9. Implementation support is constant, with expansion of efforts accompanied by proportionate increases in support;

10. Implementation efforts are initially limited to a few schools and extended later to others;
11. Participants at all levels recognize that change takes time, and plan efforts accordingly;
12. Implementation efforts are monitored, documented, and evaluated formatively and summatively.

These elements are supported by a growing body of recent research aimed at helping answer questions of *how* to create effective schools. The correlates are implemented in various ways depending on the idiosyncrasies of each school. Variations in *how* the correlates are effected can be attuned to school cultures and provide opportunities for principal leadership.

Studies such as that by Firestone and Wilson (1985), noted earlier, suggest ways that principals can lead their schools into the effective schools movement. For example, High (1984), building upon French and Raven's (1959) work, found that principals in effective urban schools relied most on expert and referent power in their schools. Principals in other schools relied less on expert and referent and more on other bases of social power, such as involvement or legitimate authority. Principals in effective schools were more active and visible than were principals in other schools; they led by doing. Similarly, Keedy (1983) observed principals in effective rural schools and found that they used norm-setting strategies in their schools. The most frequent norm-setting techniques used were human relations, modeling, and being a resource provider. The combined results of these two studies identify ways that principals can move their schools into the effective schools mode.

Now that educators are attending to positive aspects of effective schools they are comparing their findings to some current literature from business and industry. Spady (1984), Clark et al. (1984), and others have noted striking similarities between the eight basic principles of America's best-run companies, as described by Peters and Waterman (1982), and the approaches taken in the effective schools' work. The parallels may not be exact, but are interesting. In Figure 2.4 a synopsis of SHAL efforts is compared both to the eight basic principles identified by Peters and Waterman (1982) and to the composite of thirteen characteristics of good schools noted by Purkey and Degen (1985: 4–6). The apparent similarities suggest that there are some common elements of success in at least two institutions—education and business.

SOME CONCLUDING THOUGHTS

The effective schools emphasis is a positive approach to school improvement. The correlates of effective schools can be seen as variables

Eight Basic Principles *(Peters and Waterman)*	Effective Schools/Project SHAL *(Numerous Sources)*	Thirteen Characteristics *(Purkey and Degen)*
Bias for action	Get on with it. Let's try it out.	
Stay close to the customer	Surveys, Open house, Volunteers. Monitor pupil progress. Involvement.	• Parental and community
Autonomy and entrepreneurship	Building-level focus. Principal as leader. Teacher responsibility (key committees).	• Building-level leadership • School-based inservice
Productivity through people	Involve *all* staff. Climate conducive to learning. Staff development.	• Collaborative planning and collegial relationships
Hands-on, value-driven	Strong central office support. Expectations. Recognize achievement. Praise. Publicity. Success stories.	• Order and discipline • Sense of community • Recognition of academic success
Stick to the knitting	Basic skills emphasis. Slogans and logos (Study Hard And Learn). Climate.	• Maximized learning time • Curriculum articulation and organization
Simple form, lean staff	Direct access to central office and support staff. Building-level management.	• District-level support • Staff stability
Simultaneous loose-tight properties	Few goals/many methods. Common vision but flexibility by buildings to accommodate school cultures and communities.	• School-site management • Clear goals and high expectations commonly shared

FIGURE 2.4 Similarities among SHAL Efforts, a Composite of Thirteen Characteristics of Good Schools and Eight Basic Principles of Successful Companies.

that can be manipulated for future study and can be adjusted to coincide with varying school cultures. The correlates constitute partial answers to the "what" questions in school improvement. Study of effective schools projects (e.g., SHAL) and the results of other recent studies (e.g., High, 1984; Keedy, 1983) are providing answers to the "how" questions for school improvement. Effective schools approaches, although needing further refinement and study:

- Offer promising avenues for school improvement.
- Provide substance of building-level in-service for teachers.
- Provide content for district-wide in-service for school administrators.
- Offer content for preservice preparation programs for teachers and administrators.

The effective schools emphasis has educators seeking "what works" to make schools better, and trying to combine results into a conceptual framework that recognizes such key elements as the culture of individual schools, the need for rewards, and the need for a climate or environment that supports the goals of education. Yet we are constantly reminded of the need for a vision of better schools. According to Rutherford (1985), effective principals "have clear, informed visions of what they want their schools to become ... " (p. 32). Improvement through effective schools approaches starts with a vision of what a good school should be—a vision of better schools. Principals must see that vision, feelingly.

REFERENCES

Achilles, C.M.; Young, R.; Leonard, J.; Codianni, A.; High, R. (1983). "The change process in real life: Tracking implementation of effective schooling elements in Project SHAL." Paper at AERA, 4/83. Montreal: ERIC:ED 231039.

Achilles, C.M.; Young, R. High, R. (1985). "Tracking the implementation of three years of effective schooling elements in Project SHAL." (1981–1984). Paper at AERA, Chicago, April.

Achilles, C.M., and Young, Rufus, Jr. (1985). "Effective schooling implementation takes time, but results grow: Project SHAL replication/implementation model field test." Paper at AASA, 3/85, Dallas. 36 pp., 6 appendices.

Brookover, Wilbur B., et al. (1982). *Creating effective schools*. Holmes Beach, Fla.: Learning Publications.

Brookover, Wilbur B., Beady, C.; Flood, P.; Schweitzer, J.; Wisenbaker, J. (1979). School social systems and student achievement: Schools can make a difference. New York: Praeger.

Charters, W., and Jones, J. (1973). "On the risk of appraising non-events in program evaluation." *Educational Researcher*, 2(11): 5–7.

Clark, D. L.; Lotto, L.S.; Astuto, T.A. (1984). "Effective schools and school improvement: An appraisal of some recent trends." *Educational Administration Quarterly*, *20*, 3:41–68.

Colton, David L. (1985). "Vision." *National Forum*, *65*, 2(Spring):33–35.

Cuban, L. (1983, June). "Effective schools: A friendly but cautionary note." *Phi Delta Kappan*, *64*, 10: 695–96.

Donmoyer, R. (1985). "Cognitive anthropology and research on effective principals." *Educational Administration Quarterly*, *22*, 2(Spring): 31–57.

Edmonds, R.R. (1979). "Effective schools for the urban poor." *Educational Leadership*, October, pp. 15–24.

Firestone, W.A., and Wilson, B.L. (1985). "Using bureaucratic and cultural linkages to improve instruction: The principal's contribution." *Educational Administration Quarterly*, *21*, 2(Spring):17–30.

French, J.R., and Raven, B. (1959). "The bases of social power." In *Studies in social power*. Edited by D. Cartwright, pp. 150–67. Ann Arbor, Mich.: Research Center for Group Dynamics, Institute for Social Research, University of Michigan.

Hall, G., and Loucks, S. (1977). "A developmental model for determining whether the treatment is actually implemented." AERA *Journal*, 14 (3).

High, R.M. (1984). *Influence-gaining behaviors of principals in schools of varying levels of instructional effectiveness*. Unpublished doctoral dissertation, University of Tennessee, Knoxville, *DAI* vol. 45, no. 10: 3040, A84.

Keedy, J.L. (1983). *Norm setting as a component of principal effectiveness*. Unpublished doctoral dissertation, University of Tennessee, Knoxville, *DAI* vol. 43, no. 9.: 2846, A83.

Kirst, M.W. (1983). "Effective schools: Political environment and educational policy." *Planning and Changing*, 14, 4(Winter): 234–44.

Mackenzie, D. (1983). "Research for school improvement: An appraisal of some recent trends." *Educational Researcher*, 12, 4(April): 5–16.

Mazzarella, Jo Ann. (1985). "The effective high school principal: Sketches for a portrait." *R & D Perspectives*, CEPM, University of Oregon, Eugene. (Winter), 8. pp.

Peters, T.J., and Waterman, R.H. (1982). *In search of excellence*. New York: Harper & Row. (Warner Books, paperback)

Purkey, S.C., and Smith, M.S. (1983). "Effective schools: A review." *Elementary School Journal*, 83: 427–52.

Purkey, S.C., and Degen, S. (Spring, 1985). "Beyond effective schools to good schools: Some first steps." *R & D Perspectives*, CEPM, University of Oregon, Eugene. 8 pp.

Rowan, B.; Bossert, S.T.; Dwyer, C.D. (1983). "Research and effective schools: A cautionary note." *Educational Researcher*, *12*, 4(April): 24–31.

Rowan, B. (1984). "Shamanistic rituals in effective schools." *Issues in Education*, *2*, (Summer): 76–87.

Russell, J.S.; White, T.E.; Maurer, S.D. (1985). "Effective and ineffective behaviors of secondary school principals linked with school effectiveness." Paper at AERA, Chicago, Ill.

Rutherford, W.L. (1985). "School principals as effective leaders." *Phi Delta Kappan*, 67, 1(September): 31–34.

Rutter, M.; Maugham, B.; Mortimer, P.; Outson, J.; Smith, A. (1979). *Fifteen thousand hours: Secondary schools and their effects on children*. Cambridge, Mass.: Harvard University Press.

Sirotnik, Kenneth A. (1985). "School effectiveness: A bandwagon in search of a tune." *Educational Administration Quarterly*, *21*, 2(Spring): 135–40.

Spady, W. (1984). "Exchanging lessons with corporate America." Report of an interview. *Thrust*, October, pp. 18–22.

Weber, G. (1971). *Inner-city children can be taught to read: Four successful schools.* Council for Basic Education, Occasional Papers, (October), 18.

3

The Work of Principals:
A Touch of Craft[1]

ARTHUR BLUMBERG

==========

INTRODUCTION

Elsewhere (Blumberg, 1984), I have written about what I consider the fallacy of thinking about administration (or, by extension, leadership) or the work of administrators in terms that imply it is an applied science or an art. Instead I proposed that what administrators do may be most appropriately thought of as practicing a craft and, further, that I was not merely engaged in semantic nit-picking; that the concept of administration-as-craft has implications that were ultimately useful in ways that were not found in the scientific or artistic metaphors. In this chapter it is my intent to develop the image of the school principal as a craftsperson, a person whose thought processes when confronted with problematic situations are markedly similar to those of people who are engaged in the practice of what we consider to be the traditional crafts—potters, woodcarvers, or weavers, for example.

The chapter is organized around the following topics:

- a brief review of the arguments against thinking of either the scientific or art metaphors as appropriate to a principal's work.
- a consideration of the meaning of the "work" of principals.
- how the metaphor of craft fits the work of principals.
- some examples of how the use of the craft metaphor might be used for the professional growth of principals.

NOT A SCIENCE AND NOT AN ART

The history of the efforts and hopes of creating a science of school administration is a long one. Its systematic roots can probably be found in the early years of this century when quantitative methodology made its appearance on the educational scene. Cubberley (1947), for example, rather implies that it was Edward L. Thorndike who was responsible as "In 1904 [he] made the beginnings of a new method of attack by applying statistical procedures to social and educational problems... " (p. 692). Professors of educational administration soon took up the scientific cudgel as if, perhaps, to beat the problems of the schools and school administration into submission. And, though most of the research at that time had to do with fiscal issues, Cubberley also notes that "These early studies marked the beginnings of a long train of related investigations... which have laid the basis of standard textbooks and for the scientific study of the problems of city and state school administration" (pp. 692–93).

A sampling of the beginnings of this "long train of related investigations" can be found in the Strayer and Thorndike (1913) publication *Educational Administration: Quantitative Studies*. A statement from the Preface notes its purpose: "The selections quoted or summarized in this volume are deliberately chosen from the work that has been done at Teachers College, Columbia University, in the application of quantitative methods to school problems." Given that by 1913 Teachers College had started to assume its position as a dominating force in the study of education, it must have been no small thing to have two of its prestigious professors lend their names and reputations to the notion of developing a science of administration. And Cubberley, once more, undoubtedly influenced by the scientific management ideas of Frederick Taylor, noted in the Preface of *The Principal and His School* (1923):

> The technique of school organization, administration, and supervision, from the point of view of the principal, has now been sufficiently worked out that there is a definite body of concrete experience and *scientific* information which should be taught to those who are looking forward to becoming principals of elementary schools.... (p. vi. Emphasis added.)

> The organization of education during the past ten or fifteen years has gone forward by leaps and bounds, and there is every reason to think that the next ten to fifteen years will witness an even greater development in the *scientific* organization of the instructional process. (p. vii. Emphasis added.)

Space here prohibits the continued tracing of the hard science tradition in educational administration. Suffice it to say, though, it became firmly entrenched and continues, particularly in the research universities, in unabated fashion, though not without questions being raised about its relevance for the people who do the work of administering schools. Suffice it also to say that the impact on practice of the huge numbers of studies that have been conducted in school administration has been less than overwhelming—which I think is an understatement. Bridges, for example, in his review of the research on the school administrator from 1967 to 1980, writes "... the research seemed to have little or no practical utility. In short, there is nothing compelling to suggest that a major theoretical issue or practical problem relating to school administrators has been resolved by those toiling in the intellectual vineyards since 1967" (p. 25). My position, as should be evident, would be to make a similar statement about what transpired in the "intellectual vineyards" prior to 1967, particularly with regard to practice. At the very least, support of perhaps the most important kind for this position can be found merely by talking to practicing school administrators and asking them what it is they think about when they confront their daily work problems. One will have to listen long and hard before one hears any reference to anything that resembles a science of administration.

If not administration as science, then what? The "fallback" position seems to be administration as art. Here is the comment of Griffiths (1977) at a conference on research in administration, "... there is much in administration that is outside the scope of theory. The practice of administration is largely an art and reflects the personal style of an administrator and the environment in which he functions" (p. 53). That seems reasonable enough except that it, too, is not very helpful if we are interested in conceptualizing an image of a school administrator that would have some relevance for someone who is one. Consider, for example, how art is conceived by a well-known philosopher of art. Croce (1976) tells us that art is found in the expression of something called "lyrical intuition" and reflects the apprehension of "the pure throb of life in its ideality" (p. 557). Further, "... it is not circumscribed or limited by service to any practical purpose whatever..." (p. 561). This is pretty heady stuff and further, if we subscribe to Croce's last sentence, as I do, it eliminates the possibility of administration being an art. Administration is nothing but activity engaged in the service of a practical purpose. Where are we then if what purports to be the science of administration has little relevance for an administrator's work and the metaphor of administration as art is one that does not adequately represent that work? Interestingly, two other philosophers help us.

Collingwood in *The Principles of Art* (1938) provides a clear starting place. Book I of his text is entitled "Art and Not Art" and its first chapter is "Art and Craft." The distinctions are clear. Briefly, the craftsperson wishes to make something, has the end product in mind, and the skills to produce it. Not so the artist who, though he or she has skills, does not have in mind the production of a product, but the expression of something that might be called an imaginative vision. What an artist does is in the service of self—to express an imaginative vision. What a craftsperson does is to make something useful,[2] and this idea currently fits the work of a school principal.

While rejecting Collingwood's sharp distinction between art and craft, Howard, in *Artistry: The Work of Artists* (1982), furthers our understanding by taking the position that what artists *do* is craftwork and they learn to do what they do by learning a craft. The practice of a craft involves knowing what one wants to do, learning skills and techniques, developing know-how through experience, applying rules of thumb, practice, criticism, and so forth. In some cases it may involve understanding of scientific phenomena, but it is not science. As Howard puts it in a concluding remark, "Though science can inform, it cannot displace the practical perspective..." (p. 198). If nothing else, the perspective of a school principal needs to be practical—and that is also the perspective of the craftsperson.

All this has been, perhaps, an overly brief conceptual argument aimed at setting the stage for thinking of the work of principals as a form of craftwork; as a craft that involves the deliberate and prudent use of self to resolve day-to-day problems as well as those that are long-range. It will have to suffice at this point, however.

THE WORK OF PRINCIPALS

However the work of principals is described—what they are expected to do or what they, in fact, do—is dependent on the perch from which one chooses to view it. For example, I have on my desk the job description of an elementary school principal. It charges her with the responsibility of "leadership of the entire program of the elementary school, including personnel and activities." The document then goes on to enumerate nine general areas of responsibility which are elaborated by twenty-eight specific tasks or functions. One can hardly escape the feeling, in this case, that the "perch" was a textbook (read "professor") that may have been modified to fit the specific preferences of a superintendent. Does it describe the work of a principal? Probably, in some very general fashion. At the very least, it is a document for public consumption, serving as a handy response to concerned citizens, perhaps, when they ask just what it is that a school principal does. Is it important to the principal? The answer was provided by her response when I asked her if she had a job description and, if so, might I have a copy of it. She said, "Gee, I guess so. I'll have to see if I can find it."

The point is not, of course, that her job description never had any meaning for her, but that it has no particular relevance either for what she does on a day to-day basis nor for how she does it. We may be sure, for example, that she doesn't review it each morning on her way to school. Further, her "Gee, I guess so" reply rather suggests that it is not meaningful to her in the long run, either.

I must backtrack just a bit, lest I appear unduly cynical. I do not mean to imply by these comments that job descriptions for principals are useless. It is only that if we are interested in inquiring into what principals *do*, how they sense problems, how they diagnose them, or how they approach them, for example, such job descriptions provide little help.

Another way to understand the work of principals is from their "perch." How do they think about what it is they do? Over a period of time, as a means of engaging groups of principals in a sort of light-hearted way in discussion of their job, I have asked them to think in metaphorical terms about it. The list of metaphors so produced now numbers sixty-three and I'm sure it could be expanded. Here is a sample chosen at random: fire fighter, detective, super-teacher, tolltaker, quarterback, Red Cross worker, psychiatrist, distance runner, coach, judge, choreographer, paper chaser, hospital orderly, prostitute, professor. The metaphor has been described by Eisner (1985, p. 226) as "the archenemy of the stock response" and, if nothing else, this list makes the point well when it is compared with, I suspect, any job description—by any definition, a "stock response" document. A metaphor, of course, is a figure of speech and not reality. But this list starts to lend a type of reality to the daily work-life of school principals that we do not find in textbooks. Further, it places this reality in the context of some of the essential humanity of the principal. Though we may smile at the notions of the fire fighter or prostitute, for example, we also cannot escape sensing a certain amount of pathos in them. Is this the meaning of "leadership of the entire program of the elementary school"? We would have to answer, "Yes, at least in part."

A somewhat closer view of a principal's work can be obtained by engaging principals in lengthy discussions of what they do. Blumberg and Greenfield (1986) provide an example of this approach in their study of some out-of-the-ordinary principals. What emerged was an image of idiosyncrasy of worldview laced with themes of commonality of what these people were like. And though the results are interesting and perhaps even important, they do not provide a greal deal of clarity about what it is that principals do.

One can, of course, in interviews with principals become much more clinical about their work than did Blumberg and Greenfield, and inquire in depth into specific events that occurred in their work. The problem with reports such as this, interesting though they may be, is precisely that they are reports of events that occurred through the eyes of the reporter. And it must be noted, this is as close as we can come to some, perhaps most, of the events and circumstances that transpire in the course of a principal's work.

Keeping this last sentence in mind, what we are left with, it seems clear, if we wish to move as close as possible to clarifying and understanding the work of principals, is, of course, the commonsense thing— to observe them at their work and to talk with them about it. The literature (Wollcott, 1973; Willower and Kmetz, 1982—for example) provides several interesting illustrations of this approach. What we find, for the most part, is an image of people who spend their days in a highly fragmented manner, moving from one problematic situation to another, having a minimum of time to devote to these situations and even less time to reflect on them. The montage that is thus created gives one pause in thinking about the "perch" of the writers of job descriptions.

There is, though, another way of thinking about this montage that, while not a picture of systematically related activities, lends some internal coherence to them and forms a global, work-oriented view of what school leadership is all about. That is, it is not about any single thing, but about a number of things, some closely related and some seemingly not so, but all of them necessary for the life of a school. They may involve situations that, on the face of it, seem mundane or trivial—simply being visible when school dismisses, for example, so that youngsters will be able to board school buses with minimal problems. Or, they may involve matters that have serious potential impact on the lives of adults: dealing with a teacher or, perhaps, a subordinate administrator who is seen as incompetent.

In other words, the position taken here is that everything a school principal does and how well he or she does it is somehow related to the viability, or lack of it, of a school as an educational organization. It is these "everythings" that describe the work of school principals. This way of thinking, based on observations and discussions, suggests that these "everythings" may be thought of as activities that are aimed at:

- keeping things going as peacefully as possible
- dealing with conflict or avoiding it
- healing wounds
- supervising the work of others
- developing the organization
- implementing educational ideas

Some of these activities, as has been noted, are hard for the outsider to observe. Some may involve only a brief "okay" on the telephone.

Some may involve fine skills of empathy. Some may involve subtle and political combat with the superintendent. Some may require months of persistent, frustrating attention. Whatever—it is with the idea that the "doing" of these things is a craft that is exercised by a principal in his or her idiosyncratic way that the balance of this chapter is concerned. And this with the caveat that the most that can be hoped for in these pages is the development and illustration of a useful concept.

A POTTER AND A PRINCIPAL

In this section my aim is to make more explicit the idea of the work of a school principal as the exercise of a craft. I do this by way of an analogy that compares the thoughts about her work of a traditional craftsperson (a potter) and those of a school principal as he reflected on a student discipline problem with which he had dealt during the course of a working day. Analogies, of course, break down, as will this one. But the point, I believe, will be made if the reader will try to understand that what is important is the way people think about their work. It is the way people think about what they do that enables us to understand their concept of what it is they are about. These thoughts, as it were, tell us about their "psyche."

What follows are brief and edited protocols of interviews held with the two people mentioned in the previous paragraph. They represent, of course, a sort of mini-N = 2 case study, thus raising questions of reliability and validity regarding the generalizability of any inferences that may be made from them. However, numerous conversations I have had both with a variety of traditional craftspeople and with school principals concerning how they think about their work suggest that the thoughts expressed by these two people are quite representative of a way of thinking that is widely, perhaps universally, shared.

First, in an interview with the potter held on a pleasant lawn on a summer's day on Cape Cod, I started with simply, "Talk with me a bit about what you think about as you start making something out of clay."

The potter:

First, you think about what you want to be your end product, in general terms. Is it going to be practical, non-usable, a fun project, or is it just going to be an experiment? I think you structure it that way. Then you think about the materials, what kind of clay you want to use and this depends on what you want to make. Some clays are high fire and some are low fire; some are very sturdy and some are very delicate. And the character of the clay you use affects the tools you use. If what you're making isn't structurally sound, you have to start all over again. You have to watch out for air bubbles. Sometimes you sense that something's wrong and sometimes you see it. You almost always have some evidence—an air bubble that will make it explode in the kiln, for example. Sometimes you feel it in the clay. You continually make adjustments in what you're doing according to the way you sense things are turning out. The firing starts a whole other process. You have to fire what you've made, glaze it, and fire it again. It can be just what you want after the first firing and then you can mess up the glazing.

The interview with the principal of a middle school was held at the end of a school day. I had spent the day with him, following him around and observing him deal with any number of situations. The particular circumstance to which we attend involved a girl who had been referred to him for cutting classes the previous school day and spending most of the time hiding in one girls' lavatory after another. There is a tragic background to the incident. A classmate of this girl had committed suicide, and it was the day after the funeral when she cut her classes. She had then been referred to the principal. The reason she gave was that she had been grieving over the suicide and had not been able to attend to her school work. The discussion—the principal's work—between the two of them lasted for about twenty minutes. Here is the principal reflecting on that discussion:

One of the things that's important is the time of year. We're starting June and she had been in the office several times during the year. So I know her. But it was difficult because of the suicide. You just don't know whether kids are playing that there's a lot of grief or if there really is. Her mother said she wasn't particularly close to the girl. There were two things I was trying to get to. One, what was the appropriate way to deal with the situation and, also, what was the consequence that fits what she did. What I wanted her to walk out of here knowing is that she's responsible for the decision she makes. When she makes a choice to miss class that there are consequences. The classes are worthwhile and she has to make them up. And I also wanted her to know that the system will provide help for her if she's truly grieving. I gave her a pass so that she could come down and see a counselor any time she wanted to. Part of it is calling her bluff and the other part is, if she's sincere, she can go ahead and get help. You never know for sure about the bluffing. So you let them know that you're listening to them so that they know what their feelings sound like. From there, you can pretty much get an indication of what's going on. It's a matter of covering every base. I pretty much focus on dealing with the here-and-now with kids so that they start to understand the logic of the consequences of their behavior. Kids have to feel like they have their time to be listened to. I think I know when I've been good at what I do when I sense a kid has started to understand what I have on my mind.

What is important to understand about these two brief examples of people talking about their work is not the nature of the work itself, but the parallelism of the thought processes of the potter and the principal. That is, an analogy is an analogy—"a resemblance in some particulars between things that otherwise are unlike." So we attend to the resemblances.

The potter thinks about and has an image of what she wants the end product to look like or what function it will serve. What she does and how and with what she works depends on that initial image. The same holds true for the principal. The potter gives thought to the type of clay she will use to craft her product. The principal, though having no choice about the "material" with which he has to work, gives thought to both the individual involved (i.e., the "material") and the situational context as they may affect how he thinks and what he does. Both give attention to the tools they intend to use and this, too, is related to the image of what they want to "make." The potter and the principal are both aware of circumstances that may cause a shift in what they are doing—or may mean that they have to start crafting their project over again. Both seem to have a sense of the "needs" of their materials. And they both have a "nose" for when things are turning out well or poorly and for the cues that present them with evidence about how things are going. Both know when they have done a good job.

All this, of course, has been too brief for the reader to get a depth of feeling for the richness and the complexities of what is involved in the thinking of these two craftspeople as they reflected on their work and how they go about it. Brief though it may be, the analogy is intended to serve as a living example of the conceptual point made earlier—that as we start to conceive of the work of principals (or other administrators) as a craft, we also are enabled to rid ourselves of the notion that there is such a thing as a science of administration and that in order to be a good principal, one must understand and apply that science. In a way, this is simply a plea for us to recognize the reality of school administrative life for what it is. For example, one will have to search a long time, I believe, before one finds an administrator, a good one or a poor one, who will be able to cite the scientific basis for what he or she does. By the same token, I have never known an administrator who will not be able to talk with you about how he or she goes about the work and the practical rationale for doing things the way he or she does them. The rationale will have all the earmarks of someone engaging in a craft.

There is a more important reason for thinking of the work of principals as a craft than simply the intellectual honesty of it all. It is that thinking of it this way (as not a science and not an art) helps to demystify it and make it knowable in terms that can be readily communicated to others—in terms, for example, that the principal who was quoted above let us know about what he did and why he did it.

Let us take another example, quite different than the previous one, that involved one principal's use of self in a craftlike way in a student disciplinary situation. The situation may be properly categorized as an example of instructional leadership or, as earlier noted, implementing an educational idea. Implementing an educational idea, of course, is typically a long-term proposition. One cannot very easily observe and talk about what happened as in the case with the discipline problem. One must rely on the principal's retrospective analysis of things, thus, as noted earlier, opening up problems of self-report data. Nevertheless, we work with what we have, and what we have here are some comments taken from a lengthy interview with an elementary principal of a rural school who wanted to develop a program of computer instruction on the intermediate level in her school. Again, then, what follows is a brief and edited protocol of the interview followed by an analysis of it:

> I felt a need to provide some kind of computer instruction and awareness for both staff and students, but I didn't want to get swamped. The district had no budget for it, so if it was to happen, I would have to make it happen. I knew I would have to work slowly. I started with the idea that I would have to become computer-literate first. I purchased $5000 worth of equipment in my home by convincing my husband I was buying it for his business, but really knowing I was buying it because I wanted to become somewhat computer-literate before I could even begin to suggest that other people in my district become so. I was able to persuade a local business to donate a computer and some good software. I also tapped a lot of resources of other schools that had computer programs and I attended a conference at my own expense. I wrote a grant for equipment and we were funded. Teachers were very skeptical about it all and I recognized those attitudes. I started with the kids before I started with the teachers. I was thinking about all the arguments that people would have about why we don't need computers in the school and why we shouldn't be bothered by them. I listen closely for cues all the time. I'm a good listener. So I was anticipating all these arguments, but I was also becoming more conscious of the need to do something. So I was thinking about how I was going to resolve that. I was thinking about strategies that would get people to buy into it or, at the least, not oppose it. And I think that's what led me to think about starting with the kids first. They would be my entree into the faculty. I ran a minicourse for fifth and sixth graders. They went back to their rooms all excited and the teachers became curious. I knew the kids would be easier to capture. I've had that experience before—that is, working through the kids to get teachers excited. I've used this strategy before—working with one group to get something from another. That really seems to work for me, but I don't know where I learned to do that. I think it was probably trial and error at some point. But there was never

any conscious intention to learn something. Anyhow, I did a lot of careful planning about the computer lab. In my own mind, I knew what I wanted, but I really didn't share it with the Board because if I had told them we needed twenty computers, it would have seemed exorbitant and the idea would have simply been rejected as being foolish and unreasonable. But little by little we did it, including a volunteer staff development program for teachers which was so-so. I took part in the program, too. I was a learner along with them because I knew that would be important to their accepting the idea. They had to see me struggling along with them. We now have a computer lab with twenty machines and a full-time staff member, too.

Just as how one thinks about and describes the work of principals depends on the perch from which it is viewed, so the analysis and interpretation of an anecdote such as this one depends on one's perch. The scientific viewpoint hardly seems appropriate or, if it is, I am hard put to think what it might be. Likewise, to think of what was related above from an artistic framework (teasing out the "lyrical intuition" or "expressive imagination" that was involved) hardly seems productive. One could, of course, view the anecdote from a problem-solving or planning perspective and use analytical concepts deriving from either of those frameworks. This would be closer to the reality of the situation. The bias here, though, is to think about this brief anecdote of a principal engaged in implementing an educational idea as that person working at her craft, because the idea of craft, as well as dealing with problem solving and planning, makes room for an understanding of the unique use of self in problematic situations. And this, I believe, is what the work of principals is all about.

Consider, then, this analytical framework which is an elaboration of some thoughts expressed previously. The work of a craftsperson involves:

1. *Knowing what the final product should look like*—"I felt a need to provide some kind of computer instruction and awareness of both staff and students."
2. *Understanding the nature and idiosyncrasies of the materials to be worked with*—"The district had no budget for it, so if it was to happen, I would have to make it happen." "Teachers were very skeptical about it all and I recognized those attitudes." "In my own mind, I knew what I wanted, but I didn't want to share it with the Board because if I told them we needed twenty computers, it would have seemed exorbitant and the idea would have simply been rejected as being foolish and unreasonable."
3. *Having appropriate skills and techniques at hand*—"I listen closely for cues all the time. I'm a good listener." "I was able to persuade a local business to donate a computer and some

good software." "I wrote a grant for equipment and we were funded."

4. *Learning and using one's own experience and the experience of others*—"I tapped a lot of resources of other schools that had computer programs and I attended a conference at my own expense." "I knew the kids would be easy to capture. I've had that experience before...." "I've used this strategy before—working with one group to get something from another. I don't know where I learned to do that."

5. *Applying rules of thumb to one's work*—"I knew I would have to work slowly." "I started with the idea that I would have to become computer-literate first...because I wanted to become computer-literate before I could even begin to suggest that other people become so." (The rule of thumb here might be, "If you want to change the world, start with yourself.")

Clearly, there was much more involved in this principal's craftlike implementation of an educational idea than I have been able to illustrate. Indeed, the lengthy interview that was held revealed numerous examples, some of them quite subtle, of thinking and behavior that could be categorized in a manner similar to what has been illustrated. But the point here is that what this chapter is about is the development and illustration of a useful concept for understanding the behavior of school administrators and not an in-depth analysis of that concept as it appears in action. This point notwithstanding, some additional comments need to be made about the situation that has just been briefly described and analyzed.

First and critical to the argument is the fact that this principal, though she did not conceive of herself this way, thought and acted as if she were indeed a craftsperson at work, much as did the principal in the discipline case that was discussed. She had an image in mind of what she wanted to "make"; she was aware of potential "bubbles in the clay"; she possessed a set of skills that enabled her to shape things the way she wanted them to look; and she was guided by some rules of thumb that enabled her, slowly, to produce the final product. Further, at one point in our interview, she noted that what had been produced (the computer lab and the accompanying instructional program) was not "final" in the sense that it need no longer be attended to. It would need continual attention, using a way of thinking not unlike that of the potter who talked about the problems that may occur in the process of glazing something made of clay.

Second, we are left with the question of, Where did she learn to do what she did? Traditional craftspeople usually have had teachers—masters of the craft, perhaps—who guide them, coach them, and subject their work to helpful criticism. Such was not the case here nor has it been with numbers of other administrators with whom I have spoken. Though some have had administrator models after whom they have patterned themselves, few can recall having been taught—but they all have learned. The principal here, for example, when remarking on her strategy of using one group to get something from another, said, "I don't know where I learned to do that." But learn that strategy she quite clearly has and in a way that enables her to do some things she might not otherwise be able to do.

Here is another example of the same thing involving a different principal. It is an example of engaging in instructional leadership by delaying (and perhaps scuttling) a proposed curriculum change. What occurred was this: The principal had been on sabbatical leave to study for an advanced degree. In his absence the director of instruction had pushed for a radical change in part of the curriculum and he was supported by the superintendent. The change was to take place in the September following the sabbatical leave. The principal and his teachers felt the change was uncalled for and also had data on student outcomes to prove their point. This availed them little. The principal recounted:

> So I ended by saying, "If you really want us to devote the hours and the staff time it would take to put together a successful program for September, I'm willing to give you the time. But it will mean a lot of money. Otherwise, I'll be glad to plan for it the following September." I didn't want to be an agitator or appear negative, but I didn't want it to happen as they planned. I was trying to shape the superintendent's stance on the matter. I knew that the money issue would be the one that would probably carry the day. It did. I felt like a conquering hero. I felt like I was playing bridge and had just made a splendid finesse.

And then came my question, "Where did you learn to do something like that?" The answer was, "I don't know. I can't put my finger on it. It's just something I acquired through the years."

I do not intend to imply by these comments that the craft of being a principal cannot be taught, that it is all simply a matter of random trial-and-error learning. To the contrary, part of what makes a craft a craft is that it can be taught—or, at least certain elements can be taught. It is possible, to mention a few, to teach skills and techniques of listening, leading group discussions, planning, ways of understanding and diagnosing problematic situations and conflict management. But, in all likelihood, what cannot be taught is how one best uses oneself, and this is the essence of the principal's craft. It can probably only be learned as one reflects on one's experience.

A third comment needs to be made concerning the argument I have made. It has to do with the idea of "baggage" (Blumberg, 1984). What

I refer to here is the idiosyncratic social, psychological, and intellectual history that each principal brings with him or herself to the job. It has to do with the things we value, our dominant ways of relating to people, our tendencies either to rush into new situations or, perhaps, hold back, our needs for power or to be submissive, and so forth.

Here are a couple of concrete examples, framed as questions, of what I mean by "baggage." In the case of the computer lab anecdote, what was it that influenced this principal to make this an important thing to do? Certainly, every principal has not taken on that task, and her story provides abundant evidence that she was under no pressure to do so. But she did it. For glory? I doubt it. The idea was something that somehow she found attractive, and my hunch is that the attractiveness of it was related to some rather deep-seated system of valuing that she brought with her to her job. For sure, she would be thought of as highly in her district as she is had she not embarked on that venture. So there's a bit of mystery to it. And then there is the second case, that of the principal who refused simply to submit to the superintendent's wishes about curriculum and effectively blocked them, at least temporarily. How come? Why didn't he simply submit? Many principals would have rushed to comply. Was he merely being stubborn? If so, whence his stubbornness?

The essential point to be made from all of this is that part, and perhaps a large part, of how a principal approaches his or her job, the goals that emerge, the manner in which he or she approaches and deals with parents, teachers, students, and fellow administrators, the cues to which he or she pays attention or ignores, cannot be understood, if it ever can, without taking into consideration each principal's "baggage": his or her peculiar way of relating to and making sense of the work-world in which they live. In their study of out-of-the-ordinary principals noted earlier, Blumberg and Greenfield (1986) make this point clearly, though not in the same terms. That is, though each of these principals and the schools in which they presided were considered to be highly effective, each was also different. And the differences seemed clearly to reflect their own life history—the "baggage" of each principal involved.

IN CONCLUSION

My aim in this chapter has been to propose that the work of school principals may be most profitably conceived of as a craft—not as an applied science or as an art; that the thought processes of principals at work are similar to those people who work at traditional crafts; and that what the principal's craft involves is the simultaneous use of self as a judgment maker and as a tool in the vast array of circumstances that arise daily in a school and over the long run. Some of the situations are relatively matter-of-fact, requiring only brief and, perhaps, patterned responses with only minimal judgment being exercised. Many of them, though, are anything but matter-of-fact. They mandate responses that are not patterned, judgments that are delicately thoughtful and many times, perhaps, quite agonizing. Further, regardless of the character of the judgments made, it is probable that one's idiosyncratic intuition and valuing system play a major role in the process.

This position that I take about the work of principals as a craft is not an anti-intellectual one that simply brushes aside all we have learned since people started to think, study, and write about schools. Quite the opposite, I believe that thinking about what principals do and how they do it in the terms I have suggested is a rather exquisitely intellectual enterprise. It has been and continues to be for me, at least.

All this notwithstanding, the appropriate question whether asked out of genuine interest or cynicism is, "So what?" Would it make any difference to anything in the schools if people said, "Let us consciously think of ourselves as working at a craft. Let us think of ourselves, as all serious craftspeople do, as professionals in practice who are continually trying to become more skillful—even creative—in what we do?" Obviously, I think it would make a difference, but just as obviously what I suggest is by no means the panacea for whatever troubles us about the schools.

Although it is also clear to me that if the craft idea of principaling were to be taken seriously, it would change the character of administrative preparation programs and of the work of university professors whose interest is inquiry about administrative behavior, here I will be concerned about what changes might occur in the life of principals on-the-job. I will sketch out three possible scenarios. As a point of departure, I use some of the central ideas discussed in Schon's (1983) important book, *The Reflective Practitioner*. Schon's book is subtitled "How Professionals Think in Action." (It fits rather well with the thrust of this chapter on the craftlike thought process of principals at their work.) He writes of the crisis of confidence in professional knowledge and the limits of technical rationality as it is supposed to form the basis for the thinking and action of professional practitioners but appears to fall far short of that goal. From here he develops the ideas of knowing-in-action (a sort of intuitive "know-how") and reflection-in-action, the thinking we do about doing something. He also touches briefly on the idea of reflection-*on*-action. Through it all, his concern is the development of a knowledge base for professional practice through a focus on "an analysis of the distinctive structure of reflection-in-action" (p. ix).

The focus of *The Reflective Practitioner* on reflection-in-action and this chapter's concern with the principal as a craftsperson link nicely together and form the framework for these concluding remarks. The idea is to propose some images of situations in which these two ideas are brought together in the work life of a principal. Further, these images are based on the knowledge that a principal's behavior, much of which occurs out of public sight, is only rarely (if ever) subjected to the kind of knowing discussion that a potter, for example, might hold with a fellow potter about an object that has been made out of clay.

Scenario 1. Two principals agree that one day a month each of them will "shadow" each other from the moment the person to be shadowed arrives in school until the workday is finished. They will both have done some reading about the reflection-in and -on action process and about the processes of craftlike thinking. They also will have practiced, perhaps in workshops, skills of reflective discussion. The shadower keeps notes or possibly uses a tape recorder concerning what appears to be critical or even not so critical incidents during the day. He or she also keeps notes on events that occur that appear part of long-term happenings in the school.

After the principal's workday is over, the two of them, making sure they have several hours available do something that principals rarely do, talk with each other, the shadower taking the role of a non-critical inquirer about the thoughts and actions of his or her colleague. In this discussion it is the inquirer's role to understand and, in the process, to help the other understand better his or her thinking about the way he or she had engaged in the craft of the principalship that day. The understanding achieved might be confirmatory of the prudence of action judgments that were made or might form the basis for alternative judgments in the future. The discussion might turn to the value base of certain decisions so that the "working" principal could articulate to self some underlying themes that appear to underly his or her behavior. Another probable outcome of this scenario is a simple one. Both principals will feel less isolated.

Scenario 2. The principals of a school district decide to hold a series of their own developmental programs. The subject matter of these programs is built around detailed, written cases of problematic situations that have been confronted by the principals. The process of the sessions is much like those described above and, as in the previous case, the principals have studied about the elements of reflection-in-action and craftlike behavior. They have also practiced holding reflective conversations. That is, they engage with each other in reflective discussion of action in an effort to learn more about how they practice their craft.

This scenario lacks the immediacy of experience that characterizes the first. It also depends on self-reports and not on-the-spot observations. However, these disadvantages may be compensated for by the fact that the total "principal-body" of a school district may start to develop a shared basis for understanding and improving their practice of their craft.

Scenario 3. I think that the first two scenarios are capable of being implemented without too much difficulty. This one would be quite difficult to implement and might involve a high degree of risk for the principal. But its payoff might be correspondingly higher. It involves the possibility of a mix of the first two. The essential difference would be that members of the faculty of the school would replace the principal's peers as observers and data collectors. They might take turns shadowing the principal, taking into consideration his or her needs for privacy or confidentiality at times. Or the principal might prepare detailed written cases as in the previous scenario. The teachers would have studied the ideas of craft and reflection-in-action in a manner similar to the principals. They would then, in large or small groups, hold reflective conversations with their principal concerning how he or she thought the craft of principaling was practiced in that school.

As I noted, this is a high-risk venture. But there are three potential payoffs that could be of great value. First, a school could become more open. Teachers would have a better understanding of the principal's thinking and action. The principal might also get greater understanding of the way teachers think. Second, the process might model a way that the principal could engage teachers in reflective discussion of *their* craft. Third, teachers might feel encouraged to replicate the process among themselves.

In retrospect, a more deep-seated aim of this chapter has been to cast some bread upon the waters.

NOTES

1. Though this chapter is concerned with school principals, the metaphor of craft is applicable to all fields of professional practice.
2. Some people who work in traditional crafts consider themselves, quite appropriately, to be engaged as artists. What they do fits Collingwood's "imaginative vision" idea quite well.

REFERENCES

Blumberg, A. (1984). The craft of administration. *Educational Administration Quarterly*, 20, 4: 24–40.
Blumberg, A., and Greenfield, W. (1986). *The effective principal*, 2d edition. Newton, Mass.: Allyn and Bacon.

Collingwood, R. (1958). *The principles of art.* New York: Oxford.

Croce, B. (1976). In A. Hofstatter and R. Kuhns, eds., *Philosophies of art and beauty.* Chicago: University of Chicago Press.

Cubberley, E. P. (1923). *The principal and his school.* Boston: Houghton Mifflin.

Cubberley, E. P. (1947). *Public education in the United States.* Boston: Houghton Mifflin.

Eisner, E. W. (1984). *The educational imagination.* New York: Macmillan.

Griffiths, D. E. (1979). Another look at research on the behavior of administrators. In G. L. Immegart and W. L. Boyd, eds., *Problem-finding in educational administration.* Lexington, Mass.: D. C. Heath.

Howard, V. A. (1982). *Artistry: the work of artists.* Indianapolis, Ind.: Hackett.

Strayer, G. D., and Thorndike, E. L. (1913). *Educational administration: quantitative studies.* New York: Macmillan.

Willower, D. J., and Kmetz, J. T. (1982). The managerial behavior of elementary school princials. Paper presented at annual meeting of American Educational Research Association, New York.

Wolcott, H. F. (1973). *The man in the principal's office: an ethnography.* New York: Holt, Rinehart & Winston.

4

Moral Imagination
and Interpersonal Competence:
Antecedents to
Instructional Leadership

WILLIAM GREENFIELD

INTRODUCTION

The purpose of this chapter is to understand more fully the concept of "vision," a quality that is closely associated with the success of efforts by instructional leaders to make schools more effective. Instructional leadership refers to actions undertaken to develop a productive and satisfying work environment for teachers and desirable learning conditions and outcomes for children. While such leadership may be provided by teachers or by supervisors and administrators at the district level, it is generally viewed as a special responsibility of the school principal.

The chapter is organized into three parts. The first examines briefly the history of the idea of instructional leadership; the second offers a conceptualization of instructional leadership as "values in action," and explores the ideas of moral imagination and interpersonal competence as antecedents to effective leadership; and the final section presents a framework describing conditions related to the development of these personal qualities in school principals. The chapter concludes with a discussion of implications and recommendations for school districts and administrator preparation programs.

A BRIEF HISTORY

More and better "instructional leadership" is invariably the exhortation one hears in calls for reform and in attendant prescriptions for school improvement (Shoemaker and Fraser, 1981; Edmonds, 1982; Sweeney, 1982; Block, 1983). While this is so, the idea of instructional leadership has remained a muddle for much of this century (Strayer and Engelhardt, 1920; Cunningham and Gephart, 1973). It is one of those great ideas that convey hope and the possibility of progress, but that actually has provided little useful guidance. The idea connotes multiple and ambiguous meanings. It is an idea that has the ring of truth to it, yet it confuses and confounds us as we struggle to explain or enact its meaning in concrete action terms. It is an idea that historically has derived its meaning indirectly, by reference to results rather than to specific actions.

Examples from the literature in educational administration are suggestive of the appeal of the idea to the reform-minded, to those who believe that instruction in public schools can be improved. While not using the specific phrase, this ideal is evident in Cubberley's early assertion that "as is the principal, so is the school" (1929:294). His admonition that "the knowledge, insight, skill, and qualities for helpful leadership of the principal of the school practically determines the ideals and standards of achievements of both teacher and pupils within the school" (p. 295), conveys a now familiar theme: the school principal is a critical actor on the school scene, and the effectiveness of instruction and achievements by children can be tied directly to efforts by the school principal to lead, manage, and supervise teachers and school programs.

In 1954 Mackenzie and Corey noted that the principal was viewed as the "instructional leader of his school" (p. 103) and, more recently, DeBevoise (1984) suggests that instructional leadership means "those actions that a principal takes, or delegates to others, to promote growth in student learning" (p. 15). Sergiovanni (1984) refers to "leadership forces" that "can be thought of as a means available to administrators, supervisors, and teachers to bring about or preserve changes needed to improve schooling" (p. 6).

The point in mentioning these writers' thoughts about instructional leadership and school improvement is not to deride the validity of their observations but, to the contrary, to note that the twofold theme of instructional leadership and school improvement has a long history among public educators, and that this idea is as potent today as in the 1920s. However, despite the passage of time and the numerous calls for "more and better" instructional leadership during the past eighty years or so, the idea itself remains ambiguous, and evidence supporting any sort of direct cause-and-effect relationship between the effort of school principals and the accomplishments of teachers and pupils remains muddled to a large degree (Purkey and Smith, 1983; Rowen et al, 1983; Murphy et al, 1983).

Where does this leave us? Shall we toss out this idea and invent some substitute metaphor? I think not, for if nothing else, the idea has value as a rallying cry to action—it conveys the hope and the possibility of more effective schools, and it suggests that the school principal has a central part to play as the drama of school reform continues to unfold. I believe both of these notions are true: that schools can be improved and that school principals can play an important part in those efforts. However, we need to get beyond the rallying cry. Exhortations alone will not result in more and better instructional leadership. This appears to be occurring as educational researchers and inquiring school administrators more closely monitor and examine the actual work of school principals and the activities and outcomes of teaching and learning (Bossert et al., 1982; Bridges, 1982; Dwyer, 1984).

PERSONAL QUALITIES OF THE PRINCIPAL

The thesis advanced in this chapter is that an understanding of the antecedents to effective instructional leadership can be gained by focusing more attention on understanding the personal qualities of individuals—the knowledge skills, beliefs, and personal dispositions characterizing the individual teacher or school principal—and the relationships between those qualities and the demands and characteristics of the work situation itself. That is, the presence or absence of certain personal qualities may influence the ability of the individual to be effective in specific work environments. For example, numerous studies describe the work environment of the principalship as highly ambiguous, suggesting that individuals with a high tolerance for ambiguity will be more likely than others to cope effectively with such a situation, (Foskett, 1967; Goldhammer, 1971; Wolcott, 1973; Byrne, Hines, and McCleary, 1978; Gorton and McIntyre, 1978; Dwyer, Lee, Rowan, and Bossert, 1983; and Morris, Crowson, Hurwitz, and Porter-Gehrie, 1981).

Studies of the work of school principals and effective schools increasingly point to the significance of aspects of the work itself and contextual properties of the school, its environment, and its history as important determinants of the activities of principals and teachers and instructional outcomes for children (Cuban 1984; Manasse, 1985; Dwyer, 1984). However, personal qualities of the individual teacher or the principal continue to receive limited attention, by researchers and by those concerned with staff development programs and associated efforts aimed at improving the day-to-day performance of professional educators. The issue is not to study traits, attitudes, and other individual characteristics per se (Bridges, 1982), but rather to understand the relationships between the knowledge, skills, and dispositions of individuals and characteristics of the situation in which they work. This strategy assumes that individual effectiveness in a given situation is in large part a function of the degree of match between the demands of the situation and the knowledge, skills, and dispositions of the individual (Becker, 1964; Schein, 1978).

While relationships between the personal qualities of school leaders and elements of the school work culture and organizational context are not well understood, evidence does suggest that the character of the principal is central to leading a school effectively (Blumberg and Greenfield, 1986). Blumberg and Greenfield's initial study (1980) identified vision, initiative, and resourcefulness as three key elements associated with a principal's effectiveness and resulted in the development of a "grounded" or middle-range theory of leading a school. Given certain features of the role of principal which derive both from the larger system and from the school itself, Blumberg and Greenfield speculate that several personal qualities characterize the principal who would lead a school well:

- Being highly goal-oriented and having a keen sense of clarity regarding instructional and organizational goals;
- having a high degree of personal security and a well-developed sense of themselves as persons;
- having a high tolerance for ambiguity and a marked tendency to test the limits of the interpersonal and organizational systems they encounter;
- being inclined to approach problems from a highly analytical perspective and being highly sensitive to the dynamics of power in both the larger systems and in their own school;
- being inclined to be proactive rather than reactive—to be in charge of the job and not let the job be in charge of them;
- having a high need to control a situation and low needs to be controlled by others—they like being in charge of things and initiating action;
- having high needs to express warmth and affection toward others, and to receive it—being inclined toward friendliness and good-natured fellowship; and
- having high needs to include others in projects on problem solving, and moderate-to-high needs to want others to include them.

(1986: 181–185)

Their discussion of the results of a follow-up study of the principals who participated in the original investigation emphasizes the "embeddedness" of the principalship in the school culture, and lends additional support to the idea that the personal qualities of school principals are instrumental determinants of their success in coming to terms with a school's culture, the value of orientations of teachers as a social group, and the larger organizational and community context in which the school is situated (1986).

Although there has been only limited study of the specific "qualities of person" presumed to characterize those who would enact an instructional leadership conception of the principalship (DeBevoise, 1984), current images of that role usually contain three key ideas: (1) that the effective principal holds an image or a vision of what he or she wants to accomplish; (2) that this vision serves as a general guide for the principal as he or she sets about the activities of managing and leading a school; and (3) that the focus of the principal's work activity should be upon matters related to instruction and the classroom performance of teachers (Manasse, 1985; Strother, 1983). Like many others, I agree that a school principal can and should be instrumental in determining the direction and effectiveness of school programs, and that "vision" is a critical antecedent to effective leadership. However, assuming for the moment that these assertions are plausible and that they could be verified empirically, an important twofold question remains: How does one evolve a vision regarding organizational arrangements and/or instructional programs, and how does one articulate it to others and influence them to act to achieve that vision?

The purpose of the next section is to examine the concept of "vision" and to explore its fuller meaning vis-à-vis the nature of leadership in schools. The discussion will then turn to a consideration of factors that may be instrumental in the development of school administrators capable of "vision" and committed to leading schools and improving instruction.

INSTRUCTIONAL LEADERSHIP: VALUES IN ACTION

Instructional leadership refers to actions undertaken with the intention of developing a productive and satisfying working environment for teachers and desirable learning conditions and outcomes for children. Such leadership is effective to the extent that these broad purposes are achieved in a particular school or school district. The discussion to follow is centered on instructional leadership by school principals, though it is believed that the elements and conditions to be described are also relevant to instructional leadership by teachers, department heads, and others committed to school effectiveness.

Two aspects of the work situation of principals appear critical. First, decisions must be made and actions must be taken, usually in the face of competing and conflicting norms. That is, the standards by which others will judge whether the chosen decision or action alternative is appropriate or effective may be unknown, unclear, or may be different from those employed by the principal. Second, the principal's work-world is a highly interpersonal one. Frequent verbal exchanges and face-to-face interaction with teachers, students, parents, supervisors, and other adults on the school scene (aides, custodians, cafeteria workers, and security personnel, for example) characterize much of the work of a principal. The capacity of a principal to influence instructional and organizational arrangements thus depends to a large degree upon his or her ability to work effectively with and through people.

Embedded in the concept of instructional leadership is the idea that there is both a factual and a value component to action. Decision or action alternatives always require the assignment of values to facts and the exercise of judgment in arriving at an alternative—to embark upon one line of action versus another, or to choose one decision alternative over another (Simon, 1957). These often are choices of habit and may not necessarily involve deliberate and conscious choice between competing facts and values, but action always requires that a judgment be made. Whether by habit or by deliberation, judgments are made as values are assigned to facts and as decision or action alternatives are evaluated (Dewey, 1957).

Instructional leadership as it is conceived here thus involves the assignment of values to facts and the necessity to select one decision or course of action over another. Decisions and action alternatives often confront the principal with competing standards of goodness—the criterion one uses as the basis for judging that one alternative is to be preferred over others. Will it be a standard efficiency, friendship, good educational practice, convenience, political expediency, or some other standard? In this sense there is a moral component to action, and principals or others engaged in instructional leadership may frequently be confronted with moral dilemmas. The concept of "moral imagination" is discussed next to suggest aspects of the processes by which one evolves a "vision" regarding the educational or organizational arrangements in one's school.

Moral Imagination

Moral imagination refers to the inclination of a person to see that the world, in this case the school and the associated activities of teaching and learning, need not remain as it is—that it is possible for it to be otherwise, and to be better (Green, 1984). It is the ability to see the discrepancy between how things are and how they might be—not in terms of the ideal, but in terms of what is possible, given a particular school situation. This is the element of "imagined" possibility.

It is "moral" imagination because the discrepancy, the possibility envisioned, is rooted in an awareness of and a commitment to the standards of good practice, of effective schools and good teaching, that characterize membership in the normative community of educators. Thus it is "moral" in that it is the application of some standard of goodness that illuminates the discrepancy between the present and what is possible, and better.

Vision, then, results from the exercise of moral imagination. The latter is a process that involves observation of the current state of affairs in a school and the making of a judgment as to whether or not the current state is satisfactory. Implicit in the activity of making a judgment is the application of some standard of goodness. It is a consideration of what is observed in light of the standard applied that results in the decision to leave things as they are, or to try and change them for the better. Engaging in this process is thus requisite to the development of a "vision" of what might be both possible and better, in a particular school situation.

Given the decision to pursue some more desirable alternative, relative to what is observed in the present, the principal must then act to realize those objectives. He or she must articulate the vision to others, and move others to action aimed at achieving or at least working toward the desired state. Because the school setting is essentially a social situation, the principal's primary means of influencing what happens in a school is to work with and through teachers and others. "Interpersonal competence" thus is central in articulating one's vision to others and in influencing others to act on that vision.

Interpersonal Competence

The daily work of the principal is characterized by an endless series of brief interpersonal encounters and exchanges with students, teachers, parents, superiors, and others (Peterson, 1978). To paraphrase a recent study of principals, "talk is the work" (Gronn, 1983). The medium of the work is verbal, and it frequently involves face-to-face interaction (Wolcott, 1973). The social order negotiated by the principal is highly complex and often is characterized by competing norms and expectations, and it is not unusual that misunderstandings, conflicts, and miscommunication occur (Dwyer et al., 1984 & 1985; Lortie, Crow, and Prolman, 1983; Morris et al., 1981).

Interpersonal competence refers to the knowledge and skills that enable an individual to shape the responses he or she gets from others (Foote and Cottrell, 1955; Argyris, 1962). In an extension of that idea, Weinstein (1969) conceptualizes interpersonal competence as the interrelation of ten basic elements:

> Interpersonal task—The response one actor is intending to elicit from another.

Interpersonal competence—Being able to achieve interpersonal tasks.

Lines of action—What one actor actually does to elicit a desired task response from another.

Encounter—Any contact between people that involves an interpersonal task by at least one party to the exchange.

Situation—All the potentially meaningful stimuli present in an encounter.

Defining the situation—The process by which participants in an encounter select and organize situational stimuli into a coherent understanding of what is actually occurring during an encounter.

Projected definition of the situation—These are lines of action by one actor intended to influence another actor's definition of the situation.

Working consensus—This is the definition of the situation to which participants in the encounter jointly subscribe.

Situational identity—All relevant situational characteristics determining who the actors are and what they represent to one another.

Identity bargaining—The process by which actors influence their own or each other's situational identity.

The last concept, that of identity bargaining, is pivotal (Weinstein: 757). Identity bargaining is the process through which one shapes the situational identity projected and maintained for one's self and for others, and it is this situational identity that determines one's ability to influence another; that is, to get the desired response. The challenge for the principal is to develop a working consensus among teachers as to what the situation is and what needs to be done given that definition of the situation.

Critical to successful identity bargaining is the ability of the principal to take the role of the other and to predict the effect of certain lines of action on the other. Being able to establish and maintain an identity that will enable one to influence another successfully requires the ability to view and understand the situation from the other's perspective (Goffman, 1959). This is what enables a principal to determine which lines of action will be most effective in eliciting the desired response. Being able to influence a teacher successfully thus depends to a large degree upon being familiar with an extensive set of possible lines of action to enact.

School contexts differ and what is possible in one setting may not be possible in another. A school in a relatively homogeneous rural farming community, with stable student enrollment and low faculty turnover, represents conditions that differ in many respects from those one might find in an inner-city school populated by poor children and characterized by high turnover among both students and faculty. They each represent somewhat different potentials regarding what might be achieved instructionally or in terms of organizational arrangements. Similarly, all teachers are not the same, and each will differ to some extent in how he or she defines a given situation and in terms of the resources he or she might possess in the form of certain knowledge, skills, or attitudes. What works with one teacher in a given situation may not be effective in another situation, or with a different teacher.

Being interpersonally competent therefore requires that one have in his or her possession a fairly extensive set of possible lines of action to enact. The idea of being interpersonally competent as a principal thus implies not only a good deal of familiarity with the work of teachers, but also requires that the principal be knowledgeable about the viewpoints that teachers hold of themselves, their students and colleagues, and their work.

To summarize the discussion to this point, two major ideas have been suggested as the cornerstones of effective instructional leadership. The ability to exercise "moral imagination" underlies one's capacity to develop a compelling vision regarding what it is possible and desirable to achieve in a given school situation, vis-à-vis more effective instructional practices and organizational arrangements. "Interpersonal competence," the ability to elicit desired task responses from another, refers to the knowledge and skills needed to influence teachers and others in desired directions.

In each instance a judgment must be made. One must apply some standard of goodness as the basis for deciding upon a preferred course of action. The chosen course of action may be aimed at eliciting a desired task behavior from another in the immediate situation, such as influencing a teacher to experiment with an alternative method of instruction or another way to manage student behavior. On a larger scale, it may be aimed at cultivating or maintaining a more encompassing "vision" of what is possible and desirable in a given school, vis-à-vis organizational and subgroups' norms and practices associated with effective instruction, improved school-community relations, or other activities or outcomes. In both cases, standards of goodness are applied and a judgment is made.

Neither the exercise of moral imagination nor being interpersonally competent occurs in a contextual vacuum. In both cases one is constrained by and must be sensitive to the realities and the limits characterizing a particular school, a group of students, or a particular teacher or group of teachers. The exercise of moral imagination thus is the ability to see the discrepancy between how things are and how they might be—*not* in terms of the ideal, but in terms of *what is possible* given a particular individual, group, or school situation.

In order to lead a school well it is proposed that one must have a "vision" of what is desirable and possible in that school's context, and one must also be able to mobilize others to work to achieve those possibilities. Leading a school thus requires that one be knowledgeable about and committed to the standards of good educational practice, and that one be interpersonally competent and thereby able to articulate those possibilities to others, and to move others to action to work toward those goals.

SOCIALIZATION FOR INSTRUCTIONAL LEADERSHIP

How do instructional leaders became interpersonally competent, and how do they develop their capacity to exercise moral imagination? If, indeed, these two personal qualities are antecedent to one's ability to lead a school, can their development be guided or cultivated by a school district or by a professional preparation program in educational administration? The writer believes that the second question can be answered affirmatively, and that knowing how to cultivate these two qualities of leadership depends upon answering the first question—how are these qualities developed, by what process? Socialization theory offers a number of useful ideas and serves as a general framework guiding the discussion to follow.

Socialization refers to the process and conditions that mediate the acquisition of knowledge, skills, beliefs, and personal dispositions required to perform a given role satisfactorily (Brim and Wheeler, 1966). The processes by which this occurs can be differentiated into those that are formal and those that are informal. *Formal processes* refer to role-learning situations in which both the role of learner and the material to be learned are specified in advance. One example is a professional preparation program designed to train and develop prospective school administrators. Another example is found in staff development programs and in-service education activities sponsored by school districts and professional associations.

Informal socialization processes refer to those in which neither the role of learner nor the material to be learned are specified. One example is the process encountered by a newcomer to the school setting. Although neither the "learner" role nor the "lessons to be learned" are formally specified in advance, the rookie teacher quickly learns the do's and dont's of what it means to be a teacher in that school. The informal group norms are passed on fairly quickly by "old hands," and the rookie who deviates from those norms is likely to experience difficulty in gaining acceptance by the group. Another example is the informal learning that occurs as one makes the transition from teaching to administration. Upwardly mobile teachers take on more and more of the values and orientations of the administrator group, and begin to develop administrative skills and values as they engage in administrative activities and interact more frequently with administrators (Greenfield, 1985a). In both cases the learner role and the material to be learned are not clearly specified—yet much role-relevant learning nevertheless occurs.

In addition to these formal and informal role-learning processes, socialization theory points to important variations in the "content" to be learned. Socialization outcomes can be characterized as moral or technical. *Moral outcomes* refer to the sentiments, beliefs, standards of practice, and value orientations characterizing the reference group in which one holds or seeks membership. *Technical outcomes* refer to the instrumental knowledge and skills required to perform satisfactorily tasks associated with a given role.

Moral and technical learning outcomes can be influenced by formal as well as informal socialization processes. In educational administration, as in many other fields of practice, efforts to develop the capabilities of prospective practitioners tend to emphasize technical knowledge and skills, and depend primarily upon formal rather than informal processes. However, moral socialization outcomes generally receive little explicit attention through formal processes, and thus the development of beliefs, values, and role-relevant sentiments and personal dispositions tends to occur informally in school settings. As a result, what one learns is highly variable and depends upon the character of the individuals with whom one associates, what kind of work one does, and the culture that characterizes a particular work group or school setting (Greenfield, 1985b).

Four basic relationships describe the conditions that influence the socialization of school administrators, and these are depicted in Figure 4.1 as the interaction between the nature of the material to be learned (moral and technical) and the processes by which such learning occurs (formal and informal). Cell I represents the current focus of formal efforts to help school administrators acquire the technical knowledge and skills needed to perform administrative tasks and duties. The examples reflected in this cell are illustrative of the kinds of formal activities employed to influence the technical role-learning of administrators. Cell II suggests potential sources of formal moral development, but tends not to be fully exploited in current practice; the formal learning that occurs is likely to be rather limited in scope and rarely is an explicit socialization target in either graduate programs or in-service programs.

Cells III and IV represent informal, on-the-job learning opportunities, with technical knowledge and skill being the focus in Cell III, and group norms, individual values, and standards of practice being the focus in Cell IV. These two cells represent the most complex learning conditions for two reasons. First, the material itself is not formally specified. What is learned comes through informal association with others and as a result of doing particular tasks. Second, in actual practice there is often a moral dimension to the technical skill or knowledge to be acquired. In other words, some techniques or "ways of doing things" are preferred over others. They may or may not be more ef-

Socialization Outcomes

	Technical	Moral
Formal	Cell I: • Technical knowledge and skills in preparation programs. • Workshops sponsored by professional associations • Staff development activities in school districts • Administrative internships	Cell II: • Codes of ethics • National reports on excellence and reform • Standards of practice promoted by professional associations • Simulations, role-playing and modeling focused on values and standards
Informal	Cell III: • Learning the ropes (the tasks) • Sponsor-protege relationships • Engaging in administrative duties • Committee assignments at the school and district level	Cell IV: • Learning the ropes (the group's norms) • Aspiring to become an administrator • Associating with administrators • Resolving value conflicts

*(Left vertical axis label: **Socialization Processes**)*

FIGURE 4.1 Socialization Processes and Outcomes in Educational Administration (Based upon Brim and Wheeler, 1966).

fective in an empirical sense, but they frequently are assumed to be effective, and they almost always are viewed as "appropriate" or as "better" than another alternative. This may occur for several reasons. The emphasis on some skills but not others, and the value attributed to some facts and not others may be influenced by various elements: a school's history and its immediate context; the culture of the work group; the values and dispositions of influentials in the setting; traditions within the community; and perhaps the reality that a given practice "works"—or at least appears to work given the criteria applied by the actors involved.

The preceding discussion identified formal and informal processes by which the development of moral imagination and interpersonal competence are believed to occur. The framework depicted in Figure 4.1 suggested that the knowledge and skills requisite to developing and articulating a "vision" of desirable instructional and organizational arrangements in a school have both a technical and a moral component, and, to the extent that one develops these personal qualities, they tend to be learned informally, rather than deliberately.

IMPLICATIONS AND RECOMMENDATIONS

The school is a normatively complex and ambiguous organizational setting wherein one encounters numerous moral dilemmas. A principal is regularly confronted by the necessity to take action or make a decision in the face of competing and often conflicting standards of goodness; hence, the importance of the ability to exercise moral imagination. Further, the school situation is essentially social in character, and if the principal is to influence instructional and organizational arrangements, he or she is constrained by the necessity to work closely with and through people; hence, the importance of being interpersonally competent. The discussion to follow suggests that the two personal qualities of moral imagination and interpersonal competence can be deliberately developed and cultivated, and that graduate preparation and staff development and in-service programs can be more effective than they currently are in helping prospective instructional leaders develop these qualities.

Developing Moral Imagination

Moral imagination requires technical skills in observation and analysis as well as formal knowledge about alternative standards of good practice—the criteria by which one judges the desirability of a given situation, relative to what is possible. The technical skills of observation, data collection, and analysis could be the focus of formal learning activities in Cell I, and proficiency would be fairly easy to determine. Standards of good practice, the criteria applied in the process of determining the value of alternatives and judging which alternative is to be preferred, would be the province of formal learning in Cell II. Proficiency regarding an individual's knowledge of standards (normative as well as empirical) and skills in developing and defending competing arguments related to those standards, could be assessed rather easily through oral or written examination, or perhaps through evaluation of a number of short "position papers" written by the candidate.

It is not suggested that prospective or practicing administrators be indoctrinated, but rather that they be deliberately introduced to alternative empirical and normative standards of effective practice, and that they be provided with formally designed opportunities to apply those standards in simulated conditions: to practice resolving value conflicts; to engage in discussions of standards; and to prepare defenses of the relative merits of one standard of practice over another. In short, formal moral socialization efforts (Cell II) would attempt to assure that school administrators become informed of competing standards of good practice, and that they have opportunities to practice making and defending their decisions regarding the alternatives they believe would be most desirable in given situations.

Administering and leading a school requires actions and decisions, and doing so involves reliance on both moral and technical knowledge and skill. It is proposed that providing administrators with deliberately conceived opportunities to acquire and use knowledge about competing standards of good and effective practice will increase their capacity to exercise moral imagination, and will increase the likelihood that they will be able to administer and lead a school well.

Developing Interpersonal Competence

How do administrators develop interpersonal competence? The dominant mode at present occurs informally as depicted in Cells III and IV, although it is true that limited opportunities exist in some preparation programs and through some in-service programs (workshops in conflict management, communications, and interpersonal skill development, for example). However, those formal opportunities that do exist are for the most part found in only a few preparation and in-service programs, and the focus is likely to be limited only to the interpersonal *skill* dimension.

As described in the preceding section, interpersonal competence calls not only for certain skills, but also requires a great deal of formal and informal *knowledge* about the work activities and perspectives of the person whom one desires to influence. Thus, to be interpersonally competent as an instructional leader, one needs certain skills as well as a great deal of *knowledge* about teachers, the teaching task, and teachers' views of themselves, their students, and their work. A substantial formal knowledge base exists for all of these areas, and much could be done in formal (Cell I) types of activities to introduce individuals to this knowledge and to provide them with opportunities to practice using that knowledge *and* the related interpersonal skills.

While the centrality of interpersonal competence to influencing others in a school setting may seem obvious, it is an aspect of the principal's role that is largely unattended to by those concerned with understanding the nature of leadership in schools. This aspect of the work of principals requires a critical set of skills and knowledge that are basically ignored by those concerned with selecting, training, and developing school administrators.

The discussion thus far has suggested several points of intervention through formal processes. It is also possible to intervene in informal processes, and to do so without reducing the special "potency" that accompanies such learning conditions. The key strategy available to school districts, which is where the bulk of the informal learning occurs, is to attend more carefully to the general conditions associated with the processes employed to recruit, select, and develop prospective and practicing administrators. Interventions might occur in several ways: by being sure that recruits have many practice opportunities to make judgments about instruction and organizational arrangements and to influence teachers; by being sure that district and school expectations for administrator and teacher practices are clearly communicated and reinforced, and that they reflect what is known empirically about effective practice; and by being sure that prospective leaders are exposed to good role-models—those who have demonstrated their capacity to exercise moral imagination and their interpersonal competence with teachers and others. The basic issue is not to "formalize" the informal, but rather to capitalize on what is known to occur informally by shaping and structuring the circumstances through which those learning processes unfold.

CONCLUSION

The purpose of this chapter has been to call attention to the importance of the personal qualities of instructional leaders, and to suggest that it is possible to identify those qualities and to intervene in their development. Vision was noted as an important element in leading and managing a school, and moral imagination and interpersonal competence were discussed as lower-order concepts associated with that element of instructional leadership.

The ability to exercise moral imagination, and thereby to be able to develop and articulate a vision of what is possible and desirable in a school situation, is the foundation upon which the moral authority of the principal rests, and which enables a principal to lead a school well. While authority of position provides the principal with an institutionalized base for influence, it is not a sufficient basis for leading a school. Yet too often it appears to be the only basis used by principals, and thus many attempts to improve the school are resisted or aborted.

Several points of intervention were noted whereby school districts and professional preparation programs might influence the development of these and other personal qualities. The school is a sociocultural situation and instructional leaders must work with and through people, in a context of competing standards of goodness, to influence school programs and learning outcomes for students. This reality of the administrator's work-world has not been addressed to any great extent by researchers or by those concerned with increasing the effectiveness of school administrators.

More attention by researchers to understanding the connections between the personal qualities of administrators and their effectiveness at leading and managing schools promises to yield much useful knowledge about the nature of leadership in schools. Efforts by school districts and by professional preparation programs to intervene more deliberately in the processes by which administrators learn their roles promises the possibility of increasing their capability to be effective in leading and managing instruction.

REFERENCES

Argyris, Chris (1962). *Interpersonal Competence and Organizational Effectiveness.* Homewood, Illinois: Dorsey Press.

Becker, H. S. (1964). "Personal change in adult life." *Sociometry, 27,* no. 1, (March, 1964): 40–53.

Block, A. W., Ed. (1983). *Effective schools: A summary of research.* Arlington, Va.: Educational Research Service.

Blumberg, A., and Greenfield, W. D. (1980). *The effective principal.* Boston, Mass.: Allyn and Bacon.

———. (1986). *The effective principal,* 2d. ed. Boston, Mass.: Allyn and Bacon.

Bossert, S.; Dwyer, D.; Rowan, B.; and Lee, G. (1982). "The instructional management role of the principal." *Educational Administration Quarterly, 18,* (3) 1982: 34–64.

Bridges, E. (1982). "Research on the school administrator: the state of the art, 1967–1980." *Educational Administration Quarterly, 18* (3) 1982: 12–33.

Brim, Orville, G., Jr., and Wheeler, Stanton. (1966). *Socialization after childhood: Two essays.* New York: John Wiley & Sons.

Byrne, D.; Hines, S.; and McCleary, L. (1978). *The Senior High School Principalship. vol. I. The National Survey.* Reston, Va.: National Association of Secondary School Principals.

Cuban, L. (1984). "Transforming the frog into a prince: Effective schools research, policy, and practice at the district level. *Harvard Educational Review, 54,* (2) May, 1984: 129–51.

Cubberley, E. P. (1929). *Public school administration.* New York: Houghton Mifflin Company.

Cunningham, L. L., and Gephart, W. J. Ed. (1973). *Leadership: The science and the art today.* Itasca, Ill.: F. E. Peacock Publishers.

DeBevoise, W. (1984). "Synthesis of research on the principal as instructional leader." *Educational Leadership,* February, 1984, pp. 14–20.

Dewey, J. (1957). *Human Nature and Conduct.* New York: Random House.

Dwyer, D.; Alpert, B.; Lee, G.; Barnett, B.; Filby, N.; Rowan, B. (May, 1985). *Jonathan Rolf and Larkspur Elementary School: Instructional leadership in an affluent suburban setting.* San Francisco, Calif.: Far West Laboratory for Educational Research and Development.

Dwyer, D.; Lee, G.; Barnett, B.; Filby, N.; Rowan, B. (November, 1985). *Emma Winston and Roosevelt Elementary School: Instructional leadership in an inner city setting.* San Francisco, Calif.: Far West Laboratory for Educational Research and Development.

———. (November, 1985). *Grace Lancaster and Emerson Junior High School:*

Instructional leadership in an urban setting. San Francisco, Calif.: Far West Laboratory for Educational Research and Development.

———. (November, 1985). *Frances Hedges and Orchard Park Elementary School: Instructional leadership in a stable urban setting.* San Francisco, Calif.: Far West Laboratory for Educational Research and Development.

———. (November, 1985). *Ray Murdock and Jefferson Elementary School: Instructional leadership in a rural setting.* San Francisco, Calif.: Far West Laboratory for Educational Research and Development.

———. (November, 1985). *Florence Barnhart and Kirkland Junior High School: Instructional leadership in an inner city setting.* San Francisco, Calif.: Far West Laboratory for Educational Research and Development.

———. (November, 1985). *Louis Wilkins and Berry Hill Elementary School: Instructional leadership in a suburban setting.* San Francisco, Calif.: Far West Laboratory for Educational Research and Development.

Dwyer, D.; Lee, G.; Rowan, B.; Bossert, S. (1983). *Five principals in action: Perspectives on instructional management.* San Francisco, Calif.: Far West Laboratory for Educational Research and Development.

Dwyer, D. (1984). "The search for instructional leadership: Routine and subtleties in the principal's role," *Educational Leadership,* February, 1984, pp. 32–37.

Edmonds, R. (February, 1982). Programs for school improvement: A 1982 overview. Michigan State University.

Foote, M., and Cottrell, L. (1955). *Identity and interpersonal competence.* Chicago: University of Chicago Press.

Foskett, J. (1967). *The normative world of the elementary school principal.* Eugene, Oreg.: Center for the Advanced Study of Educational Administration.

Goffman, E. (1959). *The presentation of self in everyday life.* Garden City, N.Y.: Doubleday & Co.

Goldhammer, K. (1971). *Elementary principals and their schools.* Eugene, Oreg.: Center for the Advanced Study of Educational Administration.

Gorton, T., and McIntyre, K. (1978). *The senior high school principalship, vol. 2. The effective principal.* Reston, Va.: National Association of Secondary School Principals.

Green, T. (1984). *The formation of conscience in an age of technology.* Syracuse University, Syracuse, New York: John Dewey Society.

Greenfield, W. D. (1985). Being and becoming a principal: Responses to work contexts and socialization processes. Paper presented at the American Educational Research Association Annual Meeting, Chicago, March 31–April 4, 1985.

———. (1985). The moral socialization of school administrators: Informal role learning outcomes. *Educational Administration Quarterly, 21,* (4) Fall, 1985: 99–120.

Gronn, P. C. (1983). Talk as the work: The accomplishment of school administration. *Administrative Science Quarterly, 28,* (1983): 1–21.

Lortie, D. C.; Crow, G.; and Prolman, S. (May, 1983). The elementary school principal in suburbia: An occupational and organizational study. National Institute of Education Final Report, U.S. Department of Education, (Contract No. 400–77–0094).

Mackenzie, G. N., and Corey, S. M. (1954). *Instructional leadership.* New York: Bureau of Publications, Teachers College, Columbia University.

Manasse, A. L. (1985). Improving conditions for principal effectiveness: Policy implications of research. *Elementary School Journal, 85* (3), January, 1985: 439–63.

Morris, V.; Crowson, R.; Hurwitz, E; and Porter-Gehrie, C. (1981). *The urban principal: Discretionary decision-making in a large educational organization.* Chicago: University of Illinois at Chicago Circle.

Murphy, J.; Hallinger, P.; and Mitman, A. (1983) Problems with research on educational leadership: Issues to be addressed. *Educational Evaluation and Policy Analysis, 5,* no. 3, (Fall, 1983): 297–305.

Peterson, K. (1978). The principal's tasks. *Administrator's Notebook, 26* (8), 1978: 1–4.

Purkey, S., and Smith, M. (1983). Effective schools: A review. *Elementary School Journal 83,* 1983: 427–52.

Rowan, B., Bossert, S; and Dwyer, D. (1983). Research on effective schools: A cautionary note. *Educational Researcher, 12,* (4) 1983: 24–31.

Schein, E. H. (1978). *Career dynamics: Matching individual and organizational needs.* Menlo Park, Calif.: Addison-Wesley.

Sergiovanni, T. J. (1984). Leadership and excellence in schooling. *Educational Leadership,* February 1984, pp. 4–13.

Shoemaker, J., and Fraser, H. (1981). What principals can do: some implications from studies of effective schooling. *Phi Delta Kappan,* November 1981, pp. 178–82.

Simon, H. A. (1957). *Administrative behavior.* 2d ed. New York: Free Press.

Strayer, G. D., and Engelhardt, N. L. (1920). *The classroom teacher.* New York: American Book Co.

Strother, D. B., Ed. (1983). *The role of the principal.* Bloomington, Ind.: Phi Delta Kappan.

Sweeney, J. (1982). Research Synthesis on Effective School Leadership. *Educational Leadership,* February, 1982, pp. 346–52.

Weinstein, E. (1969). The development of interpersonal competence. In the *Handbook of Socialization Theory and Research,* edited by D. Goslin, Chicago: Rand-McNally.

Wolcott, H. F. (1973). *The man in the principal's office: An ethnography.* New York: Holt, Rinehart, & Winston.

PART TWO

Leading and
Managing Schools

Despite its attractiveness as a slogan guiding the efforts of reformists, instructional leadership is an elusive concept and offers little guidance about the actual nature of leadership in schools. Much of the research literature emphasizes the importance of instructional leadership as a vehicle through which the classroom performances of teachers can be improved, but provides few clues about those factors that mitigate the difficulties of observing teachers more closely and more frequently. Similarly, studies of instructional leadership and effective schools pay scant attention to the plethora of noninstructional demands on school leaders, nor do most studies consider the effects of district-level mechanisms of control and influence on the enactment of instructional leadership.

The chapters in Part Two place the concept of instructional leadership in perspective by noting the broad range of activities associated with leading and managing a school and making instructional programs more effective. In Chapter Five Ginny Lee describes the work of one junior high principal, revealing that there are many "routine and non-routine activities" associated with leading and managing a school, and that many of those are only indirectly related to classroom instruction. In a marked departure from prevailing conceptions of school improvement strategies, Robert Wimpelberg proposes in Chapter Six that most schools, if left to their own devices, are not likely to improve. He explores a "central role for central office," describes the importance of instructional leadership at that level, and concludes that the success of efforts to improve schools on a district-wide basis hinges upon direction and support by the central office.

In Chapter Seven Judith Little and Tom Bird discuss the objective realities mediating efforts by school principals to supervise teachers more closely, and more frequently. The contingencies surrounding such efforts are described in detail, and the chapter concludes with recommendations regarding training and support for instructional leadership "close to the classroom." Part Two concludes with an examination of district-wide influences on the ability of principals to lead and manage schools well. Kent Peterson describes six mechanisms of control and discusses how they shape the enactment of instructional leadership in schools. He concludes that the motivation levels of principals to improve schols can be shaped through careful design of district-level control systems by central office administrators.

While much of the reform literature in education emphasizes the importance of building-level leadership targeted directly on improving the instructional effectiveness of classroom teachers, the perspectives provided in Part Two suggest that the work of instructional leaders encompasses a broader range of activities, that many of those are only indirectly related to instruction, and that district-level forces can be instrumental in shaping the motivation and the abilities of principals to improve their schools.

5

Instructional Leadership in a Junior High School: Managing Realities and Creating Opportunities[1]

GINNY V. LEE

OVERVIEW

Those of us who wish to understand better the work of the secondary school principal in providing instructional leadership face a task for which current knowledge raises as many questions as it suggests useful strategies. Research has provided little specific information about how the leadership behavior of principals actually shapes the operation of school organizations and influences student outcomes. In addition, most recent literature discusses findings about elementary school principals, and their applicability to the secondary level is an important and unresolved question.

Current interest in the principalship has been fueled by studies of effective schools (see, among others, Weber 1971; Armor et al., 1976; Brookover and Lezotte, 1977; Edmonds, 1979; Venezky and Winfield, 1979; Wynne, 1981). This well-known body of research stresses the importance of "strong administrative leadership" for success (Edmonds, 1979). Yet, this work has been criticized for both conceptual and methodological shortcomings (Bossert, Dwyer, Rowan, and Lee, 1982; Rowan, Bossert, and Dwyer, 1983), including its failure to specify "how a principal should exercise this leadership to coordinate and control the instructional program" (Bossert et al., 1982, p. 36).

Additional concerns have been raised by other studies that have examined the principalship. Newburg and Glatthorn (1983), for example, conducted a qualitative study of four principals and concluded that "for the most part principals do not provide instructional leadership" (p. v). Similarly, Morris, Crowson, Hurwitz, and Porter-Gehrie (1982) concluded from their study of twenty-four principals that "instructional leadership . . . is *not* the central focus of the principalship" (p. 689).

These conclusions are not surprising when one considers the perspectives of the studies. In both analyses the concept of instructional leadership was framed within an implicit rational and bureaucratic model of schools; the researchers examined only those activities in which principals were directly and formally concerned with instruction and teacher supervision. This perspective ignores the capacity of the principal to influence instruction through indirect actions that support teaching and learning, through the culture of the school (Firestone and Wilson, 1983) and through the use of routine activities (Dwyer, Lee, Rowan, and Bossert, 1983). Other criticisms of current research on the principalship include the failure of studies to consider the antecedents and consequences of principals' activities (Bridges, 1982; Greenfield, 1982).

The limitations of current research for understanding how principals exercise influence are compounded when we consider questions about elementary and secondary school leadership. Commonly held beliefs among school personnel and researchers maintain that elementary and secondary schools differ in ways that have significant implications for principal leadership. For example, differences in organizational structure (Cuban, 1983) and in participants' sense of shared purpose and goals (Firestone and Herriott, 1982) have been cited as factors influencing how applicable studies of elementary school principals are to secondary school administrators.

Yet, assumptions that secondary principals face different leadership demands from elementary leaders because of the influence of size, complexity, and other factors may not be warranted. Hall, Hord, Rutherford, and Huling (1984) have pointed out that a surprising number of high schools are smaller than elementary schools. In many elementary schools special programs (e.g., Chapter 1) increase organizational complexity with respect to staffing patterns, curriculum, and instructional practices.[2] Features of the school such as these, which vary across levels, are likely to influence the range of activities that principals adopt in carrying out their leadership roles. Indeed, studies that have examined both elementary and secondary principals tend to support the idea that leaders at both levels draw upon the same repertoire of behaviors in carrying out their work (Dwyer et al., 1983; Morris, Crowson, Porter-Gehrie, and Hurwitz, 1984).

Although existing research leaves us with many unanswered questions about secondary school leadership, such unresolved issues can guide our continuing efforts to understand better the relationships between school leaders and school programs and operations. Strategies for such understanding must capture the complexity of the principal's work and must connect the school leader's activities with contexts and consequences. These strategies need to consider indirect avenues of principal influence, the contribution of school culture, and the cumulative effect of routine activities for shaping teaching and learning. Analysis must illustrate ways in which principal's activities are related to particular characteristics of their school organizations that may (or may not) be regularly associated with school level.

The case that follows aims at meeting the above criteria as it portrays in detail an example of secondary school leadership. This study of Grace Lancaster and Emerson Junior High School is one of a series of leadership stories derived from a yearlong investigation of principals in elementary and junior high schools. These intensive ethnographic studies were conducted in urban, suburban, and rural schools to examine the instructional management role of school principals in varied settings. They represent the culmination of four years of work by the Instructional Management Program of the Far West Laboratory for Educational Research and Development to examine how principals coordinate and control instructional programs and processes under diverse conditions.

During the year spent at Emerson Junior High our field study activities employed a variety of strategies for gathering data about the school and the work of Principal Lancaster. The multimethod approach combined features of previous research on principals, including Mintzberg-type studies (e.g., Martin and Willower, 1981), interview studies (e.g., Blumberg and Greenfield, 1980), and other qualitative work (e.g., Morris et al., 1984; Newburg and Glatthorn, 1983). The use of multiple methods at multiple levels of the school organization allowed us to examine the activities of the principal, the relationships among various elements of the context, and the meanings that organizational members attached to the principal's behavior. Data collection involved forty-five visits to the site, lasting between two and ten hours each. The field record that accrued totaled hundreds of pages of field notes, transcribed interviews, summary observations, and documents.[3]

These voluminous records contain an extensive and intensive view of the principal's world. In condensing these data for this chapter, the chosen strategy was to provide the reader with a first hand portrayal of Principal Lancaster at work to illustrate directly her leadership of Emerson Junior High. With this aim in mind, the bulk of the remainder of the chapter describes a typical day for Lancaster. Two additional sections complete the portrayal of her leadership: an introduction to

Emerson—its setting, clients, and staff—summarizes the context of the principal's work; and the concluding analysis section discusses the meanings and consequences of her actions. Taken together, these three sections capture the complexity of Lancaster's work and the relationships between her actions, the setting of Emerson Junior High, and the outcomes she was striving to attain.[4]

AN INTRODUCTION TO EMERSON JUNIOR HIGH

One of the fourteen junior high schools in the urban district of Waverly, Emerson Junior High School was a former elementary school that had been expanded over several decades to serve students in grades 7, 8, and 9. The facility occupied a city block and was bounded by a tall, rusting, chain-link fence. Most of the classrooms were located in four buildings that, together with the gymnasium, enclosed an open patio area where students congregated at lunchtime. This area and the two playing fields behind the gymnasium were blacktopped. Six "portable" classroom structures, situated alongside one of the playing fields, completed the physical plant.

Despite the additions of classrooms over the years, Emerson's plant was inadequate for the number of students it served. The limitations and liabilities of the old, overcrowded facility were evident throughout. Nearly all of Emerson's teachers shared classrooms, and most were not able to use their rooms during their conference periods. Several teachers had no space to call "home" and pushed carts of instructional materials from room to room, migrating as often as five times a day. In the small main office, teachers, students, support staff, parents, and visitors often found themselves in traffic jams. The library was so crowded that the librarian had resorted to issuing numbered tickets to thirty-five students each morning, allowing them to use the facility comfortably during the noon period.

In spite of the crowding, Emerson enjoyed a strong, positive reputation within its attendance area and within the district as a whole. The district's open enrollment policy allowed thirty students from outside Emerson's attendance area to enroll each year. About 225 applications for those thirty openings were submitted for the 1982–83 school year. Another indication of the school's reputation was that two nearby colleges regularly placed their education students at Emerson to practice teaching in an urban setting. The principal reported that, despite the demands of this urban experience, these novices "always prefer[red] the experience at Emerson" to their subsequent semester of practice in suburban schools.

During the 1982–83 school year Emerson enrolled about 1200 students. The composition of this group was 42 percent Black, 31 percent

Asian, 19 percent White, 5 percent Spanish-surnamed, and 3 percent other. About 20 percent of these students were the children of professional parents. Another 18 percent of the school's families were recipients of public assistance. Although one teacher remarked that the social or economic status of students was independent of race, ethnicity was still a strong bond among students. On the patio during lunch youngsters tended to eat with others of the same racial or ethnic group. Two instructors reported clashes between native, limited-English-speaking Asian students and foreign, non-English-speaking Asian students.

Standardized test scores in basic subjects for Emerson's students were above national norms, ranging from the 54th to the 65th percentiles in language, reading, and mathematics on the Comprehensive Test of Basic Skills (CTBS). In addition, scores for seventh graders, who participated in the district's testing program for basic competencies, showed 95 percent of them demonstrating mastery of basics in reading, written expression, and math.

Emerson's students enrolled in core subjects of English, mathematics, social studies, science, and physical education. Those with limited skills in English enrolled in English as a Second Language (ESL); some of these students also received bilingual instruction in math and social studies. In addition, students chose from a wide range of electives: art, crafts, typing, three foreign languages (French, German, and Spanish), homemaking, industrial arts (wood, metal, and drafting), music (vocal, band, and orchestra), and computers. This broad elective program was one of Emerson's distinguishing features, and teachers credited the principal for its high quality. Lancaster herself said that she believed the elective program was one key to keeping students interested and involved.

In addition to its formal curriculum, Emerson also offered a variety of cocurricular activities, many of which Lancaster had initiated. One of her favorites was "Rap Up," in which student discussion groups met weekly with adult facilitators who were not Emerson staff members. Lancaster had also hired a counselor who established a peer tutoring program for students. Along more recreational lines, dances, a student lounge, and lunchtime sports were available. Organizations such as student council, the state scholarship federation, a drama club, and a Ping-Pong club provided other opportunities. Additionally, Emerson's teachers promoted students' participation in various contests outside of school; and several hundred music students performed on many occasions outside their classes.

During the 1982–83 year Emerson employed fifty teachers. The group was 72 percent white and 64 percent female. Besides the principal, two assistant principals, four counselors, a librarian, and a school nurse provided support for the teaching staff. Staff members were experienced for the most part, with more than 80 percent of them having over seven years of experience.

Emerson's teachers were, on the whole, tolerant and supportive of each other. They rarely spoke negatively or critically about each other, and they accommodated a variety of ideas about how schools and classrooms should operate. Positive relations among staff members were reinforced by annual parties at Christmas and the end of the year. These traditional events, which included classified personnel and former Emerson staff, were eagerly anticipated and well attended.

Among the strongest proponents of such social occasions was Grace Lancaster, Emerson's principal for the past twelve years. Lancaster had spent virtually all of her professional years in education in the Waverly School District as a high school teacher, teacher-counselor, vice-principal, and dean of girls. A lively sixty-three years, she attended to the day-to-day details of Emerson's operation with a great deal of energy, enthusiasm, and humor.

Lancaster's leadership of Emerson was an enactment of several fundamental beliefs that she held about schools and about the principalship. In her view, schools should be "service-oriented" organizations in which "people are the most important." In carrying out this view, she maintained, "You have to be available and you have to be visible...and approachable." She also considered it important to be able to do more than one thing at a time, to "accomplish three things as you walk down the hall." Lancaster spent much of each day in the corridors, on the patio, in the students' cafeteria, and in front of the building, talking to teachers, parents, and students, listening to their concerns, and attempting, whenever possible, to accommodate their desires.

Lancaster's flexibility and willingness to subordinate bureaucratic demands to individual needs were appreciated by staff, students, and parents. Teachers described her as "supportive," "accessible," "humane," "not nit-picky," and a "strong leader but flexible." According to others, she "trust[ed] the teachers" and "want[ed] the best for the students here." Students gave examples of how Lancaster had given them personal attention regarding problems with their schedules, teachers, or other students; they valued her availability and promptness in providing help, and they emphasized her warmth and fairness in dealing with them. Parents found that her responses to their questions or problems were always immediate, attentive, and helpful; she followed through on issues until matters were resolved satisfactorily.

Lancaster's beliefs, with their emphasis on the importance of individuals over bureaucracy, shaped many of her daily routines and interactions. The next section describes a typical day for Lancaster at Emerson as seen through the eyes of an unobtrusive observer. The "day" as it appears here is in reality a composite, constructed from segments of several different days. The incidents, however, are representative and create a vivid and accurate impression of life at Emerson and the actions of Lancaster in leading her organization.

A DAY IN THE LIFE OF GRACE LANCASTER

Every morning before classes began at Emerson Junior High School the main office was a flurry of activity. All of the teachers passed through this small area to pick up keys and mail; substitutes checked in and received their assignments; and students often came in with individual problems. Overseeing all of these activities was Emerson's principal, Grace Lancaster. As she stood behind the counter in her two-piece dress, Lancaster was clearly the person in charge. While she observed, she also filled out assignment sheets for substitutes, answered staff members' questions, and because it was still early in the school year, oriented new staff members to school routines.

Yet, despite the many demands on Lancaster's attention, her style was personable rather than businesslike. She smiled as she greeted each teacher, and she even took the time to hold brief conversations with some of them; while she talked, she typically placed one hand on her listener's arm and tilted her head to the side in her customary fashion, creating a momentary bond amid the surrounding bustle.

Fifteen minutes before the start of first period, Lancaster left the office to help supervise students on their way to classes. She assisted several seventh graders who were having problems opening new lockers, and she coached one youngster through the various turns and stops of the combination lock until he succeeded in opening the dented metal door himself.

Two rings of the school's bells signaled Lancaster that she was needed back in the main office. There, one of the two secretaries informed her that a substitute had not yet arrived. Lancaster asked an English teacher standing nearby, who the principal knew had a first-period conference hour, if she could help cover the class. The teacher replied that she would be available in a few minutes. In the meantime, Lancaster hurried across campus to the classroom, unlocked it, let the children in, examined the absent teacher's lesson plan, and began looking for the necessary lesson materials, not all of which were with the plan. When she failed to find the materials, Lancaster left the English teacher in charge and headed for a social studies classroom to borrow some materials from one of her teachers.

Crossing the patio to this teacher's classroom, Lancaster intercepted a student on her way to the nurse's office with a toothache. Since the nurse was not on campus that day, Lancaster determined the severity of the problem and redirected the girl to her counselor. She then continued her errand to borrow some maps. By the time she returned to the class, the substitute was there. Lancaster filled her in regarding the lesson and distributed materials to the students; as she did so, she gave them verbal instructions for completing the assignment and explained how the skill involved was one required on their district proficiency examination. At 9:15, approximately halfway through the first period, the students were finally at work, and Lancaster returned to the main office.

In the office Lancaster met the journalism teacher, Helen Young, who was upset because her journalism class had been combined with her creative writing class as a result of low enrollments. She complained that this arrangement was too demanding and did not provide students with the best learning opportunities. Lancaster gently pointed out that the increased enrollment this year made it difficult to justify small classes. "You're telling me my class will stay like this for the rest of the year," Young replied. Lancaster said that this was not so and explained how and when the matter would be settled; in the meantime, she suggested, Young might make the combination work by having the journalism students work on the literature magazine. The teacher rejected the suggestion and left unsatisfied.

At the beginning of second period Lancaster visited an overcrowded bilingual math class, one of several classes with sixty or more students as a result of unanticipated school enrollments. The district was assigning substitutes each week as a temporary remedy until final staffing decisions would be made. Lancaster checked these overcrowded classes regularly to assist where needed and to demonstrate to the regular teachers her awareness of the problem.

The teacher had divided the students into two groups, one of which would work with the substitute in another room. Lancaster hurried to unlock the room. She remained in the hall outside directing stragglers and reminding students not to disturb other classes.

When Lancaster returned to the main office shortly after ten o'clock, Jim Lambert, one of her two assistant principals, told her that a seventh grader had chipped a tooth during a fight. The boy was now in Lambert's office, and he asked the principal if she would mind going to the attendance office for the boy's registration card. As she was about to do so, Lancaster met two new student teachers. She stopped to ask how they were doing and to have them fill out emergency information cards. She then completed her errand and took the card into Lambert's office, where the boy was describing the fight. The student paused in his story and asked her to leave because he was going to have to use some bad language that he didn't want her to hear. Lancaster complied by exiting to the adjoining main office. There she immediately recounted the boy's comment to the two secretaries, chuckling quietly as she did so. Sharing humorous episodes such as this was something Lancaster regularly did with her staff.

At 10:15 a district staff member phoned Lancaster to ask if she could use a Filipino aide to do bilingual testing. The principal checked with a counselor and told the caller that three new Filipino students needed testing; she added and emphasized that she hoped the aide could test other students as well. Lancaster shook her head impatiently as she tried to persuade the person to give her a firm date on which the aide would show up. When she hung up, the matter was still unresolved.

As Lancaster emerged from her office after this call, one of the secretaries told her that a district administrator wanted all secondary school principals to bring their up-to-date enrollment lists to the central office immediately. Lancaster gave the secretary instructions for duplicating the needed documents; while this was being done, Lancaster went to check another of her overcrowded classes. Once again, she helped a substitute move half of the group to another classroom and waited until the teacher had the students settled and working before she left.

On her way back to her office Lancaster detoured into the counseling offices to inform the testing counselor of the outcome of the phone call about the Filipino aide. Back in her office, she took another call from the central office concerning thirty Japanese educators who would be touring the district the following month. Emerson was one of four schools that the district had invited them to visit for a day. Lancaster asked some questions about lunch arrangements and explained the problem of having such a large number of visitors when some of the classes were overflowing with students. She agreed to send the caller a copy of the school's bell schedule and made a note to herself to plan schedules for them in separate small groups.

At 10:40 Lancaster informed the two assistant principals of her departure and headed downtown with the enrollment lists. About half of the forty-minute trip was spent in the district office building where she commiserated with other principals who had been drawn away from their buildings by this request. She also tried to see one of the assistant superintendents, a man with whom she had worked for many years, to inform him of a child custody situation involving students at her school. Failing to make contact, Lancaster was comfortable in briefly describing the situation to his secretary, a woman she also knew well; she left a thick, sealed envelope of pertinent documents for the secretary to turn over to her boss.

When Lancaster returned to Emerson, a secretary handed her a suspension notice. Although most disciplinary matters were handled by the assistant principals, Lancaster reviewed and signed all suspension notices herself.

Lancaster used the few minutes before lunch to make a phone call to the central office to try to make some headway in securing bilingual aides. She told the secretary there that she wanted someone to "lean on" the personnel director to get his approval for assigning to Emerson aides who could speak Chinese and Vietnamese. She stressed that the assistant superintendent had been to the school himself and had seen the need.

Now Lancaster was ready to supervise the cafeteria during the students' lunch hour. Before she could leave her office, however, a little boy came in and asked for help finding a place to study. Lancaster explained to him that he could have studied in the library if he had obtained one of the thirty-five "admission tickets" that morning. Since he had not, she offered him the use of her office. As he settled himself at a table there, Lancaster exchanged grins and shrugs with the secretaries in shared amusement at the boy's earnestness.

In the lunchroom Lancaster took the place of a campus supervisor, who went to monitor outside. This left Lancaster and Esther Buckley, the other assistant principal, to oversee several hundred students. Lancaster stood near the rear of the room where she could observe all the tables. As she scanned the room for signs of disorder, she also discussed school matters with Buckley. Several times, she used her police whistle to stop students who had left trash on the floor, had not emptied their trays before depositing them on the stack, or had started to run as they were leaving the cafeteria.

About halfway through lunchtime Lancaster moved outside to the patio. There she monitored students and chatted with the grade-level counselors, who also supervised. Lancaster had established this arrangement as a strategy for facilitating students' access to their counselors; it allowed her to stay in touch with these staff members as well. She walked to the playing fields to make sure that the appropriate teachers were on duty. Along the way she greeted many students by name. In several instances she paused to chat or joke with youngsters, accompanying her words with her characteristic gesture of a hand on the person's arm. Some students reciprocated with pats and hugs of their own. Lancaster was clearly popular with the youngsters, who found her accessible and not intimidating.

As she returned to the patio area, one of the industrial arts teachers approached her about the possibility of obtaining some adult aides to help with special education students enrolled in one of his classes. Lancaster informed him that this year the district was funding only aides for limited-English-speaking students, and she asked whether he had any such youngsters in this class. When he replied in the affirmative, she said she would try to get him the requested help.

While they talked, the bell ending lunch hour rang, and the students dispersed. Lancaster spent a few minutes picking up trash students had left behind. Before returning to her office, she made a detour past the library to see how the ESL substitute was managing with the students assigned to her from another overcrowded class.

In the main office Lancaster met one of her student teachers, Becky Johnson, who was bringing a thank-you note to Lancaster for help the principal had given her when students had vandalized her motorbike. Lancaster took Johnson into her office and explained that she had told her professional sorority about the student teacher's difficult financial circumstances. She fumbled in her purse and finally pulled out a piece of paper that she handed to Johnson, explaining that her sorority sisters "asked me to give you this $50 check." Johnson was delighted, "Oh, this is really going to help. This is twice as much money as I have saved away now. I really appreciate this." The young woman gave Lancaster a warm hug, volunteered to help chaperone or supervise students, and left with a big smile on her face.

Esther Buckley then entered Lancaster's office with two nervous girls in tow. One of them, Debbie, explained that she had gone home for lunch and had run into Jennifer, visiting from out of state. Now Debbie wanted to take her friend to her afternoon classes. Lancaster first reprimanded Debbie for leaving campus without permission during lunch. She also asked what Jennifer was doing in town alone, where she would be staying, and how she had gotten here. Finally, she asked directly whether Jennifer was a runaway. The girl swore she was not, that she was supposed to be staying with her aunt. Lancaster asked for the phone number and, a couple of minutes later, repeated the request to check the girl's truthfulness. During the afternoon Lancaster would try the number several times, unsuccessfully. In the meantime she decided that Jennifer should go to her aunt's house and wait there for her aunt. Debbie should go to her classes. The girls could see each other later.

Since it was now close to one o'clock, Lancaster retrieved her lunch from the refrigerator in the lounge down the hall. As she ate in her office, she continued to conduct business by returning phone calls from the morning.

During one phone conversation a secretary came in from the main office and gave Lancaster a note alerting her to a visitor. As soon as Lancaster finished talking, she went out to greet Dr. Adam King from the central office. Dr. King would be involved in decisions concerning Emerson's need for additional staff. After ushering Dr. King into her office, Lancaster showed him her enrollment figures for each class section and indicated to him what staff she thought she would need in various subject areas. He told her that a meeting would be held the next day at the central office and that he thought he could help her.

After seeing Dr. King to the door, Lancaster chatted briefly with the secretaries about the orderliness of the building when he had arrived. Just then a boy entered and announced that the bathroom downstairs was locked. Lancaster accompanied him there, where they found the door unlocked and two boys leaving the facility. Lancaster asked if they had been holding the door shut. They said that they hadn't, and she didn't challenge them; her tone of voice, however, indicated her disapproval of this kind of horseplay.

When Lancaster returned to the main office, assistant principal Lambert intercepted her and asked in a joking manner, "Can we pray together?" She led him to her office, where he explained that he would be dealing with three sensitive discipline matters that afternoon. He described the cases to familiarize her with the situations because he realized that the parents might want to contact her directly. Later in the day Lambert would follow up on this conversation by telling Lancaster what had happened in the meetings.

At 2:30 Lancaster had an appointment with Amy Winthrop, a new mathematics teacher. Lancaster wanted to discuss the teaching objectives that Winthrop had submitted for review. Besides this, she also wanted to respond to a note Winthrop had given her expressing dissatisfaction at being assigned to one of the "portable" classrooms near a playing field.

The principal began by asking Winthrop if she had "lumped" all of her teaching objectives together in her previous elementary school experience. When the teacher said that she had, Lancaster pointed out that, for junior high, separate objectives were required for each class level. She went on to question Winthrop's uniform statements of expectations for students mastery of objectives. In some instances her 80 percent expectation might be too low, and in others too high. In addition, Lancaster had misgivings about the test Winthrop wanted to use as evidence of student achievement. District math goals were stated in terms of the CTBS, and Lancaster wondered about the comparability of the test Winthrop cited. The principal then showed the teacher some examples of appropriate objectives written by other math teachers. Winthrop asked if she could have a few days to rewrite hers, and Lancaster readily agreed.

The conversation now turned to Winthrop's problems related to her classroom. Winthrop said that the "portable" classroom was in a location subject to disruption from noisy students "hanging out" before classes or passing by during P.E. She also complained that the room was excessively cold in the morning and hot in the afternoon. Lancaster quietly pointed out that no space was available in the main building. She added that if there were problems with students outside, Winthrop should call the main office and she or Lambert would provide help.

Shortly before the end of sixth period a student entered the office with a note from Helen Young saying that a student had jabbed another student with a pen. As Lancaster read the note, Lambert glanced over her shoulder and asked, "What's she doing about it?" He started for Young's classroom, and Lancaster followed. She knew that Lambert was "on the teacher's case," and she wanted to be available to mediate if necessary. Together, they entered the room and spoke briefly with Young. The two administrators then discussed the matter in the corridor outside, with Lambert maintaining that this was a "management problem" on the part of the teacher. As he spoke, the bell rang, and students began to leave. Lambert stopped the two students who had been involved in the incident and told one of them, "We don't do things here that way." He called Young out of the room and told her that she should phone the girl's parents. Young made a face at this suggestion, and the administrators left.

Lancaster's next stop was the sidewalk in front of the building where she supervised students leaving campus at the close of each day. Both students and teachers knew that they could find Lancaster here, and this was a time for them to bring her their special requests. One student wanted to know if he could change one of his classes to an easier level. After listening, Lancaster told the boy to leave a note in her mailbox stating his request. This was a typical strategy for determining the importance of the matter for the student. Lancaster greeted other students, parents, and school staff who were leaving at the same time that she monitored the surrounding area.

Once most of the students had left, Lancaster was free to return to her office. Inside, she found Laura Chang, the volunteer who managed "Rap Up," a student discussion program. The mother of former Emerson students, Chang had been involved in this program for ten years. She helped recruit volunteer facilitators to lead groups of students in weekly discussions of school and personal issues. Chang also managed student sign-ups and placed students in groups. In any eight-week session one hundred or more students might participate. Chang consulted frequently with Lancaster, keeping her informed of how the program was proceeding. Today they discussed what groupings would be best for some of the new Asian immigrant students.

Before leaving campus for the day, Lancaster stopped by the gymnasium where a band had just finished an audition to play at Emerson dances. Lambert had been supervising, and the two administrators discussed the problem of finding live musicians who would appeal to the various racial and ethnic groups at Emerson, each of which had its own musical preferences. Lancaster herself had been responsible for restoring activities such as dances to the junior high when she was appointed principal twelve years before. Now, even though her assistant principals were in charge of student activities, she still kept abreast of them.

The last stop of the day for Lancaster was always her office, where she picked up her coat and handbag and took a last look around to make sure everything was in order. Today, as was typical, she was the last person to leave; she turned off the lights and secured the door of the main office. The night custodian, who was sweeping the corridor, greeted her; despite the demands of the day, Lancaster's manner was cheerful and cordial as she paused to chat and joke with him before heading home.

Analysis

This lengthy description of a typical day for Grace Lancaster illustrates several general characteristics of her work as principal of Emerson. Her activities were varied and disjointed; she rarely completed one task before another demanded her attention. Lancaster frequently acted in response to unanticipated situations or to questions and problems that other individuals brought to her; it was less common for her to initiate. And, in most instances, the issues with which Lancaster was involved were not directly concerned with matters of teaching and learning.

These observations about Lancaster's work in leading Emerson are consonant with findings of other researchers who have observed principals in action. Martin and Willower (1981), for example, found the principal's work to be characterized by "variety, brevity, and fragmentation" and to consist largely of "purely verbal elements" (pp. 79–80). Morris and his colleagues (1982) identified the following components in the principal's day: "school monitoring behaviors," "serving as school spokesperson," "serving the school staff internally as a disseminator of information," and "serving the school as both disturbance handler and resource allocator" (p. 689). These researchers offered this summation of their observations:

> Everything seems to blend together in an undifferentiated jumble of activities that are presumably related, however remotely, to the ongoing rhythm of purpose of the larger enterprise. (Morris et al., 1982, p. 689)

Making sense of that "undifferentiated jumble" of activities and determining the relation between those activities and the "purpose of the larger enterprise" are the keys to understanding how principals influence instructional programs and processes in their schools. In our preliminary study of principals, staff of the Instructional Management Program reported, "In all instances . . . principals had a working theory that guided their actions (Dwyer et al., 1983, p. 54). These "working theories" comprised "complex constellations of personal experience, community and district 'givens,' principals' behaviors, and instructional climate and organization variables that offered both direct and circuitous routes along which principals could influence their schools and the experiences their students encountered daily" (Dwyer et al., 1984c, p. 66).

The introduction to Emerson mentioned a number of elements in the "complex constellation" of variables that impinged on Lancaster's enactment of instructional leadership at Emerson: the inadequate physical plant; the heterogeneous student population served by the school; the academic and cocurricular programs; and the principal's experiences and beliefs. The events described in her typical day illustrated additional "givens" for Lancaster—most noticeably in relation to the Waverly district—and demonstrated some of the means by which she strove to attain her goals. The remainder of this chapter discusses ways in which Lancaster's leadership was shaped by factors in her setting, as well as ways in which she, in turn, attempted to shape the experiences of participants at Emerson. In all instances, whether she was responding or initiating, her actions were guided by the outcomes she was striving to attain and embodied her beliefs about the most effective ways to accomplish those ends.

Lancaster's goals for Emerson can be summed up in a favorite phrase of hers, "something for everyone." She liked to point out that, unlike more mobile high school students, junior high youngsters typically had nowhere to go besides school, and even the most alienated would attend. Lancaster wanted Emerson to provide all students with the kinds of classes and activities that would keep them interested and involved and would help them succeed in their studies. Teachers described her as "a student advocate [who] cares a lot about kids," and as someone who "pushes for excellence in education."

Besides wanting students to develop positive attitudes and be successful, Lancaster was also concerned about the quality of her staff's work experiences at Emerson, and she strove to create high levels of staff satisfaction. She believed that teachers made their best contributions when they experienced support from their administrators and were able to exercise autonomy in carrying out their work. She thought that these ends were best achieved by being flexible, positive, and nonauthoritarian whenever possible.

The strategies that Lancaster employed in her efforts to reach her goals relied heavily on the performance of routine activities. As she carried out the cycles of daily, weekly, and annual activities required to maintain school operations, she used those activities as opportunities to assess progress with respect to her goals and to further movement toward achieving her vision of what Emerson Junior High should be. While nonroutine decisions and efforts—such as establishing the "rap" program—had noticeable and noteworthy impact on achieving goals, Lancaster's performance of routine activities was an even more potent avenue. These responses to the most immediate and pressing demands occupied most of her time. By connecting her performance of them to her vision of schools, Lancaster developed and reinforced that vision, creating shared perceptions among school participants that contributed to the achievement of desired outcomes.

Lancaster's most routine actions included the following: communicating with staff, students, community, and the district; monitoring both the work operations and the orderliness of the school; scheduling, organizing, and allocating resources for carrying out work; and governing in matters of safety and order. Much of her leadership was directed at setting conditions for teaching and learning to take place. This was partly the result of the circumstances she faced— overenrollments, shortages of space, inadequate staffing, lack of instructional materials—that demanded attention in order for classes to operate. In this respect, her task was one of managing realities she encountered. But part of her setting conditions involved creating an environment for addressing individual wishes and needs of students and staff. Thus, as she responded to the realities of her context, she simultaneously created opportunities for students and staff to experience success and satisfaction. The discussion that follows illustrates how Lancaster's carrying out of routine activities worked to effect her vision of what a school should be.

Lancaster's actions can be described by clustering them into two broad categories: those directed toward school climate and those directed toward the instructional organization.[5] Although these areas are treated separately in the following pages, the reader should keep in mind that Lancaster's vision of schools—as "service organizations" where "people are the most important"—and her goal of "something for everyone" represent a view in which climate, teaching, and learning overlap and interact.

Lancaster's efforts to influence the climate at Emerson were concerned both with social relations and with safety and order. She maintained that, for instruction to occur effectively, both teachers and students needed to feel comfortable and happy, and this would only happen if school participants also felt safe and secure.

The size of the student population, its heterogeneity, and the overcrowding of the physical plant made adult supervision an important function at Emerson, and this task was a regular part of Lancaster's work day, as the reader will recall from the typical day. As Lancaster monitored student behavior, she preferred to correct deviations by communicating expectations. She frequently gave students reminders about rules and procedures and made requests for compliance. This strategy was sufficient for handling most types of inappropriate behavior.

Even when student infractions were more serious, Lancaster's handling of situations reflected her humanistic orientation. One day, for example, she encountered a small boy on the patio during class time wearing jeans and an undershirt. Lancaster's first question was, "Honey, where's your shirt? You're supposed to be wearing a shirt." When he told her that it was in a bag that another boy had taken, she spent the next ten or fifteen minutes helping locate the boy with the bag. The youngster's belongings were returned to him before he was expected to return to class. Some might argue that Lancaster's approach caused this student to lose valuable class time and also disturbed other youngsters during their lesson. From Lancaster's point of view, however, her approach improved the quality of time that the youngster did spend in class that hour.

It also communicated to the boy the importance that the principal placed on his personal well-being. Lancaster communicated this message in numerous ways to Emerson's students. As she supervised, her exchanges with youngsters were more frequently concerned with matters other than discipline. Teasing about their social lives, asking about their families, checking on their recovery from illnesses and injuries, and inquiring about their classes and activities were all ways in which Lancaster indicated personal knowledge of, and interest in, her students' lives.

Such interactions contributed to the high level of student cooperation that helped maintain overall safety and order. Unlike other junior highs in the Waverly district, for example, Emerson was able to maintain the district's closed campus policy without keeping gates and entrances locked during class hours; whereas other junior highs hired one campus supervisor for every two hundred students, Emerson employed two supervisors for its twelve hundred students. Another consequence of Lancaster's approach to students was their perception of her as a fair and helpful administrator and of Emerson as a good school. Youngsters who were interviewed were glad to be students at Emerson.

Lancaster's efforts to build a positive school climate encompassed staff as well as students. The strategies she used to develop and maintain positive staff relations were derived from a belief that she considered important: "An effective principal builds on the teacher's strengths, and doesn't write him nasty little notes about...weakness[es]." This belief did not mean that Lancaster was unaware of, or unconcerned about, teachers' shortcomings. She was well aware of which staff members put little effort into their lessons, failed large numbers of students, and sent the most referrals to the assistant principals. But she believed that the best strategies for working with such people were to build a positive work environment, to expose them to new ideas, and to allow them to exercise choice. Her attempts to improve teacher behavior began with providing personal and professional support and resources and favored small nudges in the desired direction over more heavy-handed tactics.

Just as she did with students, Lancaster regularly communicated to staff her personal interest in their well-being. At the simplest level her interest was expressed through her daily interactions: she was as likely to inquire about a staff member's family or weekend as she was to inquire about events at school. Her conversations often provided her with information that prompted her to take action. In several instances, for example, Lancaster organized teachers' instructional schedules to accommodate situations in their private lives. The reader will also recall her obtaining financial assistance for a student teacher. Lancaster translated her interest in staff members' personal lives into decisions and actions that communicated concretely her concern for their well-being.

Staff recognized and appreciated Lancaster's interest in them and her activities on their behalf; many considered her the best administrator they had encountered. But Lancaster's dealings with staff accomplished more than generate high levels of personal satisfaction. Her treatment of individuals was a model for teachers in their own dealings with each other and with their students. Many teachers cited her influence on their work with students, mentioning her desire to create a positive environment and address individual needs. In addition, their interactions with each other were generally positive and supportive. Staff cohesion was high, and social interaction among staff members was an important part of work life at Emerson. Subgroups and factions among the staff were not conspicuous, although there were some individuals who were less socially integrated than others. Considering the relatively large size of the staff, as well as the division of teachers into academic departments, the extent and quality of social interactions were unexpected. Lancaster herself had said, "I think our school is like a family." She was instrumental in promoting and supporting this quality at Emerson.

In much the same way that Lancaster's concern for school climate translated into actions aimed at positive staff and student relations, her concern for Emerson's standing led to a variety of activities that were aimed at maintaining positive relations with the community served by the school. She did not consider any parent request too small for her own attention. She would spend time talking to a parent about the advisability of a youngster's riding his bicycle to school as willingly as she would discuss a student's grades. In the Spring she was always available to provide tours of the campus for prospective students and parents who were concerned about making the transition from elementary to junior high school. As a result of her positive association with community members, Emerson enjoyed high levels of PTA and community support for special school activities and large numbers of applicants for admission under open enrollment.

While concern for climate was a central theme in Lancaster's leadership of Emerson, she also devoted attention to activities that were more directly associated with the instructional program. As in most secondary schools, classes at Emerson were organized around academic disciplines, and most teachers were subject-matter specialists. Within departments, instruction was only loosely coordinated and controlled. Teachers exercised a great deal of autonomy in their classrooms, and most valued this arrangement, preferring to make their own decisions about lessons.

Lancaster's involvement with instruction at Emerson during the year of this study was, to a great extent, shaped by conditions in the setting: unanticipated enrollments had resulted in overcrowded classes; there was insufficient classroom space for students and staff; financial deficits had created staffing problems and shortages of materials; and reorganization of the central office slowed responses to Lancaster's requests. Thus, many of her activities were aimed at setting and maintaining conditions so that instruction could take place. To this end she used three behaviors on a regular basis: communicating, scheduling/organizing/allocating resources, and monitoring.

Lancaster's most common activity relative to instruction was communicating. She was at the center of the network in which information about work was exchanged at Emerson. For the most part, the information that she disbursed and received was concerned with logistics; for example, she frequently answered questions about procedures and policies. She spent a good deal of time orienting parents, students, new staff, and substitute teachers. She regularly answered questions for teachers about the availability of classroom aides, instructional materials, and other resources. In many instances Lancaster acted as communicator between the central office and her staff. Apart from her formal evaluations of teachers, Lancaster's communication about work at Emerson contained few references to curriculum or to classroom practices.

Instances of Lancaster scheduling and organizing relative to instruction at Emerson were again aimed at setting conditions so that teachers and students could carry out their work. She assumed responsibility for scheduling classes, constructing the master schedule of courses each Spring and modifying that schedule in the Fall. Despite the concentration of these actions within only a few months of the year, they nevertheless represented a sizable proportion (10 percent) of Lancaster's actions overall. In carrying them out, she carefully attended to goals: she arranged classes to "protect" various electives from conflicts with other electives or requirements; she scheduled ESL classes to allow for student movements between levels without conflicting with other classes.

Similar to her other activities related to instructional delivery at Emerson, Lancaster's monitoring of work at the school focused on setting and maintaining conditions for teaching and learning. She confirmed that classrooms were staffed at the start of the day; she checked that teachers did not dismiss classes early for lunch; she determined whether long-term substitutes were managing their classes effectively.

Lancaster's monitoring of actual instruction, apart from formal teacher evaluations, was infrequent. When she covered an absent teacher's classroom for part of the period, for instance, she would check the teacher's lesson plan and provide feedback if needed. Such informal monitoring of her staff's teaching occurred, however, only when circumstances brought Lancaster into a classroom for a brief visit or when teachers invited her to special events in their classes. It was not a common practice of hers to drop in on classes simply to visit. In this respect her behavior differed from that of her elementary school counterparts, who were observed to make drop-in visits to classrooms much more frequently.[6] Although her visits were less frequent, Lancaster did use these occasions as opportunities to make suggestions. Despite teachers'subject-matter specialization, Lancaster had definite ideas about what she wanted to see in classrooms, including direct instruction and a variety of activities. She communicated this to staff whenever she had the opportunity, and staff members' comments indicated that they were aware of her expectations.

An important way that Lancaster supported instruction at Emerson was by obtaining and allocating various resources for teachers. The reader will recall her responding to the industrial art teacher's request for a classroom aide by attempting to find a way to meet his request within the constraints of current district policy. In the case of Helen Young's complaint about her combined classes, Lancaster was unable to accommodate the teacher's request for two small classes; but the principal did adjust the teacher's schedule during the second semester to provide her with a less demanding assignment. Other teachers provided examples of Lancaster's obtaining resources for them to carry out special projects and arranging for substitutes so that they could participate in professional development activities during school hours. In all of these instances Lancaster created opportunities for staff to be more effective in their work.

Many of Lancaster's efforts to obtain resources for their staff involved interaction with the Waverly district office. In general, Lancaster viewed the district's central office as suffering from a lack of leadership and as the source of more constraints than opportunities. She was experienced enough to have developed some strategies for dealing with the central office: "I'm loud and noisy and verbal....I will bug people to try to get what I need for the school." She concluded, however, that this task was becoming "increasingly difficult."

Our observations of Lancaster's interactions with the central office confirmed this perception. We observed over a period of six months, for example, a series of frustrating experiences concerning her attempts to obtain appropriate bilingual aides for her non-English-speaking students. While this was an extreme example, other situations also found Lancaster thwarted by district paperwork, schedules, policies, or lines of authority as she attempted to obtain information and resources.

Despite her dogged persistence, she was often frustrated in her attempts to resolve such matters.

Interestingly, although we observed only limited success by Lancaster in dealing with the district office, her teachers perceived her as a supportive, helpful, and effective intermediary with the district bureaucracy. They provided many examples of past successes, which they remembered and still appreciated. Teachers also mentioned ways in which Lancaster buffered them from district impositions. They knew that her stance in relation to the district office always kept Emerson's interests in the forefront. As one teacher described her, "She really knocks herself out to get the things I need." Knowing what Lancaster faced in her dealings with the district administration, most staff regarded her as doing better than most under those circumstances. Her performance in this arena over the years had earned their appreciation of her efforts, helped generate the high levels of satisfaction they expressed about working for Lancaster, and contributed to shared perceptions about general goals, values, and priorities at Emerson.

Conclusion

Emerson Junior High School was a relatively large, complex school that served a mixed student population; it was one of many schools in a large urban district in which reduced resources and recent attempts at reorganization placed demands and constraints on individual school sites. Emerson's principal, Grace Lancaster, strove to work within these contextual givens to produce and maintain her vision of what a school should be. That vision was one in which she considered responsiveness to clients and staff to be most important.

Over the twelve years of her leadership, Lancaster had shaped the structure of Emerson's regular and cocurricular programs, and the processes that operated as work was carried out, to create an organization that provided opportunities for individuals to experience success and satisfaction. Her management was driven by her belief that schools are service organizations and was characterized by flexibility and accommodation. During the year of this study much of her work was aimed at maintaining those programs and processes under difficult circumstances and at nudging the organization as a whole closer to her ideals.

Lancaster combined a nonauthoritarian leadership style with great personal warmth, humor, and caring as she shaped a safe and pleasant work environment at Emerson. Despite the size of the school and the institutional demands that she faced, she was successful in maintaining an organization in which concern for individual participants was not sacrificed to bureaucratic requirements. As a result, most individuals who were associated with Emerson shared a sense of identity with the school and worked hard to contribute positively to that identity. Many of her colleagues commented that in her years of leadership at Emerson she had put her personal stamp on the school. During the year we spent with Grace Lancaster at Emerson, we came to appreciate how deeply that stamp had been impressed and how much it was valued by those who experienced it.

NOTES

1. Preparation of this chapter was supported by a contract from the National Institute of Education, Department of Education, under Contract No. 400–83–0003. The contents of this chapter do not necessarily reflect the views or policies of the Department of Education or the National Institute of Education.

2. For case study examples of such complex elementary schools, see D. C. Dwyer, G. V. Lee, B. G. Barnett, N. N. Filby, and B. Rowan, *Emma Winston and Roosevelt Elementary School: Instructional leadership in an inner-city setting* and *Frances Hedges and Orchard Park Elementary School: Instructional leadership in a stable urban setting* (San Francisco, Calif.: Far West Laboratory for Educational Research and Development, 1984).

3. For a complete report of the methodology, see D. C. Dwyer, G. V. Lee, B. G. Barnett, N. N. Filby, and B. Rowan, *Methodology: A companion volume for the Instructional Management Program's field study of princpals* (San Francisco, Calif.: Far West Laboratory for Educational Research and Development, 1984).

4. The full-length version of this case study is contained in D. C. Dwyer, G. V. Lee, B. G. Barnett, N. N. Filby, and B. Rowan, *Grace Lancaster and Emerson Junior High School: Instructional leadership in an urban setting* (San Francisco, Calif.: Far West Laboratory for Educational Research and Development, 1984).

5. See Bossert et al. (1982) for a complete description of the theoretical model.

6. See Dwyer et al. (1984a, 1984b) for case study examples of such principal behavior.

REFERENCES

Armor, D.; Conry-Osequera, P.; Cox, M.; King, N.; McDonnell, L.; Pascal, A.; Pauly, E.; Zellman, G. (1976). *Analysis of the school preferred reading program in selected Los Angeles minority schools.* Santa Monica, Calif.: Rand.

Blumberg, A., and Greenfield, W. (1980). *The effective principal: Perspectives in school leadership.* Boston: Allyn and Bacon.

Bossert, S. T.; Dwyer, D. C.; Rowan, B.; Lee, G. V. (1982). The instructional management role of the principal. *Education Administration Quarterly,* 18, 34–36.

Bridges, E. M. (1982). Research on the school administrator: The state of the art, 1967–1980. *Educational Administration Quarterly, 18* (3), 12–33.

Brookover, W. B., and Lezotte, L. (1977). *Schools can make a difference.* East

Lansing, Mich.: College of Urban Development, Michigan State University.

Cuban, L. (1983). Effective schools: A friendly but cautionary note. *Phi Delta Kappan, 64*, 695–96.

Dwyer, D. C.; Lee, G. V.; Barnett, B. G.; Filby, N. N.; Rowan, B. (1984a). *Emma Winston and Roosevelt Elementary School: Instructional leadership in an inner-city setting.* San Francisco, Calif.; Far West Laboratory for Educational Research and Development.

————. (1984b). *Frances Hedges and Orchard Park Elementary School: Instructional leadership in a stable urban setting.* San Francisco, Calif.: Far West Laboratory for Educational Research and Development.

————. (1984c). *Grace Lancaster and Emerson Junior High School: Instructional leadership in an urban setting.* San Francisco, Calif.: Far West Laboratory for Educational Research and Development.

————. (1984d). *Methodology: A companion volume for the Instructional Management Program's field study of principals.* San Francisco, Calif.: Far West Laboratory for Educational Research and Development.

Dwyer, D. C.; Lee, G. V.; Rowan, B.; Bossert, S. T. (1983). *Five principals in action: Perspectives on instructional management.* San Francisco, Calif.: Far West Laboratory for Educational Research and Development.

Edmonds, R. (1979). Some schools work and more can. *Social Policy, 9*, 28–32.

Firestone, W. A., and Herriott, R. (1982). Prescriptions for effective elementary schools don't fit secondary schools. *Educational Leadership, 40*, 51–53.

Firestone, W. A., and Wilson, B. L. (1983). *Using bureaucratic and cultural linkages to improve instruction: The high school principal's contribution.* Eugene, Oreg.: Center for Educational Policy and Management, College of Education, University of Oregon.

Greenfield, W. D. (1982, March). *Empirical research on principals: The state of the art.* Paper presented at the annual meeting of the American Educational Research Association, New York City.

Hall, G. E.; Hord, S. M.; Rutherford, W. L.; Huling, L. L. (1984). Change in high schools: Rolling stones or asleep at the wheel? *Educational Leadership, 41*(6), 58–62.

Martin, W. J., and Willower, D. J. (1981). The managerial behavior of high school principals. *Educational Administration Quarterly, 17*, 69–90.

Morris, V. C.; Crowson, R. L.; Hurwitz, E.; Porter-Gehrie, C. (1982). The urban principal: Middle manager in the educational bureaucracy. *Phi Delta Kappan, 63*, 682–92.

————. (1984). *Principals in action: The reality of managing schools.* Columbus, Ohio: Charles E. Merrill.

Newburg, N. A., and Glatthorn, A. A. (1983). *Instructional leadership: Four ethnographic studies of junior high school principals.* Philadelphia, Pa.: University of Pennsylvania.

Rowan, B.; Bossert, S. T.; and Dwyer, D. C. (1983). Research on effective schools: A cautionary note. *Educational Researcher, 12*, 24–31.

Venezky, R., and Winfield, I. (1979). *Schools that succeed beyond expectations in teaching reading* (Technical Report No. 1). Newark, Del.: Department of Educational Studies.

Weber, G. (1971). *Inner city children can be taught to read: Four successful schools* (Occasional paper no. 18). Washington, D.C.: Council for Basic Education.

Wynne, E. (1981). Looking at schools. *Phi Delta Kappan, 62*, 371–81.

6

The Dilemma of
Instructional Leadership
and a Central Role
for Central Office

ROBERT K. WIMPELBERG

INTRODUCTION

A reasonable reading of research on schools in the last couple of decades
leads to the interpretation that schools can develop as places for excellent teaching and learning–but, left to their own devices, many of
them will not. This chapter presents that dilemma and a response to
it. We know, on the one hand, that instruction in classrooms is the
essential core activity in our educational systems and that some
schools within those systems provide serious, productive, and even
pleasing instruction for students. In such schools, the educators become fulfilled in their work. On the other hand, we also know that
many classrooms, schools, and school districts function as little more
than loose amalgams of roles and duties. What happens in them is
recognizable as "schooling" from its surface characteristics, but students and teachers accomplish disappointingly little and have few
strongly positive feelings about what they do there.

In this essay I lay out the elements of the dilemma, from the
promising pictures of extraordinarily effective and improving schools
to the apparent void of instructional inquiry and development that is
typical of most schools and school systems. Second, I map out a strategy
for responding to the instructional dilemma. This approach is founded

on knowledge gained in the effective schools research and from studies of successful school improvement projects. While both of these lines of inquiry obviously focus on the school, the proposals advanced here hold little faith in the efficacy of leadership development that relies to any significant degree on the capacities of school units. It shifts our attention, instead, to a collaboration between central office and the school. And it asserts that organizational structure and leadership logically point to a critical role for the *intermediate central office administrator*, the person who supervises and evaluates the work of schools and school principals.[1]

INSTRUCTIONAL LEADERSHIP: THE EXCEPTIONS AND THE RULE

In spite of a usual number of detractors, there is a significant spirit of optimism among educators these days. While the national commission reports point critical fingers at high rates of illiteracy, comparatively low achievement averages, and watered-down curricula, educators are finding a silver lining in the attention they draw toward education at the federal and state levels. With all of their negative conclusions, the reports can give a symbolic impetus to positive school change in local districts (Deal, 1985).

Beyond the commission reports, research on effective schools and school improvement projects reverses a decade-old conclusion from Coleman et al. (1966) that "schools don't make a difference." Instead, we have dozens of accounts of schools where children from poor families as well as diverse kinds of communities are reaching levels of achievement that surpass those predicted for them. Alongside the "snapshots" of exceptionally effective schools, we also have documented evidence of schools that have systematically improved their instructional climates, instructional delivery, and instructional outcomes. To be sure, we have to consider a number of appropriately "cautionary" criticisms that warn about methodological flaws and problems of interpretation. Nevertheless, the powerful thematic similarities that unify these research studies lend a compelling validity to concepts like instructional and school effectiveness.[2]

Amid the positive surge of research on effective and improving schools we are faced with the quandary that, as far as we know, the schools those studies lay open to us are the exceptional ones and are relatively few in number. Furthermore, most of the abstracted characteristics of effective and improving schools contradict our knowledge base about "typical" schools and school districts. Despite this realization, recommendations for improvements are pitched primarily toward the individual school, and the call to instructional leadership is sounded almost exclusively for school principals. Much of what we know about schools, however, suggests that we cannot expect to multiply success by a significant factor through these means alone. There are disjunctures between the literatures that show us the possibilities for schools and the literatures that describe their limitations, and differences emerge for each of the professional roles that could play a direct part in instructional leadership: teachers, principals, and superintendents.

Teachers

Teachers in especially effective schools and in schools that show sustained improvement appear to interact a lot with other teachers around instructional matters and maintain a high level of participation in decisions that affect instruction in their classrooms. The review of school improvement research by Clark et al. (1984), for example, reports teachers as saying that "they learn best from other teachers. Teacher-teacher interactions provide for technical and psychological support as well as personal reinforcement" (p. 58). Little (1981) found that when teachers planned their lessons together, shared pedagogical techniques, and observed one another in action, their instructional effectiveness improved. Interaction with other teachers and participation in decision-making, says Rosenholtz, give teachers "a sense of ownership of school instructional goals and buys them a stake in the future of a collective enterprise" (p. 374).

It is a commonplace understanding of most teachers, however, that they affect each other's work very little if at all, and that they stay aloof from the principal and issues of school goal-setting. Teachers share an "ethos" that keeps them ignorant of each other's performance (Lortie, 1975; McPherson, 1979). The schools they work in are called "weakly normed" organizational systems where teachers are discouraged from pressuring each other for pedagogical change or improvement (Blumberg, 1983).

Principals and teachers are often portrayed as two camps, each of which has control over a particular "zone," "domain," or "sphere" of school activities. Instruction is squarely in the teacher's zone, which means it is seldom approached collectively by the faculty or integrated into a total school program and goal system through negotiation between the principal and the faculty (Hanson, 1981).

The Principal

Even the most casual student of the effective schools literature knows the litany of qualities and behaviors that characterize the principals in exceptional schools. They press school personnel to identify and realize a school "mission"; they monitor instruction closely and encourage the efficient and effective use of instructional time; they maintain a keen awareness of the individual and collective achievement of their students and hold high expectations for them; and they take advantage of parents' interest and willingness to be involved in the school.

Just as with the teachers, however, our research data on "typical" principals do not match the characteristics of those in particularly effective schools. Studies of how principals spend their time document the fact that a very small part of it is spent on curriculum and instruction (Peterson, 1977–78; Kmetz and Willower, 1982; Martin and Willower, 1981). Teachers seldom mention principals when commenting on the people who most influence their curricular decisions (Aoki et al., 1977; Leithwood and MacDonald, 1981). Goodlad (1983) claims that principals' detachment from curriculum and instruction is due to the fact that few of them have been prepared for instructional leadership, either by their preservice or their in-service professional training, and Fullan (1982) observes that the responsibilities placed on the work lives of principals have increased drastically during the last couple of decades and are generally unrelated, if not antithetical, to instructional leadership.

Central Office

We have the largest research base on teachers and principals and a lengthy literature on the chief school superintendent. Unfortunately, we know considerably less about the instructional leadership behavior of central office supervisors and intermediate administrators, particularly if they play a role in school effectiveness and school improvement. Nevertheless, the information that can be pieced together for supervisors and superintendents mirrors our understanding of teachers and principals.

The Supervisors. One step removed from the classroom and the school are supervisors of instruction. Whether people in these positions act as "administrators" or "consultants" appears to be in a state of confusion (Ogletree, 1972); nevertheless, in either role they have the potential of their liaison role to act as "integrators" in school systems, a position from which instructional leadership could be exercised. In improving schools there is some evidence that supervisors are a significant part of a cadre of personnel dedicated to efforts at the classroom level to improve instruction and student achievement (Fullan, 1982).

Most supervisors, however, appear to have lost their traditional role of "innovator" to the school principal in the wake of school-effectiveness research and have been able to exercise their traditional "expert" authority in curricular matters less in the last two decades because of an increase in teacher knowledge and skills (Ogletree, 1972). Consistent with these observations, Gaertner (1978–79) characterizes the work of these persons as "supervision of the content of education, not supervision of the act of teaching" (p. 3). Hannaway and Sproull (1978–79) found that supervisors spend only 10 percent of their time on requests from school level managers, and a recent survey by the Association for Supervision and Curriculum Development reports that over half the elementary schools surveyed did not even have instructional supervisors they could call on in any of the subject areas they taught (Cawelti and Adkisson, 1985).

The Superintendents. We have a fairly large literature on chief superintendents and a sketchy sense, at best, of the work of line administrators between the superintendent and the school. Fullan (1982) suggests that this is because the job components for second-level superintendents are so diverse, and because of a general preoccupation with the role of the district superintendent. Nevertheless, there is a growing list of studies that point to the important role of upper-level central office administrators in improving schools (Fullan, 1982; Cuban, 1984; Clark et al., 1985). A recent study highlights the efforts of one superintendent who appears to have produced a *district* of exceptionally effective schools (Hallinger and Murphy, 1982).

For the most part, superintendents have behaved in concert with a trend that Griffiths spotted in the 1960s. "This is the idea that administrators should have nothing to do with instruction" (Griffiths, 1966, p. 102). Chief school officers, in the last two decades, have been characterized most frequently as "politician," "negotiator," or "statesman" (Button, 1966; Goldhammer, 1977; Blumberg and Blumberg, 1985) and infrequently as "instructional leader" or "teacher-scholar" (see Cuban [1976] and Hallinger and Murphy [1982] for exceptions in the literature on the superintendency). Whatever the descriptor, the modern superintendent seems to pay little direct attention to instruction. Although superintendents may take pride in curricular and instructional accomplishments and consider them essential, they themselves complain that they pay too little direct attention to what goes on in classrooms (Willower and Fraser, 1979–80). Curriculum and instruction are low on superintendents' lists of job priorities regardless of the demographics of the districts they serve (Salley, 1979–80). In the study by Hannaway and Sproull (1978–79), both the chief and assistant superintendents spent an average of less than 1 percent of their time on instruction in schools and classrooms. Pitner and Ogawa (1981) draw a conclusion from their studies of superintendents that can generalize to most other research:

If the instruction of students is taken to be the basic production process of schools, then superintendents apparently exert limited and, at best, indirect influence on organizational performance. Superintendents, it was found, attend primarily to the structural aspects of school systems such as programs, budgets, facilities, and schedules. (p. 62)

INSTRUCTIONAL LEADERSHIP: WHAT WE KNOW

The school effectiveness and improvement literatures clearly portray instructional success as an integrated process in which each professional position, from teacher to superintendent, can play a part. These are the optimistic literatures—the ones than tell us "it can be done." Studies of more random samples of role incumbents from teachers to superintendents show a countervailing tendency toward disengagement from instructional involvement. Teachers seldom interact with each other to pursue instructional improvement, and administrators at all levels are generally removed from what goes on in the classroom.

It is in the contrast between *interaction* and *disengagement* that the gap between the effective/improving schools and the "typical" schools emerges. The organizational concept of "connectedness" among roles and units in educational systems is not new. Bidwell (1965) was among the first to identify it, and Weick (1976) elaborated on its meaning even more fully. Disconnectedness in its bureaucratic sense has come into the common organizational parlance as "loose coupling," which may be defined as a lack of coordination or control between activities in one unit of the organization (a classroom, a school, a school district office) and people or activities in other units (Hanson, 1981). Some say that the bureaucratic condition of disconnectedness is not so bad; loose coupling allows individual classrooms and schools to adapt to their particular internal and external environments (Hawley, 1978), and permits the survival of the school district as a whole when it might otherwise be threatened (Weick, 1976). Others say that the informal or cultural norm of disconnectedness is precisely the condition that hurts instructional quality and school improvement the most (Little, 1981; Goodlad, 1983). Generalizations from the growing numbers of research studies on effective and improving schools seem to corroborate both positions. That is to say, linkages among roles and units based on the supremacy of hierarchy and leading to a predominance of "top-down" decisions appears to be dysfunctional, while interactive decision-making in a combination of "top-down" and "bottom-up" collaborations fosters instructional improvement.

It may be the case that the individuality of separate schools and the cellular history of the classroom cause educational researchers and interventionists to accept organizational looseness as a positive, antibureaucratic tendency appropriate in professional organizations like schools and school districts. For whatever reasons, researchers and interventionists have become preoccupied with the *school* as the natural locus of attention. To be sure, schools are nicely distinguishable units, and they constitute manageable groupings of classrooms; both conditions aid in the feasibility and controllability of research. Furthermore, racial, ethnic, and social class segregation by neighborhoods has given a historical underpinning to our tendency to separate out individual schools.The fixation on schools may also be encouraged by a wariness about the manner in which district-level administrators approach matters of instruction and school improvement. The record of their efforts to centralize decision-making and routinize improvement strategies may have made school-change proponents more comfortable with a school-by-school approach. Yet, the individualized alternative is unrealistic: to expect that a significant number of schools will act in behalf of their own improvement or that school systems can afford to hire large numbers of supplementary specialists to assist each school in the lengthy processes of positive change is to blow hope into the rush of some strong countervailing winds.

In the remainder of this chapter I argue that one powerful source of instructional leadership given too little notice in the effectiveness/improvement discussion is the central office. More specifically, in all but the very smallest school districts, the thrust for instructional leadership can come from the intermediate administrators who supervise and evaluate the work of school principals. Furthermore, instructional leadership can take the shape of a pattern of process-expectations coupled with firmly directive actions that make instructional improvements a reality, without making any particular template fit all classrooms and schools. This view,then, retains the school as the essential locus of change activity, but couples to that an equal responsibility for district administrators. The rationale for and qualities of the central-office role are presented in the remainder of this essay in the form of five propositions and their explications.

Proposition 1   *Instruction in most schools is not likely to improve unless a leadership consciousness at the district level develops in such a way as to forge linkages between schools and central office, among schools, and among teachers within schools.*

The most compelling reason to look to the central office for instructional leadership is that many classrooms and schools will not change for the better on their own. If they were naturally prone to make positive changes, we would not be studying the seemingly extraordinary conditions present when documentable school improvement takes place. In this light, the district office has the legal and moral responsibility to see that schools achieve as high a standard of performance as possible. A second and more positive reason is that cooperative learning among schools can be a powerful source of school improvement, and the district office is uniquely positioned to cultivate and coordinate extramural learning networks.

The few studies of successful school improvement that investigated the functioning of central office support these assertions. Huberman and Crandall, for example, describe the principals in successful change-oriented schools as "accelerators in cars" that are actually given their thrust and momentum by central office administrators (1982, p.80). McLaughlin and Marsh (1978) found that teachers were more committed to change projects when they sensed that district administrators were interested in them. And Fullan concludes that, "regardless of the source of change, the single most important factor is *how central office administrators take to the change*" (1982, p. 165, emphasis in the original).

Proposition 2   *The best linkages are forged, not through centralized instructional prescriptions but through an exchange process in which the central office and school administrators simultaneously challenge and support each other.*

Made aware by the school board, business interests, or community activists that school performance is intolerably low, superintendents often engage in a ritual dance of hyperrationalized, hierarchically controlled gestures (Wise, 1979). One action frequently taken in the early phases of a response to pressure is the reorganization of duties and positions for key personnel. March (1978) comments that "reorganization of administration is a favorite strategy for reform in bureaucratic organizations. . . . But the improvements realized by reorganization are invariably marginal and are often seriously confounded with other simultaneous changes" (p. 222). A second common strategy is for top-level administrators to define improvement in terms of a few quantifiable measures of productivity (such as test scores) and to create educator-proof means for achieving them. Overreliance on test scores often leads to unanticipated and destructive consequences, such as ignoring already successful schools and reducing the definition of learning to the least common denominator (Cuban, 1984). And where test results are the currency of the improvement realm, principals and teachers look for ways of securing a payoff without having to reflect on what they are really doing (Lave and March, 1975).

A viable alternative to centralized, top-down instructional coupling is a simultaneous top-down/bottom-up process in which both the central office administrator and the principal have something to say about how improvement is defined and accomplished. As Cuban (1984) characterizes it,

> ... a superintendent can direct principals in each school to set goals, plan and establish programs, assess outcomes. By directing from the top a process to occur at each school without prescribing the content of decisions, a variation on the familiar bottom-up approach emerges. In short, seeking tighter coupling of district practices to school action does not necessarily mean mandating the same effort districtwide; it can be triggered by superintendent mandate but proceed gradually on a school-by-school basis. (p. 140)

Proposition 3 *The central office personnel with the highest potential for exercising instructional leadership are intermediate administrators who have the organizational authority to supervise and evaluate principals and the expert and referent authority to support them.*

In spite of Griffith's (1966) plea for superintendents not to disengage themselves from instruction and Cuban's (1984) observation that modern effective school/change processes require "a higher than usual involvement [by the superintendent] in the district's instructional program" (p. 146), it is clear that the vast majority of the chief superintendents cannot be expected to spend most of their time in the close scrutiny of curriculum and instruction. For one thing, the sheer volume and diversity of matters that affect school systems requires that the spokesperson be a generalist and a freewheeling negotiator (Cuban, 1976; Blumberg and Blumberg, 1985). Furthermore, in all but the very smallest districts, no single person can possibly spend enough time in each setting to know it well enough to give it the kind of interactive leadership envisioned here.

There is, of course, an important role for the chief superintendent. The chief superintendent must tend to the district's political equilibrium, negotiating the effects and intentions of top-down/bottom-up leadership with the school board and teachers' union (Purkey and Smith, 1985). The chief superintendent must constantly be aware of leadership potential among those who could assume cooperative leadership with school sites. The chief superintendent must set serious expectations for the intermediate administrators and, at the same time, buffer them from the "administrivia" that can preoccupy their time.

The chief superintendent must give *careful* public exposure to instructional improvement efforts. As Cuban (1984) asserts, "no superintendent can secretly improve a school district. The source of formal authority for a superintendent's initiative is the school board..." (p. 147), but he must carefully choose the time and means for informing the board in order to protect improvement processes long enough for them to survive in an unpredictable political environment (see Burlingame, 1981). In the same spirit, the chief superintendent must become the symbolic leader of the instructional revitalization of the schools; this means that the chief superintendent must make opportunities to visit schools where good things are happening. Cuban (1984) claims that one of the most important things a superintendent can do is "take the time to acknowledge and honor academic excellence" (p. 144).

The best strategically placed and least understood candidates for instructional leadership are the intermediate central office administrators who supervise and evaluate the work of principals. As our review of the literatures concludes, we know very little about these people. Preliminary analysis of data from interviews with forty principals in the Louisiana School Effectiveness Study suggest that there are so many liaison personnel, each with his or her own discrete monitoring or support function, that no single person under current arrangements functions as the primary overseer of the school (Wimpelberg, 1985). Special program coordinators, instructional supervisors for remediation of teaching problems, building and fiscal officers, and superintendents all have some kind of sporadic contact with the school. Most often, the person who sees the school and the principal the least is the person who is empowered to make the formal and informal evaluations of the school's functioning. The "looseness" of this mode of operating also means that ineffective practice can go unnoticed and unchallenged by anyone with the authority to require change.

There is, in the end, an organizational logic to the compelling leadership role of the intermediate central-office administrator. Just as the principal is the key supervisor and evaluator of teachers and can, therefore, be perceived as the logical instructional leader in a move toward individual school effectiveness, so also is the district administrator the key supervisor of a set of schools, all of which should be set on an effectiveness course in some systematic order. Just as a principal must take the initiative if poor teachers are to be helped or removed, so too must a supervisory central-office administrator perform this difficult task vis-a-vis principals. And just as the high expectations and effort to define a mission are hallmarks of the faculty and principal in an effective school, so too are the high expectations and supportive leadership of the central office administrator necessary for an effective *district*.

Proposition 4 *The primary responsibility of the intermediate administrator is to see that every school principal develops both a technical and cultural consciousness of the school.*

At the simplest level, matters of scheduling, activity coordination, efficient resource allocation, and communication processes are parts of the "technical" management of the school. March (1978) thinks that competence in this category of managerial responsibilities is too often overlooked. He notes that much of administrative life is taken up with activities *"quite distant from those implied by a conception of administration as heroic leadership"* (p. 233, emphasis in the original). The quality of technical management either facilitates good instruction or inhibits it, and it is the responsibility of the central office administrator to know that common, technical functions are being performed adequately without undue delay and without undue preoccupation. Technical matters also involve the more sophisticated areas of pedagogy and curriculum. The central office administrator must know that the principal is aware of the achievement of the students in his/her school and knows how to get instructional resources for teachers who need them.

According to Firestone and Wilson, the cultural dimensions of the school "affect at least two aspects of thought. The first is the individual's definitions of the task. [What does it mean to teach? What are the children like who are being taught?]... The second aspect of thought is the individual's commitment to the task" (1985, p. 13). Sander and Wiggins (1985) call this dimension "administration for relevance," defining relevance as "that which is truly important, that which has value" (p. 103). Relevance, value, meaning, and goal-setting appear to be elements in the healthy and effective school. They are inherent in concepts like school mission and participatory decision-making that are generally given expression in effective schools (Rosenholtz, 1985).

Meaning and relevance are customarily trivialized in a top-down management system. For example, some districts and state departments of education now require that principals and teachers go through a procedure that results in goal statements—expressions of outcomes that are to be pursued during a given school term. Goal statements, however, are seldom statements of meaning. They are produced in an atmosphere of task accomplishment akin to the counting of books for the end-of-school inventory. And as Rosenholtz (1985) has noted in her review of effective schools, there is a difference between *professed* and *operational* goals. Schools with strong cultures give operational goals continuous and prominent attention, and sensitive principals "work the major themes that are deemed important into interactions with others" (Firestone and Wilson, 1985, p. 18). Instructional leaders among the intermediate administrators in central office will encourage and assist principals to explore the creation of meaning, relevance, and value in their schools, fostering in them as much cultural leadership as each principal is capable of assuming.

Proposition 5   *The instructional leadership role of the central office administrator requires a new kind of intimacy with schools.*

Knowing

When schools do not improve it is due, in part, to the small "data base" that the educators in them have to work with. Teachers in stagnant schools may know the entries they have written in their lesson plans and may be able to describe the typical behaviors of the students they see each day, but they may not reflect on how well their teaching is engaging the students or explore ideas about successful and unsuccessful practices with other teachers. Principals may have a vague sense of who they talked to during the last week and which "fires" remain to be snuffed out, but they may know little about the effects the school is having on students and teachers. At the most superficial level, some principals do not know how much time is spent on instruction, how instruction is conducted, or what portion of the student body is not regularly attending school. Many principals and teachers do not know how their students have performed on standardized tests until long after it matters. Unless a central office administrator has knowledge of these kinds of conditions and chooses not to tolerate them, they can persist to the detriment and frustration of students and teachers alike.

One reason that innovations devised in the central office and imposed on the school and classrooms fail to produce lasting change is that central office administrators tend to operate without an accurate knowledge base of schools and classrooms (Fullan 1982). This usually means that purveyors of solutions outside the school seldom bother to find out about the ethos, skill capacities, and emotional concerns in each school before a change effort is undertaken, and they remain just as ignorant about what transpires in each school during implementation. While these generalizations apply to central office relationships with schools when an innovation project is in progress, they are even more characteristic of that relationship during the periods of "business as usual" when no conscious attempts at improvement are underway. We know from the research of Hannaway and Sproull (1978–79) that principals and central office administrators spend little time interacting with each other and a negligible amount of time dealing with matters of curriculum and instruction. Instructional leadership is based on knowledge, and essential pieces of that knowledge must be integrated from classroom to central office.

Communication

Communication represents the media by which educators demonstrate what they already know and find out what they want to know. It is ironic that the term "communication" peppers the speeches and conversations of so many educators, yet, as the summary in the first part of this chapter concludes, educational institutions are characterized by isolation, lack of sharing and cooperation, and infrequent interactions about professional matters—in short, a highly limited state of professional communication.

If communication is defined as the exchange of information in an attempt to mutually understand and support the growth of children and adults (teachers, principals), communication becomes a trademark of instructional leadership. Fullan (1982) is unequivocal on this point:

> [Communication] demonstrates the sincerity of one's intentions as well as knowledge of the problems of change faced by system members.... Two-way communication about specific innovations that are being attempted is a requirement of success.... The district administrator more than any other individiual in the district sets the pace and tone of the climate of accuracy of communication. (p. 168)

Communication can mean a "dialogue" about school expectations (the school's inquiry into its own culture and purpose), and it can refer to the data necessary to assess students' progress. Communication can also refer to professional exchanges *among* schools, not just within them. Goodlad (1983) suggests that "it is highly desirable that several schools be grouped together in a collaborative network. Networks are particularly powerful if they cross district lines. Networking makes the flow of ideas into schools easy and cheap" (p. 77). It is the central office administrator who can facilitate communication among schools within the district and across district boundaries.

Time

Central office administrators cannot know about schools or communicate well with principals and teachers unless they devote enough time to them. Two significant dimensions of time are frequency and duration. For the concept of "time," as with "knowledge" and "communication," research on effective and improving schools is instructive, and the few studies that include central office confirm its importance.

Principals who successfully implemented new science curricula were known to monitor some teacher activities on a weekly basis and others on a daily basis (Hall et al., 1980). Natriello and Dornbusch (1980–81) found that effective supervision of teachers requires the principal to commit time to frequent follow-up observations and conferences related to teachers' weaknesses. And Cuban (1984) reports that in a New York City school improvement project, "liaisons" from central office spent a few days a week in consultation with school staff.

Along with frequency, the duration and continuity of contact are critical for the central office administrator to know a school. Goodlad (1983) has observed that "one of the things we know about institutions ...is that they tend to deteriorate when left alone" (p. 76). As Fullan (1982) puts it, "The principal as initiator can have a powerful influence on teachers provided he or she is willing to work with teachers *over a period of time ...*" (p. 145, emphasis added). It is the nature of organic processes, as opposed to mechanistic "fixes," that they require prolonged attention and sustained interaction. Furthermore, these findings hold no less true for relationships between central office administrators and principals as for relationships among principals and teachers.

INSTRUCTIONAL LEADERSHIP AT THE WAY STATION

This chapter has laid out a dilemma of instructional leadership. We know the characteristics of instructional leadership associated with remarkably effective schools and schools where improvement efforts have met with success. The behaviors and interrelationships of educators in these kinds of settings do not appear to match what we know about "typical" educators. Therein lies the dilemma. Leadership-prone educators make connections with each other; communicate about meaning and instructional techniques; know what is happening in schools and classrooms because they spend time finding out. "Typical" educators are less in touch with each other, operating within their own "spheres"; their time is spent on matters other than curriculum and instruction; cooperation and sharing run counter to their norms of isolation and withholding.

In the midst of this quandary two observations stand out: first, those who could lead a systematic effort to improve instruction school-by-school *district-wide* are the intermediate central office administrators who supervise schools and principals; and second, the organizational positions about which we have the least amount of descriptive data are those of intermediate central office administrators. The arguments in this chapter must be taken as a preface to a wider discusssion of how educational organizations will respond to the pressures for instructional improvement and an agenda for future research. We must know as much about the potential and the limitations in the roles of intermediate central office administrators as we know about principals and chief superintendents. Is there a "typical" supervisor of principals? What are the current characteristics of "middle-manager" relationships between principals and chief superintendents? How does the work of these administrators get defined? What facets of the school system at large allow and impede their acting as instructional leaders? Do intermediate administrators *want* to intervene in schools, and, if so, how are they to be helped to make a role change? Answers to these questions may tap a reservoir of instructional leadership that has not been plumbed to date. If so, it will expose a central role for central office.

NOTES

1. This research was supported by a summer grant from the Committee on Research, Tulane University.
2. Among the best reviews of the effective schools studies are the journal articles by Mackenzie (1981), Purkey and Smith (1983), Clark et al. (1984), and Rosenholtz (1985). School improvement/change studies are well reviewed by Fullan (1982) and Clark et al. (1984). And the "cautionary" literatures are well represented by Purkey and Smith (1983); Rowan, Bossert, and Dwyer (1983); and Firestone and Herriot (1982).

REFERENCES

Aoka, T., et al. (1977). *British Columbia Social Studies Assessment. vols. 1–3*. Victoria: British Columbia Ministry of Education. Cited in Fullan (1982).

Bidwell, C. E. (1965). The school as a formal organization. In *Handbook of Organizations*, edited by James G. March, pp. 972–1022. Chicago: Rand McNally.

Blumberg, A. (1983). Supervision in weakly normed systems: The case of the schools. Paper presented at the Annual Meeting of the American Educational Research Association.

Blumberg, A., with Blumberg, P. (1985). *The school superintendent: Living with conflict*. New York: Teachers College Press.

Burlingame, M. (1981). Superintendent power retention. In *Organizational Behavior in Schools and School Districts*, edited by Samuel B. Bacharach, pp. 429–64. New York: Praeger.

Button, H. W. (1966). Doctrines of administration: A brief history. *Educational Administration Quarterly* (Autumn, 1966), pp. 216–24.

Cawelti, G., and Adkisson, J. (1985). ASCD study reveals elementary school time allocations for subject areas; other trends noted. *ASCD Curriculum Update* (April 1985), pp. 1–10.

Clark, D. L.; Lotto, L. S.; and Astuto, T. A. (1984). Effective schools and school improvement: A comparative analysis of two lines of inquiry. *Educational Administration Quarterly, 20* (Summer 1984): 41–68.

Coleman, J. S.; Campbell, E.; Hobson, C.; McPartland, J.; Mood, A.; Weinfeld,

F.; York, R. (1966). *Equality of educational opportunity*. Washington, D.C.: Government Printing Office.

Cuban, L. (1976). *Urban school chiefs under fire*. Chicago: University of Chicago Press.

———. (1984). Transforming the frog into a prince: Effective schools research, policy, and practice at the district level. *Harvard Educational Review, 54* (May 1984): 129–51.

Deal, T. E. (1985). National commissions: Blueprints for remodeling or ceremonies for revitalizing public schools? *Education and Urban Society, 17* (February 1985): 145–46.

Firestone, W. A., and Herriott, R. E. (1982). Prescriptions for effective elementary schools don't fit secondary schools. *Educational Leadership, 40* (December 1982): 51–53.

Firestone, W. A., and Wilson, B. L. (1985). Using bureaucratic and cultural linkages to improve instruction: The principal's contribution. *Educational Administration Quarterly, 21* (Spring 1985): 7–30.

Fullan, M. (1982). *The meaning of educational change*. New York: Teachers College Press.

Gaertner, K. N. (1978–79). The structure of careers in public school administration. *Administrator's Notebook, 27*: 1–4.

Goldhammer, K. (1977). Role of the American school superintendent. In *Educational Administration*, edited by L. Cunningham et al. Berkeley, Calif.: McCutchan.

Goodlad, J. I. (1983). The problem of getting markedly better schools. In *Bad times, good schools*, edited by J. Frymier, pp. 59–78. West Lafayette, Ind.: Kappa Delta Pi.

Griffiths, D. E. (1966). *The school superintendent*. New York: Center for Applied Research in Education.

Hall, G.; Hord, S; and Griffin, T. (1980). Implementation at the school building level: The development and analysis of nine mini-case studies. Paper presented at the American Educational Research Association annual meeting.

Hallinger, P., and Murphy, J. (1982). The superintendent's role in promoting instructional leadership. *Administrator's Notebook, 30* (1982): 1–4.

Hannaway, J., and Sproull, L. S. (1978–79). Who's running the show? Coordination and control in educational organizations. *Administrator's Notebook, 27*: 1–4.

Hanson, E. M. (1981). Organizational control in educational systems: A case study of governance in schools. In *Organizational Behavior in Schools and School Districts*, edited by Samuel B. Bacharach, pp. 245–76. New York: Praeger.

Hawley, W. D. (1978). Horses before carts: Developing adaptive schools and the limits of innovation. In *Making change happen?*, edited by D. Mann, pp. 224–53. New York: Teachers College Press.

Huberman, M., and Crandall, D. (1983). *People, policies and practices: Examining the chain of school improvement*. Vol. 9 *Implications for action, a study of dissemination efforts supporting school improvement*. Andover, Mass.: The Network.

Kmetz, J. T., and Willower, Donald J. (1982). Elementary school principals' work behavior. *Educational Administration Quarterly, 18* (Fall 1982): 62–78.

Lave, Charles E., and March, James G. (1975). *Introduction to models in social sciences*. New York: Harper & Row.

Leithwood, K., and MacDonald, R. (1981). Decisions given by teachers for their curriculum choices."*Canadian Journal of Education, 6* (1981): 103–16.

Little, J. (1981). *School success and staff development: The role of staff development in urban desegregated schools.* Washington, D.C.: National Institute of Education.

Lortie, D. C. (1975). *Schoolteacher: A sociological study.* Chicago: University of Chicago Press.

———. (1969). The balance of control and autonomy in elementary school teaching. In *The semi-professions and their organization: Teachers, nurses, social workers,* edited by Amitai Etzioni, pp. 1–53. New York: Free Press.

Mackenzie, D. E. (1983). Research for school improvement: An appraisal of some recent trends. *Educational Researcher, 12* (April 1983): 5–17.

McLaughlin, M., and Marsh, D. (1978). Staff development and school change. *Teachers College Record, 80* (1978): 69–94.

McPherson, G. H. (1979). What principals should know about teachers. In *The principal in metropolitan schools,* edited by Donald A. Erickson and Theodore L. Reller, pp. 233–55. Berkeley, Calif.: McCutchan.

March, J. G. (1978). American public school administration: A short analysis. *School Review, 86* (February 1978): 217–50.

Martin, W. J., and Willower, D. J. (1981). The managerial behavior of high school principals. *Educational Administration Quarterly, 17* (Winter 1981): 69–98.

Natriello, G., and Dornbusch, S. (1980–81). Pitfalls in the evaluation of teachers by principals. *Administrator's Notebook, 29*: 1–4.

Ogletree, J. R. (1972). Changing supervision for a changing era. *Educational Leadership, 29* (March 1972): 507–10.

Peterson, K. D. (1977–78). Principals' tasks. *Administrator's Notebook, 26*: 1–4.

Pitner, N. J., and Ogawa, R. T. (1981). Organizational leadership: The case of the school superintendent. *Educational Administration Quarterly, 17* (Spring 1981): 45–65.

Purkey, S. C., and Smith, M. S. (1983). Effective schools: A review. *Elementary School Journal, 83* (March 1983): 427–52.

Purkey, Stewart C., and Smith, Marshall S. (1985). School reform: the district policy implications of the effective schools literature. *Elementary School Journal, 85* (January 1985): 353–89.

Rosenholtz, S. J. (1985). Effective schools: Interpreting the evidence. *American Journal of Education, 93* (May 1985): 352–88.

Rowan, B.; Bossert, S. T.; and Dwyer, D. C. (1983). Research on effective schools: A cautionary note. *Educational Researcher, 12* (April 1983): 24–31.

Salley, C. (1979–80). Superintendents' job priorities. *Administrator's Notebook, 28*: 1–4.

Sander, B., and Wiggins, T. (1985). Cultural context of administrative theory: In consideration of a multidimensional paradigm. *Educational Administration Quarterly, 21* (Winter 1985): 95–117.

Sarason, S. B. (1972). *The creation of settings and the future societies.* San Francisco: Jossey-Bass.

Weick, K. E. (1976). Educational organizations as loosely coupled systems. *Administrative Science Quarterly, 21* (March 1976): 1–19.

Willower, D. J., and Fraser, H. W. (1979–80). School superintendents on their work. *Administrator's Notebook, 28*: 1–4.

Wimpelberg, R. K. (1985). Principals in schools that show varying degrees of effectiveness. Unpublished manuscript. Department of Eductional Leadership and Foundations, University of New Orleans.

Wise, A. (1979). *Legislated learning.* Berkeley, Calif.: University of California Press.

7

Instructional Leadership "Close to the Classroom" in Secondary Schools

JUDITH WARREN LITTLE
TOM BIRD

INTRODUCTION

Principals who bear diverse responsibilities for many aspects of school operation are now being urged or told to pay greater and more specific attention to instruction—particularly to teachers' classroom practices. But the power of the school principal to influence the perspectives and practices of teaching has more often been claimed than it has been systematically described or closely analyzed. The aims of a recently completed two-year study were to advance understanding of the principal's influence on teaching and learning in secondary schools and to contribute to a practical program of training and support for school administrators.[1]

Five basic ideas guided the work on which this chapter is based:

First, schools that prove successful, even under difficult circumstances, appear to be characterized by certain workplace habits and perspectives that are profoundly influenced by school leaders. In such schools, teachers and others work closely together as colleagues and subscribe to a norm of continuous improvement (Little, 1982b; Little, in press). Classroom principles and practices are held open to scrutiny, discussion, and refinement. The advantages of collegial work, as teachers describe them, seem clear: among them are an expanded pool of ideas and materials, enhanced capacity for handling complex problems, and opportunity for intellectual stimulation or emotional solidarity.[2]

Second, the test of instructional leadership is its influence on teaching at the level of the classroom. Principals, by virtue of their position, have rights of initiative that others do not. By their actual performance they contribute to or erode the relevant professional norms. By what they say and do, reward and defend, administrators convey a set of values. They create—or limit—certain opportunities and control certain consequences. The decisions that administrators make about master schedules, budgets, teaching assignments, the use of faculty meetings, equipment and supplies, all bear upon the professional orientations and interactions of teachers.[3]

Third, without abandoning the view that leadership requires some irreducible element of character—the sheer desire to lead, and a willingness to act with courage and deliberation in difficult situations— we argue that the central patterns of instructional leadership can in fact be described at the level of principle and practice. They can be learned and taught and deliberately organized, and thus can be made part of a program for the selection, training, and support of building administrators.[4]

Fourth, instructional leadership in secondary schools is the toughest case. The requirements and demands of leadership are confounded and compounded by school size, curriculum complexity, and the scale of administrative obligations. Observing the multiple (and often competing) goals to which secondary schools aspire, and other conditions that limit joint work among teachers, some critics doubt the possibility that either administrators or teacher leaders could exert much influence on instruction.[5]

In this chapter we have held that such leaders' influence on teaching is unlikely to be felt without a substantial investment of time spent close to the classroom; thus, we have chosen to report on the classroom observation practices that make up only one part of a much larger leadership picture, but that also bring administrators and teachers more closely in contact over classroom issues. In addition, we have argued that it is unlikely that adequate instructional leadership could be exerted by even the most talented administrators working alone. While concentrating on initiative by administrators, we have described main principles and practices in ways that anticipate a broader structure of leadership by teachers.[6]

Finally, previous research (Little, 1981) has led us to believe that some professional interactions more than others have potential for developing schools with the collective capacity for improvement. While leaving open the opportunity to be surprised, we nonetheless concentrated on certain key practices, particularly those that brought persons closest to the crucial problems of teaching and learning. Most prominent among these were practices of classroom observation and feedback. We found that observation and evaluation practices brought out the demands, principles, and strategies of instructional leadership; as an illustrative case, they serve well. And as a central practice of leadership in its own right, observation served to stimulate and support teachers in advancing their practices, to help teachers apply their training and their study of teaching, and to confirm that teaching and its improvement were the main business of the school.

This chapter is organized in three sections. The first section suggests main options for instructional leadership by administrators. The options have been shaped both by our own research and by our review of the past decade of research on school-level leadership. The second section considers classroom observation as one crucial vehicle of instructional leadership and describes the actual practices employed by administrators in five secondary schools. The third section characterizes the main dilemmas that confront school leaders and district officials who choose to promote a "close to the classroom" orientation.

IMAGES OF LEADERSHIP

A principal may be said to have three main options for assuring that instructional leadership is exerted in a school. A first option is to import leadership, as by bringing in district specialists, trainers, and consultants. The principal's leadership shows in the quality of choices made regarding who is invited into the school, for what purposes, and under what terms.

In a second option, the principal can supply leadership directly, as in supervising and evaluating teachers, in leading faculty work groups, or in supplying the human and material support necessary for an innovation. Actual tactics vary widely. Some administrators take a strong stand on a set of ideas or methods: they announce their intentions to an entire faculty; they lead or organize schoolwide in-service; they design their evaluation criteria to match their intended aims. In some instances, these administrators' chosen initiatives may fly directly in the face of well-established and powerful norms regarding both instruction and the scrutiny of instruction. Other administrators build support for an idea through small groups. In a strategy that one principal describes as "buttonholing," leaders find or create arenas of interest and support among a few interested teachers, with whom they can forge agreements on teaching practices or curriculum. Together, administrators and teachers search for common ground, existing agreements, and potential partners. In so doing, they avoid direct confrontation with immovables while testing the limits and possibilities of an idea. The study groups we observed in two schools exemplified this tactic.

By either of these tactics, administrators directly involve themselves with teachers in training, planning, teaching, and classroom observation. At its best, a strategy of direct involvement engages principals and teachers in frequent, shared work on central problems of curriculum and instruction; it helps to insure that management and policy decisions will be informed by or driven by shared agreements about instructional priorities.

At its worst, the direct involvement approach outstrips the capacity of an administrator to act knowledgeably and skillfully in interactions with teachers, and spreads administrators too thin with too little to show for the effort. When events go badly, close involvement may sap energy and erode mutual respect. Teachers in one school took pride in the accomplishments wrought by two subject-area teams, but were forthright in describing the tensions between the "haves" who worked closely with the principal and the "have-nots" who were not seen (or treated) as innovators, "do-ers," "movers and shakers."

In any case, a direct involvement strategy poses tremendous problems of organization and scale for administrators who have other matters to tend. Yet judging by teachers' comments, it is a pattern that is eminently satisfying (even while sometimes taxing) when carried off well.

In a third option, the principal can organize the staff to provide leadership for each other, as in cultivating department heads as leaders, organizing peer coaching among teachers, or promoting teacher-led curricular reform. Here, the pattern of collegial interaction in the staff as a whole becomes an explicit object of leadership by the principal. Administrators concentrate on cultivating relations among the staff that would increase their collective capacity to help one another to improve. Least actively, the administrator strives only to encourage communication. Most actively, the administrator sets out to introduce new routines (e.g., the use of common planning periods for shared planning, or peer observation) or to modify roles and responsibilities (e.g., by gaining agreements that permit supervision by respected department heads). By organizing groups and by promoting teachers as leaders, administrators succeed in "making the school larger than one person" (Lipsitz, 1983, p. 284).

At its best, this team-building strategy expands the intellectual and other resources devoted to school improvement while offering new professional opportunities and rewards to teachers. By distributing instructional leadership more widely, however, it also requires a fundamental alteration in the status relations among teachers and between teachers and principals. Strains, tensions,and conflicts arise for which administrators may have only narrow interpretations ("personality conflict") and equally narrow solutions. The major strategic problem posed by a team-building strategy is the creation of an expanded structure of leadership and the legitimation of mechanisms by which teachers can emerge as leaders with respect to teaching.

The descriptions that follow exemplify most closely the second option: they portray administrators directly involved with teachers in classrooms. In very well developed cases, however, administrators and teachers tell about the training and guidance they have received as they have learned how to be useful to one another ("option 1"). And by teachers' accounts, administrators who have used classroom observations to "model" productive professional relations have set a precedent that can extend to teacher leaders. Thus, staff in one school were preparing to develop a peer coaching system ("option 3") at the time the study ended.

CLASSROOM OBSERVATION AS A VEHICLE FOR INSTRUCTIONAL LEADERSHIP

The direct observation of classroom practice is argued to be one of the critical practices by which influence on instruction and curriculum is made possible in a school. Observing and being observed, giving and getting feedback about one's work in the classroom, may be among the most powerful tools for instructional improvement and professional recognition. Whether by direct involvement or by organizing, leading, and monitoring a system of observations done by others, administrators control a potent vehicle for making schools intellectually lively places, educative for teachers as well as for students.[7]

In one of the schools in the study, classroom observation was so frequent, so intellectually lively and intense, so thoroughly integrated into the daily work, and so associated with accomplishments for all who participated, that it was difficult to see how the practice could have failed to improve teaching. In several schools, however, the observation of classroom life was so cursory, so infrequent, so shapeless, and so tentative that if it were found to affect instruction favorably we would be hard-pressed to construct a plausible explanation.

The main question concerning classroom observation is whether it is organized, practiced, and tied to consequences in ways that make the process a credible route to effective and satisfying teaching. Data on classroom observation and feedback practices drawn from the study are used here to illustrate the range of leadership strategies, and to make a case for the probable connections between those strategies and school improvement outcomes.

Organizing Observation and Feedback

In classic apple-pie fashion almost everyone in the five schools believes in the virtues of classroom observation. Getting into classrooms ranks high, at least in principle, among the priorities of all the administrators and most of the teachers who were interviewed. The actual place of observation and feedback in a larger set of institutional priorities, however, is less uniform. Schools in the study are distinguished not so much by the official endorsement administrators give to observations as by the place they accord to observation in their day-to-day work.

Confronted by many and varied demands, administrators find it difficult to establish and preserve a priority on getting into classrooms. Well-intentioned efforts may be compromised by competing obligations. In two of five case study schools almost nothing can disrupt the observation schedule or pull an administrator out of an observation. In the remaining three schools, however, observation and feedback take second place to many other tasks and obligations; in those schools nearly anything may pull an administrator out of an observation or prevent the administrator from ever reaching the classroom door. In one high school, for example, an assistant principal delayed all his planned classroom observation until the second semester in order to devote his time to establishing a system of identification cards for students.

To make shared work on curriculum and instruction a priority, the most active instructional leaders have changed their habits, their knowledge and skills, and their offices. Something had to give. Something did. Other matters are delegated, done later, done late, or ignored. That is the practical meaning of giving a high priority to instruction.

If principals are to increase substantially their attention to instruction, they also require help from their districts in modifying their job descriptions, their priorities, their routines, and their offices. In one district principals' demonstrated ability to observe knowledgeably in classrooms is given considerable weight in principal selection and evaluation. In early stages of introducing high-quality classroom assistance, principals were also supported by a combination of formal training and an informal support group.

Versions of Observation and Feedback

A central issue here is whether observation and feedback, as presently organized in a given school, have a plausible connection to teacher quality, the overall level of pedagogical skill, and the level of professional investment and commitment.

The versions of observation ranged from "dropping in and out" to systematic, structured observations organized as part of a sequence of direct assistance to teachers. In some respects, drop-ins and structured observations must be seen as alternative choices, each with its own rationale and each requiring a considerable investment of time. In none of these schools do administrators attempt to do both.

Dropping in and out of classes was said, by those who did so, to establish administrators' presence and to provide administrators with a comprehensive view of instruction in the building. These administrators remained relatively uninvolved in teachers' daily professional work or in teachers' plans for professional development, generally trusting in an experienced faculty to do a competent job. The main benefit of the strategy, according to teachers, lies in the orderly tone established for students when administrators are frequently present in the hallways.

In schools in which systematic observation prevailed, administrators displayed no less faith in teachers' abilities and motives. In explaining their emphasis on classroom-based assistance, they stressed the complexities of teaching and the advantages to be gained for the school and the teacher when those complexities could be unraveled jointly.

In all schools teachers reserved their highest approval ratings for observation-evaluation options that were more extensive and demanding than those which, in teachers' reports, their administrators were actually using. The findings invite the interpretation that teachers support rigorous observation procedures that can hold teachers accountable for their practices, *when those same practices also support them and provide them recognition for their work in the classroom.* This is distinct from evaluation practices directed primarily to detecting and correcting poor performance.

Time for the Classroom. The impact of observation rests heavily on how often it happens and how long it continues.

How Many and How Often? In some schools, observation is a routine part of teachers' interactions with administrators. At one high school, on most days, at least one of the three administrators is in at least one classroom for a structured observation. Altogether, the administrative team completes close to three hundred structured observations with a faculty of approximately fifty during the school year. At a junior high in the same district, administrators each observe two or three classes a day, most days of the year. At that rate, they complete between five and six hundred observations each year with a faculty of about fifty.

The risk of too little observation is that it cannot possibly add up to a mechanism for the improvement of teaching, though other purposes can be served (e.g., insuring "visibility," or conveying administrators' interest in "what's going on"). Still, teachers' beliefs about the worth of classroom observation are more likely to develop from rumor than from direct experience in some schools. When structured observation occurs once every five years (as it does for most teachers in two of the high schools, and for many in a third), it is unlikely that observers and observed will have the requisite mutual understanding or the shared language for describing and analyzing what is seen.

An alternative dilemma arises from the attempt to squeeze many observations into a single day. At one large high school the principal says that he aims for ten observations a day. He was observed on several days to spend at least ten minutes in each of five classrooms. One might ask whether ten observations can in fact be "focused" in a manner that will be seen by teachers as useful. To increase the number of observations in the interest of "getting into classrooms" may seriously limit the prospects that feedback will demonstrate the kind of concreteness, focus, reciprocity, and deference needed to make teachers willing and thoughtful participants.

How Long? The length of a classroom observation distinguishes most clearly the place that observation occupies across schools. In some schools special circumstances are required to produce an observation longer than twenty minutes of a single classroom period. To observe for an entire period, or to observe two days in a row, would signal some dissatisfaction on the part of the administrator and would call for explanation to the teacher.

In other schools it takes special circumstances to limit an observation to as *little* as twenty minutes of a single class period. In schools where observation is considered a necessary component of joint work on teaching, teachers expect administrators to observe long enough to insure a grasp of their intentions and practices. The teachers' preference, often, is for observation that coincides with the beginning of a curriculum unit, and that lasts long enough to see instruction unfold over several days. In such schools an observer's failure to return for a second (or third or fourth) day would be considered rude and would call for an explanation to the teacher.

Focus. Teachers' faith in observation and feedback rests in part on the understandings and terms they share with observers. Do teachers and observers share a sense of focus and topic? Is the intended focus conceptually sound and practically appropriate? Are the procedures adequate to produce fair judgments and meaningful commentary?

Formal teacher evaluation criteria (one version of a "focus") do not begin to exhaust the inventory of topics, interests, and problems that do or might bring teachers and others together in the classroom. In one junior high, for example, informal "study groups" spawned innovative projects that gave focus to classroom visits. Over a five-year period teachers and administrators examined and reexamined basic approaches to curriculum, classroom organization, instructional planning, instructional delivery, and student or program evaluation. Together, they revised the math and English curricula, organized schoolwide efforts to learn and apply techniques of proactive classroom management, and designed experiments in cooperative learning. In each case a continuous cycle of observation and talk gave meat and meaning to the group's intentions. In early stages, at least, these "cycles of innovation" had little informal relation to teacher evaluation.

Nonetheless, a principal's inescapable obligation to evaluate makes it sensible to examine the issue of focus in light of evaluation criteria and their application. The five schools do not differ appreciably in the specific criteria they employ when administrators evaluate teachers. They do, however, differ in their treatment of those criteria—in the amount of effort administrators and teachers devote to figuring out what each criterion "looks like" in practice, in their efforts to get clarity and consistency among observers in a single school, and in the degree to which the terms used form a coherent vocabulary that administrators and teachers use to describe the work of the classroom. Thus, administrators and teachers in two schools take pride in having built a "shared language" over a period of time, while admitting that they still sometimes struggle to understand one another. In the remaining three schools administrators and teachers find the stated criteria generally sensible as they appear on paper, but they are engaged in no systematic efforts to use and refine the language of the criteria in in-service sessions or in the discussions that precede or follow an observation.

Method. Across the five schools there is considerable variation in the methods used for classroom observation and in the kinds of evidence and interactions those methods generate. Here, too, the distinctions between "what's right and what's rude" differentiate among schools. In two schools it would be rude to enter a classroom without a pad or observation form; by taking detailed descriptive notes, observers argue that they are creating the "data" without which a thorough discussion is not possible, and that they are fulfilling a professional obligation to work as hard at observing as the teacher is working at teaching. In three schools, by contrast, it would come as a surprise to teachers if an administrator were to record notes steadily throughout a lesson. Those who take no notes during a class argue that to do so would limit their ability to "see everything" and would make teachers uncomfortable. One principal relies on notes constructed later in his office, insisting "you might not believe that I can remember everything, but I can." The issue here may not be whether researchers find such a claim credible, but whether teachers do.

Teachers typically admired—and sought—rigorous observation methods, used thoughtfully and imaginatively. (One teacher comments that "comfort and improvement aren't always compatible.") Teachers in schools with frequent observation place heavy emphasis on the development of shared understandings and shared language. The notes taken in a class, they say, help to build precisely such understandings and such language. They help to create "thick skin" and a tolerance on both parts for classroom performances (and observation conferences) that are sometimes rough, unpolished, and clumsy. While principals in most schools agree to delay observations until a teacher has a class "settled down," the principal of one junior high school began observations on the very first day of school, concentrating his efforts on two teachers he expected would have difficulty getting the year off to a smooth start. Both teachers credited his assistance in classroom management with helping them establish an orderly environment in the first two weeks of school. Hardly gluttons for punishment, teachers in that school nonetheless deliberately seek observation when they believe they have something to learn from an observer:

> "I wish there were more observations. This semester I'm trying out a new unit on heroes with a lot of team learning. I so wanted him here when I tried it out. He tried but he couldn't make it. But if he does give you time, you know it's going to be quality time."

Establishing Professional Relations

By each interaction they have, teachers and administrators confirm or erode the set of professional norms and relations on which steady improvement rests. Interactions close to the classroom carry particular weight, promising both high gain and high risk. In the words of one recent review, "Closer to the classroom is also closer to the bone, closer to the day-by-day performances on which personal esteem and professional standing rest" (Little, in press). Each instance of shared work on matters close to the classroom constitutes an opportunity to establish, confirm, modify, or jeopardize the necessary social relations.

Some professional relations more than others support the close scrutiny of classroom practice, permitting work on teaching practices without damaging teachers. These professional relations are remarkably resilient, sturdy enough to withstand debate and disagreement. Satisfying and productive professional relations are expressed by teachers as matters of "trust," "respect," and the absence of "threat." Our task has been to unravel such terms, to make them less mysterious, less bound to traits of character and more interpretable as situated acts that might be learned and practiced.

Unlike close friends and families, teachers and administrators cannot generally rely on long histories to insure that they intend no harm to one another. To establish trust in one another, they must find a substitute for the intimacy of close family ties.

The trust in others' intentions, and specifically in their intentions not to do one harm, is, of course, fallible under any circumstances. The extraordinary tentativeness with which observation and feedback were discussed in some of the study's schools is testimony to the frailty and uncertainty of good intentions as a guarantor of success.

Three instrumental conceptions of trust emerge from our interviews and observations. Each is relevant to instructional leadership because each provides a means of viewing trust as a product of shared work, rather than its precondition.

Trust in predictability of procedures and criteria enables persons to make a start together by entering into explicit agreements about form and ground rules, or "what event this is." Some teachers stressed their faith in a clear (though not exhaustive) set of criteria and a procedure that took the mystery and one-sided subjectivity out of observation. One teacher proposed that thorough notes taken during an observation might provide a basis for sorting out disagreements, making him more confident in the observation process.

Trust in shared understanding arose as teachers and their leaders talked long, often, and in detail about life in the classroom, and as they studied together to develop common language and a shared knowledge base for making sense of teaching and learning.

Trust in shared obligations made the relationship fully reciprocal. The solidarity of a group seems to depend on some sense that its members—administrators, department heads, and teachers—are equally invested, equally at risk, equally rewarded, and equally energetic. To the extent that observation and feedback have taken hold as powerful practices in these schools, it is largely by virtue of fostering mutuality and reciprocity in interactions. By taking the time to learn how to observe, by working hard during classes to observe thoroughly, by inviting feedback from teachers on ways to improve their observations, administrators in some schools have shown themselves to be as invested in the examination of teaching as they expect teachers to be. In addition, reciprocity has been established by insuring that both teachers and administrators can exert influence over most or all aspects of the observation process, ranging from the selection of the observer, to the range of criteria and curiosities addressed in the observation, to the topics and procedures employed in giving feedback.

Thus, administrators balance their authority to observe or evaluate with an obligation to do so knowledgeably, skillfully, and fairly. Teachers at one junior high recounted with considerable clarity (and with no embarrassment) the critiques of their teaching made in recent observation conferences. In that school it was known by all that demands for improvement would be matched by support from both administrators and other teachers.

The requirements of reciprocity and deference are emerging as critical factors in the value attached to observation and feedback. The necessary social relations are crucial, and are strengthened or weakened in the day-by-day interaction among administrators and teachers. The following five-part description summarizes the *minimum* demands for social interaction placed on a teacher and one who would observe the teacher's work usefully.[8]

- Initially, the observer must *assert* the knowledge and skill needed to help a practitioner of a complex craft. The very least assertion that can be made is something like, "I can make and report to you a description of your lesson that will shed new light on your practices and thus help you to improve them." Even as the "least assertion," this is a substantial claim to knowledge, skill, and discipline. The question is what training and experience, either in teaching or in observation, would permit an administrator or other observer to make that assertion in good faith. In most schools there is no body of carefully examined and shared experience on which the claim could be founded.
- Simultaneously, the teacher must *defer* in some way to the observer's assertion, first by acceding to the observation, then by teaching in a manner that reveals something of the teacher's intentions, thinking, and skill, and finally by listening carefully and actively to the observer's descriptions, interpretations, and proposals.
- Having made a claim in the first place, the observer must now *display* the necessary knowledge and skill. The observer must work as hard to capture the teaching as the teacher is working to do it. The observer must make a record of the lesson that is convincing and revealing to the teacher of the lesson, or propose an interpretation of classroom events that makes sense to the teacher, or must offer credible and feasible alternatives to the practices that the teacher used.
- The teacher must *respond* to the observer's insights and proposals, ultimately by trying some change in behavior, materials, perspectives on teaching, or role relations with students. Such changes are known to require effort, discipline, and courage, but if they do not occur then observation is fruitless.
- The *observer's performance must improve* along with the teacher's and by much the same means: training, practice, and observant commentary by someone who was present. Observation cannot be more simple than the teaching it supports. If the observer does not advance along with the teacher, the observer's assertions of knowledge and skill gradually are falsified. And the central premise of observation—that mutual examination of professional practices is necessary and good—is shown to be a lie.

Practices of reciprocity and deference preserve personal and professional integrity while exposing ideas and practices to close study and evaluation. We have observed ways of talking and acting that tend to reassure persons that they are not being attacked even as their practices are subjected to rigorous scrutiny. We term these ways "deferential" because they address the person's work role; they address expectations for behavior, actual behavior and consequences, and give due respect to qualifications, experience, skills, and the complexity of the job.

It has seemed to us that these ways of speaking and acting have made it possible for teachers to join in more rigorous examination of teaching practice. The practices of deference thus become tools of instructional leadership, creating "trust" as a product of shared work rather than as its necessary precondition. The practices will be familiar to students of communication, interpersonal relations, and group interaction: they call for persons to concentrate on ideas and practices rather than people, to emphasize description before judgment, and to aim for precision and concreteness over generality. For us, the learning of these tools as personal skills is only a start in instructional leadership. The crucial question is whether they are made powerful norms—shared expectations for behavior—in schools.

Consequences of Observation and Feedback

Over time, the importance that administrators attribute to classroom observation is either confirmed or questioned on the basis of known consequences—whether observation "makes a difference" in the quality of professional work or in the nature of personnel decisions. Teachers and administrators alike argue that observation and feedback ought to serve a range of professional ends, ranging from substantive improvements to career rewards. Viewed as instruments of program development, observation and feedback ought to advance the "public" character of teaching, the integrity of the school program, and the pace and sense of innovation. Viewed as instruments of professional development, observation and feedback ought to expand teachers' repertoire of practices and enhance their ability to discover, articulate, and apply pedagogical principles. When tied to teacher evaluation, observation and feedback ought to confirm a set of professional values as well as satisfy a set of bureaucratic requirements.

Acknowledging other relevant purposes (e.g., personnel management), we concentrate here on the prospects that observation will add to teachers' knowledge, skill, confidence, and commitment and will add to the quality of the school program. At issue, according to teachers and administrators, is the nature of professional standards that are invoked and achieved, the nature and distribution of rewards or other sanctions, and the ability of administrators to influence either. In two

ASPECTS OF OBSERVATION	LEVEL OF "CLOSE TO THE CLASSROOM" LEADERSHIP	
	High (2 schools)	*Low* (3 schools)
VERSION OF CLASSROOM CONTACT	Systematic observation and feedback	Drop in and out
TIME	4-day, full lesson observation cycles twice a year, and on request	Hallway sweeps; ten minute visits during formal evaluation
FOCUS	Negotiated jointly: increase in type and difficulty over time	District evaluation criteria only
METHOD	Complete descriptive record/annotated tapes	Observer's choice: range from "sit and watch" to short summary notes
TRAINING FOR OBSERVERS	Formal observation training Informal support group	Voluntary training
PROFESSIONAL RELATIONS BETWEEN TEACHER, OBSERVER	Relations based in principles of reciprocity with regard to focus and method	Relations based authority: obligations and rights surrounding evaluation
TEACHER TESTIMONY	High praise and commitment: leaders in the classroom are thorough, knowledgeable, and useful	General disinterest: leaders' visits to the classroom are infrequent, lack depth

FIGURE 7.1   Illustration of "Close to the Classroom" Leadership in Five Schools

of the five schools teachers credit observation practices with building greater overall conceptual sophistication, technical competence, and collective capacity to improve; in three schools teachers only rarely attribute new ideas or refined skills to the observation process.

DILEMMAS AND CHALLENGES IN "CLOSE TO THE CLASSROOM" LEADERSHIP

So far, we have reported how classroom observation and feedback might be organized and pursued in a manner that plausibly affects teaching and learning. These patterns of organization have been summarized in Figure 7.1. We have projected a range of personal and institutional benefits that such organization might yield. We now turn our attention

How long will it take to observe each of 80 teachers
once if observations are done at the rate of:

OBSERVERS	One a week	Three a week	Five a week
Principal alone	2 years	27 weeks	16 weeks
Principal and one assistant principal	40 weeks	13 weeks	8 weeks
Principal and two assistant principals	27 weeks	9 weeks	5 weeks
Principal, AP and four department chairs	Variable rates for administrators and chairs, e.g., three a week for administrators and once a week for chairs would require 8 weeks		

FIGURE 7.2   A Small Illustration of Possibilities for Expanding Observation and Feedback

to four inevitable challenges that schools and districts face in organizing professional work conditions in this manner.

Scale of the Task: Time and Skill

To do observation and feedback in a meaningful fashion may stretch a small administrative team very thin, even assuming they are in agreement about the worth of the practices and feel an obligation to use them. As a matter of sheer numbers, an administrative staff numbering two, three, or four faces a major challenge in organizing observations for faculties ranging from fifty to one hundred or more teachers. Teachers claim that they do not begin to have faith in an observer's grasp of their teaching in less than three visits. In Figure 7.2 we have illustrated this problem using a hypothetical staff configuration of eighty teachers and three administrators. A principal working alone to introduce high-quality observation has an almost impossible task. A principal and assistant principal who each observe one teacher a week will take the entire school year to reach every teacher at least once. The same team observing once a day can reach everyone at least every eight weeks.

The more complex the curriculum and the more sophisticated the instructional practice, the greater are the technical demands on the observer and the harder it is to do a credible job of observation. In getting into classrooms for purposes of improvement, administrators encounter certain objective realities. Studies of school improvement and school effectiveness suggest that the tasks of improvement are well beyond the capacity of administrators to lead alone, just as they are beyond the capacity of teachers to resolve independently.

Structure of Leadership

When school improvement is seen primarily as an increase in a school's collective capacity to pursue systematic improvements over long periods of time, demands on leadership are multiplied. These demands probably exceed the capacities of even skillful administrators, but could be more nearly met if the present school leadership were augmented by teacher leaders proficient not only in teaching but also in support of other teachers.

To organize a school for direct, traceable influence on teaching appears to require a form of organization in which leadership is broadly distributed and by which collegial work among teachers is given direction, continuity, and depth. In secondary schools one pattern has been to invest team leaders or department chairs with special authority for organizing and leading team work, or specifically for doing classroom observations, teacher supervision, and (in rare instances) teacher evaluation.

Nonetheless, the options for expanding the group of observers are governed in part by prevailing perceptions of teachers' and chairs' appropriate roles. Differential roles among teachers run counter to long-standing egalitarian traditions in schools and in the profession at large.[9] There appear to be few mechanisms in schools by which teachers can come to defer to one another on matters of teaching, or by which exemplary teachers can emerge as leaders with rights of initiative on curriculum and instruction. Asked about the possibilities for introducing peer observation, or systematic observation as a part of the department chair's role, the chairs who were interviewed were almost uniformly conservative in their replies. The closer a proposed practice comes to calling for critique or evaluation of another's teaching, the more it incurs the disapproval of teachers. In subsequent survey responses teachers were more receptive of the idea of observation by their peers or department chairs in schools where administrators had paved the way by establishing a high standard for classroom observation. The initiative with regard to new professional practices, it appears, remains with the principal; exploiting the resources of the office, the principal may introduce the social norm and demonstrate the technical skill that legitimizes the practice and opens the door to its use by teacher leaders.

Training and Support

Leadership close to the classroom is both a difficult undertaking and a considerable departure from traditional practice. At present, there is some reason to believe that the demands being placed upon principals far outstrip the support being offered them. In this study administrators who succeeded in making classroom observation a potent instrument of improvement and recognition had received training and support of three kinds.

First, administrators were assisted by their districts to become familiar with the most up-to-date advances in classroom management and organization, learning theory, instructional planning and delivery, student testing and evaluation, curriculum design, and other areas. By expanding their own substantive knowledge, they had something to offer teachers and demonstrated their own commitment to continuous professional development.

Second, administrators received training in methods of classroom observation and feedback. The methods they learned were considered by teachers to be "thorough and professional," and in taking the trouble to learn them they communicated their commitment to doing observation well.

Finally, the administrators themselves organized an informal support group that met monthly for problem solving and strategizing. These sessions provided ongoing implementation support, with topics ranging widely from matters of skill and technique to matters of policy, program, and organization.

Together, these options form an impressive program of training and support that offers administrators a fair chance to enter classrooms successfully.

Policy Support: Principal
Recruitment, Selection, and Evaluation

The long-term prospects for leadership with a close-to-the-classroom orientation will be shaped by a district's policies regarding the recruitment, selection, and evaluation of principals. In one of the two districts studied here district policies neither offered incentives nor exerted pressures toward productive observation and evaluation. In the second district, however, prospective administrators were required to describe their preparation for classroom observation; principals were evaluated for the quality and frequency of their classroom observations; and principals with a reputation for extensive, successful classroom assistance held the highest status and received the most informal recognition.

CONCLUSIONS

During a two-year study we searched for instructional leadership in secondary schools. The good news is that we found it. Some schools stand out for the manner in which administrators and influential teachers have organized the work life of the school to devote time, thought, energy, and budget to the steady improvement of curriculum and instruction. These are schools in which a pattern of principles and practices is clear, and in which academic and other gains appear to have followed from administrators' and teachers' work with one another. The bad news is that such principles and practices are rare, even in some schools with an established reputation for instructional leadership. One possible explanation for this apparent dearth of instructional leadership is that the research methods and concepts may have been inadequate to the task, that more subtlety may have been required to uncover the nuances of leadership in process. It seems reasonable, however, to propose that practices so subtle as to escape detection by researchers who are actively seeking them are also likely to escape the notice of teachers who have other matters on their minds.

Instructional leadership suggests close involvement among administrators and teachers in classrooms. Specific practices of classroom observations and feedback have served in this paper as a vehicle for exploring patterns of instructional leadership. While such practices by no means exhaust the possibilities for administrators to exert influence on teachers' professional norms and classroom performance, they are among the practices that bring administrators and teachers most closely into touch with central challenges of classroom life. As a touchstone, they seem appropriate. They distinguish schools from one another and reveal a set of leadership principles that can serve as the basis of further inquiry and demonstration programs of training and support.

NOTES

1. The research on which this chapter is based was supported by the National Institute of Education under grant number NIE-G–82–0020, completed in 1985 (Bird & Little, 1985). The two-year study began with case studies of five secondary schools in the first year. Survey studies were conducted in eight schools in the second year. This chapter concentrates on the first-year findings from three large urban high schools, and from a high school and junior high school in a small city. Descriptions of the districts and individual schools are contained in the full report.

Although this chapter reports the findings of one specific study, it has also been shaped by the growing literature on the principalship. In the full report we take account of comprehensive reviews of the literature (Bossert et al., 1982; Greenfield, 1982; Persell, Cookson and Lyons, 1982; Leithwood and Montgomery, 1984) and of selected recent studies that examine the influence of principals on teachers and teaching (Dwyer et al., 1983; Keedy, 1982; Morris et al., 1981; Noblit, 1979; Metz, 1978).

2. "Quality of work life" issues have assumed new prominence in the education literature of the 1980s, as crucial outcomes ranging from student

achievement to teacher retention have been traced to the professional environment of the school. Schlechty and Vance (1982) advise us to consider whether schools are attractive places to pursue a career. Other researchers examine the norms of collegiality and improvement that undergird successful schools (Little, 1982b; Rosenholtz and Kyle, 1984). Union leaders turn their attention to the professional restructuring of schools (Shanker, 1985). And state commissions bent on reform include professional work conditions on their agendas (California Commission on the Teaching Profession, 1985).

3. Our emphasis here is on the way generally effective strategies and tactics are marshalled specifically to achieve effect on teachers' professional norms. That emphasis distinguishes this study from studies that map the broad, diverse territory of principals' work lives, e.g., Wolcott (1973), Morris et al. (1981).

4. The popularity of principals' institutes and principals' centers is one sign of support for the view that skillful school leadership can be taught. The Harvard Principals' Center, Vanderbilt University's two-week summer institute, and Far West Laboratory's Peer-Assisted Leadership Program are only three of many examples.

5. Cusick (1980, 1983) offers one of the most exhaustive, detailed, and persuasive analyses of the institutional disincentives for collaborative work among teachers and assertive close-to-the-classroom leadership by principals in secondary schools. Feiman-Nemser and Floden (in press) examine disincentives and constraints rooted in the history and culture of teaching. See also Metz (1978), and Martin and Willower (1981).

6. State and local initiatives to expand professional opportunities and rewards have begun to place teachers in leadership positions of an unprecedented number and type (Schlechty, 1984; Southern Regional Education Board, 1984; Career Ladder Research Group, 1984). Conditions in the school, the district, and the occupation that would support the emergence of leadership in teaching by teachers have been examined at greater length in Bird and Little (in press), "How Schools Organize the Teaching Occupation," and Bird and Little (1985), *From Teacher to Leader*.

7. In a keynote address to a conference on effective schools Lee Shulman introduced us to this broader image of a school as an institution of learning for all who spend their days there (Shulman, 1983). We have added the claim that the resources of the principal's office can be selectively used toward that end.

8. The following five points were introduced originally in the essay, "How Schools Organize the Teaching Occupation" (Bird and Little, in press). That essay, together with others commissioned by the California Commission on the Teaching Profession, is scheduled to appear in a forthcoming special issue of *Elementary School Journal*.

9. For an analysis of the dilemmas that surround the development of teacher leadership roles, addressed to state and local policymakers, see Bird (1985), *The Mentor's Dilemma: Prospects and Demands of the California Mentor Teacher Program*.

REFERENCES

Bird, T. (1985). *The mentor's dilemma: Prospects and demands of the California Mentor Teacher Program*. San Francisco: Far West Laboratory for Educational Research and Development.

Bird, T., and Little, J. W. (1985). *Instructional leadership in eight secondary schools.* Final report to the National Institute of Education. Boulder, Colo. Center for Action Research.

————. (1986). How Schools Organize the Teaching Occupation. *Elementary School Journal*, 86(4), 493–511.

Bossert, S. T.; Dwyer, D. C.; Lee, G. V.; Rowan, B. (1981). *The instructional management role of the principal: A preliminary review and conceptualization.* San Francisco: Far West Laboratory for Educational Research and Development.

Career Ladder Research Group. (1984). *Career ladders in Utah: A preliminary study (1984).* Career Ladder Research Group, University of Utah, and School/Community Development Section, Utah State Office of Education.

Cusick, P. A. (1980). *A study of networks among professional staffs of two secondary schools.* East Lansing: Michigan State University.

————. (1983). *The egalitarian ideal and the American high school: Studies of three schools.* New York: Longman.

Dwyer, D.; Lee, G.; Rowan, B.; Bossert, S. (1983). *Five principals in action: Perspectives on instructional management.* San Francisco: Far West Laboratory for Educational Research and Development.

Feiman-Nemser, S., and Floden, R. (in press). The culture of teaching. In M. Wittrock, ed., *Handbook of research on teaching.* Washington, D.C.: American Educational Research Association.

Greenfield, W. D. (1982). *Research on public school principals: A review and recommendations.* A paper commissioned by the National Institute of Education, contract number 81–02–08. Kent, Ohio: Kent State University.

Keedy, J. L. (1982). *Norm setting as a component of principal effectiveness.* Unpublished doctoral dissertation, University of Tennessee, Knoxville.

Leithwood, K. A., and Montgomery, D. J. (1984). *Patterns of growth in principal effectiveness.* Paper presented at the annual meeting of the American Educational Research Association, New Orleans.

Lipsitz, J. (1983). *Successful schools for young adolescents.* New Brunswick, N.J.: Transaction Press.

Little, J. W. (1981). *School success and staff development: The role of staff development in urban desegregated schools.* Boulder, Colo: Center for Action Research.

————. (1982, August-September).The effective principal. *American Educator*, pp. 38–42.

————. (1982b). Norms of collegiality and experimentation: Workplace conditions of school success. *American Educational Research Journal*, 19(3), 325–40.

————. (in press). Teachers as colleagues. In V. Koehler, ed., *Educators' handbook: Research into practice.* New York: Longman.

————. (1985). Emerging leadership roles in teaching—lessons from teacher advisors. *Educational Leadership* (forthcoming).

Martin, W. J., and Willower, D. J. (1981). The managerial behavior of high school principals. *Education Administration Quarterly*, 17, 69–70.

Metz, M. H. (1978). *Classrooms and corridors: The crisis of authority in desegregated secondary schools.* Berkeley: University of California Press.

Morris, V. C.; Crowson, R. L.; Hurwitz, E., Jr.; Porter-Gehrie, C. (1981). *The urban principal: Discretionary decision-making in a large educational organization.* Chicago: University of Illinois at Chicago Circle.

Noblit, G. W. (1979). Patience and prudence in a southern high school: Managing the political economy of desegregated education. In R. C. Rist, ed., *Desegregated schools: Appraisals of an American experiment*, pp. 65–88. New York: Academic Press.

Persell, C. H.; Cookson, P. W., Jr.; Lyons, H. (1982). *Effective principals: What do we know from various educational literatures?* Paper prepared for the National Institute of Education under contract no. NIE-P–81–0181. New York: New York University, Department of Sociology.

Rosenholtz, S., and Kyle, S. (1984, Winter). Teacher isolation: Barrier to professionalism. *American Educator*, pp. 10–15.

Rowan, B.; Dwyer, D. C.; Bossert, S. T. (1982). *Methodological considerations in studies of effective principals.* Paper presented at the annual meeting of the American Educational Research Association, New York.

Schlechty, P., and Vance, V. (1982). Recruitment, selection and retention: The shape of the teaching force. Paper prepared for the National Institute of Education Invitational Conference, *Research on teaching: Implications for practice*, Airlie House, Va.

Shulman, L. (1983). A perspective on effective schools. Keynote address, *Making our schools more effective: A conference for California educators.* San Francisco: Far West Laboratory for Educational Research and Development.

Southern Regional Education Board. (1984). *State actions: Career ladders and other incentive plans for teachers and administrators.* Atlanta: Southern Regional Education Board.

Wolcott, H. (1973). *The man in the principal's office: An ethnography.* New York: Holt, Rinehart & Winston.

8

Administrative Control
and Instructional Leadership

KENT D. PETERSON

INTRODUCTION

The work of school principals takes place within the organizational boundaries of school districts. Within these boundaries various sets of interactional processes, structural elements, and organizational systems shape, constrain, and support the activities and the normative world of principals. Many of these organizational elements impinge upon the instructional leadership of principals. For example, the system of administrative control used in a school district can have a substantial influence on the instructional leadership of principals.

Systems of control can in important ways either enhance or restrict the ways principals work to improve instruction. In this paper we will describe the characteristics of administrative control over principals and suggest the ways these controls constrain, direct, and shape behaviors, goals, and values, and motivational states associated with effective instructional leadership. Using data from recent research on control in educational organizations and studies of instructional leadership, we will suggest how controls can influence the instructional leadership in schools. Suggestions for improving these systems will be described.

ADMINISTRATIVE CONTROLS IN SCHOOL DISTRICTS

While early descriptions of educational organizations suggested that control and coordination linkages were often weak or attenuated (Hannaway and Sproull, 1978; Weick, 1976), more recent research supports Lortie's (1969) contention that control is zoned, comprised of both tight and loose linkages (Peterson, 1983, 1984). The combination of tight and loose controls constrains and shapes the work of principals.

In order for organizations to survive and grow, they must have members, employees, and workers who work in coordinated fashion to produce the necessary goods or services. But neither coordination of tasks nor work activity are givens; sometimes one unit or individual does not know what others are doing, sometimes persons are unwilling or unable to work cooperatively with others, sometimes individuals have nonorganizational goals they are trying to maximize, and sometimes members lack the motivation to apply requisite energies to important tasks. For all of these as well as other reasons, administrators establish systems of control that are designed to insure that persons in the organization coordinate activities, cooperate on tasks, focus their energies and resources on organizational goals, and are motivated to achieve those goals.

Organizational control systems are comprised of several different types of control mechanisms. These different control mechanisms, working together to channel and direct the work of subordinates, form a web of influence over a wide variety of decisions, behaviors, and norms. In this chapter we are primarily concerned with their influence over instructional leadership.

Six different mechanisms of control have been identified. Four are hierarchical: supervision, input control, behavior control, and output control. Two are nonhierarchical: selection-socialization and environmental control. Examples of each type of control have been found in studies of administrative control of principals (Murphy, Peterson, and Hallinger, 1984; Peterson, 1984). Each control mechanism can affect the ways principals enact instructional leadership.

SIX MECHANISMS OF CONTROL

One of the most widely used mechanisms of control is supervision. Supervision involves the direct observation of a subordinate's work at the site followed by positive or corrective feedback about the work. While more common at the classroom level, it is found in varying degrees at the managerial level.

The importance of input control in nonprofit organizations was first noted by Newman and Wallendar (1978). Input controls channel and limit the amount, use, and flow of money and personnel to schools. Imbedded in budgetary rules and personnel policies, these controls affect managerial autonomy and resources in all areas.

Behavior control, sometimes called bureaucratic control or performance control, includes standardization of work in rules and directives, plans and procedures, and mechanization of specific tasks. While Weber (1958) was one of the first sociologists to detail the central role of this control in bureaucracies, others (Blau, 1955; Ouchi, 1977) suggest that this control forms only a small part of control systems for managers in organizations.

Output control, found in the control systems of most organizations, involves monitoring outputs, outcomes, or results, evaluating those outputs against some standard, and finally providing feedback concerning the quantity or quality of output production. This mode of control is relatively simple and uncomplicated when outputs are easy to measure accurately and goals are clear and specific. The "outputs" of principals and schools are both hard to measure and are often quite ambiguous. The use of output control to influence and guide the work of educational managers is therefore more challenging.

The final two mechanisms are nonhierarchical in that their influence derives either from norms and values internal to the principal or from pressure brought by agents outside the organization. Selection-socialization, first noted by Lortie (1969), is a form of internalized supervision. It exists when superiors select principals who are socialized to the norms and values of the administrative role and the district or when superiors actively socialize or indoctrinate these administrators to insure that their norms and values are congruent with those of the district. Selection-socialization is common in the shaping of professionals and managers in many corporations (Peterson, 1984).

In contrast to the internal locus of influence from selection-socialization, environmental control occurs when agents from outside the organization are permitted by superiors to actively influence persons within the school or company (Ouchi, 1977, 1979). With environmental control in educational settings, parents act as monitors of school effectiveness and efficiency, transmitting information to the central office. In addition, the central office uses the degree of public support as one of several criteria on which principals and schools are evaluated. Thus, the environment indirectly shapes the work of principals and their evaluations.

CONTROL SYSTEMS

The overall system of control in school districts is comprised of the total application of these six control mechanisms. In a randomly selected sample of elementary school districts the author (Peterson, 1984) found a particular pattern of controls. First, principals were constrained by multiple controls with no single control exerting dominant sway. Multiple controls secured principals in a rather pervasive web of constraints. In addition, as Lortie (1969) has suggested, these systems were "zoned" with tighter constraints over administrative tasks and looser constraints over the instructional domain, particularly in how the principal exerts instructional leadership. Finally, these systems of control afford a balance of control and autonomy "... with principals constrained through the evaluation of outputs and the mandatory accomplishment of administrative tasks but permitted considerable autonomy in the selection of means to achieve ends, in the choice of tasks to attend to, and in the selection of key personnel" (Peterson, 1984 p. 594).

The use of the six mechanisms of control delineates the kinds of direction, constraint, and formative functions at work in school districts. Supervision in the elementary districts studied by Peterson (1984) tended to be infrequent. The median fell at nine visits per year by superintendents. As expected, input controls over budgets and teacher transfers were prevalent, but principals reported considerable discretion over the hiring of teachers.

The use of behavior controls involved specification of required reporting and meeting attendance, formalization of teacher evaluation, as well as standardization of curriculum objectives and textbooks. In general, "... superiors employed behavior controls over tasks in the administrative and instructional domains that were relatively easy to specify and standardize, while the more abstract aspects of the instructional domain were less tightly constrained by this control" (Peterson, 1984, p. 588). Principals did not perceive themselves to be highly constrained by behavior controls.

Output control was perceived to be a more potent constraining force. While almost half the principals reported that achievement tests were *not* administered in their schools, most principals felt that they were held accountable for results. The results varied considerably with "public reaction" and "student performance" mentioned as important to superiors by almost equal numbers of principals.

Selection-socialization was a relatively important method of controlling principals. Hiring and assignment of principals suggest that superiors may be seeking individuals who share the norms and values of the region, the district, and the administrative role, who have had prior opportunities to develop administrative skills, and whose selection will support the reward system of the district (Peterson, 1984).

Finally, superintendents appear to have incorporated elements of the environment into the control systems of the district. The community and parents are seen as part of the district monitoring system, and their opinions and reactions to the school are viewed by principals as criteria used when they are evaluated (Peterson, 1984).

Control systems in instructionally effective districts may be somewhat different. In a case study of effective districts Murphy et al. (1984) found that while control systems in these districts employed multiple controls, had zones of tight and loose constraints, and provided a balance of control and autonomy, there appeared to be a more coordinated, more directive approach to guiding principals' work in the instructional arena. For example, in many of the districts school district goals were used as the basis for school and classroom goals. In addition, central office administrators based training, supervision, and evaluation of principals and teachers on a clearly articulated model of instruction and set of curriculum objectives. Finally, the superintendents in several of these districts played key roles in modeling proactive leadership and attention to the instructional mission of the district. They visited schools frequently, announced their expectations, and rewarded principals who ran successful schools. In short, supervision, behavior controls, and output controls seemed to be more rigorously applied in more effective districts. In these districts control systems probably had a more potent influence on principal instructional leadership than did those features of control systems in a randomly selected set of districts.

INSTRUCTIONAL LEADERSHIP

In trying to assess the affect of control systems on instructional leadership one needs to define what is meant by instructional leadership. Such a definition (several have been proposed in this volume alone) should be detailed and clear, but not all-inclusive of the work of principals. A broad approach has been taken by Murphy, Hallinger, Weil, and Mitman (1983) who posit ten functions of instructional leadership. We take a somewhat more focused approach.

For the sake of this discussion we view instructional leadership as being composed of six sets of behaviors that actively facilitate achievement-related behaviors in schools and classrooms. These behaviors derive from Villanova and others (1982) and include: (a) regularly observing teachers and providing feedback, (b) monitoring student progress by reviewing test results with teachers, (c) working with teachers to build a coordinated instructional program, (d) promoting staff development by securing resources and finding opportunities for growth, (e) communicating to teachers their responsibility for student achievement, and (f) acting as an information node and instructional resource person by regularly discussing matters of instruction with individual teachers and at faculty meetings. While other functions may facilitate student achievement, we will of necessity only focus on the ways control systems affect these behaviors.

Recent research has also identified other aspects of the principalship that are associated with high-achieving schools. In a fine summary of this research Manasse (1985) suggests that effective principals have a "vision" of what their school should be, possess a commitment to purpose, take initiative, are adept at discretionary decision-making, and provide symbolic leadership for staff, students, and community. These findings suggest that effective principals have goals, values, and norms related to student achievement and have the internal motivation necessary to engage actively in the management and leadership of the school. In short, effective instructional leaders engage in behaviors that foster strong programs; possess goals, values, and norms related to improving teaching and learning; and have strong internal motivation. Systems of organizational control can affect all of these attributes.

FUNCTIONS OF CONTROLS

Controls can affect instructional leadership in at least three ways. First, some controls may be *directive*, detailing what a principal is to do, to decide, or to plan. Second, some controls may be *restrictive*, setting the limits on resources, time, decisions, or actions which may be taken. Third, some controls may be *formative*, shaping the norms, attitudes, values, and motivational structure of the principal. While controls have primary functions, they may function in more than one way depending on how they are enacted.

The six major control mechanisms direct, restrict, or form the behaviors, goals, and motivational states of principals. Supervision is predominantly a directive control, used to prescribe behavior and communicate expectations. Superintendents may also use supervisory visits to shape the goals and norms of principals. Input control is primarily restrictive in that it limits the resources available to principals and their schools. Behavior control directs the work of principals, but also may restrict the time available for instructional activities by requiring time to be spent in meetings and preparing reports. Output control directs the work of principals by specifying the outputs to produce or the objectives to reach. It may also shape the goals and norms of demonstrators by setting and reinforcing sets of expectations regarding outcomes of schools. Selection-socialization is a powerful formative control, used to shape the goals, values, and norms of principals. Finally, environmental control acts in both the directive and the formative mode. When parents enter the school and tell principals what they want to occur in the school or complain about a teacher or a program, it is a directive control. Over time these contacts and the use of the environment by the superintendent in monitoring and assessing principals will tend to shape the goals and values of school leaders, promoting the internalization of environmental-organizational goals and values.

Overall, use of these six controls can substantially influence the behaviors, goals, and values, and motivations related to instructional leadership. But in analyzing the potential influence of these controls we must keep several considerations in mind. Individual controls may differentially affect instructional leadership. The strength of influence over instructional leadership may vary across controls. Use of some controls may be more effective for short-term changes, while others are more effective for promoting long-term change. Finally, superintendents must be aware of the cumulative effect of control *systems*, and the ways controls combine, when applying controls.

In looking at controls in the following sections, we will note how they affect key actions, normative structures, and social-psychological states of principals. Specifically, we will discuss the affect of control on behaviors, goals, and values, and the internal motivation of principals.

Control and Instructional Leadership Behaviors

The use of behavior controls and output controls can increase the amount of time principals spend formally monitoring teachers' work, discussing test results with teachers, and working with teachers to build a coordinated curricular program (or seeing that other professionals provide these functions). Establishing rules and procedures for these activities (application of behavior control), though, may set minimal limits on the activity. By assessing outcomes of these actions (the quality of teacher evaluations, assessments by teachers of principals' leadership) and rewarding effectiveness (output control), principals will be held accountable for the actions, but can work toward higher goals for their schools.

If superintendents want to insure that instructional leadership is enacted, then more *formative* controls are necessary. For example, one could socialize principals into norms of collegiality and select those who can set high expectations, diagnose instructional problems, and provide basic knowledge about teaching. Individuals with internalized norms and instructional expertise may not need their actions constrained by more directive controls (such as rules and procedures of instructional leadership), but will act in these ways based on their goals and values, applying knowledge to problems as they arise.

Directive controls are most effective when tasks are easy to specify and standardize, with little need for discretionary decision-making. In contrast, when tasks require application of discretion to complex problems (for example, in the provision of informal staff development), formative controls which have instilled internalized sets of norms, values, and knowledge are more likely to produce effective and efficient instructional leaders.

CONTROL AND THE GOALS OF PRINCIPALS

While some administrative controls directly influence the behaviors of principals in their work as instructional leaders, others influence the goals held by and sought by these administrators. The ways managers spend time, allocate resources, and initiate improvements depend to a large extent on the goals they hold for themselves and their organization. Effective principals have a vision of what they want their school to be and take initiative in attaining a viable school culture. Much of the stimulus for the decisions they make, the energy they apply to the school, and the time they spend comes not from demands from superiors, pressure from parents, or grievances by teachers but from their deeply held goals for the school. Formative controls can shape the composition of the administrative team, selecting principals who share certain goals for schools and socializing principals to share the goals of the district.

Selection-socialization is the primary control that shapes the goal structure of principals, but three others—supervision, output control, and environmental control—can also affect the specificity, content, and crystallization of administrative goals. How is this accomplished?

Supervision, direct observation of principals' work followed by feedback, can shape the goals principals attend to, spend time achieving, and use as guides for their interactions with teachers. During visits a superintendent may, like other school leaders (Little, 1982), *announce* his or her expectations for principals and teachers, *model* the behaviors desired, and *indoctrinate* the principals into the norms and values the superintendent holds. Superiors can do this by sanctioning subordinates for not sharing certain values, rewarding subordinates who express shared values, and by persuading them to take on certain values. Both verbal and nonverbal messages communicate the importance of the set of goals and values that are central to the district's social system.

Output controls also shape the goals of principals. Recent research on organizational control and the evaluation systems of principals and teachers (Harrison, 1985; Natriello and Dornbusch, 1980–81; Peterson, 1984) point to the complex set of outputs for which principals believe their superintendents hold them accountable, and to the problems associated with ambiguous evaluation standards. In these studies principals report that they believe superintendents hold them accountable for a wide variety of outcomes, including public reaction, student performance, as well as building maintenance and school climate. In some instances principals report that they have no clear idea of what is most important from their superiors, but that they try to intuit what will be the focus of their evaluation. The clear communication of goals not only increases satisfaction with evaluations, it increases the time and attention spent reaching the goals that are articulated (Natriello and Dornbusch, 1980–81; Turcotte, 1974). In short, when superintendents clearly articulate the goals and criteria used in evaluations, principals are more likely to work toward those goals and, over time, to internalize those goals for themselves. Thus, clear and specific use of output control will shape the goals of principals. When these goals deal with instructional leadership, then principals are more likely to spend time in this role.

These studies, though, suggest that principals do not always view instructional improvement as the central goal of their work. Rather, many believe that keeping parents and teachers happy and not "making waves" is more important. When this is the case, principals will spend time and develop goals focused on keeping the public satisfied rather than on program improvement.

Finally, environmental control shapes the work of instructional leadership through the strong influence of community members whose goals, expectations, and demands impinge upon principals. This control is primarily formative, for the pressure and demands from community groups mold the goals of principals, particularly when superiors formally or informally use parents as sources of information on school functioning and their opinions as criteria of effectiveness. Principals may change their goals and behaviors in response to demands from the environment. When the environment values and expects a strong instructional program and leadership from the principal, then the principal will need to respond to these pressures. Alternately, when the community is more concerned with classroom discipline, orderly hallways, and clean stairways, principals may reshape their goals to conform to these expectations.

Superintendents may either support competing district goals that counter those of parents, or they may use parent influence to reinforce shared goals for principals. In instances where parents and superintendents demand strong instructional programs, principals are more likely to act as instructional leaders.

In all of these ways control systems shape the goals of principals, goals which may either focus on instructional efficacy or on other elements of school success. But, as we have noted, some controls are more effective in promoting principal goals focusing on instructional leadership. Furthermore, some controls foster rapid change in goals—output control, for example—while others such as selection-socialization take longer to shape the goals of principals, but may have greater long-term effect on their goal structure.

CONTROL AND PRINCIPAL MOTIVATION

The degree to which principals are motivated to improve instruction in their schools is the key to effective instructional leadership (Blumberg and Greenfield, 1980; Manasse, 1985; Peterson, 1985). Administrators may have the skills and knowledge to improve schools, but if they do not have strong internal motivation they may spend their time in less challenging and less demanding activities. A high level of motivation will increase their initiative (Blumberg and Greenfield, 1980), their commitment to purpose (Manasse, 1985), and their willingness to press for continuous improvement of the instructional program. Principals without a high level of motivation are more likely to be reactive, to facilitate the interests and purposes of others, and to focus on organizational stability and maintenance rather then organizational change and amelioration. Though principals come to their positions with certain psychological predispositions, the level of motivation they feel may be affected by the nature of organizational controls, controls which can differentially dampen or stimulate preexisting levels of motivation.

The use of some forms of control as well as the overall pattern of control may lessen principal motivation to improve schools. Extensive application of directive controls may decrease principals' beliefs that they can achieve specific, short-term goals. Close supervision, specific requirements for spending money, comprehensive use of job descriptions, frequent memorandums, and detailed directives, combined with extensive use of management by objectives may communicate to principals that they are not trusted to make effective plans, professional decisions, and provide quality leadership. These actions may lower principals' expectations that they can be effective [expectancy in Vroom's (1964) terms] and thus lower the force of their motivation. Seemingly weak directive controls can combine into a strong "web of control" (Peterson, 1984) that can deplete motivation and make principals dependent on central office for instructional leadership and the stimulus for change.

It does not follow that districts should relinquish all control to activate the highest levels of principal motivation. Rather, a subtle balance of control and autonomy (comprised of carefully integrated directive, restrictive, and formative controls) could provide the right conditions for high principal motivation focused on instructionally relevant actions, decisions, and plans.

What might such a system of control look like? First, supervision would be extensive in the early years of the principalship, with much attention focused on shaping values and providing concrete, positive feedback on those actions of the principal that are promoting instructional success. Superintendents would communicate high expectations for quality instructional leadership on the part of the principal. As experience increased, supervision would be less directive and more formative, primarily reinforcing shared values and offering supportive feedback about performance, with particular attention to the ways the principal has been able to reach many of the objectives sought.

Input controls, where legally or politically possible, would be flexible enough to allow principals the right to allocate monetary resources and personnel to deal with specific problems at the school level. As the principal develops greater motivation and skill, restrictions would lessen, thus adding further encouragement for principals to take initiative and search for novel solutions to old problems.

Behavior controls should not be extensive as the nature of principals' work makes standardization of processes and behaviors problematic. During the beginning years of the principalship, memorandums and directives could provide useful ideas for ways to solve problems and frameworks for understanding the underlying processes of administration. In this way behavior controls could help the neophyte principal gain skills and confidence in administration, increase his or her awareness that administration can be learned and that actions can be proactive in spite of the inherent pressures and demands from within and without the organization. With increased skills and a belief that principals can in large part control their managerial day, their expectancy—the belief that they can reach immediate goals— would increase, thus increasing their force of motivation. Eventually instrumentality—the belief that by achieving a set of initial outcomes one will eventually achieve a secondary set of outcomes—will also increase as the principals see how actions they initiate combine to reach secondary, longer-term goals for their schools.

Judicial use of output control could also increase the motivation of principals. If superintendents and principals cooperatively specify a set of outputs or objectives to be reached, develop reliable and valid measures of those outputs, jointly monitor the achievement of outputs, and then analyze together the reasons why some outputs were not up to standard, then new principals and some veteran principals may increase their expectancy and instrumentality. This would occur as they see how their behavior produces valued outcomes.

Superintendents can increase the motivation of principals by initially selecting individuals who are highly motivated, by supporting and rewarding motivation and proactive behavior, and by developing a district culture that supports motivated instructional leadership rather than one that supports leadership focused on organizational maintenance and stability. Finally, superintendents may foster more proactive behavior and motivation by differentially buffering principals from the pressures of community groups and parents. By supporting the demands of parents for strong instructional programs and buffering principals from demands for less important arenas, superintendents may increase a principal's focus on the instructional domain.

In sum, central office administrators may shape the motivation levels of principals through careful design of control systems. Control systems that promote the development of skills and knowledge, provide opportunities to increase the sense that one can achieve immediate goals, help principals understand how reaching immediate goals and completing daily tasks make it possible to attain long-term goals, and that inculcate norms and values related to instructional leadership, high levels of student learning, and ongoing improvement will increase the motivational level of school leaders. With high levels of motivation principals are more likely to have a commitment to the vision of their school, take greater intiative in leading the faculty, be more adept at discretionary decision-making and actively managing the resources available to foster school improvement.

SUMMARY AND CONCLUSIONS

Administrative-level controls over principals will in a variety of ways affect behaviors, goals, and values, and motivation related to instructional leadership. Let us suggest points to consider in viewing the relationship between control and instructional leadership.

First, individual mechanisms of control differentially influence instructional leadership. Some effectively prescribe activities the principal is to follow, while others shape the goals and values of the principal—either towards or away from instructional leadership. Some provide discretion for principals to enact the leadership they select, while others limit the potential behaviors that an instructional leader could enact.

Second, some controls are more potent under certain conditions or situations. Some controls are more effective with new principals, while others are better for experienced school leaders. Some controls are adequate when principals share the instructional goals of the district, while others are better when instructional goals are in conflict.

Third, some control mechanisms are better for promoting short-term change in principal instructional leadership, while others are designed to effect long-term change. Changing procedures for teacher supervision and evaluation can be quickly implemented, while instilling goals and values of collegiality and ongoing improvement take considerable time and effort.

Finally, superintendents need to be aware of the ways controls can function as directive, restrictive, or formative forces on principals, forces which must be shaped and molded to the specific needs of the district. Additionally, superintendents need to know that these various functions will differentially affect instructional leadership behaviors, goals, and values related to instructional improvement, and the motivational level of principals. By applying this information to the design and application of organizational control, superintendents can foster improved instructional leadership on the part of principals. Given the nature of principals' work, the problems of multiple, hard-to-measure goals, and the structure of schools, superintendents and policymakers may want to try to influence and change principals using a more comprehensive approach rather than a narrow one focusing on the application of one or two methods of control. By viewing control as a combination of multiple, interlocking methods of influence they can provide the needed balance of control and autonomy that allows principals to be instructional leaders and to function effectively in a role demanding discretionary actions, complex decisions, and comprehensive planning.

REFERENCES

Blau, P. M. (1955). *The dynamics of bureaucracy.* Chicago: University of Chicago Press.

Blumberg, A., and Greenfield, W. (1980). *The effective principal.* Boston: Allyn and Bacon.

Hannaway, J., and Sproull, L. S. (1978). Who's running the show? Coordination and control in educational organizations. *Administrator's Notebook, 27,* (9), 1–4.

Harrison, W. (1985). *Evaluation systems for principals.* Nashville, Tenn.: Peabody College of Vanderbilt.

Little, J. W. (1982). Norms of collegiality and experimentation: Workplace conditions of school success. *American Educational Research Journal, 19,* 325–40.

Lortie, D. C. (1969). The balance of control and autonomy in elementary school teaching. In *The semi-professions and their organizations,* edited by A. Etzioni, pp. 1–53. New York: Free Press.

Manasse, A. L. (1984). Improving conditions for principal effectiveness. *Elementary School Journal, 85,* 439–63.

———. (1984). *A policymaker's guide to improving conditions for principals' effectiveness.* Alexandria, Va.: National Association of State Boards of Education.

———. (1985). Improving conditions for principal effectiveness: Policy implications of research. *Elementary School Journal, 85,* 138–62.

Murphy, J.; Hallinger, P.; Weil, M.; Mitman, A. (1983). Instructional leadership: A conceptual framework. *Planning & Change, 14,* 137–49.

Murphy, J.; Peterson, K. D.; Hallinger, P. (1984). *The administrative control of principals in effective school districts.* Paper presented at the annual meeting of the American Education Research Association, Chicago.

Natriello, G., and Dornbusch, S. M. (1980–81). Pitfalls in the evaluation of teachers by principals. *Administrator's Notebook, 29,* (6), 1–4.

Newman, W. H., and Wallendar, H. W. (1978). Managing not-for-profit enterprises. *Academy of Management Review, 3,* 24–31.

Ouchi, W. G. (1977). The relationship between organizational structures and organizational control. *Administrative Science Quarterly, 22,* 95–113.

——. (1979). A conceptual framework for the design of organizational control systems. *Management Science, 25,* 833–47.

Peterson, K. D. (1983). *Mechanisms of administrative control in educational organizations: An exploratory study* (Contract No. NIE–6–0619). Washington, D.C.: National Institute of Education.

——. (1984). Mechanisms of administrative control over managers in educational organizations. *Administrative Quarterly, 29,* 573–597.

—— (1984, April). *An organizational perspective on career movement.* Paper presented at the annual meeting of the American Education Research Association, New Orleans.

——. (1985, April). *Obstacles to learning from experience and principal training.* Paper presented at the meeting of the American Education Research Association, Chicago.

Turcotte, W. E. (1974). Control systems, performance, and satisfaction in two state agencies. *Administrative Science Quarterly, 19,* 60–73.

Villanova, R.; Cauthier, W.; Proctor, C.; Shoemaker, J. (1982). *The Connecticut School Effectiveness Questionnaire.* Hartford, Conn.: State Department of Education.

Vroom, V. H. (1964). *Work and motivation.* New York: John Wiley.

Weber, M. (1958). Bureauracy. In *From Max Weber: Essays in Sociology,* edited by H. H. Gerth & C. W. Mills, pp. 196–244. New York: Oxford University Press.

Weick, K. E. (1976). Educational organizations as loosely coupled systems. *Administrative Science Quarterly, 21,* 1–19.

PART THREE

School Cultures and Contexts

One of the most severe limitations of the research and policy literature on effective schools and instructional leadership is its failure to consider the influence of school culture and context on the activities and orientations of students, teachers, and administrators. The culture of the school and the particular context in which the school is located mediate the leadership role of school principals and others. The school's history, the values and beliefs of teachers, and the nature of the school's social, political, and economic environment are but several examples of factors that can shape and constrain the nature of leadership in schools, and the success of strategies intended to make a school more effective.

The chapters in Part Three place the concept of instructional leadership in perspective by revealing the multitude of factors that come into play in shaping a school and influencing the success of efforts to lead and improve schools. In Chapter Nine David Dwyer and Louis Smith chronicle the "life-cycle" of one school. They discuss the importance of history and the influence of changing community demographics, changing student populations, and changes in school leadership, illustrating that the significance of leaders' roles cannot be understood apart from the larger systems and flows of events that surround their actions. Philip Hallinger and Joseph Murphy, in Chapter Ten, discuss the influence of school level, staff composition, instructional technology, and district environment on instructional leadership. They describe how these and other aspects of the school organization and its social context shape the school's mission and how the instructional program is managed by school leaders.

In Chapter Eleven Douglas Mitchell examines incentives shaping the work efforts of teachers, and suggests that neither teachers nor students find the incentive system of the school strong enough to elicit the level of dedication and intensity of effort needed for the kind of performance expected of them. These conditions represent major obstacles for instructional leaders and their efforts to improve schools. Part Three concludes with a discussion by Terrence Deal who suggests that there may be many good reasons why school principals do not devote the level of attention to instruction that is prescribed by much of the literature on effective schools. He describes other important dimensions of the principal's role and illustrates how these are shaped by aspects of school context and culture. The chapter concludes with the speculation that if principals spend too much time on instructional matters they may very well jeopardize their ability to respond to other important demands associated with leading and managing a school.

While the results of research indicate that schools can be effective and that instructional leadership is associated with improving schools, caution must be exercised in generalizing such conclusions to schools in different community and historical contexts. Schools are shaped by their larger environments, and by the values, beliefs, and standards of participants. Actions to improve schools are mediated by aspects of the school's culture and organizational context, and what works in one school may fail in another. Studies that compare and contrast schools in different settings can reveal much about the nature of leadership and instruction in schools, and such strategies are needed if a more useful and generalizable knowledge base about school effectiveness and instructional leadership is to be developed.

9

The Principal as Explanation of School Change: An Incomplete Story

DAVID C. DWYER
LOUIS M. SMITH

THE LEADERSHIP DEBATE

James MacGregor Burns speculated that most men and women are subject to a bias in their thinking, an assumption that " 'great men' *do* make history" (1978, p. 51). He pointed to the fact that versions of this theory have long been supported in folklore wherein the fate of humankind is decided by battles waged between kings and princes, gods and demigods. Equally pervasive is the tendency for the mass media to emphasize the impact of leaders' actions in the determination of local, national, and world events. We are surrounded, then, with sagas of great men and women who are said to have dramatic effects on individuals, organizations, and societies.

This bias may have helped to set the stage for the unprecedented amount of attention that has recently been focused on the school principal. For better or worse, principals are being viewed as one of schooling's best bets for reform. A number of outspoken researchers have supported this view, arguing that strong leadership is a factor that is clearly associated with effective schools (Armor et al., 1976; Blumberg and Greenfield, 1980; Brookover and Lezotte, 1977; Clark, Lotto, and McCarthy, 1980; Edmonds, 1979; Lipham, 1981).

There are, however, other opinions expressed in the literature.

Peterson (1978), Pitner (1982), and Sproull (1979) found that the work of principals is varied and fragmented, providing little support for the contention that principals are dynamic, programmatic leaders. Shoemaker and Fraser (1981) pointed out that few of the studies that argue that strong leadership is essential for successful schooling actually set out to study the role of the principal. And Rowan, Bossert, and Dwyer (1983) warned of several methodological and conceptual shortcomings in the principal effects and effective schools literature. Thus, contention rather than consensus characterizes the research findings about principals and their ability to shape successful schools.

This paper provides another view of school leadership, one obtained by considering the succession of leaders in one school over a fifteen-year period. The assumption has been made that this circumstance provides a natural laboratory in which questions about leadership can be investigated. As such, it joins numerous studies, mostly accomplished in business, industry, or sports organizations, that have attempted to yield new insights about leadership employing the succession strategy. (For a review of this body of work, see Hall, 1977.) We believe this approach helps to put the importance of school leaders in perspective.

LEADERSHIP IN PERSPECTIVE

In 1971 Louis Smith and Pat Keith published *Anatomy of Educational Innovation* in which they presented the findings of a participant observation study of the radically conceived Kensington Elementary School, which had been built in a small midwest community that they called Milford. The report chronicled the people and events involved in the school's inception in 1964. In 1979 we had the opportunity to return and, once again, examine records, observe, and interview faculty about their daily work (Smith, Dwyer, Kleine, and Prunty, 1983). In addition, we tracked down the original faculty and interviewed them about their lives and careers since their Kensington experiences.

When Kensington School first welcomed students through its doors, it represented a unique blend of architecture, people, ideas, and pedagogy that Smith and Keith captured in their initial chronicle about the school's opening year:

> The setting was the Kensington School, a unique architectural structure with open-space laboratory suites, an instructional materials center, and a theatre. . . . The program exemplified the new elementary education of team teaching, individualized instruction, and multi-aged groups. (1971, p. v)

On our return, fifteen years after these words were written, we found that the innovative program had been entirely abandoned. The open architecture, featured in Kensington's design, had been closed; walls had been built between most of its classrooms. In sharp contrast to the values of individualism and self-realization that had marked the instructional goals and ideology of the staff in 1964, the 1979 staff was primarily concerned with reading, math, and discipline; the school had become a bastion for back-to-basics values and goals.

During our fifteen-year absence, Kensington had been led by three principals. A fourth began his tenure during the second year of our study. As we reconstructed the school's history, the stories of these four men seemed to offer a plausible explanation for the transformation of the Kensington innovation into the traditional elementary school that we found. But as the investigation continued, it became apparent that a much more complex web of persons, situations, events, and even serendipity lay behind Kensington's departure from its original conception. We begin the Kensington saga, then, by recounting this principal strand, the stories of principals Shelby, Edwards, Hawkins, and Wales.

The Shelby Era

The first person to occupy the office of principal at Kensington was Eugene Shelby. He was hired by the superintendent and brought to the Milford district to open the new school. He remained for just under two years, leaving midway through the Spring semester. This fact is indicative of the growing problems he faced as leader of the Kensington innovation. In part, some of his problems while at the school are accounted for by the fact that he was viewed as a "deviant newcomer" (Smith and Keith, 1971, p. 123) to the district by other Milford principals; he was never able to obtain the support of his peers.

Within Shelby's first year, conflict developed between him and his staff; Shelby professed a preference for a "bottom to top" or democratic leadership style, yet some teachers felt that he had developed an increasingly directive stance as the year wore on. Some colleagues characterized him as "intensely analytical" and "passionate in the pursuit of rationality." Others felt that Shelby's ego was too involved in his work. Other views of Shelby included his uncanny ability to "sell" his program and building. A staff member reflected that Shelby virtually "brainwashed parents" with the positive aspects of the program. The larger Milford district, however, remained unconvinced. The image we were left with was of a man filled with a true belief in the new elementary education, who came to Milford an outsider and left relatively unchanged.

Shelby's intellect, vision, and personality dominated the first two years of the school, as was recounted in detail in the Smith and Keith account. Ironically, his staff held him in greater esteem after his departure from the school; they created a larger-than-life memory of their first principal (Smith and Keith, 1971, pp. 12–15). Yet, fifteen years later, the overwhelming reaction of the 1979 faculty was to joke: "Eugene who?" The very absence of comment about him was telling in itself. In contrast, one principal's name arose continually and unsolicited—Michael Edwards.

Edwards's Revisionary Decade

Michael Edwards was born and raised in Milford's neighboring, metropolitan city. He took his first teaching job with Milford in 1949 at an elementary school. In 1956, at age thirty-one, Edwards was promoted to principal at the Field Elementary School where he served just under ten years. Those who worked with him described his last couple of years at Field as a time of staleness and boredom. Shelby's untimely resignation from Kensington provided Edwards with a needed respite. From a field of six applicants, Edwards emerged the new Kensington principal.

During the first few months of his tenure Edwards immediately faced problems. The group of innovative teachers brought together originally by Shelby refused to rally around their new principal. Seventeen of them resigned at the end of the school year, which forced Edwards into a busy summer of recruitment but permitted him the chance to build his own staff. He chose both beginning and veteran teachers, and most came from within the Milford district.

The six hundred students who entered Kensington the following Fall encountered the replenished staff and other changes as well. One of the staff members recalled that face-off:

> The kids were not allowed to make as many choices. [In Shelby's era] they were allowed to make choices all day long, and choices in important things such as "Do I want to go to math class today, or do I want to go out and play?"

She recalled her surprise at how easily students adjusted to the new order when Edwards simply said, "This is the way we're going to do it now." She also remembered how pleased youngsters were to have their very own textbooks, an indicator of just how radical the original Kensington innovation was. These modifications in curriculum and instruction appeared to have been carried out swiftly and smoothly. District curriculum guidelines were adhered to more closely; teachers used more direct instructional methods; and students' learning activities were more scheduled and routine and less independent. These alterations endured throughout Edwards's first six years at Kensington.

With these changes in curriculum and instruction, modifications were also made in the physical plant: the original "perception core" became a "resource center," for example, and the covered play shelter was walled with brick to become the lunchroom and gymnasium. The first interior wall to divide Kensington's instructional spaces was built in the school's basic skills area, ending the total openness of Kensington's original design. Overall, however, the school retained its airy feel, and visitors interested in its innovative design streamed continuously through the building. Edwards, however, spent much less time with these guests than had his predecessor.

Over and above the instructional and physical changes at Kensington, there were major differences in the personalities and leadership styles of Shelby and Edwards. Although both principals were described as "child-centered" by the staff, only Edwards was able to integrate that philosophy successfully with the school's program and defuse the community's earlier disapproval. He led by example, demonstrating his ultimate concern for children. As one teacher reminisced:

> I think all in all that his philosophy rubbed off on a majority of the teachers ... that you can love a child and teach him. They don't have to be punished.

The divisiveness and conflict that marked Shelby's era were gone. Edwards allowed the teachers considerable autonomy in instructional matters. The frequent faculty meetings and the night and weekend planning sessions that characterized the school's opening years under Shelby all but disappeared. In contrast to Shelby, who maintained an administrative aloofness from his staff, Edwards placed little social distance between himself and his teachers. Parties, banquets, celebrations, and general good humor were part of his formula for a cohesive and hardworking teacher/principal team.

Despite Edwards's propensity for more structure in Kensington's program, he was an innovator in his own right. Though not in the "alternative of grandeur" (Smith and Keith, 1971, p. 104) style of Shelby, Edwards encouraged his staff to try new ideas and to experiment with curriculum. He was supportive of teachers' ideas and also took the initiative to bring opportunities for change and renewal into the building. One teacher reported, "He was always searching for new things and better ways to do things."

The situations and attitudes described above represent the "golden years" of Kensington School. Unfortunately, those golden years were short-lived. Edwards's health began deteriorating while at the same time drastic population shifts were occurring within the Milford School District. These two factors, at least in the eyes of the teachers, contributed greatly to changes that occurred both during Edwards's last years and during the terms of succeeding principals.

The proportion of white to black students attending Kensington School was dramatically altered. At one point there were twenty-four white students at the school for every black student attending. Only four years later the ratio was one white student to two black students. One teacher, remembering this transition, shared her impressions:

> Just the noise. All right, six years ago, never would you have found this. If [my team teacher] and I were sitting in the classroom where we were visible,... our kids would not say a word.
>
> The different language... I remember the first time we heard someone was "mellin" with somebody. "Mellin," I thought, "Oh dear, how do I face this one?" I come to find out it was "messing with," you know, "bothering," you know, "upsetting." Maybe I build this up too much, okay, but I was confused. I didn't understand. I wanted somebody to help me.
>
> And then the fights. We were not used to that at all. And you'd be sitting in the classroom teaching when all of a sudden two of them would jump up and start going at it. One time I got between two of them, and I really got hit and it was the last time. I backed off and I said I would never do that again.

Whether this teacher's perceptions of the changes in her students over the years were accurate, marred by frustration and apprehension, or simply enhanced by the passage of years is not really the point here. The fact is that such perceptions held by the teaching staff at Kensington led to new demands on the principal. Those demands had consequences for the instructional program as well as the physical plant. Another teacher commented about this period:

> In those first years I don't ever remember having a child who read below fifth-grade level, and having them at fifth-grade level was rare. So now, all of a sudden, you had this whole bunch that—you had to revamp your thinking, you know, you couldn't teach them as a whole group. You had to revamp completely.

Another teacher joining this conversation said:

> Yeah, that's sort of when the "divisions" and all that fell by the wayside.

"Divisions" referred to the continuous-progress grouping arrangement used at the original Kensington instead of the more traditional grade level organization. The first teacher continued:

And more and more teachers requested walls. That was the first thing they thought—I say they thought, "If I have two walls, one on each side, it will be better."

Thus, the radical shifts in pedagogy and plant that we found on our return to Kensington began with the fears of the staff who suddenly faced a large number of students they did not understand. Their urgent need to find ways to cope with the new student group drove them back to what was most familiar and to what seemed to offer hope for the most control: self-contained classrooms, rigid curriculum, and tight— even coercive— discipline.

During this time of teacher adjustment and changing conditions, Edwards's health worsened. Despite his illness, he insisted that he would see the school through its trying times. He still believed in his philosophy and program, but as a principal who believed that he must respond to his staff, he made concession after concession to the clamoring teachers. The walls continued to go up.

One teacher recalled the way in which Edwards's faithful staff closed ranks about their ailing leader during this crucial period.

> We watched him die is what we really did. We watched the man that used to run up the steps and run down the steps barely able to get up, and have a very difficult time getting down. But never did he lose his finesse, his class, his ability to make a decision, or uphold someone, or to tell them they were wrong.... And even when he was in the hospital... his only desire was to get back to this school, because it was his school, this was his responsibility... and all this time we had problems. We had classroom problems, fights, knives, you know, we had problems.

Edwards, then, held fast to his child-centered beliefs, hoping they would bear for Kensington's new students the same fruits that they had for students of earlier years. Shortly after his death, in appreciation of his dedication, the community and district renamed the school the Michael Edwards Elementary School.[1]

Marking Time: The Hawkins Years

Kensington's next principal was William Hawkins. He had grown up in a small rural community where he eventually taught and served as a principal before coming to Milford in the late 1950s. He recalled the urgency around his appointment to Kensington:

> One day the superintendent walked in and said, "I've come after you to go to Kensington School as Mr. Edwards's assistant. He's ill and I want you to go over there this morning." Mr. Edwards had gone to the hospital

that morning and he died four days later. I never did even get to see him. So I took over cold here.

Hawkins's first tour of his new school shocked him and he reacted quickly. His actions were very different from those that his predecessor might have taken:

> The first morning I come into school, out in front on the circle out here and up on the hill, there must have been 150 kids playing right out in the streets where the cars were coming in. I walked around the building and broke up three fights the first time around. I suspended three children, I think, that first week.

> Every time I would call a parent, practically, their theory was "You've got to use a paddle up there at that school," and I hadn't been used to doing that. . . . But after a while, I finally decided that that was the way you had to do it. . . . But anyhow, that was what I saw the day that I come over here.

Hawkins's administration of Kensington School was complicated by many factors that he had never before faced. Transience of the school's families produced a turnover rate of pupils that peaked during his tenure. In the 1978–79 school year, forty-nine students enrolled in the school and 102 left, a fluctuation of fully one third of that year's student body. The first-time enrollment of Vietnamese children who spoke no English added to Hawkins's burden but, from his point of view, this problem paled in comparison to the one created by the number of children with learning disabilities who attended Kensington. In his candid manner Hawkins recalled:

> I . . . referred, I would say, twenty-five kids to Special District. And all the children that we refer just about after they've tested them, come up with learning disabilities. There are more learning disabilities than you can imagine in a school of this size.

Hawkins wished to lower the teacher-to-student ratio at the school, hoping to help the students with learning difficulties, but he encountered another serious problem that limited his options:

> Money. . . . Most changes cost money. This district is a very poor district, operating on the same tax level they operated on in 1969. Here it is 1979.

New state and federal regulations further affected Kensington. The state mandated that a standardized test of basic skills be given in all districts yearly. Hawkins feared this would limit Kensington's instructional prerogatives. In addition, state laws governing corporal punishment were changed, confusing the students and the community. And finally, an order from the Equal Employment Opportunity Commission forced the hiring of Kensington's first black teacher. Hawkins commented:

> The EEOC caused us to start hiring black teachers, I guess. I started asking for black teachers when I first came over here, but it didn't take the EEOC long until someone had reported us and now we have to hire one black teacher for each two white we hire.

Although Hawkins approved of the new hiring practice, he did not believe that this practice alone necessarily solved any problems. His first black teacher expressed the same helpless dismay with the students as did most of the other teachers. Hawkins described his attempt to utilize the new teacher as a consultant in dealing with difficult children.

> So I called her and asked her about this problem, and she said, "Well, how could I answer your question, because I was not raised like [these students] were."

Despite Hawkins's concern for the school and its students, he did not believe he could turn the school around. He was near the end of his career in education when we returned to Kensington and, like Edwards, his predecessor, Hawkins suffered debilitating health problems. His perception of his capacity was influenced by that fact.

> Two years ago next week, I had a heart attack and have been ill with this ever since—missed probably forty days this year—with being ill. So I have not been able to really put too much pressure on in changing the situation around here and knowing that I would only be here for two years.... It takes vim and vigor to really make changes. You've got to really be able to prove to them that you believe in what you are doing.

Thus the Hawkins years can best be described as marking time. This third principal was a gentle, friendly man, beset with health problems at the end of his career. His roots were small-town, rural, Southern. He followed a principal who had stamped the school indelibly. Kensington and its immediate neighborhood continued to change at a rapid pace during Hawkins's brief tenure.

The Current Head: Jonas Wales

Jonas Wales, Kensington's current principal, had grown up in the South, where he had developed both his drawl and his interest in education.

He had begun his teaching career in a rural elementary school but soon moved to a neighboring high school where he taught mathematics. During these years he completed a masters' degree and became an elementary school principal for four years. Wales followed a colleague to the Milford district in 1965 and was hired to teach math in a junior high school. Over the next six years, he continued to teach and formed an important liaison with the social studies teacher across the hall, the future superintendent of the Milford district. He also served for one year as an interim principal in Milford. After that opportunity, he taught for two final years before receiving the invitation to join the Kensington staff as principal.

From Wales's point of view, his interim principalship had been an important stepping stone to Kensington. He described that year simply: "I got the job done in the way [the district administration] wanted it done." During this time he was able to establish himself as a team player and he believed that had paid off when the Kensington principalship became available. As he talked further about his assumption of command, he stated his view of Kensington's primary problem.

> [The administration] offered the school to me and I talked to some of the people and after that I recognized that discipline was not as strict, as regulated . . . as I would like it to be. . . . Basically, I wanted [the school] to get settled down, to get into a certain mode that I wanted it in.

When asked to describe that mode, Wales spoke of his traditional education philosophy and of the way he perceived his role as principal.

> Well, the mode that I would like to have is a philosophy I have about teachers. Teachers are to teach and my job as principal is to coordinate that and to alleviate any problem that interferes with that. . . . I view myself not as a boss, exactly, but as a person who's here to help and that's what I try to do as far as discipline and getting [teachers] supplies, whatever things like that will help them, I try to do.

Wales made it clear, moreover, that he saw the school system as a hierarchy in which he and others had very specific roles.

> I've always been in the mind that a superintendent sets the tone for the district and the principal sets the tone for a school and the teacher sets the tone in the way he's going to run the classroom. . . . It makes no difference to me whether [kids] are black or white, they're students and we educate them.

Wale's straightforward views about education translated into several direct strategies for running his school.

First, he was very aware of the importance of his faculty. He simply said, "I cannot do their job." Keeping his crew working smoothly, then, was one goal to which he devoted much energy. He employed several means to that end.

In the area of hiring Wales relied on instinct, making sure that prospective staff members would fit into both his worldview and the social system already in place at Kensington. His comments regarding the hiring of one of his teachers revealed this approach.

> What I do is try to hire a person who fits my concept of music or P.E. or seventh grade...whatever...and who will fit into the building with as little turmoil as possible. In my opinion it is necessary for a faculty to... get along basically in order to have a good teaching situation in the building. If you have a lot of bickering and fighting, I think it hurts your educational program so I always try to pick someone who will fit into the building.

His concern for integration of a new teacher into the existing faculty social system led to Wale's second strategy for keeping the staff working happily, maintaining esprit de corps. As he explained:

> I try to keep a give-and-take with each one of the teachers individually, myself, and always try to be on good terms with them....Most of [the faculty] has been here quite a while and get along very well. However, there are some hot spots here and there for which I try to find some happy [middle] ground that everybody will be at least mediumly pleased with.

The importance of give-and-take between principal and teacher was recognized by Wales, but in matters he considered important, he was willing to make decisions and stick to them even if they were unpopular with the staff. Wales appeared, however, to apply an intuitive cost-benefit analysis in situations in which his decisions might be unpopular. Despite his opposition to the school's traditional Halloween festivities, for example, he understood that eliminating the celebration would cost too much for what it would gain.

> Most of these things...[are] just fun and games. And fun and games are all right as long as they add to the instructional program, but if they don't, then I'm opposed....If I had a way to do so, I'd do away with [the Halloween celebration]. But I don't know that you could do that without causing more upheaval than it would be worth in the long run.

Wales also maintained staff morale by supporting his teachers in difficult situations. In parent-teacher conflicts, for instance, he applied a simple rule: the teacher was always right. In addition, he relieved the teachers of lunchroom supervision by performing this duty himself. He was always very visible in this role, pacing among tables with a paddle protruding conspicuously from his back pocket. His posture left no doubt that order was the rule of the day.

Wales's preoccupation with discipline was perhaps best explained under the same rubric of promoting harmony within his school and among his faculty. It was the other significant aspect of "keeping the system running." Spanking students was not uncommon. Suspending offenders, although distasteful to Wales, became more routine. Detention, holding students after regular school hours, was instituted over the objection of at least one of his outspoken teachers.

Wales clearly believed that children were at school to learn. He linked this belief to his premise that "teachers were to teach." He saw these points as tenets of his self-termed "traditionalism" that hinged on tight discipline within the school and a faculty with high morale. All of this fit well within the bounds of the superintendent's, the board's, and the community's expectations.

There were, of course, some problems. Many of them were generated in Kensington's larger institutional and community context, and Wales felt they were largely beyond his control. First on Wales's list was his discomfort with a county program that provided classes for children with diagnosed learning or behavioral difficulties. Wales perceived the program to conflict with other routine instructional activities at the school and yet, according to his understanding of the law, he could not interfere with the special program's agenda.

Another problem stemmed from Wales's inexperience with elementary curriculum, particularly in the area of reading. This problem was worsened by the overwhelming number of children who required remediation at the school.

> Now, in this building, we have 141 youngsters [one third of the school] who qualify for special reading help. The reading teacher is required by law to only take 50, so my philosophy has been to take them as young as we can. . . . I also asked the reading teacher not to take any students that are involved in the Special Services Room in which the limit is 30. So it's possible of those 141 students to get some sort of remedial help . . . for 80 of them.

Despite his best intentions, sixty-one students who qualified for special reading help would not receive remedial training. This problem stemmed partially from the law which restricted class size but partly from district inequalities. The following illustrates this latter point:

> *Observer:* Can you make a pitch to central office for more reading help?
>
> *Wales:* Yes, I can make a pitch, but I would not anticipate receiving another reading teacher.

Observer: Are there other schools in the district with significantly fewer reading problems?

Wales: Oh, yes. I'm sure that's true in some of the eastern schools.[2]

Observer: Is there any equity argument about that? Can you make an argument that somebody will listen to?

Wales: I've never known anything to happen like that.

It is interesting to note that in both of these instances of problems that frustrated Wales, the actual authority to solve the issues lay beyond his grasp. State and federal laws and district-level decisions hampered problem-solving steps that Wales wished he could take.

We see, then, several sources of constraint on a principal's authority and his ability to make and act on a decision. First, we noted the "give-and-take" between leader and faculty; there were areas into which Wales would not tread. Second, several instances of state and federal constraints were seen. Third, Wales's comment that "the superintendent sets the tone" illustrates district restrictions and implies limits set by the board of education. Fourth, this principal's limited knowledge of elementary curriculum and county, state, and federal regulations hampered his ability to choose and act. And last, in Wales's opinion, the districts's own financial problems as well as inequities between schools within the district severely limited his choices.

At the end of Wales's first year at Kensington, another district elementary school was closed. For a time he and his staff worried that he would be replaced by the more senior principal from the closing school. When our study concluded, however, Wales remained principal of Kensington.

Summary

Thus far, we have recounted portions of the Kensington saga that illustrate the once-innovative school's gradual return to the "old Milford type." We have recounted the procession of four principals through the Kensington organization, and we might be tempted to attribute the school's programmatic shifts to them. Shelby, an outsider, opened the school, hired the first faculty—also mostly outsiders, imbued the staff and the program with radical educational and organizational ideals, sold the program to his community, and left the school after eighteen months in search of new horizons.

Edwards, an insider in need of a new challenge, stepped in to wrestle with the problems Shelby had left behind. Edwards's inability to coalesce the original faculty around his more moderate ideas led to the resignations of seventeen teachers, which, in turn, allowed him to hire a core of more moderate teachers from within Milford's ranks and set the stage for program reform.

Edwards's ill health and untimely death during a period of community flux opened the principal door to two more insiders, both conservative educators by any standard. All remnants of Kensington's innovative and auspicious beginnings disappeared as they were replaced with traditional textbook curriculums, self-contained classrooms, paper-and-pencil instruction, and strict discipline.

Within the walls of Kensington, this analysis of the organization's shifts during the past fifteen years seems plausible, even persuasive. Yet it is an incomplete analysis, an incomplete story. Even the telling of the principal strand hinted at other forces, other determinants at work in the school's context: changing economies, population shifts, court rulings, and state and federal regulations represent a few. The next section extends the analysis, widening the spotlight to broader arenas and once again begging the questions: Do leaders make a difference? If so, how much?

CONFOUNDING THE LEADERSHIP STORY: KENSINGTON'S HISTORICAL AND CONTEMPORARY CONTEXT

In Smith and Keith's (1971) look at Kensington in 1964, they focused on the school itself; with few exceptions, they limited their analysis to the interactions of participants within the school. On our return trip, we found that this school and classroom perspective was insufficient to explain how Kensington had changed. Any issue we examined carried us into wider circles of inquiry: circumstances at the school were tied to district events, and district decisions were influenced by changing boards, shifting community composition, and waning economic tides. Further, the proceedings of both Milford and Kensington were influenced by county, state, and national events and policy changes. Finally, history with its embedded traditions and beliefs— particularly at the local level—was also seen to intrude in the Kensington story.

In this light, our notions about leaders and their effects on the school were altered. Events in Kensington's history which at first seemed to represent the consequences of intentional, creative, and individual actions were soon entangled in other kinds of change growing out of personal and political interests, activities of other organizations, and forces that emanated from larger systems. One direct result of this perspective was the asking of a new question: Why had the Kensington School appeared at all in the Milford district? The pursuit of an answer to this question revealed a far more complex explanation of Kensington's change than the story of leadership succession already presented.

We began our search with records that stretched back to Milford School District's beginnings. The course of this search revealed that the individuals who committed themselves to the implementation of a creditable school system were traditionalists at heart who pursued the best of what conservative ideas about education always represent. The one exception was again an outsider—Dr. Steven Spanman, a Milford school superintendent and the designer of the Kensington dream. Spanman arrived at Milford in an extraordinary period of national euphoria and infected the community with that spirit despite local conflict. In the ultimate flow of Milford's history, however, his contribution made only a small ripple as the district's conservative bent was swelled by an apparent return nationally to more provincial values.

In 1928 Milford appointed its first superintendent of schools, Mrs. Claire Briggs. That event, though far removed in time from the Kensington School, began the lineage of superintendents who acted to shape the district and its schools. Only two superintendents filled the position between Mrs. Briggs and Dr. Spanman who set the stage for Kensington's construction. The first, Fred Grey, served from 1930 to 1935. He died unexpectedly, a young man. Walter McBride followed him and held the office for twenty-seven years. McBride assumed the office during the Great Depression and remained at the post beyond the cold war period and Sputnik's far-reaching launch. The end of McBride's tenure and its circumstances bear critically on Kensington's origin and its eventual reversion to the old Milford type.

In the wake of the Great Depression, World War II, and a tremendous growth in population, a once-rural, sleepy Milford was awakened by a boom of housing and school construction. In this context community members were concerned about the school district's capacity to manage the new pressures generated by the changing times. Within the district's administrative ranks and the board of education, "old hands" were being replaced by younger, more energetic individuals. These shifts generated considerable controversy.

In the Spring of 1961 a paralyzing conflict evolved. Three new board members, each without previous board experience, were elected. Their addition to the six-member board gave the upper hand to the community element that sought to modernize the district and office of the superintendent. By unanimous request, the new board called for the resignation of McBride, citing that he "had failed to carry out board policies and procedures." No specific examples were listed with the accusation. Milford School District's perennial leader refused to comply.

The impasse was significantly affected by the unprecedented action

of a young social studies teacher, Ron George. As president of the local
teachers' organization, he requested that the National Educational Association (NEA) enter into the district's dilemma as an impartial, fact-
finding commission. The NEA responded to George's letter and issued
a statement to the president of the Milford Board of Education, which
in part read:

> The undignified treatment to which Mr. McBride has been submitted does
> not affect him as an individual alone—it is considered an affront to all the
> professional personnel in the school system. Under the circumstances the
> Board of Education has nothing to lose and considerable to gain in finding
> a solution to the situation that will remove a good deal of the bitterness
> from the present conditions and make possible an immediate step toward
> a more wholesome administrative situation.

Eventually, an agreement was reached between Superintendent Mc-
Bride and the board that responded to a set of guidelines issued by the
NEA. The superintendency was vacated and McBride was hired for the
remainder of his original contract as a consultant to the district. One
who worked with McBride commented that he was reassigned office
space that amounted to not much more than a "broom closet." The
resolution of this incident led to the search for the next superintendent.

Following an NEA recommendation, an outside commission was
established to search for a new superintendent who had not been involved in the district's conflict. The decision to act on that recommendation precluded the possibility of hiring a Milford insider for the
job. This action further resulted in the hiring of a group of consultants,
a contemporary version of the national "old boys network," by the
Milford board. This group trained, selected, and controlled the careers
and job placements of most of the major superintendencies in the
country. Their choices for Milford's chief executive position were
bright, young, ambitious, and cosmopolitan men with outstanding
qualifications. These key events in the transition from McBride to his
successor set the occasion for the ripple in the traditional stream of
Milford's history that included the designing, building, and staffing of
the Kensington School.

To resume our chronology, the McBride era closed in a time of
community growth and optimism—eight new schools had been opened
during his administration. The nation, too, swelled with pride from
early space-flight successes and a successful standoff with Russia over
missiles in Cuba. The nation's public eagerly anticipated Kennedy's
"New Frontier."

In this era, a majority of Milford's Board of Education—but not
all— sought a new, young, dynamic superintendent to lead the district
in this hopeful time. As a result of the outside consultants' nomina-

tions, Steven P. Spanman, Ed. D., burst upon the scene ready and willing for a challenge. Interpersonally, he was impressive and charismatic. He was described by a cohort as "a man who could talk the birds out of the trees." He promised to bring quality, future-oriented education to the boys and girls of Milford.

Milford's community newsletters give a fascinating view of the Spanman era. Spanman's editions provided a striking contrast with the routine reporting of bus schedules, high school sports calendars, homecoming events, etc., of previous issues. Instead, his sweeping headlines portrayed an educational utopia down the road and around the very next corner. In an early edition he urged his staff to prepare for the future:

> New ideas, new ways of living and new technology require new and equally challenging ideas in education. Teachers must be aware of their added responsibilities because of these changes.

The impact of Dr. Spanman on the small Milford community was nothing less than spectacular. In two short years he arrived, found fertile soil for his ideas, and proceeded at a blinding pace to commit the district to a million-dollar construction agenda. He entertained national educational figures, placed the district in the national media limelight, involved his teachers in an ambitious and exhausting in-service program, altered the traditional district curriculum, and rallied parents to his causes. As Smith and Keith (1971) indicated in their earlier account, his pace was too fast for many and his parade was left behind. Essential to that parade were the old Milford administrators. As an outsider, he was never able to rally them to his cause.

It remains speculation whether Dr. Spanman read the handwriting on the wall—the shifting political and economic climate in the district—or whether opportunity knocked fortuitously, but, still only thirty-five years old, he was provided a face-saving exit; he received an opportunity to spend a year with the National Foundation, a prestigious, innovative educational organization. He never returned to Milford. Kensington, of course, had been built; the building was Spanman's legacy to the district.

In an important board election disgruntled members who had earlier resisted Spanman's persuasions were joined by two new members. Both were supporters of the earlier, more traditional McBride perspective on schooling. Thus, the power shifted; the stage was once again set for traditionalism.

Dr. Ronald George quietly became superintendent of Milford on May 27, 1966. One of four candidates from inside the district, Dr. George had taught elementary and junior high school in the district for a dozen years and recently had completed a doctorate in education at a nearby university. His uneventful rise to superintendent was in contrast to his earlier district activities—Ronald George had been the militant young leader of the teachers' organization that had sought outside help in dealing with the McBride conflict.

Dr. George's activities in that conflict had earned him an infamous place in the record of the board's proceedings. Their minutes clearly indicated that they had not entirely approved of his intervention.

> Mr. Henderson moved that junior high school teacher, Ronald George, not be re-employed for the school year 1962–63, because of his contemptuous attitude toward board members, his irrational behavior in public, and his totally unprofessional behavior. Mr. Obermeir seconded the motion.... The motion failed.

George was able to hold on, retain his position, and gain stature over the next few years through the teacher organization. The same power shift that indicated the end of the line for Spanman created the opening for George. It is ironic that he was both instrumental in the process that led to the hiring of Spanman with the resultant liberal change in district agendas, and, as Spanman's replacement, became the leader of the district's conservative re-consolidation. At the conclusion of our study, George remained Milford's superintendent.

Milford's "back-to-basics" period began earlier than did the national trend. The cluster of tighter control and discipline, self-contained classrooms, use of textbooks as curriculum, and assign-study-recitation teaching methods that characterized George's agenda for the schools was also part of the mandate from the board presented to George at the time of his appointment. This reemergence of traditionalism presented no problem because the majority of Spanman's appointments had departed. This meant, in effect, that Dr. George's central office staff were individuals, as was he, from the earlier McBride era. They were localists and conservative educators in the best sense of those words.

The pace of events in the Milford district slowed in the first part of Dr. George's continuing tenure. Kensington was the last school built in the district. For a while, conflicts over bond issues and tax levies took on a less pressing and emotionally charged quality. The size of the district's student body continued to grow but at a slower rate. The teaching staff was still riding on the salary increases of previous years, inflation was under reasonable control nationally, and the fact that purchasing power was gradually eroding was little noticed. This period coincided with Kensington's golden years under Mr. Edwards.

In our view, some of the most important variables that altered this relative lull in Kensington's shifting environment and greatly influenced the school's program were demographic changes. In the second half of George's tenure those forces influenced all aspects of the district's business; again, they seem borne on currents generated in the nested systems of Milford's and Kensington's context; they are forces over which the leaders of the school and district had no control.

On our return to Milford as this study began, those changes were immediately apparent to Smith. In his fifteen-year absence Milford had undergone a transformation through extensive land development. With nostalgia, he recognized a stable and small farm at one corner of Kensington's play yard, but few other reminders of Milford's rural roots remained. Numerous apartment complexes, shopping malls, subdivisions of small, inexpensive homes, and greatly expanded roads and highways characterized most of the community in 1979.

Much of this wave of construction coincided with a countywide boom in business and industry and the white middle-class migration from a nearby metropolitan city to the suburbs. But the bulk of large apartment complex construction came later, beginning around 1964. In the middle years of the 1970s the Milford community was qualified for federal housing support which made the apartments affordable for minority families who sought better living conditions than those provided by deteriorating areas in the city. Over the next few years, as previously mentioned, the student population in Milford altered quickly and drastically; Kensington's student body shifted from less than 4 percent to 60 percent black. The community as a whole became segregated with a major highway separating the predominantly white neighborhoods from the few integrated and the predominantly black areas.

During this flux, there were many instances of school boundary changes in the district, but one set of schools in the district remained white while others became 60 to 95 percent black. Despite the number of black students in the Milford schools in 1979, a black person had never been elected to the Milford Board of Education. Two black women had run for election but had been overwhelmingly defeated. Districtwide, there was one black administrator, as assistant principal. The district remained dedicated to a neighborhood concept of schooling, despite federal and state efforts to assure integration.

Beyond the racial issues confronting Milford on our return, the community was suffering a declining population and faced a gloomy economic outlook. After the boom period, businesses and industries had died out or moved, seeking greener pastures. The result for the school district was a declining tax base. Attempts to levy higher tax rates on property owners had been overwhelmingly defeated year after year. Rising inflation rates, reduced revenues, and fewer numbers of students brought about several school closings. The school closings resulted in the loss of jobs for teachers. These layoffs, combined with the district's inability to raise teachers' salaries, fueled militant demands by the teachers' organization. Such was the context of the Kensington School that we found in 1979.

Against this backdrop of history and contemporary conditions, Kensington's departure from its original conception can be posed. It is our contention that the lucidity of the leadership explanation of Kensington's changes pales considerably in the light of this longitudinal and contextual perspective.

CONCLUSION

The innovative Kensington is gone. We related the changes in structure, organization, instruction, and beliefs that occurred at Kensington during its fifteen-year conversion to a traditional, back-to-basics school. We also presented an account of the succession of Kensington's four leaders. The story illustrates that leaders can have an impact on the life of an organization. Shelby was able to bring his dream for schooling to life in as unlikely a place as Milford; Edwards struck a philosophic and programmatic chord that provided a productive harmony between community, staff, and students; Wales, too, after a long period of instability at Kensington, brought order to the organization by legitimating and enforcing a traditional elementary school program that aligned with the district's and community's views about schools and instruction.

A historical and contextual view of the school, however, revealed that the Kensington saga was a small part of a larger tale and that the actions of Kensington's leaders were significantly affected by their far-ranging contexts. Shelby began his dream at Milford only because Superintendent Spanman set the stage. Spanman was able to prepare the way because he had serendipitously arrived at the right place at the right time; no other period in Milford's history presented the opportunity for the same economic or ideational support. The golden era attributed to Edwards coincided with a lull in the community's turbulence: for a time the population was settled, economic conditions were relatively stable, and the school's white, suburban, middle-class families provided Kensington with eager, compliant students. Wales came to the school bearing the law-and-order message of the superintendent and board and began his tenure with a faculty fatigued by their long struggle in a troubled school that had been without strong administrative support for eight years. Two of the three transitions in leadership at the school had occurred because of the whims of nature: Edwards died of cancer, and Hawkins suffered a debilitating heart condition. In short, taken in the broader historical and contextual perspective, the Kensington story leaves us more with an image of men swept by events than of leaders artfully guiding or shaping their organization.

Thus, we are arguing the importance of holistic studies of organchizations and their histories. We contend that one cannot understand the significance of leaders' roles without considering the larger systems and flows of events that surround their actions. In this, the view of leadership gained from the study of the Kensington school joins the conclusions of those who argue that the apparent effectiveness or ineffectiveness of leaders is ultimately tied to contextual factors and that many of those factors lie beyond leaders' control (Brown, 1982; Dwyer, 1984; Dwyer, Lee, Rowan, and Bossert, 1983; Eitzen and Yetman, 1972; Galbraith, 1974; Gamson and Scotch, 1964; Gouldner, 1954; Lieberson and O'Connor, 1972; Rowan and Denk, 1983; Salancik and Pfeffer, 1977).

Implicitly, we have come to accept a contextualist root metaphor rather than a formalistic, mechanistic, or organic one (Pepper, 1942; Sarbin, 1977). At the same time, we do not wish to abandon entirely our search for causal explanations of change in organizations. The result is our embrace of theories of social interaction as potent tools for understanding change (Dwyer, 1981; Smith and Dwyer, 1980). We want to argue that organizations operate through the social interaction of two or more actors who are perceiving, thinking, wishing, feeling, acting beings, and who are also aware of their own histories and contexts. These actors play different roles that are dependent on their immediate context. Each affects the other and together they shape their realities (Berger and Luckmann, 1966; Blumer, 1969).

In this light, Kensington's four principals were important agents who helped to shape the organization. As they communicated with their superintendents for advice, support, and direction, the school developed in very different ways. Similarly, as they talked with their teachers, seeking information and ideas or contributing support and direction, the Kensington program changed. In addition, however, our narrative reveals many other individuals, events, and serendipitous occasions that also significantly influenced Kensington's direction over the years.

Thus, we find that the notion of multiple causation is an important social science concept. We have been enamored with Zetterberg's (1965) phrase for this, "inventory of determinants." In our effort to capture the contexts of Kensington's changes over time, our inventory grew exponentially. Change occurred not because of one person's dictum, but as the result of discussion, argument, and wrangling in multiple arenas and among scores of people. We do not mean this pejoratively. Rather, we are emphasizing the straightforward point that nothing is simple. Oppenheimer (1955) colorfully drew the same conclusion:

> Human behavior is like a centipede, standing on many legs. Nothing that we do has a single determinate. (p. 10)

Finally, then, we return to our initial questions: Do leaders make a difference? and if so, how much? Our story indicates that Kensington's leaders influenced their organizations. In most instances, their effects appear dramatic when the school is viewed over a short span of time and as an entity unto itself. In all instances, however, any notion of strong, effective leadership erodes when a larger, longer perspective is taken. Kensington's leaders led within the limits defined by their contexts. None affected his larger context; instead, each was swept along by it.

POSTSCRIPT

Two years after the conclusion of this study Kensington School, once a beacon for educational reform, was permanently closed. A small article in a Midwest newspaper reported that the Milford Board of Education had made this decision after determining that compliance with new regulations governing the removal of asbestos insulation from public buildings was not cost effective.

NOTES

1. For purposes of clarity, we will continue to call the school Kensington.
2. These are schools that lie on the other side of what Milford teachers call the "Holy Highway." This major avenue serves as a distinct racial and economic boundary between Milford neighborhoods.

REFERENCES

Armor, D.; Conry-Osequera, P.; Cox, M.; King, N.; McDonnell, L.; Pascal, A.; Pauly, E.; Zellman, G. (1976). *Analysis of the school preferred reading program in selected Los Angeles minority schools.* Santa Monica, Calif.: Rand.

Berger, P. L., and Luckman, T. (1966). *The social construction of reality: A treatise in the sociology of knowledge.* New York: Anchor Books, Doubleday.

Blumberg, A., and Greenfield, W. (1980). *The effective principal: Perspectives in school leadership.* Boston: Allyn and Bacon.

Blumer, H. (1969). *Symbolic interactionism: Perspective and method.* Englewood Cliffs, N.J.: Prentice-Hall.

Brookover, W. B., and Lezotte, L. (1977). *Schools can make a difference.* East Lansing, Mich.: College of Urban Development, Michigan State University.

Brown, M. C. (1982). Administrative succession and organizational performance: The succession effect. *Administrative Science Quarterly, 27,* 1–16.

Burns, J. M. (1978). *Leadership.* New York: Harper Colophon Books, Harper & Row.

Clark, D. L.; Lotto, L. S.; McCarthy, M. M. (1980). Factors associated with success in urban elementary schools. *Phi Delta Kappan, 61(7),* 467–70.

Dwyer, D. C. (1981). Ideology and organizational evolution: A comparative study of two innovative educational projects. Unpublished doctoral dissertation. St. Louis, Mo: Washington University.

———. (1984). The search for instructional leadership: Routines and subtleties in the principal's role. *Educational Leadership, 41(5),* 32–38.

Edmonds, R. (1979). Some schools work and more can. *Social Policy, 9,* 28–32.

Eitzen, D. S., and Yetman, N. R. (1972). Managerial change, longevity, and organizational effectiveness. *Administrative Science Quarterly, 17(1),* 110–16.

Galbraith, J. K. (1974). The U.S. economy is not a free market economy. *Forbes, 113,* 99.

Gamson, W., and Scotch, N. (1964). Scapegoating in baseball. *American Journal of Sociology, 70* (1), 70–71.

Gouldner, A. (1954). *Patterns of industrial bureaucracy.* New York: Free Press.

Hall, R. H. (1977). *Organizations: Structure and process* (2d ed.). Englewood Cliffs, N.J.: Prentice-Hall.

Lieberson, S., and O'Connor, J. F. (1972). Leadership and organizational performance: A study of large corporations. *American Sociological Review, 37(2),* 117–30.

Lipham, J. A. (1981). *Effective principal, effective school.* Reston, Va.: American Association of School Principals.

Oppenheimer, R. (1955). Prospects in the arts and sciences. *Perspectives USA, 2,* 10–11.

Pepper, S. (1942). *World hypotheses: A study in evidence.* Berkeley, Calif.: University of California Press.

Peterson, K. (1978). The principal's task. *Administrative Notebook, 26,* 1–4.

Pitner, N. J. (1982). *Training of the school administrator: State of the art.* Occasional Paper. Eugene, Oreg.: University of Oregon, College of Education, R&D Center for Educational Policy and Management.

Rowan, B.; Bossert, S. T.; Dwyer, D. C. (1983). Research on effective schools: A cautionary note. *Educational Researcher, 12,* 24–31.

Salancik, G. R., and Pfeffer, J. (1977). Constraints on administrator discretion: The limited influence of mayors on city budgets. *Urban Affairs Quarterly, 12(4),* 475–98.

Sarbin, T. R. (1977). Contextualism: A world view for modern psychology. In *Personal construct psychology, Nebraska symposium on motivation, 1976,* edited by J. Cole. Lincoln, Nebr.: University of Nebraska Press.

Shoemaker, J., and Fraser, H. W. (1981). What can principals do: Some implications from studies of effective schooling. *Phi Delta Kappan, 63(3),* 178–82.

Smith, L. M., and Dwyer, D. (1980). *Federal policy in action: A case study of an innovative urban education project.* Occasional Paper. Washington, D.C.: National Institute of Education.

Smith, L. M.; Dwyer, D. C.; Kleine, P.; Prunty, J. (1983). *Innovation and change in American education, Kensington revisited: A fifteen-year follow-up on an innovative elementary school and its faculty* (vols. 1–6). A Final Report. Washington, D.C.: National Institute of Education.

Smith, L. M., and Keith, P. (1971). *Anatomy of educational innovation.* New York: Wiley.

Sproull, L. (1979). Managing education programs: A micro-behavioral analysis. Unpublished paper.

Zetterberg, H. (1965). *On theory and verification in sociology* (3d ed.). Totowa, N.J.: Bedminster Press.

10

Instructional Leadership in the School Context

PHILIP HALLINGER
JOSEPH MURPHY

Over the past fifteen years the notion that leadership in organization is situational has reached the status of a truism. Few would argue against the assertion that a leader must take the particular characteristics of the organizational setting into consideration when acting. Common sense, as well as numerous studies, confirm that contextual variables such as organizational size, staff characteristics, technology, and environment influence the nature of organizational leadership.

Despite this development, research in educational administration has paid relatively little attention to the impact of the organization on school administrators (Bridges, 1977, 1982). Most models of educational leadership are unidirectional. They attribute the effectiveness of the organization to the leader without considering the nature of the school context and its influence on the actions of school leaders (Bossert, Rowan, Dwyer, and Lee, 1982). This inattention to the school context is especially apparent in discussions of the principal's role as instructional leader. Researchers have consistently interpreted the finding that effective urban elementary schools are characterized by strong instructional leadership to mean that strong leadership by the principal is a prerequisite for improving schools (e.g., Brookover et al., 1982; Lipham, 1982).

This interpretation is reflected in the structure of school improvement programs. These typically carve out a uniform role for the principal regardless of the school context (Farrar, Neufeld and Miles, 1983). Even if strong instructional leadership is necessary to generate improvement in poor, urban, elementary schools, the appropriate style of instructional leadership in other schools may vary depending upon a number of organizational (e.g., staff composition) and environmental (e.g., district support) factors.

In this chapter we examine the relationship between the organizational context of schools and principal instructional leadership. We discuss this relationship with respect to several contextual variables including school level, staff composition, technical clarity and complexity, and district context. Our primary focus, however, will be on analyzing ways in which the social context of schools influences the instructional leadership of principals. Our observations are not prescriptive; rather they are offered as propositions for digestion by practitioners and as starting points for future research.

LIMITATIONS OF RESEARCH
ON INSTRUCTIONAL LEADERSHIP

A growing body of research has examined the effectiveness of principals and their schools (Bossert et al., 1982). This research serves as the knowledge base for many school improvement and principal training programs. As a result, principals are now being expected to play a more active instructional leadership role than has been the case in the recent past. It is assumed that this activity will improve schoolwide instructional processes and student learning. We believe, however, that the efficacy of these efforts to improve schools by applying leverage at the level of the principalship is threatened by four limitations of the research base.

First, studies of principal leadership and school effectiveness have not utilized research designs that allow for the specification of a causal relationship between principal leadership and school outcomes (Bossert et al., 1982). Most of the research has used case study (New York State, 1974; Venezky and Winfield, 1979; Weber, 1971), ethnographic (Donmoyer, 1985; Dwyer, Lee, Rowan, and Bossert, 1983), or correlational designs (Biester, Kruse, Beyer, and Heller, 1984; Glasman, 1984; Jackson, 1982; O'Day, 1984). As Bossert and his colleagues (1982) have noted, it is possible that the "perceptions of strong leadership [found in this research] result from the process of becoming an effective school" rather than from the behavior of the principal (p. 36). Thus, the interpretation that effective principals produce effective schools has yet to be substantiated.

The second limitation is also related to the issue of research design. Almost all of the studies have investigated schools at a single point in time. Even the case studies typically do not take place over a period of time greater than one school year. Researchers have not looked at the process by which principals promote change in student achievement, merely at the characteristics of schools that are instructionally effective. This limits our understanding of how to create effective schools and, more specifically, of the principal's role in promoting school improvement (Cuban, 1984).

The third limitation of the research on effective principal leadership concerns the population of schools that has been investigated and the outcomes used to assess organizational effectiveness. Almost all of the effective schools studies have investigated poor, urban, elementary schools and used student achievement as the sole criterion for assessing effectiveness. Even if we accept principal leadership as a causal factor, it is still unclear whether those leadership styles that are "effective" in this specific population of schools will have a similar impact in other types of schools (e.g., high schools). There is even less certainty that leadership behaviors designed to promote student achievement will also contribute to the realization of other organizational goals (e.g., noncognitive student outcomes) or other dimensions of organizational effectiveness (e.g., innovation). Thus, prescriptions to "make your school more effective" that are based upon these findings may lack validity in schools that pursue different goals or that vary in the population of students served.

Finally, instructional leadership is seldom defined in concrete terms. In only a few studies is this domain of leadership operationalized in terms of specific policies, practices, and behaviors initiated by the principal (see for example Dwyer et al., 1983; Hallinger, 1983; Hallinger and Murphy, 1985a, 1985d; Jackson, 1982; O'Day, 1984). This limitation has implications for both research and practice. The lack of operational definitions makes it difficult to compare findings across research studies. It also leaves an important question unanswered: What should a principal do in order to be an instructional leader?

These limitations of the research base make it difficult to draw conclusions about the impact of principal instructional leadership. The first two limitations serve as a caution to those who would cast the principal in the role of the white knight, heralding in an era of radically improved schools. Despite renewed optimism concerning the potential impact of principals, several influential researchers have argued for a less heroic role for school administrators in recognition of the many organizational constraints under which they operate (Bridges, 1977; March, 1978; Weick, 1982). The third and fourth limitations provide the basis for the remainder of this chapter in which we explore the relationship between the school context and principal instructional leadership behavior.

ORGANIZATIONAL CONTEXT
AND INSTRUCTIONAL LEADERSHIP

The literature on organizational leadership focuses attention on numerous personal, organizational, and environmental factors that influence administrative behavior. Here we discuss selected organizational and environmental factors under the rubric of "contextual variables." Several contextual variables have been studied sufficiently so that propositions can be generated concerning their impact on principal leadership. These include the complexity of the instructional technology employed by the school, the nature of the district context, staff composition, and school level. We note in advance that the presentation of these variables as discrete factors with independent effects on principal behavior may give a distorted view of organizational leadership. In reality, these variables interact with one another to create an overall context within which principals act.

Clarity and Complexity of Instructional Technology

The technology of an organization is the process it employs in order to accomplish its goals. In education, the technology designed to produce student learning is the curriculum and instruction to which students are exposed. Organizational theorists maintain that two aspects of an organization's technology—clarity and complexity—have an impact on the behavior of managers (Thompson, 1967). In educational organizations these two characteristics of the instructional technology influence the degree to which managers coordinate and control the work of teachers (Cohen and Miller, 1980; Hannaway and Sproull, 1978–79; March, 1978; Peterson, 1985).

Clarity refers to the extent to which the instructional process is understood and can be specified. Schools vary in the clarity of the instructional technologies they employ. Traditionally, most schools have utilized an unclear technology (March, 1978; Weick, 1982). Individual teachers select the mode of instruction and implement their own conception of the curriculum. This has resulted in the use of a wide variety of instructional techniques within any given school, reflecting the belief that no one method of teaching is better than another.

Two relatively recent developments have made it possible for schools to utilize instructional technologies characterized by higher degrees of clarity. First, research on effective instruction has found that, under certain conditions, teaching models that emphasize direct instruction by the teacher result in greater gains in student achievement (Rosenshine, 1983). The use of one of these models may enhance the clarity of instruction. Another finding with similar implications concerns curricular coordination. Coordination of curricular objectives with materials and test instruments also results in increased student achievement (Cooley and Leinhardt, 1980; Eubanks and Levine, 1983; Venezky and Winfield, 1979; Wellisch et al., 1978). These findings suggest that technical clarity may increase when a school staff uses a coordinated approach to teaching a particular subject, adopts a preferred model of instruction, or specifies and teaches the components of the curriculum.

The clarity of the school's technology creates a context for principal leadership. In situations characterized by greater clarity, closer supervision is possible and may have positive results. The highly directive instructional leadership exercised by principals in effective schools is, to some degree, made possible by the greater clarity of the technology used in these schools. Effective urban elementary schools emphasize a limited number of learning outcomes, break the curriculum down into a set of common instructional objectives, coordinate those objectives with testing, and use a somewhat more uniform approach to instruction. For example, the staff in an effective school might participate in a schoolwide staff development program in teaching expository writing. Once they have been trained in this instructional approach, the principal is able to specify the components of writing instruction that will be analyzed in classroom observations. Although teachers will emphasize a common framework, the specification of a method of instruction adds clarity to the school's instructional technology. This makes it possible for the principal to provide more valid assessments of classroom instruction (Bridges, 1984).

In cases where the instructional technology is more nebulous, highly directive instructional leadership behavior can be counterproductive. Close supervision of instruction in the absence of a clear understanding and policy concerning the components of the curriculum or effective classroom instruction may result in high levels of administrator-staff conflict (Cuban, 1984). In such contexts principals should emphasize indirect types of leadership behavior. These might include symbolic, facilitative, or political strategies (Deal and Celotti, 1980; Duckworth, 1981; March, 1978; Peters, 1980).

Complexity refers to the degree to which the instructional processes of the school require interdependence and coordination among the teaching staff. The complexity of the instructional technology utilized by schools also varies. For example, the departmentalized curricular organization of secondary schools is more highly differentiated than the traditional form of elementary school organization. Similarly, schools that participate in categorically funded programs exhibit greater complexity. These schools must adopt specific instructional, monitoring, and reporting procedures not required of other schools. Instructional techniques such as team teaching also result in greater complexity as teachers are more interdependent than their counterparts in traditionally organized schools.

In each of these examples the increased complexity of the school's technology affects the principal's instructional leadership role. Evidence from several studies suggests that increased complexity necessitates increased coordination on the part of the principal (Cohen and Miller, 1980; Wellisch et al., 1978). Both the repertoire and frequency of coordinating behaviors should increase in schools that utilize more complex methods of organizing and delivering instruction (Cohen, Miller, Bredo, and Duckworth, 1977; Deal and Celotti, 1980; Duckworth, 1981; Wellisch et al., 1978). Interestingly, in educational organizations increased technical complexity is not necessarily accompanied by increased control on the part of principals (Cohen et al., 1977; Cohen and Miller, 1980).

These findings suggest that the nature of the instructional technology employed by the school affects the instructional leadership role of the principal. More specifically, the degree to which principals should attempt to control instruction is affected by the clarity of the school's curricular and instructional processes. The principal should consider: How broad are our learning goals? What are the beliefs and practices of the staff with respect to the teaching process? How diverse are the instructional methods used by teachers in the school? In general, a high degree of principal control over instructional processes seems less appropriate in contexts characterized by wide diversity of instructional goals and methods.

The principal's role in coordinating the school's program is tempered by the complexity of the instructional technology. In general, increased complexity demands greater coordination. It is important to note, however, that there are at least three routes by which the principal can increase coordination. First, the principal can assume a more active and central role in curricular coordination. This seems to be the strategy employed in instructionally effective elementary schools (Bossert et al., 1982). Second, the principal can delegate authority to assistant principals, department heads, special program coordinators, or grade leaders (Gersten and Carnine, 1981). Here the principal maintains responsibility for coordinating the overall educational program but is less directly involved in carrying out the routine tasks. Third, the principal can increase coordination by offering additional opportunities for staff interaction in professional activities such as staff development and curricular planning (Cohen et al., 1977; Little, 1982; Rosenholtz, 1985). The effectiveness of a particular strategy will depend on the nature of the school's instructional program as well as on other contextual variables such as school size and school level.

District Context

The role of the district office in promoting instructional improvement has received rather limited attention from researchers (Bidwell and Kasarda, 1975; Bridges, 1982; Hallinger and Murphy, 1982; Hart and Ogawa, 1984; McCormack-Larkin and Kritek, 1982; Murphy and Hallinger, in press). Thus, relatively little is known about the impact of the district context on principal leadership. Recent attempts to apply the effective schools findings at the district level, however, suggest that the district administration does have a role in both providing and promoting instructional leadership (Cuban, 1984; Rowan, 1983).

The district context influences principals in at least three complementary ways. First, district support is often linked with successful efforts to implement innovations in schools (Berman, 1984; Finn, 1983; Purkey and Smith, 1983a). Actors at the school site seek signals from the district office to assess the commitment of the superintendent and district staff to the implementation of a particular innovation (Berman and McLaughlin, 1978). It is logical to assume that the majority of principals are more likely to engage in instructional leadership behavior under conditions of district support than in its absence.

District support can take the form of additional resources, staff training, technical assistance, better information, or increased authority. One resource that principals need in order to fulfill their instructional leadership responsibilities is time. The district can address the problem of scarce time by adopting policies that delineate the job priorities of the principal. Similarly, the district can increase the efficiency of principal time by providing remedial assistance for commonly occurring teaching deficiencies (Bridges, 1984). Principals may also need additional skills in order to effectively carry out their instructional leadership responsibilities. The district can encourage professional development and offer instructional leadership training to principals. District staff can provide technical assistance to principals in the analysis and interpretation of test scores and in the coordination of curriculum. Districts can also make better information available to principals through the administration of annual community opinion surveys. Recent findings further suggest principals may need additional authority if they are to be held accountable for school improvement (Bridges, 1984). In particular, they may need greater authority in the selection of staff (Teddlie, Falkowski, Stringfield, Dessalie, and Garvue, 1984).

A second strategy districts can use to promote principal instructional leadership is to change the district culture and make excellence in teaching top priority (Bridges, 1984). Numerous descriptive accounts of superintendent job behavior convey the impression that curriculum and instruction occupy a relatively low priority at the top of the organization (Hannaway and Sproull, 1978–79; Pitner and Ogawa, 1980; Willower and Fraser, 1979–80). This norm is reflected in the work activity of principals. They too spend most of their workday on managerial tasks that are unrelated to instruction (Cohen and Miller, 1980; Deal and Celotti, 1980; March, 1978; Weick, 1982). The superintendent can begin to change the district context for instructional improvement by providing symbolic leadership, modeling the type of behavior most highly valued by the organization. District goals, standards, policies, reward systems, and superintendent behavior communicate the district's expectations and priorities with respect to the job role of the principal. Preliminary reports indicate that comprehensive attempts by superintendents to change the district context can have effects at the school site (Hallinger and Murphy, 1982; McCormack-Larkin and Kritek, 1982; Murphy, Hallinger, and Peterson, 1984).

The third way in which the district can influence the instructional leadership of principals is through the manipulation of formal and informal controls. In general, district offices have not exercised much control over principals, particularly in the areas of curriculum and instruction (Deal and Celotti, 1980; Hannaway and Sproull, 1978–79; Peterson, 1985; Rowan, 1983). Tentative results, however, suggest that districts can bring about districtwide instructional improvement through increased coordination and control of principals (Murphy, Hallinger, and Peterson, 1985; Rosenholtz, 1985). Superintendents hold principals accountable for spending more time on the tasks associated with instructional leadership. Systematic assessment of principal instructional leadership is one way of communicating accountability (Bridges, 1984; Hallinger and Murphy, 1985a).

Despite the small direct effects of school district organization on student achievement (Bidwell and Kasarda, 1975; Hart and Ogawa, 1984), there is little doubt that the district context shapes the leadership behavior of principals. As noted elsewhere, however, the process of translating findings concerning effective schools into district programs is complex and not without potentially negative consequences (Cuban, 1984). Current efforts to implement instructional management programs at the district level will provide needed information regarding specific ways in which variations in district organization affect the work of principals.

Staff Composition

The primary assumption underlying contingency models of leadership is that no one style of leadership is appropriate to all situations or contexts. To be effective, leaders must adapt their behavior to the characteristics of subordinates and to the specific organizational context (Fiedler and Chemers, 1974). In schools the staff characteristics that most directly influence the leadership behavior of principals include structural factors, personal characteristics, and organizational attitudes.

Structural factors describe the characteristics of faculty members as a group, such as average age, educational level and years of experience of the faculty, and staff stability. Although there are few clear-cut prescriptions, it has been suggested that these structural conditions influence how principals coordinate and control the work of teachers. In an observational study of five principals, it was found that the two principals who were least intrusive in the teaching-learning process supervised the most experienced staffs. Those principals with more directive leadership styles had either less mature staffs or lower levels of staff stability (Dwyer et al., 1983). This and other studies of organizational control in schools (Cohen et al., 1977) suggest a working hypothesis. As teaching staffs mature and stabilize, the leadership strategies of principals will shift from formal directive approaches to more informal, indirect leadership styles.

The most commonly studied personal characteristic of teachers is intelligence, generally measured by scores on standardized tests. Researchers have noted that verbal ability is the only personal characteristic of teachers that is consistently and positively related to student learning (Bridge, Judd, and Mook, 1979). Although research on the relationship between teacher intelligence and principal leadership style is limited, the available evidence argues for differing approaches to leadership based upon teacher intellectual ability. For example, writers in the area of developmental supervision argue that principals should vary their leadership style when supervising teachers with differing abilities to think abstractly. It is suggested that less directive supervisory styles are appropriate with teachers who possess higher abstract thinking skills. Teachers with less abstract thinking ability may require more directive supervisory behavior (Glickman, 1983).

Since the earliest formulations of situational models of leadership, organizational theorists have argued that leadership style should vary with the organizational attitudes of staff. When staff commitment to the organization is either relatively high or low, directive types of leadership are appropriate. When the supportiveness of the staff toward the manager is moderate, less directive, more personalized leadership activity appears to be more effective (Fiedler and Chemers, 1974). Again, looking at the implications of teacher commitment for instructional leadership, developmental supervision advocates suggest the following: where commitment is weak, more control needs to be exercised by the principal. Where such commitment is high, less directive, more collaborative behavior is appropriate (Glickman, 1983).

School Level

School level is a prominent yet poorly understood characteristic of American public schools (Firestone and Herriott, 1982). Educators tend to underestimate the impact of differences between elementary and secondary school organization on school leadership. This inattention is reflected in the structure of school improvement programs, few of which make allowances for the level of schooling (Farrar, Neufeld, and Miles, 1983).

There is, however, growing concern over the tendency to generalize findings on principals gleaned from studies of elementary schools to their counterparts in secondary schools. One cause for concern derives from the paucity of systematic studies of secondary school principals in general and instructional leadership in particular (Mazzarella, 1985). Few findings regarding the impact of elementary school principals have been validated at the high school level. This lack of data is particularly troubling in light of evidence that different strategies and activities characterize successful school improvement programs at the elementary and secondary levels (Berman, 1984).

A second avenue of concern arises from studies that examine differences in the organizational characteristics of elementary and secondary schools. Secondary schools differ from elementary schools in several important respects, including goal structure, administrative organization, student and faculty characteristics, curricular organization and delivery, and linkages to parents and the community. Although the empirical evidence remains thin, initial conclusions drawn from analyses of these organizational differences suggest that prescriptions for strong instructional leadership derived from elementary school studies may simply not apply at the secondary level (Firestone and Herriott, 1982; Mazzarella, 1985; Purkey and Smith, 1983b).

This inference does not mean that instructional leadership is unimportant in junior and senior high schools. There is evidence that strong administrative leadership does contribute to secondary school success (Rutter, Maugham, Mortimore, Ouston and Smith, 1979). Instructional leadership in secondary schools may, however, differ in two related ways. First, secondary school principals cannot rely on the same type of direct leadershp activity utilized by their peers at the elementary level. In high schools the larger staff and student populations, the multileveled organizational structure, and the specialized subject area knowledge of teachers all limit the principal's ability to be personally involved in all aspects of instructional management. Instead, the principal must rely more on indirect, facilitative, and symbolic modes of expression, providing direct intervention in selected situations (Bridges, 1984; Firestone and Herriott, 1982; Firestone and Wilson, 1985).

The second difference was suggested earlier in our discussion of technical complexity. The secondary school principal will carry out the instructional leadership role by delegating certain instructional leadership functions to vice principals, deans, and department heads (Gersten and Carnine, 1981). Curriculum coordination, instructional supervision, and monitoring of student progress must be accomplished partly through the work of other administrative staff. Thus, at the secondary level the principal must insure that the critical instructional leadership functions are performed even in the absence of direct leadership.

SCHOOL SOCIAL CONTEXT
AND INSTRUCTIONAL LEADERSHIP

Thus far we have examined the impact of several organizational variables on principal instructional leadership. In this section we look more closely at ways in which the social context of schools influences the instructional leadership behavior of principals. The term *social context* refers to the socioeconomic status (SES) of the student and community population served by the school. Common indices used to determine the nature of the school social context include the occupational status, educational attainment, and income level of parents; the percentage of students from families receiving aid to families with dependent children (AFDC); and the percentage of students receiving free or subsidized lunches. Social context is relevant to understanding the organization and management of schools because these measures of student socioeconomic status correlate highly with measures of student achievement and educational attainment (Bridge, Judd, and Moock, 1979; Coleman et al., 1966). Students from lower-class backgrounds typically achieve less in school and do not advance as far in the educational system as their counterparts with middle- and upper-class backgrounds (Levine, 1979).

Explanations for the relative lack of success of students from low-income backgrounds center on at least three factors. First, students from low- income families receive fewer educational opportunities in the home. They are exposed to fewer educational materials such as books and have fewer opportunities to partake of cultural activities which support the body of knowledge taught in schools. Second, the community context of low-income families does not emphasize academic success and places a lower value on educational attainment. Third, the home, school, and community communicate relatively low expectations of the student with respect to academic achievement. Both the structure of the school program and the behaviors of school staff and parents communicate the message that the failure of students to succeed in school is acceptable, if not expected. In wealthier communities student achievement and attainment in school is expected and reinforced to a greater extent in both the school and community.

These findings led to the national effort to raise the achievement levels of lower SES students, particularly those from urban backgrounds. The effective schools studies have identified characteristics of schools in which students from poor, urban backgrounds succeed.

These studies consistently find that instructionally effective schools provide a climate of high expectations for student achievement. The curricular structure, academic policies, and staff practices in these schools communicate the message that student mastery of a substantial body of academic skills is expected. Principal instructional leadership is thought to be a key to the success of these schools serving the urban poor.

Instructional leadership in these effective schools is composed of three dimensions of principal job behavior: defining the school mission, managing the instructional program, promoting a positive school learning climate (Hallinger, 1983). Each dimension is comprised of more specific job functions that the principal must carry out as the instructional leader (See Hallinger, 1983, and Hallinger and Murphy, 1985a, for detailed descriptions of this framework). These dimensions of instructional leadership are being emphasized in many school improvement and principal training programs.

As we noted earlier, however, the fact that these findings result primarily from research on poor, urban, elementary schools leaves their applicability to middle- and upper-income schools in question. Additional studies have begun to examine the characteristics of schools that are successful at teaching students from middle- and upper-income communities. This research suggests that social context influences several school-effectiveness factors, including principal instructional leadership.

In this section we examine ways in which principal instructional leadership seems to vary in different social contexts. The primary source for many of our comments is a study of effective California elementary schools of varying socioeconomic status (Hallinger and Murphy, 1985c, 1985d); findings from related studies are also discussed. We organize this discussion of principal instructional leadership and school social context in terms of the three dimensions of instructional leadership mentioned above.

Defining the School Mission

The importance of developing a clear organizational mission has been substantiated by research on effective schools (Purkey and Smith, 1983b) and organizational cultures (Deal and Kennedy, 1982). A clear mission provides a framework of underlying values for organizational activities. The mission serves as a source of identification and motivation for members, bonding them to the organization. It guides the activities of semiautonomous workers, such as teachers, in the absence of close supervision. A mission may be written or unwritten; its power derives not from its form, but rather from the awareness of and acceptance of the mission by the organization's members.

Effective schools maintain a clear academic mission and focus (Purkey and Smith, 1983b). Unlike schools more generally, instructionally effective schools consciously commit their resources to a limited set of cognitive goals. There is also a higher degree of consensus among the staff as to the means that will be used to pursue those goals. In effective schools the mission also serves a socialization function. As new members enter the organization, they are socialized to a schoolwide philosophy that assumes a high degree of coordination and consistency in the policies and practices of teachers (Rosenholtz, 1985).

As a result of these findings, most school improvement programs encourage principals to develop explicit schoolwide academic goals as an initial step in the school improvement process. It is further suggested that these goals be selected from a limited number of options. On the surface, this appears to be a reasonable inference. There is evidence, however, that indicates a need for caution before developing a uniform mix of goals for all schools. A substantial body of research concludes that an organization's mission must conform to the demands of its environment (Deal and Kennedy, 1982; Emery and Trist, 1965; Thompson and McEwen, 1958; Weick, 1982). Educational organizations are particularly sensitive to the numerous, shifting preferences of their constituents (March, 1978; Weick, 1982). Thus, it is important that these preferences be reflected in the school's mission.

Social class has a significant effect on the educational expectations and preferences of parents. Parents of different social classes prefer schools to address different educational goals. Parents in lower-class communities often prefer an emphasis on social and vocational goals, while those in wealthier communities prefer schools to concentrate on the development of intellectual skills (Hills, 1961; McDill et al., 1969). These varying preferences influence the goals that schools actually pursue and the corresponding structure of their educational programs (Hallinger and Murphy, 1985c; Hills, 1961; Levine, 1979; McDill et al., 1969; Wayson, 1966).

The effective schools research suggests that effective low SES schools, in a sense, emulate higher SES schools by giving greater weight to the pursuit of academic goals. The emphasis on academics translates into school policies and practices that reflect high expectations and promote higher achievement. Despite this similarity, there are still differences between successful lower and higher SES schools in the nature of their mission. The differences appear to lie primarily in the breadth of their mission, the degree of goal consensus among staff, and the extent to which the mission is explicitly defined. These differences have implications for the principal's role in developing a mission suitable to the school's social context.

Effective low-income schools focus on a highly limited mission: improving instruction in basic reading and mathematics skills (Brookover and Lezotte, 1979; Venezky and Winfield, 1979; Weber, 1971). They often translate their mission into a few explicitly stated, school-wide academic goals (Brookover and Lezotte, 1979; Glenn and McLean, 1981; Hallinger and Murphy, 1985b). A critical feature of this goal orientation is the delimitation of a few priorities that supersede all others.

A clear academic mission is also an important ingredient for success in schools serving middle- and upper-income students. Although these schools operate in an environment of higher academic expectations, this does not insure the existence of a clear mission. Numerous environmental pressures expand and dilute the mission of all public schools, regardless of the social context. As Boyer (1983) and Goodlad (1984) have noted, the American public "wants it all" when it comes to schooling. Thus, even schools in wealthier communities often find it difficult to limit their mission to the pursuit of academic goals.

Evidence from the California effective schools study, however, indicates that successful schools in wealthy communities do maintain an academically oriented mission. The staff in these elementary schools described their mission as "promoting academic learning" or "emphasizing a traditional curriculum" (Hallinger and Murphy, 1985b). Although this suggests a sense of educational purpose similar to that found in effective low-income schools, the mission in these higher SES schools addressed a broader array of intellectual skills. Mastery of basic cognitive skills was viewed as important, but was almost accepted as a given. Thus, these schools emphasized the development of a more varied set of academic and intellectual skills than in the effective low-income schools. This broader mission was reflected in the schools' curricular and instructional programs.

Social context also seems to affect the degree of goal consensus needed to bring about school improvement. In low-income schools a high degree of consensus on the school's mission and the means for attaining that mission is important (Estler, 1985; Hallinger and Murphy, 1985b; Purkey and Smith, 1983b). Thus, it is not surprising to find that effective low SES schools often translate the mission into discrete measurable goals (Clark, 1980; Glenn and McLean, 1981; Weber, 1971). The process of defining the mission in terms of explicit goals provides an opportunity for the staff to have input as to the substance of the school's mission. This can add to the staff's awareness of and sense of commitment to the mission. The definition of goals also provides explicit criteria for making resource allocation decisions and can serve as performance standards against which to measure school progress (Brookover et al., 1982; Rowan, 1983; Wellisch et al., 1978).

It is important to note, however, that the explicit definition of school goals does not guarantee the development of a clear mission

(Estler, 1985; Hallinger and Murphy, 1985b). Many schools, particularly ones serving low-income students, are required to develop measurable goals as a condition for participation in special federal and state compensatory education programs. Yet, the laundry list of goals that results from such participation seldom reflects or generates a schoolwide mission. Too often these goals lie unused in the principal's file cabinet.

It is in developing, communicating, implementing, and sustaining the mission that the principal plays a key role as instructional leader. The principal must insure that schoolwide policies and practices, as well as the job behavior of the administrative staff, reinforce the values inherent in the school's mission (Deal and Kennedy, 1982; Estler, 1985; Hallinger and Murphy, 1985b).

We noted that successful higher SES schools pursue a more broadly defined mission than effective low-income schools. It also seems that school success in wealthier social contexts requires less consensus concerning the actual content of the mission and means for achieving it (Estler, 1985; Hallinger and Murphy, 1985b, 1985c). This is reflected in the finding that effective upper-income schools are also less likely to translate their mission into specific goals and objectives. Therefore, although instructional effectiveness in wealthier social contexts seems related to an academic focus, it is still unclear how that mission is developed. It may be that the principal plays a less formal, but just as important, mission-building role in these schools. Additional empirical research is needed to understand the process by which higher SES schools develop a clear academic mission.

We conclude that the social context does influence the nature of the school mission. The principal's leadership role in developing the school's mission and in defining schoolwide goals also appears to vary according to the social context of the school. Whereas we noted that instructionally effective low-income schools are characterized by strong administrative involvement in goal development, principals in successful high SES schools appear to exert less authority in this area.

This finding presents somewhat of a paradox in light of earlier studies of social contexts and school goals. Our discussion suggests that effective low-income schools succeed, in part, by focusing on an academic mission, rather than on the social and vocational goals often preferred by low-income communities. While we might expect this discontinuity between school and community values to result in conflict, this does not appear to happen. Preliminary evidence suggests the opposite. Academic success in low-income schools breeds pride in the community and higher academic expectations among parents. This begins a process of mutual support and reinforcement. Thus, our earlier discussion in which we viewed low SES schools as emulating the academic orientation more prevalent in high-wealth contexts may begin a process of transforming the school social context.

Managing the Instructional Program

This dimension refers to the principal's role in managing instruction and coordinating the school's curriculum. Supervision is the job function most commonly associated with the principal's instructional leadership role. Instructional leadership involves close attention to this function regardless of the school's social context. Principals in effective schools have a high degree of credibility with teachers in the areas of curriculum and instruction and are frequent visitors to classrooms (Hallinger and Murphy, 1985d; New York State, 1974; Venezky and Winfield, 1979; Wellisch et al., 1978; Weber, 1971). Beyond these general similarities, however, the supervisory style used by principals does appear to be influenced by the social context.

In effective low SES schools principals play a highly directive role in the selection, development, and implementation of curriculum and instructional programs (Venezky and Winfield, 1979; Weber, 1971). They have a clear vision of how the school should be organized and tend to exercise relatively tight control over classroom instruction. They are forceful in establishing high expectations and standards for staff and students and in holding themselves and staff accountable for student achievement. Teachers describe these principals as being a major factor in the school's success, the key to turning the school around (Hallinger and Murphy, 1985c).

In contrast, principals in successful high SES schools exercise less direct control over classroom instruction. They orchestrate more from the background, allowing teachers greater autonomy with respect to instructional decision-making. These principals maintain a close watch over student outcomes, but tend to exert control over classroom instruction only when results fall below expected levels. Although teachers describe these principals as strong instructional leaders and as important actors, they do not identify them as "the key" to school success (Hallinger and Murphy, 1985b).

The different content of the mission in effective higher and lower SES schools is reflected in the principal's role as curriculum coordinator. Effective low SES schools focus on a limited set of learning objectives in order to achieve a high level of instructional effectiveness. The principal insures that students are exposed to material that addresses the objectives on which they will be tested (Cooley and Leinhardt, 1980; Venezky and Winfield, 1979; Wellisch et al., 1978). The principal also maintains continuity between the regular program and the special compensatory education classes. Successful high SES schools offer a broader set of curricular offerings, but participate in fewer compensatory education programs. The principal still assumes an active role in coordinating the curriculum, but may be less directive in the implementation of the curriculum in classrooms (Hallinger and Murphy, 1985c).

The principal's instructional management role also includes attention to the allocation and use of instructional time. In effective low SES schools the principals insure that teachers focus on the mastery of basic reading and mathematics skills. To facilitate this, they allocate more time for instruction in reading and math. For example, in one study a third grade teacher was describing an effective education activity center in the rear of her classroom. She regretted that there was so little time to use it with her students. When asked why, she responded that her principal expected teachers to spend as much time teaching reading, writing, spelling, and math as was necessary to obtain mastery of basic skills, even if that meant the entire day. The emphasis on implementing such a narrowly defined program was less acute in the successful high SES schools (Hallinger and Murphy, 1985c).

Thus, the instructional management role of principals appears to vary in specific ways according to the social context of the school. The preliminary research in this area suggests that principals in effective low SES schools exercise a more directive supervisory role than principals in wealthier school contexts. Explanations for this variation in instructional leadership behavior suggest the school context as a possible causal factor.

In many cases principals enter low SES schools with a mandate to change. Dissatisfaction with student achievement and school climate is often apparent and the focus of discussion. This is less likely to be the case in wealthier school contexts in which student achievement may be lower than desired, but is still above the "red zone." Thus, low SES schools probably represent a more congenial context for strong leadership than higher SES schools. Both formal and informal norms within the schools allow the principal in a low SES school to assume greater authority than the principal in a higher SES context (Rowan and Denk, 1984).

Promoting a Positive School Learning Climate

The third instructional leadership dimension concerns the principal's role in establishing a climate of high expectations for student achievement. The finding that effective low SES schools hold high expectations for their students is perhaps the most widely publicized finding from the effective schools literature (Brookover and Lezotte, 1979; Purkey and Smith, 1983b; Rutter et al., 1979). Several recent studies indicate that, despite this finding, the social context influences both the nature and source of a school's academic expectations.

In effective low SES schools the principal and teachers hold high, but reasonable, expectations for their students. They expect all of their students to master basic reading and math skills. They do not, however, expect as much from their students as staff in schools serving students in wealthier communities (Hallinger and Murphy, 1985c; Teddlie et al., 1984). As we have already noted in our discussion of school goals and instructional management, effective low SES schools attempt to do a few things very well. These schools do not, however, attempt to convey the same breadth or depth of knowledge that is addressed in effective high SES schools.

The source of expectations also seems to differ. Whereas principals in successful high SES schools sustain the high expectations that prevail in the community context, principals in effective low SES schools must build high expectations without the benefit of continuing community input. Parents in poor communities are less well schooled and are often only tangentially involved in the life of their schools (Hills, 1961; McDill et al., 1969; Wayson, 1966). In a low SES school the principal often becomes the key actor in developing and sustaining high expectations on the part of school staff (Murphy, Weil Hallinger, and Mitman, 1982). The principal must insure that the climate of low expectations that prevails in the school's environment is halted at the school's doors. In part, this involves accepting responsibility for the achievement of students since there is little likelihood of student success if the school staff does not push students to achieve (Brookover and Lezotte, 1979).

The picture differs dramatically in schools located in wealthier communities. Principals and teachers in these schools identify parents as the primary source of the school's expectations (Hallinger and Murphy, 1985c). There is an implicit assumption among teachers in such communities that the children of professional parents will succeed in school. Teachers feel tangible pressure in this regard, noting that parents are vociferous if their child's progress does not meet their expectations. In these schools the principal plays the role of a sustainer and translator of community expectations, rather than a builder. Since high expectations already exist, the principal's tasks are to make sure that expectations are clear and consistent, and to translate them into appropriate school policies and programs (Hallinger and Murphy, 1985d; Murphy et al., 1982; Rowan and Denk, 1984; Teddlie et al., 1984).

The expectations of a school can also be viewed through the type of reward system used to reinforce student achievement. Evidence from the California study suggests that principals in effective low SES schools develop more elaborate and unified systems of student reward and recognition than their counterparts in high SES schools. Teachers in effective low SES schools reward students more frequently and rely more heavily on tangible public rewards for student accomplishments.

The principal makes frequent use of assemblies, honor rolls, and public lists to recognize students for academic achievement, academic improvement, citizenship, and attendance (Hallinger and Murphy, 1985c).

In contrast, the effective upper-income schools in this study offered few tangible school or classroom rewards for students. The principals also maintained looser linkages between classroom and school reward systems. The teachers often spoke of tangible rewards for achievement with disdain; one teacher typified this norm when she remarked, "we're not an M & M school" (Hallinger and Murphy, 1985c). This reflected the expectation that students in high-wealth communities should be able to succeed without frequent or tangible rewards. These teachers felt that reasonable amounts of verbal praise, good grades, and the intrinsic satisfaction of learning should be sufficiently motivating and rewarding for students.

These differences in the structure of schoolwide reward systems can be traced back to variations in the social context. Students in low-income schools generally have fewer of the prerequisite skills necessary for academic success, and in many cases place a lower value on schooling. In such cases the principal must take systematic measures to reward and publicly recognize students for the behavior that the school seeks to promote. Students in wealthier communities generally come to school with a higher level of readiness skills, a more positive academic orientation, and higher parental expectations. This combination of factors leads the school staff to hold higher expectations and enables students to experience success in school more quickly. Learning becomes rewarding and less dependent upon frequent extrinsic rewards. Thus, the principal in a high SES context may need to resort to fewer concrete rewards in order to promote high expectations than the principal in a lower SES context.

A discussion of the impact of social context on school learning climate would be incomplete without attending to the principal's role in linking the school and the community. Parental involvement in schools varies greatly in different social contexts (Becker and Epstein, 1982; McDill et al., 1969). In general, parents in wealthier communities are more involved in the school program than parents in poorer communities. The pattern of low levels of parental involvement is even found in the studies of effective low-income schools. Despite this finding, many school effectiveness researchers advocate strengthening ties between the home and school in school improvement efforts (Brookover et al., 1982; Purkey and Smith, 1983b; Teddlie et al., 1984). Additional information from the California study sheds some light on the role of the principal in linking the home and school (Hallinger and Murphy, 1985c).

In the high SES schools principals involved parents in many aspects of the educational program and obtained their support in a variety of ways. Parents contributed their time as office and classroom aides, their money to support expansion of the school's programs, their labor to build fixtures in classrooms, their expertise to raise additional funds for the school program, and their energy to assist in organizing school-wide festivals. In the wealthy communities a critical aspect of the principal's leadership role entailed mediating parental expectations of the school. These principals acted as boundary spanners, linking the community and the school. They were constantly seeking efficient ways to involve a population that took great interest in the school and that had substantial resources to offer. A significant portion of the principals' time was devoted to integrating the parents into the school in an effective manner.

In the effective low SES schools the principals expended relatively little energy involving parents in the life of the school. Typically, there was a history of limited parental interest in the school, and school staff had come to expect little from the community in terms of substantive support. The sporadic efforts of staff to involve parents and the lower expectations of parent support reflected the notion of a trade-off among limited resources. The teachers felt that the energy needed to obtain and sustain parent involvement would be better spent working with the children. In these schools the principals acted as buffers, carefully controlling access to the school and filtering outside influences that might dilute its effectiveness. Thus, the school was rather isolated from the community, particularly during the early stages of the im-provement process. As the school began to improve, principals began to encourage higher levels of interaction between the school and the community.

These observations, though tentative, suggest that the principal's role in developing a positive learning climate in schools is highly sen-sitive to the nature of the social context. Probably the most interesting implication with respect to this dimension of instructional leadership concerns the manner in which schools react to the expectations of the social context. Principals must be acutely conscious of the types of expectations that the school fosters. In contexts where high expecta-tions do not prevail in the community, a greater burden falls on the principal and teachers to create those within the school. In school contexts where high expectations already exist, the principal must insure that those are sustained by the school. In both cases, the school needs to translate high expectations into educational programs that are appropriate for the particular educational context.

CONCLUSION

In this chapter we examined a variety of ways in which the context of the school influences the instructional leadership role of the principal.

The genesis of this effort was a concern over the uniform application of findings from studies of principal effectiveness conducted in poor, urban, elementary schools to other school contexts. Our analysis leads us to conclude that instructional leadership is not a simple, one-dimensional construct. Our findings support researchers who argue that leadership is context-dependent rather than uniform in nature. More specifically the results support the proposition that principals need to consider the organizational context in which they work in developing an appropriate style of instructional leadership.

The factors considered in this chapter interact in the actual school setting to create a context for principal action. Thus, the nature of the school's technology, the type of district support, the characteristics of the teaching staff, the school level, and the social context combine to form a complex constellation of forces mediating instructional leadership by the school principal. The findings reviewed here represent a starting point for the development of contingency models that can be used in the study of instructional leadership and school change.

REFERENCES

Becker, H., and Epstein, J. (1982). Parent involvement: A survey of teacher practices. *Elementary School Journal, 83*, 85–102.

Berman, P. (1984). *Improving school improvement: A policy evaluation of the California school improvement program, vol. 1.* Berkeley, Calif.: Berman Weiler Associates.

Berman, P., and McLaughlin, M. (1978). *Federal programs supporting educational change, vol 8: Implementing and Sustaining Innovations.* Santa Monica, Calif.: Rand Corporation.

Bidwell, C., and Kasarda, J. (1975). School district organization and student achievement. *American Sociological Review, 40*, 55–70.

Biester, T.; Druse, J.; Beyer, F.; Heller, B. (1984). Effects of administrative leadership on student achievement. Paper presented at the annual meeting of the American Educational Research Association, New Orleans.

Bossert, S.; Dwyer, D.; Rowan, B.; Lee, G. (1982). The instructional management role of the principal. *Educational Administration Quarterly, 18,* 34–64.

Boyer, E. (1983). *High school: A report on secondary education in America.* New York: Harper & Row.

Bridge, R.; Judd, C.; and Moock, P. (1979). *The determinants of educational outcomes.* Cambridge, Mass.: Ballinger.

Bridges, E. (1977). The nature of leadership. In *Educational administration: The developing decades,* edited by L. Cunningham, W. Hack, and R. Nystrand. Berkeley, Calif.: McCutchan.

———. (1979). The principalship as a career. In *The principal in metropolitan schools,* edited by D. Erickson and T. Reller. Berkeley, Calif.: McCutchan.

———. (1982). Research on the school administrator: The state of the art, 1967–1980. *Educational Administration Quarterly, 18,* (3), 12–33.

———. (1984). *Managing the imcompetent teacher.* Eugene, Oreg.: ERIC Clearinghouse.

Brookover, W., and Lezotte, L. (1979). *Changes in school characteristics coin-*

cident with changes in student achievement. Michigan State University, East Lansing.

Brookover, W.; Beamer, L.; Efthim, H.; Hathaway, D.; Lezotte, L.; Miller, S.; Passalacqua, J.; Tornatzky, L. (1982). *Creating effective schools: An in-service program for enhancing school learning climate and achievement.* Holmes Beach, Fla.: Learning Publications.

Clark, D. (1980). An analysis of research, development, and evaluation reports on exceptional urban elementary schools. In *Phi Delta Kappan, Why do some urban schools succeed?* Bloomington Ind.: Phi Delta Kappa.

Cohen, E., and Miller, R. (1980). Coordination and control of instruction. *Pacific Sociological Review, 23,* 446–73.

Cohen, E.; Miller, R.; Bredo, A.; Duckworth, K. (1977). *Principal role and teacher morale under varying organizational conditions.* Stanford Center for Research and Development in Teaching. Stanford University, Stanford, Calif.

Coleman, J.; Campbell, E.; Hobson, C.; McPartland, J.; Mood, A.; Weinfeld, F.; York, T. (1966). *Equality of educational opportunity.* Washington D.C.: U.S. Office of Education, National Center for Education Statistics.

Cuban, L. (1984). Transforming the frog into a prince: Effective schools research, policy, and practice at the district level. *Harvard Educational Review, 54,* (2), 129–51.

Deal, T. and Celotti, L. (1980). How much influence do (and can) educational administrators have on classrooms? *Phi Delta Kappan, 61,* 471–73.

Deal, T. and Kennedy, A. (1982). *Corporate cultures.* Reading, Mass.: Addison-Wesley.

Donmoyer, R. (1985). Cognitive anthropology and research on effective principals. *Educational Administration Quarterly, 21,* (2), 31–57.

Duckworth, K. (1981). *Linking educational policy and management with student achievement.* Center for Educational Policy and Management, University of Oregon, Eugene.

Dwyer, D.; Lee., G.; Rowan, B.; and Bossert, S. (1983). *Five principals in action: Perspectives on instructional management.* Far West Laboratory for Educational Research and Development, San Francisco.

Emery, F., and Trist, E. (1965). The causal texture of organizational environments. *Human Relations, 18,* 21–31.

Estler, S. (1985). Clear goals, instructional leadership and academic achievement: Instrumentation and findings. Paper presented at the annual meeting of the American Educational Research Association, Chicago.

Eubanks, E., and Levine, D. (1983). A first look at effective schools projects in New York and Milwaukee. *Phi Delta Kappan, 64,* 697–702.

Farrar, E., Neufeld, B., and Miles, M. (1983). *A review of effective schools programs: Effective schools programs in high schools; implications for policy research and practice.* Final report prepared for the National Commission on Excellence in Education, (ERIC Document No. ED 228 243).

Fiedler, F., and Chemers, M. (1974). *Leadership and effective management.* Glenview, Ill.: Scott, Foresman.

Finn, C. (1983). *Strategic independence: Policy considerations for enhancing school effectiveness.* Washington D.C.: National Institute of Education.

Firestone, W., and Herriott, R. (1982). Prescriptions for effective elementary schools don't fit secondary schools. *Educational Leadership, 40,* 51–53.

Firestone W., and Wilson, B. (1985). Using bureaucratic and cultural linkages to improve instruction: The principal's contribution. *Educational Administration Quarterly, 21,* (2), 7–30.

Gersten, R., and Carnine, D. (1981). *Administrative and supervisory support functions for the implementation of effective educational programs for low income students.* Center for Educational Policy and Management, University of Oregon, Eugene.

Glasman, N. (1984). Student achievement and the school principal. *Educational Evaluation and Policy Analysis, 6,* 283–96.

Glenn, B., and McLean, T. (1981). *What works? An examination of effective schools for poor black children.* Harvard University Center for Law and Education, Cambridge, Mass.

Goodlad, J. (1984). *A place called school.* New York: McGraw-Hill.

Hallinger, P. (1983). Assessing the instructional management behavior of principals. Unpublished doctoral dissertation, Stanford University, Stanford, Calif.

Hallinger, P., and Murphy, J. (1982). The superintendent's role in promoting instructional leadership. *Administrator's Notebook, 30,* (6).

——. (1985a). Assessing the instructional management behavior of principals. *Elementary School Journal, 85.*

——. (1985b). Defining an organizational mission. Paper presented at the annual meeting of the American Educational Research Association, Chicago.

——. (1985c). Instructional effectiveness and school socio-economic status: Is good for the goose, good for the gander? Paper presented at the annual meeting of the American Educational Research Association, Chicago.

——. (1985d). Instructional leadership and school socio-economic status: A preliminary investigation. *Administrator's Notebook, 31.*

Hannaway, J., and Sproull, L. (1978–79). Who's running the show? Coordination and control of instruction in educational organizations. *Administrator's Notebook, 27,* (9).

Hart, A., and Ogawa, R. (1984). An examination of the effect of superintendents on the instructional performance of school districts. Paper presented at the annual meeting of the American Educational Research Association, New Orleans.

Hills, J. (1961). Social classes and educational views. *Administrator's Notebook, 10,* (2).

Jackson, S. (1982). Instructional leadership behaviors that differentiate effective and ineffective low-income urban schools. Paper presented at the National Reading Association Convention, Chicago.

Levine, D. (1979). The social context of urban education. In *The principal in metropolitan schools,* edited by D. Erickson and T. Reller. Berkeley, Calif.: McCutchan.

Lipham, J. (1982). *Effective principal, effective school.* Reston, Va.: American Association of School Administrators.

Little, J. (1982). Norms of collegiality and experimentation: Workplace conditions of school success. *American Educational Research Journal, 19,* 325–40.

McCormack-Larkin, M., and Kritek, W. (1982). Milwaukee's project RISE. *Educational Leadership, 40,* 16–21.

McDill, E.; Rigsby, L.; and Meyers, E. (1969). Educational climates of high schools: Their effects and sources. *American Journal of Sociology, 74,* 567–86.

March, J. (1978). American public school administration: A short analysis. *School Review, 86,* 217–50.

Mazzarella, J. (1985). The effective high school principal: Sketches for a portrait. *R & D Perspective.* Center for Educational Policy and Management, University of Oregon, Eugene.

Murphy, J., and Hallinger, P. (in press). The superintendent as instructional leader: Findings from effective school districts. *Journal of Educational Administration.*

Murphy, J.; Hallinger, P.; and Peterson, K. (1985). Administrative control of principals in effective school districts. Paper presented at the annual meeting of the American Educational Research Association, Chicago.

Murphy, Weil, Hallinger, & Mitman, 1982. Academic press: Translating high expectations into school policies and classroom practices. *Educational Leadership, 40,* 22–27.

New York State. *School factors influencing reading achievement: A case study of two inner-city schools.* Albany: Department of Education, Office of Performance Review, 1974.

O'Day, K. (1984). The relationship between principal and teacher perceptions of principal instructional management behavior and student achievement. Unpublished doctoral dissertation. Northern Illinois University, Dekalb, Ill.

Peters, T. (1980). Symbols, patterns and settings: An optimistic case for getting things done. In *Readings in managerial psychology,* edited by H. Leavitt, L. Pondy, and D. Boje. Chicago: University of Chicago Press.

Peterson, K. (1985). Mechanisms of administrative control over managers in educational organizations. *Administrative Science Quarterly, 29,* 573–97.

Pitner, N., and Ogawa, R. (1980). Organizational leadership: The case of the school superintendent. *Educational Administrative Quarterly, 17,* 45–66.

Purkey, S., and Smith, M. (1983a). *Educational policy and school effectiveness.* Wisconsin Center for Educational Research, University of Wisconsin, Madison.

———. (1983b). Effective schools: a review. *Elementary School Journal, 83,* 427–52.

Rosenholtz, S. (1985). Effective schools: Interpreting the evidence. *American Journal of Education, 31.*

Rosenshine, B. (1983). Teaching functions in instructional programs. *The Elementary School Journal, 83,* 335–51.

Rowan, B. (1983). *Instructional management at the district level: A conceptual framework.* Far West Laboratory for Educational Research and Development, San Francisco.

Rowan, B., and Denk, C. (1984). Management succession, school socio-economic context and basic skills achievement. *American Educational Research Journal, 21.*

Rutter, M.; Maugham, B.; Mortimore, P.; Ouston, J.; Smith, A. (1979). *Fifteen thousand hours: Secondary schools and their effects on children.* Cambridge Mass.: Harvard University Press.

Teddlie, C.; Falkowski, C.; Stringfield, S.; Desselle, S.; Garvue, R. (1984). *Louisiana school effectiveness study: Phase two, 1982–84.* Baton Rouge: Louisiana State Department of Education.

Thompson, J. (1967). *Organizations in action.* New York: McGraw-Hill.

Thompson, J., and McEwen, W. (1958). Organizational goals and environment: Goal setting as an interaction process. *American Sociological Review, 23,* 23–31.

Venezky, R., and Winfield, L. (1979). *Schools that succeed beyond expectations in teaching reading.* Newark, Del.: University of Delaware.

Wayson, W. (1966). Source of teacher satisfaction in slum schools. *Administrator's Notebook, 14,* (9).

Weber, G. (1971). *Inner city children can be taught to read: Four successful schools.* Washington D.C.: Council for Basic Education.

Weick, K. (1982). Administering education in loosely coupled schools. *Phi Delta Kappan, 63*, 673–76.

Wellisch, J.; MacQueen, A.; Carriere, R.; Duck, G. (1978). School organization and management in successful schools. *Sociology of Education, 51*, 211–26.

Willower, D., and Fraser, H. (1979–80). School superintendents and their work. *Administrator's Notebook, 28*, (5).

11

Teaching Incentives: Implications for School Leadership

DOUGLAS E. MITCHELL

We must see power—and leadership—as not things but as *relationships*.
We must analyze power in a context of human motives and physical
constraints. If we can come to grips with these aspects of power, we can
hope to comprehend the true nature of leadership—a venture far more
intellectually daunting than the study of naked power.

James MacGregor Burns, 1978, p. 11.

INTRODUCTION

Problems of leadership are at least as serious in the public schools as
in any other sector of contemporary life. Neither targeted use of tax
money, coercive legal policies, nor intense public criticism have proven
powerful enough to produce desired improvements in the performance
of the schools. The weakness of recent reform efforts lies, in large part
at least, in their inadequate understanding of the problems of leadership
and motivation. Neither teachers nor students find the incentive system of the school strong enough to elicit the level of dedication and
intensity of effort needed for the high performance that is expected of
them. It now seems certain that generating enhanced work incentives
for both teachers and students is the single most important ingredient
in any successful school improvement program.

Leadership in the public schools, as in any other complex organization, rests on a willingness and ability to understand the motivations of those who are expected to follow. As Burns (1978) noted, leadership consists of linking the motivations and aspirations of organizational members to the overall goals and basic operational norms of the organization. This linkage makes possible the development of an effective incentive system within the organization—one that arouses and directs the actions of organizational members. Successful development of such incentive systems is among the most complex and difficult problems facing any leader.

This chapter is devoted to an analysis of the problems of incentive and motivation in the schools. The analysis is built around a study of fifteen elementary school teachers whose work was observed over a period of several months and who were asked to talk about their work in a series of interviews spaced over the observation period. (For a full report on this study see Mitchell, Ortiz, and Mitchell, 1983). The chapter is presented in three main sections. The first examines the key concepts of motivation, reward and incentive—exploring the cultural basis for the development of effective incentive systems in the school. The second major section reviews the work orientations and belief systems of the fifteen teachers that were studied. It shows how the incentives that guide their work are controlled by their views of the goals of education and their beliefs about how the educational process should be organized. The last major section of the chapter looks at the implications of teacher incentives for school leaders. It concentrates on the need to break the cycle of self defeat that prevents many teachers from deriving adequate rewards from their work and highlights the importance of strengthening everyone's understanding of the ultimate purposes of schooling and developing strong group solidarity or identity within schools and classrooms.

THE KEY CONCEPTS: MOTIVATION, REWARD, INCENTIVE

The literature on work motivation and control is vast and complex. As early as 1970, Lawler (1970) had identified more than 5,000 published studies of employee attitudes and motives. Several thousand additional studies have been reported since then. Despite perennial interest in these topics, however, there is still substantial confusion regarding three key concepts—motivation, reward and incentive. Though space does not permit a detailed review of these concepts here, a brief summary will help to clarify their importance for educational leadership. Motivation, reward, and incentive are, of course, closely related terms. They each address the problem of controlling social activity, but they deal with this problem from very different perspectives. To be effective school leaders must distinguish carefully among these different perspectives and take actions appropriate to each of them.

Motivation is the most general term of the three. It is concerned with the *origins* of human action and refers to the willingness of people to participate in meaningful actions and to direct their efforts toward fulfilling particular goals or purposes. Vroom provides one of the clearest interpretations of the essential meaning of the term *motivation* when he says,

> There are two somewhat different kinds of questions that are typically dealt with in discussions of motivation. One of these is the question of the arousal or *energizing* of the organism. Why is the organism active at all? ... The second question involves the direction of behavior. What determines the *form* that activity will take. (Vroom, 1964, pp. 8,9, emphasis added)

The two aspects of motivation described by Vroom are at the heart of the two most widely recognized problems affecting the quality of teacher work performance: emotional burnout and technical competency. Teacher burnout represents a failure of motivation in the first of Vroom's two areas—energizing action. Burnout is characterized by a lack of energy and a generally reduced willingness to make the effort required to be effective. Burned out teachers are frequently competent, in the sense that they know how to be effective in the classroom, they have simply lost the *will* to work up to their capacities.

Teacher competency is quite a different matter. Though emotionally burned out teachers are frequently called incompetent, incompetency results from the failure of motivation in the second domain identified by Vroom—the proper forming or shaping of action. Incompetent teachers lack direction or adequate technique, not simply the needed level of energy to discharge their responsibilities successfully.

Knowing that teacher effectiveness problems are the result of inadequate or inappropriate motivation does not, of course, tell us very much about how to solve them. To improve teacher motivation we need to know how leadership can improve the energy level and give greater precision to particular activities. In short, we need to know how leaders could turn loose energy or better inform the actions of teachers. There are, of course, many different answers to this question—they begin with improved teacher recruitment and training strategies and include regulation, supervision, and enforcement of legal policies governing teacher work responsibilities. The simple truth, however, is that the best way to improve motivation is to make work more rewarding. To do so we need to understand what rewards are available to teachers and how their distribution is controlled.

Rewards, rather than addressing the origins of human action, are connected to its *consequences*. A reward is any experience that is received as compensation for our actions. Compensation, of course, has both a positive (reward) and a negative (punishment) meaning. The term *reward* can be used to carry both of these meanings, however. Thus, a reward is any experience that produces pain or pleasure, frustration or fulfillment, dissatisfaction or satisfaction.

Whether or not a reward will affect motivation is problematic in several important respects. First, the value of any given reward is subjectively defined by its recipient—one person's reward may be another's punishment. This point was highlighted by Weick (1966) when he pointed out that some workers view physical exertion, and the resultant perspiration, as a distasteful punishment (the result of the biblical curse requiring man to earn his bread by the "sweat of his brow"), while others view it with pride and satisfaction as a display of their prowess or moral righteousness.

In addition to the problem of uncertainty regarding their subjective meanings, there is a problematic connection between getting a reward and taking any particular action. This problem exists at both the objective and subjective levels. Objectively, there is always at least some degree of uncertainty about the consequences of an action—great effort fails to produce results, employers fail to meet payrolls, pride in completing a difficult job does not result in the joy that was anticipated, a work group that promised camradarie and fellowship turns out to be tension laden and contentious.

Subjectively, the link between performance and reward is even more problematic. The "pyramid climbing" corporate executive finds that promotions produce new demands and fresh reminders of still higher places to aspire to rather than pleasure and satisfaction at current successes. Salary increases can be seen as small compared to subjective estimates of our worth and thus come to symbolize being underpaid rather than highly valued.

A widely recognized distinction between *extrinsic* and *intrinsic* rewards is especially important in education. Intrinsic rewards are those that arise directly from engaging in particular activities (like the pride of workmanship or sense of accomplishment that arises from doing good work). Extrinsic rewards (such as money, social position, or increased authority) are detached from the work itself and are conveyed *for* particular actions rather than *in* their execution. There is virtually unanimous agreement in the literature on rewards that teachers are more powerfully affected by intrinsic rewards—particularly their sense of responsibility for student learning and their enjoyment of warm social relationships—than by extrinsic rewards delivered after their work has been observed and evaluated by others (such as pay differentials, social status, or public recognition). For a fuller discussion of this issue see especially Lortie (1969, 1975), Miskel (1974), Spuck (1974), Miskel, et al. (1980), Sergiovanni (1967), Thompson (1979), and ERIC (1980, 1981). This is an especially important aspect of teaching because, as several scholars have noted, overreliance on (or inappropriate use of) extrinsic rewards can seriously damage workers' capacity to derive intrinsic satisfaction from their work, and can even reduce their willingness to perform needed tasks (see, for example, Deci, 1972, 1975; Herzberg, 1966; Kesselman, et al., 1974; Larsen, 1982; Martin, 1978; Miller and Hamblin, 1963; Notz, 1975; Ouchi, 1981).

The importance of intrinsic rewards for teachers is a particularly nettlesome problem for school managers because the most potent of these rewards—a sense of responsibility for student learning and the feelings of warmth and closeness that come from working with a group of responsive and appreciative children—are controlled by students rather than school officials. For most teachers, the meager resources for reward and punishment typically under the control of school administrators are quite limited compared with the capacity of students to make their work meaningful or distressing. It is this problem of control over the delivery of rewards that brings into focus the important concept of incentives.

Incentive is the least well understood concept in the literature on work motivation. Many authors use the concepts of reward and incentive interchangeably, speaking of both as the experiences that follow the performance of various work activities. For example, Clark and Wilson (1961), in a frequently cited article, define "material incentives" as "tangible rewards; that is, rewards that have a monetary value or can easily be translated into ones that have." (p. 134). This statement, and countless others like it, invite confusion. Incentives are rewards, to be sure, but that is not their distinguishing feature. The distinction between a reward and an incentive lies not in the *content* of the experience, but in the attention given to the *method of distribution*. Rewards are used as incentives when their distribution is planned and controlled in such a way that recipients can *anticipate* receiving the rewards if they take particular actions. Which is to say, there are two critical dimensions to the process by which various experiences contribute to the work motivation of teachers (or any other workers). First there is the "reward-value" of these experiences; that is, the amount of satisfaction/dissatisfaction, pain/pleasure, frustration/fulfillment that they are capable of producing. Though this reward-value is subjectively determined, experiences with a higher reward-value have a higher impact on motivation. But there is a second dimension to this process that is even more important. The "incentive-value" of these experiences that motivate work behavior has to do with how they are distributed, not with the amount of impact on individuals when they are encountered.

In most of the current debate about improving teaching incentives primary attention is being given to the potency of various rewards to energize or direct teacher work efforts. Too little attention is being given to the fact that rewarding experiences are mediated through a system of distribution that can very substantially affect their impact on teacher motivations. The distribution process (the incentive system of the school) is much more complicated than is generally recognized. There are, of course, the ordinary problems of uncertainty regarding whether teachers will actually receive the rewards that they expect. This is one of the reasons teachers organized into unions to bargain collectively with school districts and force them to sign contracts guaranteeing salaries and working conditions. And there are all the subjective problems associated with any type of reward; disappointment that rewards are less satisfying than expected or that they are given for actions that are more difficult or distasteful than originally thought.

But two factors affect the incentive-value of any reward; these are rarely considered and yet enormously important in determining how much they contribute to teacher motivation. The first is the fact that distribution of the crucially important intrinsic teaching rewards is not under the direct control of school managers or policymakers. Hence, school leaders can only indirectly control the extent to which teachers feel rewarded for their efforts. Second, and even more important, many of the most valued rewards available to teachers cannot be separately distributed to individual teachers and thus cannot serve to differentially motivate individual work efforts.

This last point was outlined in a general way by Lawler (1977) in an essay on different reward systems in industry. He pointed out that many different rewards, including wage payments, can be structured to reward *group* behavior or entire *organizations* just as easily as they can be attached to the efforts of specific individual workers. For example, it makes perfect sense to talk of using "tax incentives" to control such corporate activities as capital investment or energy conservation, but it does not seem right to talk about these as "rewards" for individual workers. Tax incentive systems have a demonstrable effect on corporate motivations, and they work very well to influence the performance of entire organizations even when individual workers are not differentially rewarded.

When it comes to schools, this relatively abstract point about group and organization level incentives is made more concrete if we think about two types of incentives first identified by Clark and Wilson (1961)—"purposive" and "solidary" incentives. By "solidary incentives" these authors meant that many workers are motivated by experiences such as "conviviality," "group membership," "maintenance of social distinctions," and similar social experiences that can only be made available if an entire group experiences them together. To the extent that workers are motivated by social relationships that develop in the workplace, they cannot be rewarded as single individuals—social groups must be nurtured and they must collectively experience these group solidarity or group identity rewards.

Similarly, "purposive" incentives are only available on a collective basis. Only in this case the collectivity is the entire productive organization. As Clark and Wilson (1961, p. 135) put it,

> Purposive, like solidary, incentives are intangible, but they derive in the main from the stated ends of the association rather than the simple act of associating.

Purposive incentives are those rewards that are reaped when an organization reaches the goals for which the members have been brought together. The sacrifices made in political parties, religious organizations, or military campaigns are to a substantial extent motivated by the fact that members in these organizations have accepted the ends of the organization as their own and feel rewarded when goals are reached, victories won.

The solidary and purposive incentives described by Clark and Wilson are at the very core of the intrinsic rewards identified by many scholars as the most powerful motivators for teachers. It cannot be emphasized enough that the important feature of these incentives is the fact that they cannot be given selectively to individual teachers, no matter how well they perform. They must, by their nature, be granted to work groups or entire organizational units.

As described in the next section, the data collected from fifteen elementary teachers clearly indicate that how teachers understand the purposes of schooling, and whether they take social solidary rewards from their relationships with children or with other adults in the school directly controls the availability of the most important teaching rewards.

THE INCENTIVE SYSTEM IN ELEMENTARY SCHOOLS

To explore the incentive system that mediates the flow of intrinsic rewards to teachers we spent a full academic year repeatedly observing and interviewing fifteen elementary school teachers. We asked about their joys and frustrations, their teaching strategies and persistent problems, how they learned to teach and how they compared their present assignments with those remembered or anticipated in other work settings. As our understanding grew, we looked for commonalties and differences in the overall orientations of these fifteen teachers that would illuminate their obvious differences in work style, levels of success and enjoyment of their work. The result, elaborated in the remainder of this chapter, is a "grounded theory" of teaching incentives (Glaser and Strauss, 1967).

The fifteen teachers under study fell naturally into four distinct groups on the basis of their shared interpretations of six basic elements in their work. These common elements were:

1. A view of how teaching activities contribute to student learning,
2. Criteria for determining whether their teaching is successful in reaching its fundamental goals,
3. Definitions of student success and beliefs regarding how students become successful,
4. Perceptions regarding the most difficult aspect of teaching—difficult in the sense that teachers who can handle this task well are seen as really outstanding teachers,
5. Feelings about the most distasteful aspect of teaching—distasteful because it represents a perpetually unsolvable problem which constantly interferes with the work, and
6. A sense of the central mystery of teaching—the marvelous thing that makes learning possible; a thing that teachers can celebrate but cannot entirely predict or control.

These shared cultural meanings shaped the incentive system of the school for these teachers. They are especially important in controlling organization and group level incentives. At the organization level these common cultural elements provide teachers with an overall orientation toward the goals of schooling and control the flow of "purposive" rewards, and thus determine whether they gain a sense of significance and satisfaction in the performance of their teaching duties. At the group level teachers discover that sharing a common cultural definition of their work provides them with a common identity and gives rise to the sense of group solidarity that controls the flow of these crucially important intrinsic rewards.

As suggested in Figure 11.1, the four natural groups found in our sample of fifteen teachers are created by two overlapping distinctions in their overall work orientations. The first distinction arises in their views regarding the organizational mission or fundamental goals of education. The other springs from whether the teachers' group identities are primarily linked to their students or to other adults in the school. As shown in the cells of the figure, we can characterize the shared work orientation of each group and identify their common understandings of the goals and processes of schooling.

Specific elements in the cultural system embraced by these teach-

	PURPOSIVE, ORGANIZATIONAL MISSION INCENTIVES	
	Producing Achievement	Nurturing Children
	Direct Instruction, Learning as Work	Evocative Education, Learning as Opportunity
Adult-Centered	THE MASTER TEACHERS Teachers A, B, & C	THE HELPERS Teachers K, L, M, N, & O
Program-Structured	Becoming academically disciplined	Learning to cope with the curriculum
Ability-Based Work	*Success:* Getting up to grade level. *Hardest:* Reaching the difficult kids. *Distasteful:* Lack of administrative support.	*Success:* Functioning as students. *Hardest:* Imposing an order or regimen. *Distasteful:* Kid who hates being there.
Child-Centered	THE INSTRUCTORS Teachers D, E, & F Making intellectual progress	THE COACHES Teachers G, H, I, & J Exploring new worlds
Task-Structured **Interest-Based Activity**	*Success:* Kids turn on to learning. *Hardest:* Pacing the instruction. *Distasteful:* Having to discipline.	*Success:* Kids click with the teachers. *Hardest:* Emotional energy required. *Distasteful:* School organization stuff.

SOLIDARITY, GROUP PROCESS INCENTIVES

FIGURE 11.1 Alternative Teaching Work-Orientations and Incentive Systems

ers can be found in transcripts of their interviews. A few illustrations will help to clarify their thinking.

Organizational Incentives

While the teachers characterized how their work contributes to the essential purposes of the school in somewhat different ways, two broad themes emerge from our interviews and observations. One theme is clearly expressed in the following remark by Mrs. A:

> The most important consideration is probably getting up to grade level. Covering the material, not just covering it, but teaching it, really teaching it.

At another point she elaborates:

if the child can learn inner discipline and learn to accept the fact that some things are not always fun—for example, reading for some children is not fun. . . . if they at least get the attitude that there are certain things that must be done despite the fact that we don't like it—then everything else will work.

This teacher believes that schools exist to produce objective, measurable achievement gains among students. She feels that she is contributing to the mission of the school if her children are able to read easily and compute accurately using the materials prescribed for their age group in the district curriculum.

Another teacher, Mr. D, places less importance on standardized measures of achievement, but he still identifies achievement as the primary purpose of schooling:

> To me . . . it is just getting a kid to learn to like to learn, because once you get them hooked on learning they go into everything on their own. And, of course, being a good reader and knowing elementary math, those are part of the tools you have to have in order to become a good learner.

For a third teacher, Mr. E, producing achievement is explicitly identified as the major source of pride in his work,

> I think when I see a kid making progress—especially a kid that had a lot of problems before and people had just given up on him . . . If I see him make progress then I feel proud of myself. I think I feel prouder of myself than I do of him.

The views of these three teachers contrast sharply with other teachers who see child nurture or development as the central mission of the school. Though her metaphors are mixed, Mrs. I, a fifth grade teacher, poignantly articulates the child nurture mission in the following remarks:

> I see my class as "young broncos" that need to be tamed. Like I'm taking them into a new world . . . maturity, hormones, the whole thing is bubbling and I have to kind of grab them by the hand and lead them through this tunnel. A lot of them don't even know they are going through it, but eventually they will know, so I see them as like young broncos that have to be tamed and I really like the challenge.

Mr. G, a kindergarten teacher, sharpens the point:

> The most important consideration in what I teach is what I am giving them. I want to be sure they are comfortable in school. I want them to be

happy coming there. At this particular stage, if they get a lot of heavy academics it does not make that much difference because what they need to know is that school is a nice place to come to—a place where you can learn, but also a place that will welcome and make you feel like it's not drudgery. I do want them to learn, too . . . but I don't want any pressured situations for them at this stage. They don't need that. They have a lot of time to grow up and be pressured.

In her second-third grade room Mrs. L adopts a more passive form of this commitment to the child development mission of the school. She says:

I make curricular decisions, usually, by where I feel the children need help. I try to help them. I don't try too much to impose a regimen. Of course, we have a certain regimen in the curriculum that is selected, etc. But I try to let them go where they are able. And I help them where I feel they need help, and when they come and say they need help.

Of the fifteen teachers studied, six share the achievement production orientation of Mrs. A, Mr. D, and Mr. E. The other nine give primary allegiance to the child nurture views illustrated by Mrs. I, Mrs. G, and Mrs. L. The six achievement producers share three beliefs that support their commitment to this basic school mission. First, they all feel strongly that teachers—not students—are responsible for initiating the learning process. Second, they all believe that schooling is serious work—work that, even at its best, is not always fun for either students or teachers. And third, they all believe that teaching work is primarily a matter of direct instruction rather than a process of stimulating or evoking student interest and activity. That is, these teachers believe they should aggressively present materials and experiences aimed at producing specific learning outcomes embedded in the school curriculum. The emphasis is on expected student achievements, not their interests or abilities.

The nine teachers with child development orientations share the obverse of these beliefs. They each express the view that students bear the ultimate responsibility for initiating the learning process; that schools should appeal to children's interests, curiosity, or sense of play; and that teaching works best if learning is evoked from children rather than pressed upon them.

Mrs. B illustrates the achievement producers' commitment to initiating the learning process. She says:

The important consideration in my teaching is to make sure that students are grasping the concepts—whether it be math, reading, health, or whatever. And by getting feedback from them—whether in body language, verbally, or written form—I know whether or not I am doing my job, whatever subject it might be that we are working on.

I think I am being responsible for their education. I cannot dwell too much on their problems at home. I can empathize and I can see to it that, perhaps, counseling or a certain agency that could maybe provide contingency funds (if there is no one in the house) or whatever. I can do those things, but when it comes time that they are in this classroom, then by gosh, at that time I must insist that we get on with the lessons, or I could be having therapy in there all day and I would not really be doing the kids a service as far as making sure that they have math skills and reading skills.

At another point she captures the achievement producers' belief that learning involves work for both teacher and students:

There's a kind of fine line where I can be loving and caring to my kids, but also be assertive—such as, "I'm sorry that happened, Suzie, or Johnny, nevertheless, we have work to do today, now let's get on with it." I will not let their plight interfere with developing them as persons, as far as their academic work is concerned.

Notice that Mrs. B separates her concept of development from that held by the nine child nurture teachers when she adds the phrase "as far as their academic work is concerned" to her use of that term. Mrs. B, like the other achievement producers, is unequivocally committed to the proposition that schools are directed toward academic goals and are not extensions of family life or social service agencies.

Mr. E links the achievement producers' belief in teacher responsibility for initiating the learning process with an emphasis on the view that teaching and learning are serious work:

Teaching is not very redeeming at the particular moment when you're doing it. I think it is something you have to stand back, look at, and say, "Well, you know, we have done this and I can see how far they have come." And I think that with a combination class, because I have a couple of kids back from last year and see what they are like this year, that I can more or less compare the fifth grade with the fourth grade. And I can see the big difference. I can see the big gap right there and I think, "I'm doing a pretty good job after all. You know I did not do such a bad job." I think that is probably the most redeeming thing—making progress. That makes me feel really good.

"Progress"—Mr. E's word for student achievement—is seen as springing directly from the willingness of teachers and students to get down to business. Mr. E is an excellent teacher, however, the serious business is not seen as tedious and boring. He tells of a story the class was working on, saying, the kids are getting a kick out of it and I'm getting a kick out of it. It is fun to read. It is not real drab material. I don't like the picture of the school marm sitting up there in the class saying, "You're going to do this," or "You're going to do that." That would be drab.

The nine nurture-oriented teachers discussed these issues in very different terms. Mrs. I, for example, emphasizes the importance of building a relationship with the students:

I'm not here just for myself. I'm here for them, and I need them as much as they need me.... Yes, their accomplishments in, say tests or what have you, did make me happy, but I think it was more of this relationship that we had with each other because I was able to relate to them and they were able to relate to me.... it doesn't have to be a touch, or $20, or a fur coat, it can be just, "Wow, thank you very much, I really enjoyed it."

I find that this year the sixth graders who were in my class last year are coming back to see me at recess. "Do you need any help? How are you? Gee, the room looks much different from last year's." And that kind of thing. So I am going, "Wow!" I am patting myself on the back and I am feeling fantastic. I feel really great.

Mrs. H, a first grade teacher, is typical of nurture oriented teachers. She uses the concepts of right- and left-brain development to describe her conception of the link between enjoyment and learning in the classroom:

I think that children need to be involved in "doing," so that they are functioning well at both the right and left brain levels.... Sometimes it is very difficult, but their response is in how well they learn, and whether or not they are happy with what they are doing. And yet, at the same time, maintaining good discipline in the classroom so that everybody is functioning and doing—and having a good time.

To summarize: six of the teachers in this study expressed a commitment to the proposition that the primary mission of the school is the production of measurable achievement for students. The other nine teachers gave primary weight to the school's function as an agency of child nurture and development. The first group see teachers as the initiators of a learning process which is characterized by serious work and direct instruction. The latter group concentrate on indirectly evoking or awakening learning in students; they want children to like learning and to be energized by strong interpersonal relationships with their teachers.

Group Level Incentives

In addition to balancing the tension between achievement and nurture as the ultimate goals of education, every teacher in this study displayed a clear preference for one of two basic strategies for organizing their classrooms. As described more fully below, by selecting a particular approach to classroom organization, teachers determine the cultural meaning system that will be developed within the school and thus give concrete form to the group "solidary" incentive system from which they derive important rewards.

Some teachers see classroom organization in terms of school "programs" and emphasize the importance of properly placing children within these programs, encouraging or insisting upon student compliance with the program requirements. These teachers—let us call them "adult centered"—find their group identity, and thus their solidary incentives, primarily among the other adults in the school system. They believe that educational objectives, whether of the achievement production or child nurture type, are best pursued by creating a classroom environment that surrounds students with universalistic and standardized educational opportunities and expectations. They believe that education consists of a set of learning experiences that all children encounter, learn to cope with, and eventually master. Eight of the fifteen teachers in our study (i.e. teachers Mrs. A through Mrs. C and Mr. K through Mrs. O) held this perspective on classroom organization.

The other seven teachers (i.e., Mr. D through Mrs. J) see classroom organization primarily in terms of the structure and conduct of lessons rather than the implementation of programs. These teachers—let's call them "child centered"—find that solidary group incentives arise inside the classroom and are rooted in their relationships with students. They express the view that learning is more the result of "activities" than "experiences." That is, they believe that students learn through high quality engagement in particular activities and they take a special interest in creating lessons that will stimulate and direct this engagement.

The adult-centered, program organization approach is vividly captured by Mrs. A who frequently talks about "covering" or "teaching" the curriculum materials for her age group and then insists:

> I think that any kid can learn. There are certain things that must be done, whether it is an enjoyable experience or not, then all other things will fall into place.... It's all in your expectations, but I expect them to work at grade level.

Mrs. B, while not as clearly committed to this program structured approach, still reports that she gets her greatest joy from turning around the "snottiest kid you can give me." As she puts it,

> I find it very rewarding to be working with students who are showing growth. Not only academically, but as far as their attitudes, their behavior. I really turn on to the snottiest kid you can give me to be able to help that child discover self-worth and the joys of reading and being able to work out a long division problem.

Note that for Mrs. B the learning tasks—reading, working out long division, etc.—are given in the curriculum. Her job is to help the kids master these tasks.

Adult-centered teachers who take the child nurture rather than the achievement-production goal articulate the program structured approach to classroom organization somewhat differently. Mrs. L, for example, sees the issue as one of making life easier for both herself and her students, and assuring that the whole educational system becomes respectable. She says,

> if we had K–1 classes where children were put in a 1 to 10 ratio and then tested, taught or screened—so that by the time they got to third grade they could test into the third grade then . . . it would give them some feeling of "I've made third grade." And then there would be better respect for the system.

Mrs. O, though less concerned about overall school operations, still sees the clock and the schedule as important devices for organizing and controlling classroom activities. She says,

> I can determine what can get done in a class period by the actual time of the work schedule. Now some children, as we all know, are faster workers than others. Some can complete this writing lesson in, maybe, ten minutes. And for some it will take 39 minutes. So those that have not completed it will have to go on with their reading. In their spare moments they have to come back and get their writing assignment completed. . . . Those that I know could work a little faster, I encourage to complete their work at a certain time. "Look at the clock now. By the time that long hand gets to a certain number, I would like you to be through writing." Some are slow workers, but I know they are picking up now.

The child-centered, lesson teaching approach to classroom organization contrasts sharply with the program structured approach of these teachers. Mr. D articulates the starting point for the child-oriented teachers when he says,

> I love learning and I really get interested in, and turned on, to the things that I am doing in class. I expand on it . . . . I discover new things, right along with the kids.

Another of the child-centered teachers, Mr. E, describes the tension between this group's focus on teaching lessons and the adult-centered emphasis on standardized school programs,

> Certain things do have to be covered. But there are areas I like teaching. I teach a unit on weather every year, and I like that. I teach a health unit on nutrition, and I enjoy that. I enjoy teaching U.S. History because I enjoy the history of the United States. There are certain things that I just like to teach, and there are certain things I am obligated to teach.

Miss F, a special education teacher, displays this same tendency to distinguish her own lessons from the overall framework of school programs. After describing the details of her personal approach to lesson planning, she says of her small group of severely handicapped children,

> This is not a "behind" class, this is a language class...I use a language orientation to spelling...trying to get as much language into it as I can.

Some of the nurture- and development-oriented teachers are even more aggressive in their embrace of the child-centered approach to the classroom. Mrs. H says,

> When I decide what to teach—first of all, I take into consideration the children and what level they are, which seems to be different every year. Then I usually try to determine a form of presentation and introduction— something to make the lesson, or whatever, exciting; something the children will be interested in. And that also depends on the group.

Mrs. G, the child-centered kindergarten teacher also insists on adjusting program to fit children's developmental needs and current interests. She says,

> I feel that reading is important, and math is important, but I feel that learning to socialize and get along is even more important, so I guess the social aspect is very important to me....It kind of falls where it falls.... It's things that happen during the day, you know, "How did so and so treat so and so? Do you think that was the right way? What can we do to change that?"

In sum, eight of the fifteen teachers approached the classroom from an adult-centered, program-structured perspective. They see their role as one of "keeping school"—insuring that children learn the attitudes and materials prescribed by the school's curriculum. The other seven teachers operated from a child-centered perspective. They concentrated on teaching lessons, adjusting the content and style of those lessons to fit what they perceived to be the developmental needs and interests of the children with whom they worked on a daily basis.

By combining the achievement production versus child development and adult-centered vs. child-centered distinctions described thus far, we get the four teacher groups shown in Figure 11.1. As indicated in the figure, each group has a characteristic view of schooling. We have given a name to each group, one that highlights their essential motivations.

The Master Teachers. Mrs. A, Mrs. B and Mrs. C, are so labeled because they have all been recognized by their superiors as strong contributors to the school system as well as effective classroom performers. Each of the master teachers in this study had been singled out as the major confidant and consultant to their principals. Two had been appointed as teaching assistant principals. These teachers have a deep commitment to the production of achievement—a commitment which they tend to articulate in terms of "bringing the kids up to grade level." This symbol provides their basic criterion for successful teaching. They see "academic discipline" as the key element in student success. Students, these teachers believe, succeed by "getting with the program," "buckling down," and "plugging away" at their school work.

The hardest thing about teaching, as the master teachers see it, is "getting to" the hard-to-reach kids. Mrs. A talks about this problem as a matter of seeing a kid who has been "kind of squirrely" starting to become academically disciplined and doing his homework. Mrs. B describes it as helping the "snottiest kid you can give me" discover "self worth" through the "joys of reading." Mrs. C, a special education resource teacher expresses this attitude by taking pride in being able to handle children no other teachers can deal with.

Difficult kids are a challenge, but the most distasteful part of the teaching profession for these teachers is lack of administrator support. Mrs. A reports the debilitating effects of this lack of support in her previous school:

> Had I not gotten interested in working for a principal who really supported me and liked me, I probably would have become a very discontented, burned-out person, because I was getting to that point rapidly....I had worked for a number of principals, many of whom were totally non-supportive simply because I don't think they had the skills to work with people and to stroke them once in a while....I felt like it didn't really matter what I did.

The great mystery at the heart of teaching for these teachers is that the program works. By holding true to their belief in kids and in the worth of learning, these teachers find that children eventually come around; they too become, in some inexplicable way, committed to mastering the curriculum and using school learning to handle life's problems.

The Instructors.   Mr. D, Mr. E and Ms. F, combine the commitment to achievement with the child-centered, lesson structured approach to classroom organization. These teachers believe that the most fundamental teaching responsibility is the development and execution of lessons. They view teaching as a technically sophisticated, skilled craft, and they believe that students learn through active engagement in intellectually stimulating activities. Intellectual "progress" is the criterion for success for these teachers. Students who make progress enable them to "feel really good" about their work.

For these teachers, students make progress when they are given learning experiences that accurately match their needs. They know they are doing a good job when they break through the isolation of disinterest or ignorance that keeps children from being successful in school and "turn kids on to learning." The hardest part of this process— the part which is mastered only by the best instructors—is learning how to *pace* instructional activities properly. Mr. E is confident of his pacing capacities. He says, "I have mastered the daily requirements of the work, I think, just by repetition." But Mr. D is not so sure of himself. He wants in-service programs that will help him with the pacing problem by providing "something that I can bring directly back to the classroom and use." All of the instructors agree, however, that a good teacher is able to handle curricular materials competently and creatively in order to appropriately structure and accurately pace their lessons.

The persistently distasteful aspect of teaching for the instructor group is discipline. Mr. E speaks for all of them when he says,

> I hate disciplining. I don't like to discipline. It makes me crazy. I hate being confronted by kids that are belligerent....I am paid to teach. That is what I want to do.

The wonderful mystery that lies at the heart of education for these teachers is the learning process itself. Mr. D offers the typical instructor's description of that mystery when he says,

> Watching a child make a discovery is satisfying. They didn't exactly understand something and the excited voice of, "Oh, now I understand!" is one of the most satisfying things for me. And I always try to remind myself that I really don't have much to do with it.

The Coaches.   Mrs. G, Mrs. H, Mrs. I, and Mrs. J, adopt the child-centered, lesson structured approach of the instructors, but put nurture and development goals ahead of measurable academic achievement. These teachers see themselves as responsible for evoking learning responses from the children and tend to feel that being "with the children" as they explore new worlds is their most important contribution to the learning process. These teachers want to make classroom life exciting, challenging, and stimulating for the children. Like good dramatic or athletic coaches, they move back and forth between rigorous demands for student engagement in classroom activities and offering them warmth, encouragement, and a guiding hand. Success for these teachers arises, as Mrs. J puts it, "when the children's personalities are clicking with mine." These teachers speak of students as being successful when they are learning to "love," "get along" with, and "respectful" of others. This success comes, the coaches believe, if kids are made to feel comfortable rather than pressured, excited rather than bored. Their approach to lesson structuring is articulated by Mrs. J, who says,

> I feel I have to start wherever the child is. I have been in classrooms where the material is too hard or it's too easy...they start moving around....I feel that it's important to keep the level of teaching to the individual.

The most distasteful and persistent problem for these teachers was summarized by Mrs. G:

> I don't like all these other things. Things that are going along with teaching—the mandated, the meetings, the writing, the records, all these things that we have to do—all this writing down. It is taking a whole lot of time that could well be spent working with children.

It's not a tolerance for these things, however, but a high level of emotional energy that marks a great teacher in the eyes of the coaches. Good teaching is hard, they believe, "because it takes a lot out of you." Mrs. I says, with obvious pride, "even if I have used my last ounce of strength I still crawl, I still go and I think my class knows this."

The central mystery for these teachers is the growth process itself. The children unfold before them. The "hormones" flow, "maturity" develops, and new abilities emerge from within the children. For the coaches, teaching is an art form. Children's emotions, attitudes, and abilities are molded and shaped as they learn to participate in the classroom culture. Teachers may direct and coordinate the activities, but the accomplishments are the children's own through the mysterious processes of growth and development.

The Helpers.   Mr. K, Mrs L, Mrs. M, Mrs. N, and Mrs. O hold to the child nurture and development goals of the coaches, but they see school organization in terms of predetermined curricula and program structures. This group, not accidentally, contained all of the weakest teachers in the study. They define their work role as "helping" students deal with the demands of schooling which are seen as essentially like the demands that all the children will face in later life. Mrs. O illustrates the general view of these teachers that student problems are troublesome because they interfere with proper functioning of the class. She says,

> I think they are nice students. Some have different problems. I can't diagnose their problems though, because I'm not a psychologist. So, I would not dare to start diagnosing their problems, but some seem to have problems. I could not go into what their problems are. I work with them to the best of my know-how and try to get them to function as a student.

This last phrase, "function as a student," is perhaps the best way to describe the criterion for successful teaching used by the helpers. For them, teaching is successful if the children learn to cope with the demands of the curriculum and function properly as a student—that is remain cooperative and compliant, delivering recitations and assignments on time. These teachers often spoke of students "performing up to grade level." Unlike the master teachers, however, they did not feel that they were personally responsible for making this happen. Rather, like Mrs. L, they tended to ask for better assignment of students so that they would only get "children who could understand what they are supposed to do at the third grade level."

The helpers were generally suspicious that a substantial number of their students were either unwilling or unable to cope with the school program. For them, the most persistent and distasteful problem in teaching is the number of resistive and noncooperative children they must confront. Mrs. M said of her learning handicapped class, "Basically they don't want to work. It takes thinking and work and they don't want to do it." Mrs. L likes working with the children in the morning hours, but in the afternoon, "they are just about exhausted," which makes the afternoons much harder work for the teacher. Rather than seeing it as a challenge to stimulate and engage the children (as the coaches do) the helpers say things like, "when they are 'with it' we accomplish more," but on days when they are "itchy or crabby or tired," or even "days when I burn-out, we don't get much covered."

Though these teachers find much of their work distasteful, they have admiration for their colleagues who solve the hardest problem, establishing an effective regimen in the classroom. Getting the classroom organized and running smoothly they know is possible, and they are impressed when they see someone do it effectively.

For these teachers there is not much wonder and mystery in the learning process. It is more a matter of routine, almost dull, plodding through the curriculum and trying to reach the kids with what they need to pass tests and move along through the school program. When they do experience mystery, it is usually in the form of someone appreciating their efforts. They generally feel unappreciated by colleagues and superiors (a feeling that is generally accurate as far as our research team could discern). So it is a mystery to them why some people are loved and appreciated when they do not appear to work any harder.

IMPLICATIONS FOR SCHOOL LEADERSHIP

Though many important lessons for school leaders can be found in the data drawn from these fifteen elementary school teachers, three are of special relevance to the problem of building an incentive system capable of supporting high quality teaching in the public schools.

Lesson 1: Breaking the Chain of Self Defeat

A self-defeating cycle of interaction between the school's incentive system and the teachers' work motivations was found among the teachers we identified as the "Helpers." The reason for this cycle is not too difficult to understand, but breaking out of it appears to be very difficult indeed. The Helpers start work, appropriately enough, with the expectation that their work will be valued by other adults (fellow teachers, school administrators, parents and community members). They also believe that the school program is so designed that children must succeed in school in order to succeed in later life. Their concept of success is, we should note, rather diminished (probably because their personal successes in life have been modest). They generally see success as a matter of *coping* with demands rather than acquiring mastery, independence, or creativity.

These teachers do not feel that they personally create the school program. Instead, they see themselves primarily as implementers of a program developed by "experts" who are remote in time and place from their own classrooms. To this essentially adult-oriented, program-structured view of schooling these teachers add a belief that their job is to *nurture* children—helping them to accept the "real world" of the school in order to assist them in coping with the rigors of adult life embodied in its programs. But when children fail, or become alienated from the school program, these teachers are presented with a dilemma. Is the problem with the child or with the program? For the Helpers the tendency is to believe that the problem is with the children. They have too much of their own personal identities wrapped up in the validity of the existing program. Moreover, they do not feel adequate to redesign the program even where changes are needed. Hence they emotionally abandon the children and become "traffic cops" for the system—explaining children's failures as the result of limited ability, broken homes, poor preparation, laziness, or stubborn recalcitrance. Program expectations are compromised or abandoned, not because they are thought to be wrong, but because children are not "up to" fulfilling them. The result is an earnest belief that children are being helped while, in fact, they are being told in a thousand subtle ways that they are beyond help.

How large is this group of Helpers? And what can be done about them? The answer to the first question is largely speculative at this point, but at least 15 percent of the teaching work force has probably been drawn into this self-defeating incentive system. And there is no reason to be very optimistic that many of these teachers could be given a more successful set of work incentives—though it is certainly important to begin a program of research and experimentation aimed at changing their overall work orientations. The problem is that for these teachers to change their self-defeating work patterns they must either free themselves from the confines of established curricula (like the Coaches) or accept responsibility for producing measurable student achievement (like the Master Teachers). Their generally weak personal egos prevent them from accepting responsibility for the curriculum. And their general lack of success makes them resist accountability for achievement production. The shift to achievement production appears to be the more promising management strategy, primarily because it could be incorporated into a personnel program aimed at eliminating the Helpers from public school classrooms if they fail to alter their basic work orientations.

Lesson 2: The Importance
of Organizational Purpose

The second critical lesson to be drawn from our study of incentives available to elementary school teachers is that both their work efforts and their capacity to find those efforts rewarding depends in a very significant way on what they believe to be the fundamental purpose of education. Teachers who believe that their primary work responsibilities are linked to measurable student achievement approach teaching quite differently from those who give primary allegiance to more diffuse goals related to child nurture and development. It is not clear how easily individual teachers can shift their loyalties from one of these goals to the other. Nor is it clear whether the two goals can be creatively merged. What is certain, however, is that teachers who do not give the same weight to a these goals as that given by school managers and policymakers are not likely to produce the expected results. To be effective, school leaders must find ways to bring teacher thinking into line with their own views regarding the appropriate mix of achievement and nurturance goals for education. In this regard, many current reforms appear doomed to failure because they emphasize teaching *behavior* rather than teaching *beliefs* as the primary mechanism for improving school performance. The data from the teachers in this study clearly indicate that beliefs about the goals of education play a major role in motivating teachers—both in energizing their commitment to particular teaching activities and in guiding their selection of strategies for preparation and presentation of lessons.

Lesson 3: Creating Group Solidarity

The third lesson for school managers to be drawn from the fifteen teachers in this study is the most subtle, but perhaps the most important. One of the key components of the teacher incentive system is the creation of group identity or solidarity relationships for individual teachers. Teachers who identify themselves with their students are motivated to perform their work in very different ways from those who derive solidary rewards from other adults in the school. Child oriented teachers are much more inclined to approach their work through carefully crafted lessons. They have a much stronger tendency to believe that the quality of their lessons, rather than the quality of text materials or centrally designed curriculum frameworks, are responsible for the effectiveness of their work with students. These teachers accept responsibility for their students more fully, and are generally more anxious to do battle for their rights. From a leadership standpoint, the problem with these teachers is that they tend to be "loners" who do not easily accept mandated changes in curriculum, disciplinary policy, or administrative arrangements unless the changes are obviously intended to facilitate their own work. These teachers are, in short, harder to manage.

The result is a managerial dilemma. Should child-oriented teachers be freed from managerial direction and allowed to use their own judgment regarding curriculum content and teaching strategy? Or should their resistance to managerial direction be viewed as a problem to be overcome with stronger supervision and direction? The answer is complicated. Weak management countenances poor teaching by the "Helpers" and other adult-oriented teachers just as much as it supports the work of child-oriented teachers. Moreover, aggressive management threatens to draw teachers away from their commitment to children and encourage them to become adult-oriented—a process that is likely to reduce attention to lesson structure and increase the likelihood that teachers will become "Helpers" who have generally reduced motivation and poor performance.

One way out of this dilemma is to "professionalize" teaching— combining rigorous training with peer evaluation and discipline and greater authority for individual teachers. By giving teachers greater responsibility for the creation and operation of programs as well as holding them responsible for the planning and execution of lessons, it would be possible to merge their two main sources of work motivation into a powerful incentive system. But professional autonomy for public school teachers will only be tolerated by a generally skeptical public if teachers acquire and display a much stronger sense of professional responsibility for both the goals and the processes of their work. For some teachers, acceptance of professional responsibility is attractive, but for a great many more it appears to be emotionally threatening or beyond their intellectual abilities. Whether enough teachers are both able and willing to adopt a professional view of their work is not clear. Moreover, whether school board members and school managers, who for most of this century have believed that they must closely supervise a nonprofessional teaching work force, will ever be willing to allow teachers to achieve professional autonomy is even more doubtful.

CONCLUSION

This chapter has tackled the complicated issue of teacher incentives. After noting that work motivation depends not only upon the availability of potent rewards for individual teachers, but also the creation of an incentive system to deliver those rewards, data collected from fifteen elementary school teachers was reviewed to identify the nature and consequences of the incentive systems available to them. Primary attention was focused on the highly potent *intrinsic* rewards—organizational purposiveness and group solidarity—that are most important to teachers. It was noted that these rewards are mediated by the beliefs teachers have about the ultimate goals of schooling and about how classrooms should be organized. Four types of teachers were identified and described based on whether they gave priority to achievement production or child nurture educational goals and whether they used a child-oriented lesson structuring or an adult-oriented program structuring approach to classroom organization.

Three lessons for school leaders were drawn from the work incentive systems of the fifteen teachers. First, the combination of child nurture goals with adult-oriented program structures does not provide teachers with adequate work motivation. Second, in order to improve teacher incentives it is important to focus attention on the mix of educational goals that are to be pursued and to find ways to persuade teachers to adopt the goals embraced by school leaders. Third, a serious dilemma is created for school managers by the fact that child-oriented teachers do not respond easily to mandated changes in curriculum, disciplinary policy, and educational program definition. Gaining the loyalty of the child- centered teachers for centralized program decisions may have the effect of reducing attention to lesson structure and responding to the needs of individual children. It is for this reason, if for none other, that a major effort should be made to "professionalize" teaching by giving teachers a greater sense of responsibility for both program definition and classroom lesson structures.

REFERENCES

Burns, J. M. (1978). *Leadership.* New York: Harper & Row.

Creighton, D. L. (1974). Philosophies, Incentives and Education. Unpublished paper prepared under contract to the National Institute of Education (DHEW Contract No. NIE-P–74–0125).

Deci, E. L. (1972). The effects of contingent and noncontingent rewards and controls on intrinsic motivation. *Organizational Behavior and Human Performance,* 8, no. 2 (October 1972), 217–29.

––––––. (1975). *Intrinsic Motivation.* New York: Plenum.

ERIC Clearinghouse on Educational Management (1981). Motivating teachers. *The best of ERIC on educational management.* Eugene, Oreg.: University of Oregon, ERIC Document EA 013 983.

––––––. (1980). Teacher motivation. Research Action Brief Number 13. Eugene, Oreg.: University of Oregon, ERIC Document ED 196 116.

Glazer, B. G., and Strauss, A. L. (1967). *The discovery of grounded theory: Strategies for qualitative research.* Chicago: Aldine.

Herzberg, F. (1966). *Work and the nature of man.* Cleveland: World.

Kessleman, G. A.; Wood, M. T.; Hagen, E. L. (1974). Relationships between performance and satisfaction under contingent and noncontingent reward systems. *Journal of Applied Psychology,* 59, no. 3, 374–76.

Larson, E. (1982). High-performers are 'Different Folks'. Interview with Charles A. Garfield. Originally printed in the *Wall Street Journal,* reprinted in Riverside, Calif. *Press Enterprise,* January 24, 1982, p. 3.

Lawler, E. E., III. (1970). Job attitudes and employee motivation: Theory, research, and practice. *Personnel Psychology.* 23, 223–37.

––––––. (1977) Reward Systems. In *Improving Life at Work,* edited by J. R. Hackman and J. L. Suttle, chapter 4, pp. 163–226. Santa Monica, Calif.: Goodyear Publishing Co.

Lortie, D. C. (1969). The balance of control and autonomy in elementary school teaching. In *The semi-professional and their organization,* edited by A. Etzioni, chapter 1, pp. 1–53, New York: Free Press.

––––––. (1975). *School teacher: A sociological study.* Chicago: University of Chicago Press.

Martin, E. (1978). Can society pay for altruism? Or, why virtue must be its own reward. Occasional paper. Chapel Hill, N.C.: Institute for Research in Social Science, University of North Carolina.

Miller, L. K., and Hamblin, R. L. (1963). Interdependence, differential rewarding, and productivity." *American Sociological Review, 23*, 768–88.

Miskel, C. (1974). Intrinsic, extrinsic, and risk propensity factors in the work attitudes of teachers, educational administrators, and business managers. *Journal of Applied Psychology, 59*, no. 3, 339–43.

Miskel, C.; DeFrain, J. A.; and Wilcox, K. (1980). A test of expectancy work motivation theory in educational organizations. *Educational Administration Quarterly, 16*, no. 1 (Winter 1980) 70–92.

Mitchell, D. E.; Ortiz, F. I.; and Mitchell, T. K. (1983). *Work orientation and job performance: The cultural basis of teaching rewards and incentives.* Final Report to the National Institute of Education on research conducted under Grant No. NIE-G–80–0154. Riverside, Calif.: University of California, Riverside.

Notz, W. W. (1975). Work motivation and the negative effects of extrinsic rewards: a review with implications for theory and practice. *American Psychologist*, September, 1975, pp. 884–91.

Ouchi, W. (1981). *Theory Z: How American business can meet the Japanese challenge.* Reading, Mass.: Addison-Wesley.

Sergiovanni, T. J. (1967). Factors which affect satisfaction and dissatisfaction of teachers. *Journal of Educational Administration, 5*, 66–82.

Spuck, D. W. (1974). Reward structures in the public high school. *Educational Administration Quarterly, 10*, 18–34.

Thompson, S. (1979). Motivation of teachers. *ACSA School Management Digest*, series 1, no. 18. ERIC/CEM Research Analysis Series, No. 46. Burlingame, Calif., and Eugene, Oreg.: Association of California School Administators and ERIC Clearinghouse on Educational Management, University of Oregon. ERIC Document ED 178 998.

Vroom, V. (1964). *Work and motivation.* New York: Wiley.

Weick, K. E. (1966). The concept of equity in the perception of pay. *Administrative Science Quarterly, 11*, 413–39.

12

Effective School Principals:
Counselors, Engineers,
Pawnbrokers, Poets...
or Instructional Leaders?

TERRENCE E. DEAL

Overall, the effective schools literature has made its mark on education. It has rekindled our faith in the ability of schools to produce results. That, in itself, is a significant contribution, coming at a time when the performance of schools was widely questioned. Now it is commonly accepted that schools can make a difference. At least some can.

Beyond shoring up the faith, the literature has outlined some essential qualities of an effective school. It has reminded principals and teachers that they ought to: (a) agree on the core of what they are about, (b) believe that they can deliver on these basic premises, (c) create an environment that is safe and focused on essential tasks (at least part of the time) and (d) reflect occasionally to see whether what they are doing is accomplishing what they want (Cohen, 1982). These are sensible qualities. They are all worthy of attention in building any effective organization—public or private, profit-making or not. While such qualities may not always be a sufficient foundation for a top performing school, most would agree that they are necessary ingredients. Conversations and strategies that center around such desirable attributes are bound to have meritorious impact on schools, even though some educators are treating characteristics of effectiveness as something to be installed rather than to be developed from within (Deal, 1985). Despite the conceptual and methodological shortcomings of the effective schools literature, the practical applications of the findings should do more good than harm—as long as desirable qualities are approached as guidelines, rather than embraced as panaceas.

Another aspect of the effective schools literature, however, may be sending us in a counterproductive direction. A recurrent finding in studies of effective schools identifies strong instructional leadership by principals as a major force (Cohen, 1982). One review of studies of principals in effective schools suggested some reasons why. Such principals observe teachers more regularly than do their counterparts in less effective schools. They talk with teachers more about instruction, are highly supportive of teachers, and are more active in initiating evaluations of teaching or programs (Bossert et al., 1982). Research findings are taken beyond objective limits to construct a mythological language around the principalship: "the principal is key," "the principal is the gatekeeper to school effectiveness" (Little, 1982). The mythology has spawned countless efforts to develop the instructional leadership of principals and to focus their time and attention on monitoring, influencing, and improving the technical activities within classrooms.

The chief problem with shifting the attention of principals is that no one has really identified what instructional leadership is nor provided solid empirical assurance that if a principal were to do more of it, a school would perform at higher levels. Most studies that link instructional leadership to school effectiveness are not able to separate causes and effects. The essential if-then connection is not established well enough that we can assure principals that instructionally focused behavior will pay off. Many principals argue that if they were to behave in accordance with leadership prescriptions derived from the effective schools findings, their schools would deteriorate and they would eventually lose their jobs. Is this a defensive reaction of people unable to do what the new prescriptions require? Or are principals articulating something that we need to stop and ponder before rushing headlong in a direction that may do more harm than good?

This chapter sides with many principals. It argues that findings of effective schools studies with respect to the principal as instructional leader ignore important aspects of schools as organizations. The literature typically depicts schools as rational instruments that exist primarily to produce results. But there is much more to schools than their instrumental or technical role. Schools exist to serve human needs. They serve as hubs of political activity. They create meaning and serve society as important symbols. Principals who ignore needs, shrink from politics, or neglect symbols and ceremonies to concentrate on instruction may be in for a jolting surprise.

THE GULF BETWEEN WHAT PRINCIPALS ACTUALLY
DO AND WHAT RESEARCH SAYS THEY SHOULD DO

Principals lead a complex existence. Studies of their behavior document that principals spend most of their time on a wide variety of brief encounters that have very little to do with one another (Peterson, 1978). Like managers in other sectors, many of these encounters are initiated by others (Mintzberg, 1973). Most of the principal's time (91 percent in one case study—96 percent in another) is spent disciplining students, talking with teachers about noninstructional matters, dealing with parents or the community residents, or filling out forms for superiors (Peterson, 1978). Less than 6 percent of a principal's time (in these cases, at least) was spent in tasks related to instruction. These two principals spent only about twenty-five minutes in a six-hour day dealing with instruction—the technical core of a school organization (Peterson, 1978). The actual behavior of principals hardly appears as a mirror image of how the effective schools literature characterizes the ideal role.

How do we interpret the discrepancy between how principals allocate their time and prescriptions that would redirect and refocus them on matters that currently are receiving very little of their attention? One possibility is that the principals in studies of principal behavior are different from those in effective schools. If we were able to compare time allocation with measures of performance, then we might find a link between an instructional focus and school effectiveness. But many would question how much real instructional leadership exists. Most studies of principal behavior find little variance in the allocation of time to instructional versus noninstructional tasks—from one principal to another. There is also the possibility that some principals influence instruction through their noninstructional exchanges.

A second possibility is that principals spend time on noninstructional tasks because they are uncomfortable with teaching and find the classroom an alien territory. This seems odd as nearly every principal enters the role after spending a number of years as a classroom teacher.

A third possibility is that how principals allocate their time is actually functional and productive. Through experience, they may have learned something that may escape effective schools researchers. Their behavior allows them—and their school—to survive and thrive in an environment that expects more than technical performance. March (1980) finds virtue in the discrepancy between how administrators talk and how they act—the slippage between words and deeds helps them to address conflicting demands of the administrators' role. Meyer et al. (1983) find justification in the fact that principals and superintendents keep their eye focused outward on the environment while turning their backs on the technical core of the enterprise. The reversal of the customary focus allows them to tailor the symbols of the organization to fit societal demands. In environments where faith and confidence depend more on how an organization appears than on its results, an outward orientation is sensible and essential (Meyer and Rowan, 1977). In this view, principals may have intuitively found the logic that drives the social contexts they are asked to administer. Their intuitive lore may reveal sides of schools as organizations that many researchers minimize or ignore. If so, we need to articulate and examine concerns of principals in the light of various theories of organizations before we alter their role in significant ways. Otherwise, in our desire to improve the performance of schools, we may experience quite the opposite.

Schools as Complex Social Organizations

Formal education occurs within the defined boundaries of an officially sanctioned organization. State governments typically have ultimate authority in matters of education, but delegate some authority and most of the responsibility to local governing bodies. In concert with an elected or appointed chief executive, local school boards set policies and guidelines. The chief executive and district office staff see that these guidelines shape the process of education in local schools. While, in theory, each level plays an important role in influencing what happens in a school or classroom, the process of teaching and learning is ultimately determined within each local site.

There, each year, principals, teachers, students, parents, librarians, custodians, specialists, counselors, secretaries, and others intertwine official duties with special interests, rational priorities with personal quirks, and regulated authority with passion and power, to create a unique social collective. Their task is never an easy one. Schools are more vulnerable to forces outside their boundaries than many organizations. Schools also have a complicated array of constituencies they are supposed to serve. Most important, schools are asked to pursue several goals simultaneously. They are supposed to improve the cognitive abilities of students. They are flagships in society's efforts to acculturate young people into our way of life. They are asked to keep students from under feet or off the street, and to control them while on (and off) the school grounds. They are asked to channel students into career tracks and to certify them once they have passed important milestones (Spady, 1974). The challenge of creating a school that works involves much more than meets the naked eye. For those who wonder how administering an elementary school of three hundred or a high school of fifteen hundred can be so difficult, consider the circumstances that any principal has to face. Executives of corporations may deal with larger units, but the complexity of schools as social systems creates problems disproportionate to their size.

For many years researchers have studied schools as organizations. The literature is filled with head-scratching wonderment over research results that rarely seem to fit preconceived notions of how organizations ought to behave—at least according to rational standards. Creative scholars have coined terms such as "schools as loosely-coupled organizations" (Weick, 1976) or "schools as institutionalized organizations" (Meyer and Rowan, 1977) as a way of introducing new images into research efforts to help explain the anomalies.

Like researchers, many principals have often scratched their heads when newly well-defined goals are not being reflected in everyday practice or when efforts to change evaluation practices have backfired and created bigger problems than they were originally designed to solve. Reminiscent of Butch Cassidy and the Sundance Kid fleeing from a persistent posse, principals wonder "Who are those guys?" "Why doesn't my school behave the way I was taught that it should, the way an organization is supposed to?"

Underlying the confusion and surprise of both scholars and researchers is the prevailing set of images that are used to view and interpret the experience of schools as organizations. It is not that the images are wrong; the problem is that we used a limited set of perspectives to view a highly complex social system.

To understand schools as social phenomena or to reinterpret our original quandary about the gulf between how principals behave and how research says they should, we need to move toward a more pluralistic view of organizations (Bolman and Deal, 1984). At present, researchers, policymakers, and practitioners typically focus on the two obvious sides of schools as organizations: individuals or formal structure, needs or roles, morale or productivity. While each of these captures an important aspect of schools, both ignore their hidden sides: politics and culture, power and symbols, conflict and meaning. Once we examine the smoke-filled room where deals are struck, the public arena where conflicts are decided, the stage upon which issues are dramatized and transformed, or the existential substrates where meaning is anchored and created, we can develop a much richer image of schools as organizations—or of principals as leaders. We can also avoid many of the pitfalls to change that occur because we have failed to examine the hidden sides of schools as we formulate strategies for improvement or reform (Baldridge and Deal, 1983).

THE OBVIOUS SIDES OF SCHOOLS:
INDIVIDUALS AND STRUCTURE

Whether one looks at studies of schools by researchers who wish to understand them, policies crafted by policymakers who seek to improve them, or strategies forged by administrators who try to manage them, two main perspectives stand out. One focuses on the human resources of schools—the needs, skills, and attitudes of individual participants. The other attends primarily to how these human resources are arranged—the formal structure of roles or interdependencies and the goals that provide direction.

The human resource view emphasizes the importance of tailoring schools to meet the needs and skills of participants (Bolman and Deal, 1984). The primary focus is people. Problems are typically centered in individuals. Policies or management strategies based on this perspective rely heavily on training, selecting the right people for this position, or removing those that do not measure up. The primary indicator of organizational effectiveness is morale. A large proportion of the literature on schools as organizations is guided by psychological or human resource theories. Superintendents, principals, and teachers often advocate and behave in accordance with the central tenets of the human resource approach.

By comparison, the concepts and assumptions of the structural view of schools are quite different. The primary focus is productivity. Performance is seen as enhanced by articulating clear goals, encouraging specialization, specifying roles so that tasks can be approached with certainty, and controlling the technical core of activities through the exercise of authority, clear policies and procedures, and adequate measures of quality control. The key focus is on the relationship between the structure of schools and the technology of teaching. Problems arise when the two don't support each other, the various parts of the structure are out of kilter, or goals do not provide a clear direction.

The structural perspective is deeply embedded in contemporary policy and management (Bolman and Deal, 1984). Policies based on this approach advocate changes similar to those in the effective schools literature or in the recent commission reports calling for reforms in schools. Management approaches derived from this perspective encourage schools to clarify goals, to link behavior to precise objectives, to evaluate personnel systematically, and to reorganize the structure to improve productivity. A significant slice of research on schools as organizations, policies for school reform, or prescriptions for school management is guided by this approach. The notion of the principal as instructional leader with the attendant factors for effective schools is heavily emphasized by structural ideas.

Again, it is not that either of these perspectives is wrong; they are both quite useful in explaining how schools work or in developing policies and strategies for helping them to improve. The main problem is that each leaves something out; that together they do not highlight significant features of schools as organizations. To capture the hidden sides of schools, we need to entertain other less obvious perspectives.

THE HIDDEN SIDE OF SCHOOLS:
ORGANIZATION POLITICS

Political theories look at schools quite differently (Bolman and Deal, 1984). Rather than focusing on people's needs, a political perspective emphasizes their self-interests. Rather than advocating rational control exercised through authority, a political view concentrates on a nego-tiated order achieved through the exercise of power among groups and coalitions (Peterson and Wimpleberg, 1983). In any school, different interests and differential power among teachers and students, special-ists and teachers, principals and teachers, or parents and principals produce a continual cycle of conflict and stimulate an ongoing process of bargaining and compromise. Unlike the human resource or struc-tural counterparts, political theorists see conflict as unavoidable and necessary. Considerable effort is devoted to constructing arenas in which contenders can fight fairly in front of watchful spectators. Con-tests avoid street fights where people sabotage, undermine, and hurt one another—behind the scenes.

Policymakers and administrators are well aware of the need to acquire power, build coalitions, and strive for compromise. The problem is that policies and strategies in education are often formu-lated outside the arena without dealing with political realities until action is taken. Avoiding conflicts and power struggles up front often cuts down on time and turmoil in the short run, but contributes to failure over the long haul. From a political view, successful schools, like successful marriages, are full of fair fights. Successful principals are intimately and artfully involved in the politics of their schools.

THE HIDDEN SIDE OF SCHOOL
ORGANIZATION: CULTURE

Human resource, structural, and political perspectives share a common assumption: a belief in certainty and direct cause-effect relationships. Needs are knowable and, if met, enhance morale and productivity. Goals are definable and, if specified, keep an organization on course at top performance. Power is tangible and, if used wisely, can create order and get results. A symbolic perspective takes another tack (Bolman and Deal, 1984). Organizations are highly ambiguous, yet people in them crave meaning. Everyone wants to believe that his or her efforts make a difference. Most want to have faith in the overall enterprise in which they work.

Belief and faith are anchored in symbols and ceremony. People of every country create culture to make sense of an otherwise nonsensical world. They do the same in business organizations, hospitals, and schools (Deal and Kennedy, 1983). The elements of culture transformational organizations into cherished institutions (Clark, 1975). Shared values represent what the organization stands for. Heroes and heroines embody values and provide tangible symbols and role models for everyone to appreciate and follow. Rituals create physical expressions of values and give everyone the opportunity for sharing and bonding in a common implicit quest. Ceremonies provide periodic occasions where people can celebrate and appreciate their secrets and most cherished symbols or accomplishments. Stories carry values and make the exploits of heroes or heroines accessible to those inside an organization as well as to interested constituents in the external environment. Presiding over a culture assuring the continuity of shared values are priests and priestesses. Storytellers spread the lore. Gossips spread information—reliable or otherwise. From a symbolic perspective, the elements of culture form the glue that holds an organization together (Deal and Kennedy, 1982). Symbols inspire loyalty and effort. Beliefs link efforts to outcomes—accurately or otherwise. Culture fuses identity of individuals with the collective identity of the organization and serves as a focal point for maintaining the confidence and faith of outsiders (Meyer and Rowan, 1977).

Because of their ambiguous goals and intangible product, the culture of schools plays an even more prominent role than it might in other organizations. Yet if one reviews the last decade of change and reform, it seems obvious that many efforts to improve the human resources, structural, or power relations of schools have unraveled their social tapestry, fragmented their cohesion, and poked holes in their useful fictions (Baldridge and Deal, 1983; Sarason, 1971). Policymakers, steeped in a culture of their own, often unknowingly undermine the very thing that needs to be strengthened for schools to perform at higher levels. School administrators, heavily schooled in interpersonal or structural approaches to organization, find that their efforts to make things better often backfire and make things worse. To understand a school, policymakers or principals must think of it, at once, as family, factory, and jungle, or arena. But schools are also theaters and museums, special places because of what they express or say to a society about itself, not because of what they accommodate, produce, or resolve.

FOUR SIDES OF SCHOOL LEADERSHIP

A four-sided image of schools as organizations suggests that an effective school is one where: (a) individual needs are acknowledged and met, (b) a well-coordinated system of roles and relationships supports goal-directed instructional activities, (c) different interests and perspectives have been negotiated into a commonly accepted pact among contending subgroups, and (d) shared symbols and ceremonies create meaning and a sense of collective identity for those inside the schools—as well as for important constituencies in the environment. Weaknesses in any of the four dimensions can reduce a school's effectiveness—either in producing tangible results or in carrying out its less tangible expressive role.

From a multisided perspective, how principals actually spend their time has several interpretations. Let us revisit and review those tasks that occupy their attention and energy—using other lenses. In disciplining students, principals may be meeting student needs, assuring that teachers can devote more of their time to instruction, reaffirming the power of society over the individual, or carrying out an age-old ritual that signals important values to those inside or outside the school. Talking with teachers about noninstructional matters may help principals to let them know they matter as people; provide opportunities for dealing with conflicts, bargaining, or building coalitions across boundaries of formal authority; or serve as occasions for transmitting or enforcing important cultural values. Dealing with parents and local residents builds friendships, coalitions, and offers the opportunity to bring them into the meaning system of the school. Filling out forms for superiors serves as an important source of formal control, but also provides information to supplement the power of district-level staff—and serves as an important ritual reinforcing the belief that the school system is well managed and well coordinated.

In a given behavioral sequence, a number of different transactions may take place simultaneously, each dealing with a different side of the school as an organization. Some of these transactions may be directly related to the instructional dimension; others may affect instruction indirectly or serve other important organizational purposes. Neglecting any one of these facets may reduce the overall effectiveness of the school. Principals need to be instructional leaders, but they also need to attend to other leadership duties, for example, as counselors or parents, engineers or supervisors, contenders or referees, heroes or poets.

The Principal as Counselor or Parent

In the imagery of the school as extended family, the principal's leadership role is concentrated on meeting individual needs. He or she gives praise and constructive feedback to promote both satisfaction and growth. The principal listens and helps teachers and students grapple with personal strengths and weaknesses. The principal gives advice, counsel, and affection. The principal recognizes that different people have different needs and tries to respond to each individual on the appropriate level, while encouraging personal growth and development. He or she sees a robust correlation between personal needs and professional performance. Nurturing is a top contender for a principal's time and attention.

The Principal as Engineer or Supervisor

The school-as-a-factory image of the structural side of organizations emphasizes the principal's role as engineer or supervisor. As an engineer, the principal's leadership focuses on designing a system of roles and relationships that uses the talents of faculty, supports the instructional program, and allows the school to deal with its relevant environment. The principal sees to it that goals are clearly defined and widely understood. As an engineer, he or she works to assure that important tasks and responsibilities are allocated sensibly, that roles are defined well enough to minimize overlaps and confusion, and that interdependencies among specialties are sufficient for the complexity of the various tasks. In addition to creating the right parts, the principal spends considerable time making sure the parts mesh well, getting the various roles or groups to pull together, rather than to pursue narrow responsibilities and goals without sufficient integration. Much of a principal's time is spent planning, developing clear policies and procedures, coordinating roles or units (such as department heads, team leaders, or housemasters), exercising his or her authority through making decisions, resolving conflicts, or convening and overseeing meetings to coordinate the efforts of different persons or units. Meetings occupy much of a principal's time and attention. The larger and more complex the school, the more time and attention the principal devotes to coordinating strategies and duties.

As a supervisor, the principal sees to it that schoolwide goals are translated into specific operational objectives for teachers, custodians, secretaries, counselors, cafeteria workers, and others. He or she develops clear criteria of adequate performance, observes performances regularly, then holds periodic appraisal sessions in which people learn about how well or poorly they are doing as well as what they can do to improve their performance. Since a primary function of the school is instruction, much of a principal's time is spent observing and evaluating (often informally, in short spurts) classroom teachers.

The Principal as Power Broker or Statesperson

The school-as-jungle-or-arena metaphor focuses considerable attention on the role of the principal as power broker or statesperson. Each school is seen as a collection of special interest groups. The principal's main job is to mold special interests into a schoolwide coalition. This task puts the principal into a swirling vortex of power and conflict, often armed with less power than other contenders or coalitions.

The principal as power broker sees conflict as a natural by-product of collective activity. Rather than avoiding or smoothing over conflict, the principal confronts and encourages it. The main goal is to create an arena, to bring contenders from various interest groups into contact with one another, governed by rules, overseen by a referee, and in full view of the spectators. Street fights behind the scenes are to be avoided as assiduously as fistfights on the playground. Occasionally principals help warring young people "put the gloves on and work it out." Principals exercising political leadership metaphorically encourage the same behavior among squabbling adults. The principal spends considerable time in the ring dealing with conflict—as a participant or as a referee.

The principal as statesperson works to build coalitions. He or she knows the special interest groups and tries to find common ideological ground on which the groups can work together. Through subtle diplomacy, negotiation, and behind-the-scenes cajoling and compromising, the principal does everything possible to assure that special interests coexist, governed by a productive pact. The principal rarely uses his or her power directly inside the school. But internal solidarity is used freely as a bargaining chip, as scarce resources are allocated to individual schools within the district. The principal spends ample time building and maintaining important constituencies in the school community.

The Principal as Hero/ine or Poet

The school-as-drama or theater metaphor requires a principal to be a symbolic leader. He or she spends time building the culture of the school—shaping and articulating shared values, annointing and celebrating heroes and heroines, convening and orchestrating key rituals, dramatizing and revitalizing the school's identity in celebrations, spreading its merits in stories, and working hand in hand with the informal network of priests or priestesses, storytellers, and gossips to keep the spirit of the school alive and the core values and beliefs intact. As symbolic leaders, principals work diligently to present the identity of the school to outsiders, to maintain the confidence and faith of external constituencies.

As heroes and heroines, principals realize their symbolic role in representing and embodying the existential core of the school. They are creative visionaries, willing to take risks in pursuit of cherished values, and able to cling to a vision with a tenacity that is contagious to nearly anyone. A principal's symbolic influence is exercised through costume, bearing, words, and deeds. Such principals relish their role as a central player in the everyday drama that plays on the stage called school. They accentuate and dramatize the values of the school. They spend time on the stage, not in the director's office. They give everyone someone to look up to, but do not steal the show from other important cultural players.

As poets, principals articulate the important, often inaccessible dreams and visions of an organization devoted to passing on the ways of the people. They speak about their schools in artful prose, capturing the emotion and passion of the classroom or playground. They spark imagination and loyalty by connecting everyday experience with historical memories or myths and future wishes or fairy tales.

Implications for School Leadership

Our analysis of school leadership paints a complex portrait of the principalship. Principals carry out their duties in ambiguously chaotic settings. They need to pay attention to instruction. But they also must attend to individual needs, power and conflict, symbols and ceremony. How much time they spend on each of these areas undoubtedly varies from school to school or month to month. At Roxbury High School, for example, Jerome Wineger's early days as principal were focused almost exclusively on politics. As an explosive situation stabilized, his attention undoubtedly shifted to other things: building morale, improving instruction, reorganizing the administrative team, or rebuilding the traditions of the school. As the current spotlight of society focuses on education, many principals are called upon to be poets. To deter them from that side of their leadership to focus too closely on instruction may hinder our efforts to reform or to improve public education.

If one looks at principals' perceptions of how they are judged as leaders, we encounter a profile that may not be too far from reality. As Table 12.1 illustrates, principals know what is expected of them. They realize that they must attend to individual needs, school goals, organizational roles, internal politics, and schoolwide meaning as well as to the instructional side of school.

Effective principals, after all, are not much different from effective leaders anywhere—including the occupants of the United States presidency. Those who have experienced difficulty in the presidency have concentrated on one side of their leadership role leaving other aspects unattended. President Carter's structural approach was undermined by power and symbols. Teddy Roosevelt's symbolic genius was marred by inattention to changing individual sentiments and a shifting power base. Lyndon Johnson's flair for mobilizing power was muted by structural weaknesses in delivering on promises and a failure to understand the symbolism of a foreign war in the culture of America. Even Franklin

TABLE 12.1   Criteria Perceived to Be Important When Central Office Evaluates Principals

Criteria	Number of Times Category Mentioned by Respondents (N = 360)	Percentages of Respondents Listing item (N = 112)	Percentage of All Items Mentioned
1. Public reaction: parents are happy, no complaints, public relations	72	64	20
2. Teacher reaction: good morale, no grievances, teacher-principal relations	54	48	15
3. Principal and teacher compliance to district rules and procedures, including meeting attendance and paperwork	44	39	12
4. Not making waves: smooth running, few problems taken to central office, keeping superintendent informed, not raising difficult questions	37	33	10
5. Student performance and progress: test scores, academic performance	31	28	9
6. The instructional program: innovation, good programs, instructional leadership	29	26	8
7. Overall school operation, includes atmosphere and climate	21	19	6
8. Relations with students, student compliance, and discipline	14	12	4
9. Good working relations with central office	7	6	2
10. Miscellaneous #1: includes plant management, leadership style, peer relations	25	22	7
11. Miscellaneous #2: all single items	26	23	7

From K. D. Peterson, *Administrative Science Quarterly*, p. 593.

Roosevelt, whose ability across each of the four sides of leadership is legendary, encountered difficulty when he overestimated his power relative to the symbolism of the Supreme Court. Judgments about Ronald Reagan's genius in the symbolic realm are still forming. Much will depend on his ability to build political support for his programs, to address the needs of a large range of Americans, and to structure the executive staff and federal agencies so that things can get done.

For principals, the implications of the argument are straightforward. They need to understand intimately the human needs, formal structure, politics, and culture of their schools. In our work with school principals at Peabody College we find that many principals understand the psychological and sociological aspects of their schools. They are less well versed about the politics and culture. They tend to see themselves above politics and unable to deal with elusive symbols. They abhor conflict and have never thought consciously about how they might influence the identity of their schools. Principals may be right in resisting efforts to make them instructional leaders, but they need to articulate their concerns more clearly. And they need to reflect on how well their attention and time mesh with the four sides of a school that requires both. Principals need to see a school in four dimensions. They need to be flexible leaders equally adept at the roles of counselor, engineer, power broker, or poet.

Policymakers need more complex images of schools. If they wish to make them better, they have to understand why schools are the way they are. In the zeal of improving one aspect of a school, policymakers frequently overlook others. If the all-consuming problems of "implementation" addressed in the policy literature are to be eliminated, policymakers need to embrace a more comprehensive view of the phenomenon they wish to affect.

Researchers need to examine their own images of schools as organizations. Some aspects of schools are easier to measure than others. Needs and roles are typically more suited to objective measurement than power or symbols—at least that is what many psychologists and sociologists would like us to believe. But the political and cultural forces in organizations—especially in schools—exert such a powerful influence that we need some way to factor them into an analysis of variance or regression equation. Either that or we need to relax the canons of quantitative research so that we can capture important variables that are difficult to define and measure. Otherwise, research findings will send practitioners down the wrong path and our intellectual understanding of schools as organizations and our ability to predict or to improve them will be markedly diminished.

SUMMING UP: WILL THE REAL DEPICTION OF THE PRINCIPALSHIP PLEASE STAND UP?

This chapter began by highlighting the discrepancy between how principals act and how the effective schools literature says that they should.

By becoming instructional leaders, principals may very well jeopardize the leadership they need to provide as counselors, engineers, power brokers, or poets. Effective schools meet human needs, get things done, negotiate an arrangement between existing factions, and create meaning for those who learn, study, support, or appreciate them. Effective principals are those who focus time and attention on each of these areas. They see a school as a family, as a factory, as a jungle, and as a carnival. They rotate their lenses like a kaleidoscope, finding different patterns in the social world they are asked to administer. They enjoy providing leadership for each. They know better than to concentrate their efforts on one view—even if researchers and policymakers tell them that they should.

REFERENCES

Baldridge, J. V., and Deal, T. E. (1983). *The dynamics of organizational change in education*. Berkeley, Calif.: McCutchan.

Bolman L., and Deal, T. E. (1984). *Modern approaches to understanding organizations*. San Francisco: Jossey-Bass.

Bossert, S. T., Dwyer, D. C.; Rowan, B.; Lee, G. V. (1982). The instructional management role of the principal. *Educational Administration Quarterly*, *18*, 34–64.

Clark, B. (1975). The organizational saga in higher education. In *Managing change in educational organizations*, edited by J. V. Baldridge and T. E. Deal. Berkeley, Calif.: McCutchan.

Cohen, M. (1982). Effective principals. *School administrator*, November, 1982, pp. 14–16.

Cohen, M., and March J. (1974). *Leadership and ambiguity*, McGraw-Hill.

Deal, T.E . (1985). The symbolism of effective schools. *Elementary School Journal 85*(5), 601–20.

Deal, T. E., and Kennedy, A. (1982). *Corporate cultures*. Reading, Mass.: Addison-Wesley.

Deal, T. E.; Meyer, J.; Scott, W.; Rowan, B. (1983). *Organization environment: Ritual and rationality*. Beverly Hills, Calif.: Sage Publications.

Little, J. W. (1982). Norms of collegiality and experimentation: Workplace conditions of school success. *American Educational Research Journal*, *19*, 325–40.

March, J. (1980). How we talk and how we act. Unpublished manuscript, Stanford University.

Meyer, J., and Rowan, B. (1977). Institutional organizations: Formal structure as myth and ceremony. *American Journal of Sociology*, *3*, 440–63.

Mintzberg, H. (1973). *The nature of managerial work*. New York: Harper & Row.

Peterson, K. D. (1977–78). The principal's tasks. *Administrator's Notebook*, 1977–78.

Peterson, K. D. (1984). Mechanisms of administrative control over managers in educational organizations. *Administrative Science Quarterly*, *29*, 573–597.

Peterson, K. D., and Wimpleberg, R. (1983). Dual imperatives of principals' work. Paper presented at the meeting of the American Educational Research Association, Montreal.

Sarason, S. (1971). *The culture of the school and the problems of change.* Boston: Allyn and Bacon.

Spady, W. G. (1974). The authority system of the school and student unrest: A theoretical exploration. In *Uses of the sociology of education,* edited by W. W. Gordon, pp. 36–77. Chicago: National Society for the Study of Education.

Weick, K. (1976). Educational organizations as loosely coupled systems. *Administrative Science Quarterly, 21,* 1–19.

PART FOUR

Professional Development Practices and Policies

School teachers and administrators are the most important resources available to schools, and efforts to reform and improve education ultimately depend on the quality of the day-to-day job performances of education professionals. Without these individuals we do not have schools as we know them, and we cannot have effective schools unless they are staffed with persons capable of delivering the necessary level of performance. Professional development practices and policies thus constitute an important vehicle for making schools, and school leaders and teachers, more effective. Instructional leaders will face major staffing challenges in the years ahead, and as the pool of well-qualified teachers declines, it will become increasingly important to retain and develop those who do enter the occupation of teaching. The quality of school leadership is largely dependent upon the quality of the teaching work force. Most, if not all, school leaders begin their careers as teachers.

The changing character of the work force in education and increasing pressures to improve schools present school leaders with enormous personnel management and development challenges. Part Four opens with a provocative discussion by Roland Barth of the importance of teachers, and he calls for instructional leaders to tap teachers as key resources for professional development and school renewal. He describes the various ways in which teachers can contribute to efforts to improve schools, discusses how school principals can foster their own development through their efforts to develop teachers, and closes with a description of the Harvard Principals' Center and its successes as a forum for leadership development. Chapter Fourteen, by Bruce Barnett, offers a description of a specific leadership development strategy designed to capitalize on the potential that school leaders have to work together to become more effective. He suggests that school principals can help themselves and one another become more effective by developing their capacity to become more reflective about their practice. In Chapter Fifteen Diana Pounder discusses implications of

247

the growing shortage of teachers for school leaders, suggesting that the nature of the work of teachers and the working conditions in schools represent critical but virtually unexplored points of leverage for instructional improvement. Her discussion concludes with recommendations regarding how school principals can work with teachers to create conditions that make schools more attractive, satisfying, and productive work places for students and teachers.

Chapter Sixteen, by Chad Ellett, includes a description of two large-scale teacher performance assessment systems. He discusses how these practices were developed and implemented by two states and explores the implications of those systems for the instructional supervision role of school principals. The chapter concludes with a discussion of prevailing clincial supervision practices, suggesting that emergent teacher assessment practices will increase the capability of school principals to serve as instructional supervisors. Part Four concludes with a call for more effective in-service training and development for school leaders. John Daresh argues the importance of professional development and its relationship to leader effectiveness and offers numerous examples of how in-service practices can be improved. The chapter includes a succinct statement of criteria related to effective in-service and concludes with recommendations regarding what school leaders can do to facilitate the development of good programs.

The educational work force will experience dramatic changes in the years ahead, and school districts will find it increasingly difficult to attract and retain good teachers and administrators. These trends, combined with pressures for schools to be more effective, will present school leaders with major personnel management and development challenges. In order to cope effectively with these difficulties it will be necessary for educational policymakers and school administrators to consider major reforms of the working conditions in schools, professional development and evaluation policies, and personnel management practices in general.

13

The Principal
and the Profession
of Teaching[1]

ROLAND S. BARTH

Teaching other people's children has become an extraordinarily difficult occupation, made no easier by "other people" who hold little
confidence in what teachers do and who pare away the resources with
which they are expected to do it.

Teachers are dejected. A recent NEA study revealed that 42 percent
would not enter the profession again. A survey of the faculty of one
respected high school in the Boston area suggested why: teachers report
a sense of discontent and malaise; they feel unappreciated, overworked,
and demeaned as professionals. They feel little trust for or from the
administration and the public. They even feel alienated from one another. They feel trapped in their jobs, powerless to effect change, and
frustrated at the never-ending nonteaching demands.

Increasingly, schools are staffed with veteran, tenured teachers
with little horizontal or vertical mobility. For most there is little to
do next September except when they did last September, a formula for
personal and professional atrophy. Teachers are encountering times
more difficult than at any period in American education. The social
value of their work, which has fueled them through past difficulties,
no longer provides sufficient compensation and professional
invigoration.

Theodore Sizer has observed that prior to 1960 a position in public education was a "calling." The sixties and seventies was a period when education became more of a profession. In the 1980s, says Sizer, it has become a job. As a calling or a profession, education offers much to teachers and their students; as a job it offers little. Fortunately the crisis in teaching—attracting capable men and women into the classrooms, retaining them, and sustaining and replenishing them in their important work—has become an issue of national importance. At the root is the question, "Under what conditions can teaching in American public schools become less of a job and more of a profession?" Several remedies are proposed: improve all teacher salaries; compensate the best through merit pay; construct career ladders that will pay those who assume more responsibility; support the training of the best and the brightest so they will choose to enter teaching; make teacher evaluation more rigorous; and tighten teacher certification requirements.

Although these proposals promise much, all are outside-of-school remedies to inside-of-school problems. Therefore, they offer little hope of influencing the basic culture of the schools. And it is in the ethos of the workplace that the problem resides and where, I believe, the more promising solutions reside as well. The moment of truth for the teaching profession comes when the alarm rings at 6:30 a.m. How does the teacher respond? Higher salaries, career ladders, and certification requirements will have little influence upon the reaction of the waking teacher. Yet it is the level of satisfaction that teachers experience in their daily work life that, more than anything else, defines their level of professionalism.

Four years of public school teaching in Massachusetts and California and ten years as principal in urban New Haven and suburban Newton and Brookline, convince me that the nature of the relationships among the adults who inhabit a school has more to do with a school's quality and character, with the accomplishments of its pupils and the professionalism of its teachers, than any other factor. The success of a school depends upon interactions between teacher and teacher, teacher and administrator, and all school people and parents. And I am convinced that the school principal is in the best position to influence these relationships and thereby the profession of teaching. It is in support of these beliefs and in an attempt to address the question, "How can changes in the relationship among teachers and principal lead to the professionalization of teaching?" that this chapter is directed.

COLLEGIALITY

Relationships among adults in most schools are primitive, affording administrator and teacher little satisfaction or assistance. Sociologist

Dan Lortie found that in the eyes of most teachers learning, success, and satisfaction come largely from students within their classrooms and that "... all other persons (parents, the principal, other teachers) without exception were connected with undesirable occurrences. Other adults have potential for hindrance but not help." This condition of adult alienation must be redressed if teaching is to become satisfying.

Adult relationships in schools—all schools, from preschools to graduate schools—take several forms. One of them is described by a wonderful term from nursery-school parlance, "parallel play." Two three-year-olds are busily engaged in opposite corners of a sandbox. One has a shovel and bucket; one has a rake and hoe. At no time do they borrow each other's toys. Although in close proximity, and having much to offer each other, each works and plays pretty much in isolation. This description serves remarkably well as a characterization of adult relationships in schools.

But, of course, not all adult relationships in schools are independent. I observe three different forms of interaction:

Adversarial Relationships.   Recently a Boston-area principal made a sage observation: "You know, we educators have drawn our wagons into a circle and trained our guns—on each other." When adults in school interact, all too often we attack one another. It may be that adversarial relationships among adults in school make "parallel play" a welcome alternative.

Competitive Relationships.   Typically, competition takes the form of withholding. Most school people carry around extraordinary insights about their important work, hard-won insights as valuable as elegant research studies and national reports, but adults in schools have a strong reluctance to make them available to competitors for scarce resources and recognition.

Collegial Relationships.   The least-common form of relationship among adults in schools is one that is collegial, cooperative, and interdependent. Collegiality is not the same as congeniality.

Enormous risks and costs are associated with observing, communicating, sharing knowledge, and talking openly about the work we do. Yet somehow most good schools are ones where parallel play and adversarial and competitive relationships among adults have been transformed into cooperative, collegial ones.

In my own experience as principal I found ways to counter the taboo that exists in schools against collegiality. We decided to hold each faculty meeting in the classroom of a different teacher. During the first twenty minutes host teachers told us what they did in their rooms, something about the curriculum, grouping practices, and special characteristics of the class. While initially these parts of the meetings were tense, the faculty grew more comfortable as both presenters and receivers. This rather contrived activity "primed the pump" and legitimized talk about instruction.

Students were placed with teachers each spring on the basis of two considerations: Under what instructional conditions does each child in a class seem to work best? Which of next year's teachers comes closest to providing those conditions? In order to answer these questions teachers had to observe carefully each student in the class. And they had to learn something beyond faculty-room gossip about how their colleagues taught. Each "sending" teacher spent a half day during the winter observing the classroom of each "receiving" teacher. After each visit the two teachers had lunch together. This process, of course, violated the taboo against one teacher invading the sanctuary of another's classroom. But it led to fruitful and ongoing conversations, about how teacher A might handle a unique problem of student B.

It has long been my belief that the optimal number of adults working together for children is two. One teacher in a self-contained classroom gets pretty lonely and depleted. Large teams, on the other hand, spend too much time and energy in meetings, trying to achieve consensus. Teachers working in teams provide a built-in support system, an adult with whom each can talk about teaching, learning, and students. In short, teachers who work together enjoy a professional collegial relationship.

MAKING IMPORTANT DECISIONS

A second building block of teacher professionalism, one over which principals also have particular influence, is allowing and encouraging teachers to make judgments about important elements of their work. Teachers, of course, make thousands of decisions each day, but exclusion from the most critical choices about teaching leads to a pervasive feeling of inefficacy which erodes the profession. Let me give a few illustrations of decisions to which teachers can be a party and often "own."

The Decision to Be There. A good school is one where each adult has deliberately chosen to be. All too many teachers feel that school is as compulsory for them as for their students. Teachers need periodic opportunities to commit and recommit to their work, otherwise the profession becomes a job.

A request by any teacher for a leave of absence for any purpose should be granted. The teacher is requesting an opportunity to stop, reflect, replenish, and consider other options. If the teacher returns to the school, everyone wins—the teacher, students, school. If the teacher decides to leave, everyone wins. Sabbaticals would be preferable, but automatic availability of leaves of absence without pay can also help relieve the trapped feeling so prevalent in teaching. Teachers become professional to the extent that they make a genuine commitment to be there.

The Decision about What Teachers Do in the School.   As a principal, each year, after teachers had recommitted to employment, I met with each staff member and asked, "If you could decide under ideal conditions what you would like to do next year and with whom, what would it be?" I provided one boundary condition: "You must work in the school in some way with children." In short, I invited teachers to disregard all practical constraints for a few moments and reflect upon their work as educators, consider current interests, ideas, skills, and relationships, and engage in some "if only . . ." brainstorming. My objective was for all of us to come to school each September with at least one significant new element in our professional and personal lives— something to dream about, think about, worry about, get excited about, be afraid about, become and remain *alive* about.

Many teachers expressed the wish to do "the same thing" next year. But more teachers came ready to dream. A teacher aide wants to become a librarian; a teacher wants to become a principal; two teachers want to work together. It came as a surprise to us how closely we were able to comply with most of these "fantasies." The results suggest that following the best interests of teachers is often in the best interest of their students and the school.

Decisions about Spending Money.   Money is a symbol. It is also an antidote to a feeling of inefficacy. A little money is a large antidote. Each year our school was allocated about $45 per child for all instructional purposes. As principal I chose to divide the pie into twenty-five pieces by allocating a "fair share" to each teacher—$400 a year. How this money was spent was up to each individual. It could go for texts, games, food, teacher courses, field trips, or testing materials.

Many things happened. Book salespeople had to convince teachers that a product was helpful to teachers and valuable for children. Each of three fourth-grade teachers contributed $13 toward a box of geoblocks, and their students used the blocks as often as they might have had the blocks "belonged" to one class. Important decisions about teaching materials thus rested in the hands of those most qualified to make them. Teachers talked with each other about what the children were doing, even came into each other's rooms to observe, and occasionally grouped their classes together for activities with the blocks.

Now $400 isn't very much, but it's $400 more than many teachers ever see. It's meaningless to give people responsibility without giving them the resources to exercise that responsibility. In that sense, the money is almost as important as a symbol as it is for what the teachers can do with it. It's a vote of confidence. What teachers do with limited funds is what most people do with their budgets: they become very responsible and resourceful; they feel empowered.

Decisions about Curriculum. Public elementary and secondary teachers have minimal control over curriculum, but they can have more. Again, the school principal can be part of either the problem or solution for teachers. Each June I asked teachers to prepare curriculum outlines that revealed what they expected to teach. The outlines might reflect a little or a lot of the system's guidelines but above all were to be "honest." This practice shifted the teacher's role. Teachers were expected to be actively creative rather than passively compliant. While exposing themselves in this way caused both labor and risks, most teachers gladly accepted the accountability because with the costs came a large measure of control over classroom instruction.

Unlike the system's guidelines, the teachers' never meshed neatly with one another. Their curriculum outlines didn't form anything resembling a coherent blueprint for the elementary years suitable for solemn presentation at a PTA meeting. So each year we selected a different subject, science for instance, and collated each teacher's plans for the year. A huge poster in the faculty room revealed what each teacher was doing in science—and revealed some startling omissions and redundancies. Why was everyone growing bean seeds? Questions emerged. Teachers had to talk with one another, establish some priorities, and make some decisions. The curriculum began to be "articulated" because the teachers became expressive.

The biggest problem besetting schools is the primitive quality of human relationships among children, parents, teachers, and administrators. Many schools perpetuate infantilism. School boards infantilize superintendents; superintendents, principals; principals, teachers; and teachers, children. This leads to children and adults who frequently behave like infants, complying with authority out of fear or dependence, waiting until someone's back is turned to do something "naughty." To the extent teachers become responsible for their own teaching, they not only help children become responsible for their own learning, but they become professional.

SCHOOLWIDE RESPONSIBILITIES

The model of the single individual who unilaterally "runs" a school no longer works very well. Problems are frequently too big and too numerous for any one person to address alone. Schools need to recognize and develop many kinds of leadership among many people to replace the venerable, patriarchal model.

School leadership can come from principals who transform adversaries into colleagues; from teachers, who individually or collectively take responsibility for the well-being of the school; and from parents who translate a basic concern for their children into constructive actions. School leadership, then, can be considered not only in terms of roles but also in terms of functions. Teachers, principals, and parents need skills, insight, and vision that will equip them to assume responsibility for their schools.

Principals can recognize capable teachers not as competitors but as future principals, and help them develop skills that will lead to the principalship. Principals need to find ways to share with teachers as much responsibility as both are able to handle. Principals often find it difficult to delegate. But one person cannot do it all, and certainly not all well. If the principal tries, that leaves teachers uninvolved in important pieces of school life, unprepared when a principalship opens up in the next town, and not feeling very professional.

As principal I enlisted committees of teachers to be fully responsible for decisions over matters such as schedules, budgets, staff development, and, yes, fire drills. Teacher "coordinators" were appointed in each subject to mediate between the central office and the faculty while coordinating curriculum within the school.

Involving teachers as committee members and coordinators had many ripple effects. These formal responsibilities encouraged teachers to relate directly and frequently with one another over conflict-laden issues. Teachers learned that assuming responsibility for school problems frequently meant assuming responsibility for one another's problems. The title of "coordinator" made it not only legitimate and appropriate but expected that teachers help one another. And both committees and coordinators frequently determined acceptable behavior for teachers. When teachers have legitimate authority, sanctioned by the principal and faculty, they find the courage to make demands on their colleagues in one instance and to comply with their colleagues' demands on them in another.

Nonteaching responsibilities, then, can enable members of the school community to contribute their strengths and share the power, the satisfaction—and the price—of influence. This exchange contributes to the professionalism of teachers.

TEACHER AS VISIONARY

I can think of nothing so badly missing in the teaching profession as the engagement of teachers in contemplating what schools should be, what children should learn, and what teaching might become. Schools badly need inhabitants who ask "why?" Philosophers. This important function—questioning the way things are—is now filled by six- and seven-year-olds. Why are there twenty-five students in a class? Why are the upper grades upstairs and the lower grades downstairs? Why do teachers talk 95 percent of the time while 95 percent of the persons in a classroom talk only 5 percent of the time? Why indeed? We need to devise a mechanism in schools for adults constantly to consider embedded ways of doing things. And above all, we need to juxtapose the way things are with school people's visions of how they might become.

I know of no teacher, principal, counselor, or department head who does not have a sense of the kind of classroom or school he or she would like to see. Many have well-developed visions of the kinds of places in which they would like to have their own children study or in which they themselves would like to work.

All of us who entered teaching brought with us a conception of a desirable school. Each carried a valued personal vision and was prepared to work, even fight, for it. Over time our personal expectations became blurred by the visions, demands, and requirements of others. For many teachers, personal visions are now all but obliterated by external pre-scriptions. Recently I talked with a group of principals and one observed, "Its gotten so that what's me is hard to figure out." We have become so habituated to reflecting back the visions of others that what is us is hard to discern. As a principal I remember succumbing to what I called "PTA rhetoric," using words like "discipline," "rigor," "work," "basics," "respect." Good words, hard words, but none of them part of the vocabulary of my personal vision. In short, I found myself, as most other teachers and principals do, becoming obsessively practical while becoming less of a professional.

Why honor the visions of school people? I believe there are several reasons: massive research studies stand little chance of having a major and direct influence on the schools. In the loosely coupled world of the schools, adults usually act on their own conceptions of quality and rarely on the ideal of someone else. One reason to honor the visions of school people, then, is that these are the only prescriptions for school reform that have a prayer of being taken seriously and sustained.

There is a second reason. Most large-scale research studies are, by nature, a mile wide by only an inch deep. The researchers pay brief visits to many schools, with all the effect of a teabag swished through a bathtub. The visions of school people, by contrast, stem from many years' experience in only a few school settings. These experiences may be only an inch wide, but they are a mile deep. These rich insights, hammered out of years of practice, give credibility to the visions school people hold about good education. Strong tea, indeed.

A third reason I feel it essential to elicit and honor the conceptions that school people have about reforming their schools is that, as I vividly recall, the excitement of working in schools, the kicks, the satisfactions, the rewards come from studying a difficult situation and then generating one's own plan for improving things. Why should educators be placed—or place themselves—in the position of implementing the grand ideas of others, ideas with which they seldom agree? The greatest tragedy I know is to be caught every day in the position of doing something we don't want to do or don't believe in. Too many educators are playing out this tragedy—functioning as assembly-line robots whose main business is production, not learning. This condition, above everything else, diminishes professionalism in the public schools.

It's astonishing that the voices of teachers and principals are not more audible in the current discussions and debates about school improvement. Those who work in schools can no longer have it both ways, dismissing the many conceptions of quality education that currently bombard them from outside but still refusing to push forward their own visions or goals and approaches for achieving them. If teachers and principals don't want to be the dependent variable in attempts to improve the schools, they will have to become the independent variable.

How to encourage teachers to consider continuously, reflect upon, develop, and articulate their visions about how their classrooms and school might become better is a formidable job and right at the heart of what it means to be a professional. Principals have been successful in creating schools of vision-makers by becoming more conscious of their own visions, articulating them, and thereby modeling vision-making.

THE TEACHER AS LEARNER

A good school ought to be a community of learners, a place where children are discovering the joy, the difficulty, the excitement of learning, and adults are rediscovering the same. Learning is lifelong. It is not, as one teacher observed "something like chicken pox—a childhood disease that makes you itch for a while, then leaves you immune for the rest of your life."

Those who value public education should be worried about the stunted growth of teachers. Probably nothing within school has more impact upon students in terms of skills development, self-confidence, or classroom behavior. When teachers examine, question, reflect on their ideas and develop new practices that lead toward their ideals, students are alive. When teachers stop growing, so do their students. Yet the professional development of individual teachers is more than a means toward the end of delivering services to students. It should also be an end in itself. Learning enables the learner.

Most school districts operate from a "deficiency" model of adult growth. Certain skills—writing behavioral objectives, employing a new language arts program—are deemed by the central administration essential for teachers to master. Most teachers don't have the requisite skills, so after-school or release-day workshops are mandated to remedy the weakness. Staff development has thus taken the form of workshops done to someone by someone else, as in the phrase, "to in-service teachers." When a school or school system deliberately sets out to foster new skills by committing everyone to required workshops, little usually happens except that everyone feels virtuous about having gone through the motions.

School-based staff development tends to be more effective. I am convinced that greater opportunities reside under the schoolhouse roof and that a powerful force in assisting teacher growth can be the school principal. Although it's clear that a principal may have little effect, no effect, or even a negative effect upon teacher growth, it's far less clear that a principal can have a positive effect. While there seems to be widespread agreement about the potential for principals' contributions to teachers' growth, a major reason for the recent proliferation of a new educational cadre called "staff developers" is that school principals have failed to realize their enormous potential as staff developers.

There are good reasons, of course. Is it reasonable to expect the principal, the person with the capacity to terminate the professional life of teachers, to be charged with promoting professional life? The culture of schools does cruel things to teachers and to principals and their relationships. Most people I know who are beginning principals enter their new roles as advocates, friends, helpers, supporters, often former colleagues of teachers. By December of their first year they have become adversaries, requirers, forcers, judges, and setters of limits.

As an elementary school administrator in three schools, I vigorously attempted to promote the personal and professional development of teachers. I encountered many brick walls. Sometimes I was able to go around, over, under, or even through them. Equally often I bloodied my nose against them. When I began as a principal I used to think that successful staff development had occurred if teachers did what I expected them to do—follow the curriculum outlines, arrive on time, and write careful pupil evaluations. But soon I became dissatisfied with this definition and altered my conception of effective staff development to "do what I expect you to do and do it well." I expected teachers not only to teach about the Navajos but to build hogans with children, to learn Navajo dances, and to write poems about the Indians.

Still many teachers didn't seem to care. So my concept of staff development subsequently extended to something like "Do what is expected of you, do it well, and love it!" I was finding, of course, that while teachers might well follow the guidelines, they did so with all the eagerness of a child confronting a plate of spinach. I then became intent upon finding conditions over which I had control that would make it likely teachers would conform to my expanded definition. More frustration. Only recently have I begun to realize that I was engaging not in staff development but in promoting institutional compliance, not in the personal and professional growth of teachers but in, at best, "in-service training."

To be sure, it is important if an organization as complex as a school is to survive that members conform to certain expectations and norms such as teaching literacy skills and coming to school on time. But to make these norms the sole content for adult growth is to prescribe a pretty undernourished diet.

Staff development for me has come to take on quite a different meaning. It is listening in a hundred different ways for a question to emanate from teachers, usually in the form, "Here's what I want to try." And staff development means being ready to supply assistance or encouragement in a hundred different ways. I have become conscious of a taxonomy in responding to teachers:

not listening
listening
listening and hearing
listening, hearing, encouraging, and valuing the
 teachers' initiative
listening, hearing, encouraging, valuing the request,
 and agreeing to share the risks and consequences.

Any initiative emanating from a teacher, whether a request to buy 1,000 tongue depressors or to deviate from the prescribed curriculum in order to build a new one based upon last summer's trip to Alaska, carries with it powerful potential for professional growth. The way to insure that a teacher becomes a deeply engrossed student is to allow and encourage the teacher to identify the problem to be addressed. The source of the problem for adults, as for students, determines the energy and motivation that will be expended upon resolving the problem. Some call it "ownership."

Everything a principal does has potential for staff development. Through a huge number of small, daily decisions and interactions, the principal, teachers, and pupils live and work. The so-called management functions of principals—student discipline, budgets, scheduling—are the occasion, the opportunity, the stage for the principal to exercise creative instructional leadership.

Teacher as Mentor

"The knowledge base for improving schools resides in universities; practice resides in schools." I find this common conception inaccurate, simplistic, and disturbing. I know of no schoolteacher or principal who works without some organizing principle or framework—or, in university language, a theory. Theories about teaching, parent involvement, curriculum improvement, and motivation *abound* in schools.

The knowledge base for school improvement is fed by *two* tributaries—research from the academic community and craft knowledge from teachers and principals. One reason for teachers to be providers of information as well as consumers is that their craft knowledge can contribute to the betterment of schools.

A second reason for teachers to convey to other adults what they know is that by so doing they derive enormous professional satisfaction and recognition. Despite the good rhetoric about the importance of school teachers offered in recent state and national reform proposals, few teachers *feel* valued or recognized in their work. That's hardly what PTAs, superintendents, school boards, and principals convey to teachers each day. Yet, of all the pressing needs of public school practitioners, none is more vital than the need for personal and professional recognition from a society that values the product of education far more than those committed to providing it.

For teaching to become a profession, teachers must feel professionally recognized. Recognition for teachers can come from inviting them to share their craft knowledge with colleagues, from empowering them with major decisions, and from enabling teachers to become mentors to others who would like to become capable at the craft of teaching.

How can a teacher working full time in the classroom assume responsibility as colleague and mentor to other practicing teachers as well as prospective teachers? Once again, I find the principal occupies a central position.

Principals successful in unlocking the vast talents of their teachers seem to hold several assumptions: every teacher possesses strengths and insights of value to others; we should rely as much upon the strengths of public educators as upon universities and outside resources; and teachers have a great capacity to stimulate professional growth and effective practice in their colleagues. A major opportunity for the principal is to devise ways to reveal this abundance of thinking and practice so it can be more widely available to improve the school and improve teaching.

At one school where I was principal we had a contract with Brandeis University to cooperate in their undergraduate teacher-certification program. About a dozen students were placed with as many of our teachers. In addition, the teachers ran what we called "Brandeis seminars" which helped the student teachers learn instructional methodology. Each year a committee of teachers, paid by Brandeis, led these seminars. They, in turn, engaged a considerable portion of their fellow teachers as faculty for the seminars. Topics included "discipline," "observing children," "record keeping," "curriculum," and "getting a teaching job." Teachers also assisted others through the Greater Boston Teacher Center, which offered faculty-led workshops and courses.

In both of these activities teachers were paid to share their knowledge with prospective or practicing teachers. This opportunity and remuneration for it conveyed several important messages: "We are aware of the many good things you are doing; we value these things; we feel others would benefit from knowing what you are thinking and doing; we feel strongly enough about this and value your expertise enough so that we will convene the other teachers and pay you." These messages, so seldom communicated, affirm importance, dignity, and professionalism. When teachers receive this kind of recognition, they go to extraordinary lengths to justify it. They reflect on their practice, translating intuitive and unconscious behavior into more conscious, deliberate, visible information that can be useful to others. And of course, this process feeds back into extraordinary learning and classroom improvement for the teachers themselves. There is no more sophisticated form of staff development.

The issue then is not whether school people know much of value to others but, rather, under what conditions they will reveal their rich craft knowledge so that it may become part of the discussion to improve schools. Recognition is the commodity in least supply to teachers these days and the process of being helpful to others is a powerful way of conveying recognition to others as well as to oneself.

TEACHERS AND QUALITY CONTROL

Nothing kills the morale and sense of professionalism of good teachers more than bad teachers. And nothing infuriates good teachers more than no one doing anything about it. Responsibility for monitoring, evaluating, and dismissing incompetent teachers rests chiefly with the school principal who can establish high expectations for performance and insure that all move toward them.

As principal, I told teachers that there was room under the roof for everyone. I explained that in questions of goals neither parents nor teachers could make unilateral decisions. Teachers couldn't decide to omit teaching reading simply because they believe that children would learn to read. However, in questions of means—for example, how you teach reading, how you teach math—the responsibility was with the teacher, not the parents, not the principal, not the kids, and not the central office. I set two conditions. The first was that they could teach subject matter in any way they thought best providing they accepted and respected the way the teacher across the hall was doing it. The second condition was that, at least twice a year, I expected the teachers to convey to me, to one another, and to the parents that, as a result of teaching the subject in their particular way, good things were happening to children in that subject area.

Like most school principals I also engaged in the formal evaluation of teachers, required each year by the school committee. There were several familiar components. First, I observed in the teacher's classroom two or three times during the fall. Before each visit, the teacher and I shared ideas and, after the observation, more ideas. Then we each filled out the official form, commenting on work in the different subject areas and on relationships with parents, other teachers, and children. After that, we brought the two sets of forms, reflecting our perceptions, to another conference. I was always particularly interested in differences in our perceptions. When I identified difficulties, I almost always found teachers well aware of them. The last step was to incorporate both sets of observations into a final report, which went to the personnel office with a recommendation for reappointment.

Part of my own vision of teacher professionalism is that teachers accept responsibility for the performance of their colleagues. I would like to see the day when teachers, in effect, police themselves by maintaining standards of performance for their own work and that of their peers. Teaming teachers and visits to one another's classrooms are examples of moves in the right direction. We are a long way from the day when teachers maintain standards for themselves. Yet nothing better marks the coming of professionalism to teaching than the willingness and ability of teachers to monitor the performance of their colleagues.

THE PROFESSIONAL DEVELOPMENT OF PRINCIPALS

I have argued that the principal of a school occupies a position of central influence over the professionalization of teaching. Transforming relationships by developing collegiality, engaging teachers in important decisions affecting their classrooms and school, developing personal visions, becoming active adult learners, serving as mentors to other teachers and prospective teachers, and maintaining quality in their own and others' performances, are all ways principals can make good use of their extraordinary influence. Each of these characteristics contributes to the profession of teaching; collectively they define a school culture of professionalism.

The role of the principal in professionalizing teaching suggested here is, of course, not a common one. Many principals attempt to exercise an authoritarian, hierarchical kind of leadership: they arrange schedules that mandate who is supposed to be where and doing what; they maintain tight personal control over money, supplies, and behavior; and they dictate curriculum, goals, and means. An inevitable consequence of this patriarchal model of leadership—aside from a certain amount of order, productivity, and consonance—is the creation of a dependent relationship between principal and teacher. Teachers learn not to move without orders. This dependency training immobilizes teacher and principal when they both need maximum flexibility and imagination.

Principals, like college presidents these days, are effective less as charismatic authority figures than as successful coalition builders. Increasing specialization of teachers, for instance, signals that the principal can no longer be the master teacher well versed in instructing handicapped children, students who are gifted and talented, beginning reading, and advanced math.

In order not only to survive but flourish, principals must learn to share problems without worrying about appearing inadequate, to feel that adult learning is legitimate, and to become more secure about their visions, values, ideas, and practices so that they can act consistently and confidently. And all this learning requires support systems within the school, from other principals, from the central office, and from outside the system.

I have been actively engaged for the past several years in the professional invigoration of the nation's principals. For all the agreement about their importance, surprisingly little is known about their professional development.

Professional development for principals has been described by an official of one of the national principals' associations as "a wasteland." Principals take assorted courses at universities. They attend episodic in-service activities and they struggle to elevate professional literature to the top of the sedimentary pile of papers on their desks. Staff development for principals designed by state departments, large school systems, and universities is more coherent. Many of these activities stem from a common set of assumptions and draw upon a common logic:

a. find schools where pupils are achieving beyond what might be predicted by their backgrounds;
b. observe principals in those schools and find out what they are doing;
c. identify these behaviors as "desirable traits";
d. devise training programs to develop these traits in all principals;

e. enlist principals into these programs;
f. to the extent these principals successfully acquire these traits,
    students in their schools will also come to achieve at a level
    beyond what might be predicted by their social class, race, and
    family background.

I find this model simple, straightforward, compelling, and logical.
Its only major flaw is that it doesn't seem to work very well. I suspect
there may be several reasons. The assumption that "strong leadership"
is whatever results in high student test scores suggests a very limited,
and I think demeaning, view of both students and principals. Good
education is more than good scores, and good leadership is more than
generating good scores. And conditions in one school are seldom similar to those in another. To treat "schools" as a generic class is easier
said than done. A third reason is that people who run things, as principals run schools, don't want to be themselves run—especially badly.
Principals have built up antibodies to attempts by others to remediate
them. And finally, even if principals have been successfully trained by
means of these staff development activities, without sustained feedback and skillful coaching, little comes of it. The linkages from principal behavior in a workshop setting to principal behavior in a school
to teacher behavior to student learning are convoluted, and tenuous
indeed.

In our work at the Principals' Center it is becoming clearer just
why it is so difficult for school leaders to become learners. One difficulty is, of course, "I don't have time." For principals, like all of us,
this is another way of saying other things are more important and
perhaps more comfortable.

A second impediment is principals' experience as learners. Few
come to professional development activities without baggage from the
past. District in-service and university course work, for instance, have
left principals turned off. Principals resist new learning opportunities
because they have been there before and found what's there wanting.
Third, for a principal to be a learner is immoral. The purpose of schools
is to promote *student* learning. Taking $100 from the school budget
to join the Principals' Center is tantamount to snatching bread from
the mouths of babes. Think of what the school could do with $100—
teacher aides, books, magic markers. And think of what could be done
at school during those two hours of workshop. Principals are public
servants whose place is to serve, not be served—an all-too-embedded
belief in the school culture.

Another obstacle to the principal becoming a learner is that by
publicly engaging in learning, principals reveal themselves as flawed.
The world out there expects principals to know how to do it.

It is also *inappropriate* for the principal to be a learner. Learning always begins one rung on the ladder below the teacher. The moral order of the school universe places the principal in authority as knower. Principal as learner is out of place.

Finally, if principals engage in a learning experience and learn something—a new way of thinking about curriculum, a new interpersonal skill, a new idea about improving school climate—they are then faced with having to do something with it. Principals are rewarded for learning by additional work. It seems to be one of the paradoxes of professional development that it can be both energy and time depleting and energy and time replenishing.

These impediments suggest just how difficult it is for the leader to become learner. Yet, I am convinced that being a learner, a lifelong adult learner, is the most important characteristic of a school leader and of a professional. Learning is not just another on the long list of critical characteristics. The leader as learner belongs at the top of the list. Many of the characteristics, the skills most of us recognize as important for effective principals, are *learned* skills. A principal can learn how to monitor performance of pupils, to convey high expectations to teachers and pupils, and to professionalize teaching.

Learning is replenishing. We deplore teachers who do more of the same next September as they did this September and last September. I think it equally unfortunate for the principal. After several years principals tend to switch onto "automatic pilot" in PTA meetings, teacher evaluation sessions, and parent conferences—a sign of clinical death. Not only do teacher and student suffer, the principal suffers. Learning is an antidote to routinization.

And the leader as learner is critical because there is a striking connection between learning and collegiality. The most powerful form of learning comes not from listening to the good words of others but from sharing what we know with others. Learning comes more from giving than from receiving. Every principal I know is darn good at something. By reflecting on what we do, giving it coherence, and by sharing and articulating our craft knowledge, we make meaning; we learn. The best way, perhaps the only way, schools are going to improve is by school people learning from and helping other school people.

I find the most powerful reason for principals to be learners as well as leaders comes from the extraordinary influence of modeling behavior. In many schools the more important you are, the further you are removed from learning. But when the leader is learner, when the principal's learning is continuous, sustained, visible, and exciting, a crucial and very different message is telegraphed to the community: "this school is a community of learners; learning is its most important characteristic; the principal is a first-class citizen of the community of learners, the *head* learner."

THE HARVARD PRINCIPALS' CENTER

Given the importance of the principalship, what is the Harvard Principals' Center doing? A major proposition underlies our efforts. *Principals will be seriously involved in all aspects of their professional development.* It is our belief that the critical element in principals' learning, indeed, in anyone's learning, is ownership.

The idea of principals' serious involvement in their own development is deceptive. It does not appear to be particularly noteworthy or fruitful. But we are finding that the consequences of taking this proposition seriously and acting upon it is leading to some noteworthy conversations and fruitful results.

Our conviction that a principals' center must be principal-centered led to enlisting twenty-eight Boston-area principals as architects, designers, and engineers of the center. After a half year of meetings, discussions, and deliberations this group came up with several building blocks for the center, each of which to this day is surprisingly in place, attached to the cornerstone of principals' involvement and ownership.

There are no more important decisions affecting principals' staff development than those determining the content and format of activities. Principals care about narrowing the discrepancy between what they are doing and what they want to be able to do. A governance structure of an Advisory Board chaired by a principal joined by eighteen other Boston-area principals and four Harvard faculty ensures that the major voice about program will be the principals'. These discussions follow a pattern: brainstorm about issues, themes, problems about which principals want to know more (e.g., "new technologies," "dealing with diversity"); sharpen up questions for each theme (e.g., "How can a new Apple II be used both as a management tool and an instructional tool within an elementary school?", "How can the principal come to see and use differences of age, gender, race, and ability within a school as an opportunity for school improvement rather than as a problem to be avoided?"); then the Board grapples with the question, "Who knows what about these questions?" and begins to identify consultants, university professors, and principals as possible resources. Then members form groups to develop the idea, select resource persons, and devise formats. Finally, a staff member of the center, often a doctoral student interested in the principalship, takes the plan and invites speakers, secures a room, supplies wine and cheese, evaluates the sessions, and thanks the presenter.

Many observers questioned the wisdom of turning responsibility for the principals' program over to principals, fearing that their decisions, like those made by high schoolers in an "open campus" might be frivolous, irresponsible, and self-interested. This tension took the form of a question, "Will the Principals' Center offer what principals want or what principals need?"

Principals, on the other hand, with a long history as recipients of others' prescriptions, were suspicious that the center would be a disguised attempt by Harvard to "in-service" them. More of the logical model under Crimson wraps. Over time, suspicions abated as principals demonstrated rigor and inventiveness in planning programs for their colleagues and as others became caught up in their enthusiasm and in the rationale behind their judgments.

Principals, then, have had serious involvement in planning the center and developing the program. Each also makes the critical decision about whether to become a *resource* for other principals. We have engaged in a long and difficult struggle against fear on the part of both presenting and listening principals that when principals talk they will reveal not craft knowledge but war stories. But more and more principals are acknowledging the importance of what they know and finding ways of making it available to others. Observing colleagues successfully leading groups and making presentations encourages others to follow.

Each principal decides whether to become a member for a year and in which of sixty or seventy events to take part. By placing the decision for participation squarely upon each principal's shoulders, indeed, by making it difficult through costs of time and dollars, we find that those who participate want to participate. Activities are, therefore, refreshingly professional and free of back-row cynics. With the choice to attend comes an openness to learn.

By the end of the first year the Principals' Center enjoyed nearly one hundred members, but concern grew that the center was becoming an elitist organization for only "the top ability group" of principals. As had been the case with many teacher centers, "those who need it the most won't come; those who come already have it." We have watched and waited. Today the center has over five hundred members, perhaps ten percent of whom attend each session. Membership is generally representative of men, women, beginning principals, veterans, elementary, middle, and high schools—and a cross section of "ability groups." Our experience now suggests that every principal has some of "it" and every principal needs and wants more of "it."

There are other important decisions in which principals have a major hand. Although there is a great deal to learn using the schoolhouse as locus and context, principals have preferred the more neutral, protected university setting for their reflections and conversations. Principals find that a university-based center can provide a contemplative place in the ivory tower for school people as well as for academics.

The education business seems to thrive as a sorting enterprise, always attempting to narrow the range of human characteristics represented in a group. The Board has firmly tilted in the other direction, toward heterogeneity and diversity. Few activities are "grouped." The center has thereby come to occupy a rather unique place in the experience of principals. Currently members with extraordinary variety and background of ideas and experiences sit around a table. About one third are not principals at all, but superintendents, teachers, board members, university faculty, and students.

Too many attempts at professional development for principals are attempts at group growth. The assumption is that they all need the same skills before Thursday and will have them after Thursday. Principals, like other learners, have preferred learning styles, different attention spans, interests, and needs. Consequently, the Board attempts to vary activities along several important dimensions: e.g., those led by principals, Harvard faculty, graduate students, and outside consultants; long-term and short-term; small groups, large groups, and individual participation; low-risk activities (large-group addresses), modest risk (small-group discussions), and high risk (writing groups, pairing to exchange school visits). Principals can match their styles as practitioners and as learners to these different formats. In the process many are learning something about themselves as learners as well as new content and skills.

In many ways these and other decisions made by principals are obvious to students of staff development and adult growth. Obvious perhaps, but surprisingly uncommon in the lives of principals and in the halls of universities.

Four years later we can begin to see the outlines of a conceptual model for the professional development of principals quite different from the venerable logical training model:

The logic is not complicated: if we can devise ways to help principals reflect thoughtfully and systematically upon the work they do, analyze that work, clarify their thinking through spoken and written articulation, and engage in conversation with others about that work, they will better understand their complex schools, the tasks confronting them, and their own styles as leaders. Understanding practice is the single most important precondition for improving practice and the hallmark of a professional.

THE PRINCIPALS' CENTER AND THE
PROFESSIONALIZATION OF TEACHING

I have suggested that the relationships among adults within a school have a major influence upon the profession of teaching. Many of these conditions also appear to be among the outcomes for principals at the Principals' Center. For instance, the center has witnessed the development of collegiality among principals. Four years ago few suburban principals talked with urban principals; elementary folks didn't talk with high school folks, even within the same district; men administrators didn't talk with women administrators; public school personnel didn't talk with their private school counterparts; and no one talked with those in parochial schools. Now, conversations among these groups are frequent and continuous, infused with fresh vigor, expanding the repertoire of different responses to similar school problems. And that is the essence of what principals seek as they strive to improve their leadership.

"Do as I do as well as I say," is a powerful formula, as one principal suggests:

> I came away with the notion that professionals are largely responsible for their own growth and development and that the principal can best encourage and nurture this development and growth by 1) modeling, and 2) facilitating. At the beginning of the school year, I put together a portfolio of relevant readings for each teacher and have been adding to the package regularly. I've encouraged staff members to share anything that they read which would be of interest. What is desperately needed is a community of professional colleagues. Then and only then will we have a living, dynamic teaching and learning atmosphere. It's to this end that I have set my sights.

And, through the center, many principals have begun to develop and reveal visions and support the visions of others within their schools.

> The Institute gave me the opportunity to stop, rethink, reaffirm and to learn. I will now take the time to expand the community of learners here and give them every opportunity to explain and develop their visions.

No longer can principals dominate. The top-down model is too unwieldy, too infantilizing, and too unprofessional. Leaders need to set general directions and create environments, structures, and school cultures that enable teachers to discover their own skills and talents. The role must be one of enabling rather than controlling. How will principals learn this? Principals must engage in their own professional development. Principals too need replenishment and invigoration and an expanded repertoire of ideas and practices with which to respond to overwhelming demands. And even more, principals need a sense of their own professionalism.

Despite severe declines in budgets and public confidence in education, both teachers and principals will persist. Principals alone cannot make a profession of teaching. But principals and teachers working together can create an ecology of reflection, growth, and profession-alism. The relationships among teachers and principal I have dis-cussed—collegiality, shared decision-making in classrooms and within schools, personal vision, the teacher as learner and mentor, and control of the quality of teaching—are what being a professional is all about. These are the conditions that will cause teachers and principals alike to blossom rather than wilt when that alarm rings at 6:30 in the morning.

NOTE

1. The original version of this chapter was prepared for the California Commission on the Teaching Profession, April, 1985.

REFERENCES

Barth, R.S. (1980). *Run school run*. Cambridge, Mass.: Harvard University Press.

Barth, R.S. (1981). A principals' center. *Journal of Staff Development, 2* (1), May 1981.

Barth, R.S. (1982). Now what. *Principal, 61*, no. 4, March, 1982.

Barth, R.S. (1984). The professional development of principals. *Education Leadership*, October, 1984, pp. 93–94.

Barth, R.S., and van der Bogert, R. (1984). What is a principals' center? *Education Leadership*, December, 1984, pp. 92–93.

Barth, R.S. (1985). The Leader as Learner. *Education Leadership*, March, 1985.

Barth, R.S. (1985). Outside looking in—inside looking in. *Phi Delta Kappan*, January, 1985.

Barth, R.S. (1985). Principal-centered professional development. Paper deliv-ered at the American Educational Research Association, Chicago, April, 1985.

Hirsch, E.G., Ed. (1983). A conversation with Roland Barth. *Principals' prin-cipals*, vol. 2:4, April, 1983. Dallas, Texas: Ambit Publications.

14

Using Reflection as a Professional Growth Activity[1]

BRUCE G. BARNETT

In recent years the leadership role of the school principal has come under increasing scrutiny. The effective schools literature of the last decade has identified the characteristics of successful schools, pointing to the principal as an important factor for a school's efficient operation. This research has stressed that effective principals can provide leadership by setting academic goals and standards, visiting classrooms regularly, maintaining student discipline, and creating incentives for learning (Armor et al., 1976; Brookover and Lezotte, 1977; Edmonds, 1979; Wynne, 1981; Bossert, Dwyer, Rowan, and Lee, 1982).

As a result of the renewed interest in the leadership role of principals, they are expected to be the key persons for creating curricular and instructional reform in their schools (Olivero, 1982; Dwyer, 1984; Dwyer, Barnett, and Lee, forthcoming). The growing need for retraining, refining, or supporting principals' leadership skills has stimulated the development of a wide variety of in-service programs. These programs include principals' centers housed at universities and colleges, academies formed by state departments of education, and district-mandated in-service training aimed at making principals more effective instructional leaders.

One of the major problems in developing useful training for principals (and other professionals) is to insure that the training content and processes fit the everyday demands and circumstances of their job.

Recent research has suggested that the life of a principal is marked by a series of brief encounters, many of which are unrelated to one another (Martin and Willower, 1981; Morris, Crowson, Hurwitz, and Porter-Gehrie, 1982; Peterson, 1985). The nature of the job requires principals to retain bits and pieces of information that can be retrieved at a moment's notice. Events can happen in such rapid-fire order that Morris et al. (1982) concluded that a principal's actions "blend together in an undifferentiated jumble of activities that are presumably related, however remotely, to the ongoing rhythm and purpose of the larger enterprise" (p. 689).[2]

Training principals and allowing them to learn from their experiences, therefore, becomes difficult because of the brevity and fragmentation of their actions. It is difficult for them to recall the myriad events in which they are engaged or to see underlying patterns in their behavior (Peterson, 1985). The rapidity with which events occur is not conducive to reflective action and thoughtful on-the-spot response (Morris et al., 1982).

THE POWER OF REFLECTION

Although previous research of principals indicates that they have difficulty reflecting as they conduct their daily activities, there is much to suggest that reflection can be a powerful tool for allowing professional growth. Schön (1983), for example, sees reflection as a way for professionals at many levels to deal with the complexities, uncertainties, and value conflicts inherent in their jobs. He argues that the "technical rationality" approach, where scientific theory and technique are used by professionals to solve problems in their workplaces, is of limited value. The demands of many professions include ambiguity and instability such that rational approaches cannot be practically applied. Instead, he contends that "reflection in action" is an art used by many professionals in dealing with situations that involve novelty, instability, and uncertainty. This reflective process can be likened to engaging in an internal dialogue with one's self using experience, intuition, and trial and error thinking in defining and solving a problem or dilemma. Schön further indicates that this reflective process can focus on a variety of objects including the tacit norms underlying a judgment, the implicit strategies behind an action, the feelings associated with a situation, and the role being fulfilled.

The implications for using reflection as a professional development tool for principals are clear. The hectic nature of principals' day-to-day activities forces them to make a host of on-the-spot decisions. Furthermore, principals lead very isolated professional lives that do not allow them many opportunities to observe other principals in action or to learn from their colleagues (Barnett, 1985a). Therefore, a professional development program that incorporates reflection can be very powerful in allowing principals to recall the intent of their behavior, reduce the uncertainty of their actions, reduce their sense of isolation, and consider alternative ways to act.

Such a professional development program, incorporating reflection as a key ingredient of the training process, has been produced by staff members of the Instructional Management Program (IMP) housed at the Far West Laboratory for Educational Research and Development in San Francisco. This training program, referred to as Peer-Assisted Leadership (PAL), will be described in the remainder of the chapter. Following a description of the PAL training processes and procedures, attention will be given to those particular activities that stimulate principals to become more reflective about their actions, thus increasing their professional and personal effectiveness as leaders of their schools.

PAL TRAINING PROCESSES AND PROCEDURES

Two salient findings from the IMP's intensive research of principals helped to drive the conception and development of PAL.[3] First, based on our research findings, we constructed a general framework of instructional leadership describing the important elements that principals took into account when developing programs or when working with students and staff (Dwyer, Lee, Rowan, and Bossert, 1983; Dwyer, 1984). This framework, which appears as Figure 14.1, captures the overarching perspective that many principals use to insure that their schools are healthy, productive settings for students and teachers.

Second, our major data-collection procedures, shadowing (observing) and reflective interviewing, were ones that principals felt were advantageous for helping them to reflect on their actions. During reflective interviews principals were asked to clarify and comment on those actions we had seen as we shadowed them around their buildings. This process of reflective interviewing is much like holding up a mirror to a principal and asking him or her to comment on what he or she sees.

Principals reported that being shadowed and interviewed reduced their sense of isolation; they enjoyed the opportunity to talk with someone about their school, someone who was familiar with the day-to-day events and the problems they faced (Dwyer et al., 1983). Although our research activities had been intended to learn more about the work of principals, these activities were discovered to have the additional value of reducing principals' sense of isolation and of enabling them to reflect on their actions.

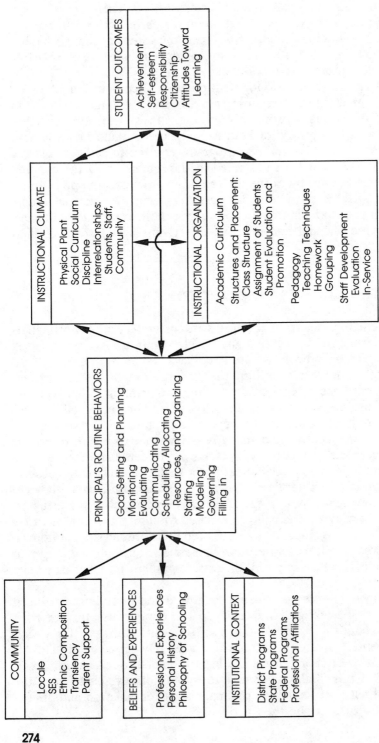

COMMUNITY

Locale
SES
Ethnic Composition
Transiency
Parent Support

BELIEFS AND EXPERIENCES

Professional Experiences
Personal History
Philosophy of Schooling

INSTITUTIONAL CONTEXT

District Programs
State Programs
Federal Programs
Professional Affiliations

PRINCIPAL'S ROUTINE BEHAVIORS

Goal-Setting and Planning
Monitoring
Evaluating
Communicating
Scheduling, Allocating
   Resources, and Organizing
Staffing
Modeling
Governing
Filling in

INSTRUCTIONAL CLIMATE

Physical Plant
Social Curriculum
Discipline
Interrelationships:
   Students, Staff,
   Community

INSTRUCTIONAL ORGANIZATION

Academic Curriculum

Structures and Placement:
   Class Structure
   Assignment of Students
   Student Evaluation and
   Promotion

Pedagogy
   Teaching Techniques
   Homework
   Grouping

Staff Development
   Evaluation
   In-Service

STUDENT OUTCOMES

Achievement
Self-esteem
Responsibility
Citizenship
Attitudes Toward
   Learning

FIGURE 14.1 The Principal's Role in Instructional Management. Principals can understand and influence the varied elements of their organizations through the performance of routine activities. Their success hinges on their ability to connect their actions to an overarching perspective of their school settings and their aspirations for students.

274

Purposes of PAL. The PAL process uses both the general framework and the shadowing and reflective interviewing procedures in order to promote more reflective behavior on the part of principals. Each PAL participant is paired with another principal; partners shadow and interview each other. They also construct models summarizing their partners' leadership styles and behaviors, using the general framework as a guide.

The name "Peer-Assisted Leadership" was chosen specifically to describe a key feature of the process—principals assisting other principals in improving their leadership skills. Because this process allows principals to watch and talk with each other, they are able to provide one another with unique opportunities to reflect upon their own actions and to understand how other principals operate in similar or dissimilar situations. Reflective action, therefore, is encouraged and supported through the goals of the program, which include helping principals to:

1. Learn and apply new ways to think about instructional leadership;
2. Analyze their own and another principal's behavior;
3. Learn how other principals lead their schools; and
4. Reduce the isolation that many principals experience by forming a collegial support system where new ideas and insights are shared.

Training Processes. The PAL training consists of a series of six full-day meetings conducted by two IMP trainers at intervals of about six weeks. At the beginning of the training, each principal selects a partner to work with throughout the entire process. During training meetings participants learn the various skills associated with shadowing, reflective interviewing, data analysis, and model building. Before applying these skills in working with their partners, participants practice working with a common set of materials. These materials consist of data from the IMP's prior research with principals; they are used to illustrate the processes for collecting and analyzing information and for practicing skills and receiving feedback.

Between meetings principals apply these skills in conducting the observations and interviews that provide the data about their partners' schools. The expectation is that each principal will conduct at least four shadows (lasting from three to four hours each) and four reflective interviews (each lasting about one hour). This training process is a sequential and cumulative one in which each skill is built upon the preceding ones. By the final meeting, principals are prepared to present models of their partners' instructional management activities to the group.

Special care is taken throughout the training process to incorporate elements that have been identified with successful training. For example, the characteristics of effective in-service training identified by Joyce and Showers (1980, 1982) are used, including: (1) presenting theory or describing the skills or strategies to be performed, (2) modeling or demonstrating the required skills, (3) practicing in a simulated and classroom setting, (4) providing structured and open-ended feedback, and (5) providing coaching to insure that the skills are applied in the work setting. The final characteristic—using coaching techniques—is used somewhat differently than Joyce and Showers (1982) have defined it. Rather than using coaching to help principals receive evaluative feedback on a particular skill, principals provide their partners with a nonevaluative description of what has been observed. Nevertheless, this nonjudgmental feedback oftentimes spurs principals to consider new ways to act and to seek advice from peer partners.

Training Content. In order to provide more detail about the substance of the training materials and activities, a brief description of each of the six meetings is provided below.

Meeting 1: General Orientation and Shadowing. This initial session orients participants to the PAL process by introducing them to the general framework of instructional management (Figure 14.1) and to the shadowing procedure. Using the structure of the general framework as a guide, partners share information about each other as a way to orient themselves to what they will be observing in each other's schools. Instruction in shadowing is provided, with an emphasis on how to take accurate, descriptive, specific notes and how to assume a nonthreatening role during shadows. Examples of exemplary shadow records, practice taking shadow notes, and feedback from the trainers are used to assist principals in grasping the purposes and mechanics of shadowing.

Meeting 2: Reflective Interviewing. In this session principals learn how to form reflective interview questions based on the observations recorded during their first shadows. Again using the general framework as a guide, participants learn how to ask and record answers to questions that clarify the intent and meaning of their partners' actions. Simulations, practice forming and asking questions, and individual feedback are provided.

Meeting 3: Advanced Reflective Interviewing and Theme Build-

ing. Using the information gathered during initial shadows and interviews, principals are taught how to expand their reflective interviewing skills by asking questions that connect the various pieces of information they have obtained. Emphasis is placed on developing questions using the structure of the general framework as a tool for organizing the information. In addition, participants begin to identify important "themes," or stories, that are emerging in their partners' schools. Again using simulations, guided practice, and individual feedback, trainers assist principals in forming appropriate and effective "advanced" questions and themes.

Meeting 4: Clustering Data by Themes—Preliminary Model Building. Participants are taught how to organize the information from their shadows and reflective interviews around the themes identified in the previous meeting. Simulations and guided practice are used to help principals cluster all the relevant information for each theme and to represent the data visually to show connections between the various bits of information.

Meeting 5: Final Model Production. Trainers assist principals in summarizing and combining their clustered theme data as the last step in producing the final models for their partners. Participants begin the final model construction, receive feedback from trainers, and learn how to make the oral presentations of their models that will be made at the sixth meeting.

Meeting 6: Model Presentations. As the culmination of the year's activities, principals orally present the written models of their partners. These models are compared and contrasted in order to demonstrate the similarities and differences between principals and their settings. Discussion also centers on the common issues that emerge from examining principals' leadership behavior.

PAL Participants. Since its inception in 1983 the PAL process has been used with principals across Far West Laboratory's service region. In the first year of operation groups of elementary principals from school districts in Sacramento, California, and Salt Lake City, Utah, participated. Each group consisted of between ten and fifteen principals. During the second year of operation additional groups of principals from Sacramento and the San Francisco Bay Area joined. These groups were comprised of elementary and junior high school principals and vice principals.

In addition, the original group of elementary principals from Sacramento continued for a second year, using their collegial support group as a way to identify, reflect upon, and try out different ways to combat common problems faced by principals. Shadowing and reflective interviewing were not used as extensively in the second year; however, principals did visit each other's schools and speak informally with one another about how they were dealing with issues such as instructional grouping procedures, computer usage, and promotion and retention policies.

ELEMENTS OF PAL THAT STIMULATE REFLECTION

As previously stated, the PAL activities are designed to allow principals to become more reflective about their own actions, thus prompting professional growth and development. As we have conducted PAL training for the last two years, we have obtained principals' reactions to the training activities and materials. Group discussions focusing on principals' perceptions have been tape-recorded and short questionnaires have been completed by the participants throughout the training. These reactions provide insights into how the various training components combine to foster principals' reflective behavior. The first portion of this section describes those activities that contribute to principals' becoming more reflective and introspective about their work; the latter portion touches on how reflection in action becomes a natural part of their everyday thoughts and behaviors.

Building a Foundation of Trust. A major assumption of the PAL training is that principals are not being judged or evaluated by their peers or by the trainers. Throughout the training this point is constantly emphasized. Participants are urged to retain their objectivity during the shadow and reflective interview processes. Shadows are for gathering a behavioral record of observed events, and reflective interviews are for obtaining the meanings attached to those events. Principals are taught to use neutral, nonjudgmental language when describing observed activities and when interviewing their partners. By suspending judgments, we believe that principals stand a better chance of building trust with one another so that they can begin to reflect upon and to examine critically their own actions.

Beginning in the first meeting, this "trust base" is developed. For example, in the initial training session, principals have the chance to obtain background information about their partners, using the general framework as a guide. Principals are urged to discuss informally what is important to them regarding each of the critical elements in the framework (represented by the different boxes in the model). The principal seeking the information does not evaluate what is being said, but asks clarifying questions in order to understand more about the important aspects of the community, philosophy, climate, instructional organization, and intended student outcomes at his or her partner's school.

Principals comment that this initial experience allows them to learn more about their partners and to develop a mutual terminology based on the general framework. In addition, principals begin to build rapport with their partners by discovering that they "share similar philosophies and approaches" and "that we all share similar problems and expectations which makes it easier to share information." In other words, principals not only begin to understand their partners' approaches, but also to realize that their peers share similar ideas and philosophies about leadership and the schooling process.

Trust and openness also are built by devoting time during each meeting for principals to express their reactions to the training processes as they are being implemented. Trainers encourage principals to voice their positive and negative reactions to shadowing, reflective interviewing, and model building. For example, before they conduct their first shadows and reflective interviews principals voice their initial concerns about taking on these new roles with their peers. Once they have conducted their first shadows and interviews, principals are encouraged to discuss the joys, frustrations, and dilemmas associated with these processes. By allowing this type of open dialogue, not only do principals learn that their ideas are valued, but they also learn how their colleagues are dealing with similar situations. This type of sharing allows a close bond to develop between principals in the group, resulting in a more trusting atmosphere where reflection can flourish.

Being Shadowed and Interviewed by a Peer.   Having a peer follow a principal around the school recording his or her everyday actions and then conduct a reflective interview to determine the meaning of those actions is intended to foster reflection. The neutral, nonevaluative stance that principals are taught to use allows a relationship of trust and acceptance to develop between partners. By being able to explain their activities and rationale without fear of being judged, principals can become more open about their intentions, goals, frustrations, and successes. This openness allows them to reflect upon their actions, leading to self-analysis and self-evaluation.

As principals describe their reactions to being shadowed and interviewed, they mention that these processes make them more reflective in several ways. First, principals continually comment that having to talk about their observed behavior forces them to "clarify" the goals and intentions of their actions. In this way, they are forced to raise to a conscious level the specific rationale for why they are behaving in a certain way. Typical comments from principals include:

> When my partner comes in and shadows me, nothing's new for me. But seeing it through his eyes and the questions he asks makes me clarify to

him and to myself.... It makes me more aware of what I'm doing. [Being
shadowed and interviewed gives me] a chance to reflect on what I'm doing
and how I'm handling things that I usually do instinctively.

Second, by reflecting on the actions that their partners have observed, principals begin to make judgments as to whether or not they
are acting in ways that are consistent with their goals and philosophies.
This can be a very rewarding experience; many principals remark that
their enthusiasm as leaders is renewed and that reflection "validates"
or "confirms" what they are currently doing. Several comments
include:

The opportunity to discuss [and] share common concerns, problems, and
solutions [has] confirmed in my own mind that what I am doing is proper.

[I've] become more verbal about what my philosophy is and why I believe
[in] what I do. Reflecting on it has ... given me a sense of knowing where
I am going.

Shadowing and Interviewing Another Principal. Besides becoming
more reflective as a result of being shadowed and interviewed, principals can gain some insights into their own styles and actions by
observing and interviewing their peers. The training activities are designed to encourage them to adopt an inquiring and open view when
watching and talking with their partners. Principals learn to observe
and question their partners in neutral, nonjudgmental ways, keeping
the general framework in mind as they attempt to understand the
meanings their partners attach to their actions. Furthermore, by training principals to identify the important emerging "themes" in their
partners' schools, they discover the relevant issues in the school rather
than making a priori decisions about what should be occurring. Encouraging principals to take an open and inquiring view about their
partners' situations allows principals to consider alternative ways to
lead their schools.

PAL participants remark that watching and talking with other principals stimulates their thoughts about their own styles and actions.
Because most principals are isolated from their peers, they rarely have
the chance to observe how their peers react to similar situations. Principals, in reflecting on what they are seeing and hearing, begin to
compare their own situations to those of their partners. Therefore, as
they consider what they are seeing and hearing from their partners,
principals project themselves into the situation, examining ways in

which they might react. This notion of comparison is evident in the following comments:

> [Having] a chance to see a principal in action brings to a conscious level similar activities that I'm doing or that I need to deal with.

> [Watching someone else] makes me question my own behavior as a principal. Am I too intense or compulsive?

> This give me knowledge of why [principals] do some of the things they do. [It] helps me to clarify my thinking and actions.

Another benefit of watching and talking with their peers is that principals' sense of isolation is reduced and they see other ways to handle situations. Not only do they consider new strategies or techniques to try at their school, but they also realize that they are handling situations in a manner similar to their peers. Once again, this experience tends to renew and energize their enthusiasm as school leaders. In other words, principals feel "validated" or "reaffirmed" when they realize they are not alone in the world and other principals behave in similar ways. The ideas of learning new strategies and receiving confirmation are illustrated in the following comments:

> I was taught ... how to make a classroom visit. I had this philosophy [and] I held it dear to my heart. And then I walked out to see this principal and she goes into the classroom in an entirely different mode. And afterwards we talked about it. I haven't had a chance to start that yet, but next year my visits will be much different than this year. Much better.

> A validation of what I'm doing in my school [has occurred] by seeing that [the] same things [are being] done by my partner.

> One of the things I've really enjoyed is having a chance to go someplace, watching somebody do what I do and standing aside not having to ... know what happened before or what's going to happen later. But just to look at that specific segment and say, "You know, that's really what I do too."

Incorporating the Instructional Leadership Framework. The general framework of instructional leadership (Figure 14.1) derived from our research with principals is used throughout the entire training process. Principals use the framework for obtaining background information about their partners, for developing their reflective interview questions, and for summarizing the data and constructing a final model of their partners. It is meant to provide a focus for organizing and understanding the wealth of information they gather during the year.

Most principals believe that the framework provides a useful way to "structure" and "focus" their observations, interviews, and model building; however, they also report that it becomes a tool for reflecting on their own actions. Because of its simplicity, principals can "keep it in mind" as they think about their own situations and actions. Comments illustrating the power of the model as a reflective device include:

> [The framework] consolidated my goals. I felt that I could look objectively at what I was doing and self-evaluate.

> [The framework] gave me insight and I was able to see my administrative style and [my] interrelated pattern [of actions].

> [The framework] forced me to clarify and ask myself questions about what I was or was not doing.

Transferring Reflection to the Work Setting. While we are interested in having principals become more reflective as they conduct shadows and interviews and as they are shadowed and interviewed, we also want this reflective behavior to become part of their regular routines. In other words, we want the reflective processes to become useful on an everyday basis, allowing principals to process information in such a way that they are acting purposefully rather than instinctively. Many principals mention that this transfer does occur, as the following quotes illustrate:

> Now what's happening [is that] I am constantly looking at myself and reevaluating myself more so than I ever did before. I did it when I was a teacher. I used to evaluate lessons. How would I do this better next time? I never really did that as a principal. I was like the boss reacting all the time. [PAL has made me] more conscious of my leadership style, how it affects [others] . . . and how they respond to it. I'm constantly reevaluating, and I had forgotten to do that.

> Now . . . I can go someplace and see something happen and I don't immediately make a judgment about it. I now process reflectively what I've seen and ask somebody to give me a little history on what's happening before I make a decision. . . . So, [PAL] has given me a route [for] reflectively examining what's happening.

SUMMARY AND CONCLUSIONS

Based on the reactions of principals who have participated in PAL, it is clear that the activities promote reflection and self-examination.

Principals state their belief that reflection is critical for making improved decisions in leading their schools. Reflection, as Schön (1983) suggests, can be a powerful tool when practically applied in the work setting. Furthermore, isolation from other principals is reduced such that principals form new support networks and renew their enthusiasm as school leaders (Barnett, 1985a).

While many of a principal's activities and interactions are brief and fragmented (Martin and Willower, 1981; Morris et al., 1982; Peterson, 1985), this training program illustrates that by becoming more reflective principals can see patterns in their behavior, analyze situations on the spot, and clarify their own goals. The argument that principals cannot be trained to use their experiences in order to examine the underlying patterns in their behavior (Peterson, 1985) seems unfounded. In short, our work demonstrates that principals can begin to make sense of the ambiguity and uncertainty in their jobs when given strategies for examining and reflecting upon their philosophies, intentions, and actions.

We believe that the interaction of the PAL activities is responsible for principals becoming more reflective. No single PAL activity is solely responsible for stimulating reflection. Allowing trust to develop between partners, being shadowed and interviewed by a peer, shadowing and interviewing another principal, becoming familiar with the framework, and building models of leadership behavior—all combine to create an atmosphere where reflection, openness, and professional growth can occur.

Keeping a nonjudgmental tone in the shadowing and reflective interviews is critical for allowing trust to develop between partners. Although many principals do ask for advice and suggestions from their partners, they request this advice rather than have it forced upon them. In this way, principals make conscious professional decisions regarding those areas in which they would like to improve. Professional development becomes personalized rather than externally mandated.

Using the trust relationship as a foundation, the shadowing and reflective interviewing processes become the main medium through which principals become more reflective. Being shadowed and interviewed are just as critical as shadowing and interviewing another principal in promoting reflective behavior. Having peers shadow and interview one another allows principals to become more aware of their overall goals and to understand the consequences of their actions. Observing and interviewing other principals provides a basis for comparing and contrasting their own styles with their partners'. Professional growth, therefore, can occur by being observed as well as observing, analyzing, and interviewing a peer (Goldsberry, 1981).

Another critical element of PAL is the introduction of the general framework of instructional leadership derived from the IMP's research of principals. Our intent in using the framework throughout the training is to establish a common language for trainers and participants. Furthermore, we use the framework as a device for helping principals organize their thinking about the complex set of factors that school administrators must deal with on a day-to-day basis. As principals become increasingly familiar with the framework, it becomes a useful device for understanding what they are seeing and hearing from their partners. Interestingly enough, the framework also is helpful for principals as they consider their own situations and circumstances. As one principal remarked, "Everything you do can fit in the model." In other words, the framework becomes what Garman (1984) refers to as an educational construal that allows principals to organize their actions and their meanings into an abbreviated, manageable form.

The ultimate power of the PAL process, however, is the fact that "reflection in action" (Schön, 1983) occurs as principals begin actively to use the reflective process on a daily basis, not just when they are being shadowed and interviewed. The often frantic nature of their jobs forbids most principals from considering alternate ways of acting, clarifying their goals, or validating that they are acting in a manner consistent with those goals. However, those who participate in PAL find themselves more naturally introspective about their work. Reflection, therefore, becomes a process that principals incorporate in considering alternate ways to act and in confirming that they are acting consistently with their own goals and visions. Not only do principals reflect on past or future events, but also on the momentary decisions they make daily. In this way, they conduct an "internal dialogue" (Schön, 1983) with themselves as they interact with teachers, students, and parents.

The current operation of PAL has focused on using reflection as a professional development tool for school-site principals; however, we believe that the shadowing and reflective interviewing procedures can be implemented in a variety of other ways. For example, this program could be used to complement and support new skills that principals are undertaking, to expose potential administrators to the rigors and demands of the principalship, and to develop reflection in other educational administrators besides principals.

PAL could be expanded in other ways to meet the needs of current or future principals. For instance, many of today's principals are facing increased pressure to develop their teacher supervision and evaluation practices. In California, for example, principals must be certified by their districts as being competent teacher evaluators. As a result, many staff development programs are arising to help nurture these skills. PAL could be used to complement these in-service training programs, providing principals with opportunities to reflect on their current practices and to learn how other principals are handling the challenge of supervision and evaluation.

Furthermore, preservice training courses at universities and colleges could teach shadowing and reflective interviewing practices so that future administrators could see how experienced professionals operate and could consider how they might handle similar situations. Therefore, the theoretical coursework that students are taking can be enriched by observing practicing administrators. In this way, potential principals could view firsthand the job demands and gain insights about how to deal with those demands.

Finally, this program does not have to be used exclusively for principals. Other administrators—superintendents, directors of curriculum, vice principals—also lead very isolated professional lives. There is every reason to believe that these educational administrators could benefit from becoming more reflective about their philosophies, intentions, and consequences of their actions.

In summary, reflection, as Schön (1983) indicates, is something all professionals can benefit from using more systematically in solving problems and making everyday decisions. The challenge for those of us in education is to nurture and support opportunities for practitioners to become more reflective. This may mean that priorities for staff development need to be rearranged; however, without having the chance to put reflection into action, educational practitioners are more likely to be reactors to situations rather than vibrant, innovative leaders in the field.

NOTES

1. The training program described in this chapter was supported by a contract from the National Institute of Education, Department of Education, under contract No. 400–03–0003. The contents of this chapter do not necessarily reflect the views or policies of the National Institute of Education or the Department of Education.

2. Research on principals conducted by Dwyer, Lee, Barnett, Filby, and Rowan (1984–85) has begun to untangle the jumble of activities principals engage in by demonstrating that there are consistent patterns in principals' routine, everyday actions. Their analyses focus on the meanings principals attach to their behavior as a way of understanding the patterns principals employ in leading their schools.

3. A more thorough description of the history of the Instructional Management Program and the rationale for creating PAL can be found in Barnett (1985b).

REFERENCES

Armor, D.; Conry-Osequera, P.; Cox, M.; King, N.; McDonnell, L.; Pascal, A.; Pauly, E.; Zellman, G. (1976). *Analysis of the school preferred reading program in selected Los Angeles minority schools.* Santa Monica, Calif.: Rand Corporation.

Barnett, B. (1985a). Reflection in action: A stimulus for professional growth. *Thrust, 14,* 48–49.

Barnett, B. G. (1985b). Peer-assisted leadership: A stimulus for professional growth. *Urban Review, 17,* 47–64.

Bossert, S.T.; Dwyer, D. C.; Rowan, B.; Lee, G. V. (1982). The instructional management role of the principal. *Educational Administration Quarterly, 18,* 34–64.

Brookover, W. B., and Lezotte, L. (1977). *Schools can make a difference.* East Lansing, Mich.: Michigan State University.

Dwyer, D. C. (1984). Forging successful schools: Realistic expectations for principals. *Educational Horizons, 63,* 3–8.

Dwyer, D. C.; Barnett, B. G.; Lee, G. V. (Forthcoming). The school principal: Scapegoat or the last great hope? in *ASCD Yearbook.* Alexandria, Va: Association for Supervision and Curriculum Development.

Dwyer, D. C.; Lee, G. V.; Barnett, B. G.; Filby, N. N.; Rowan, B. (1984–85). *Case studies of the instructional management behavior of principals.* San Francisco, Calif.: Far West Laboratory for Educational Research and Development.

Dwyer, D. C.; Lee, G. V.; Rowan, B.; Bossert, S. T. (1983). *Five principals in action: Perspectives on instructional management.* San Francisco, Calif.: Far West Laboratory for Educational Research and Development.

Edmonds, R. (1979). Some schools work and more can. *Social Policy, 9,* 28–32.

Garman, N. (1984). Reflection, the heart of clinical supervision: A modern rationale for professional practice. Unpublished manuscript.

Goldsberry, N. (1981). College consultation: Teacher collaboration toward performance improvement. Paper presented at the annual meeting of the American Educational Research Association, Los Angeles, Calif.

Joyce, B., and Showers, B. (1980). Improving in-service training: The messages of research. *Educational Leadership, 37,* 379–85.

———. (1982). The coaching of teaching. *Educational Leadership, 40,* 4–10.

Martin, W. J., and Willower, D. J. (1981). The managerial behavior of high school principals. *Educational Administration Quarterly, 17,* 69–90.

Morris, V. C.; Crowson, R. L.; Hurwitz, E.; Porter-Gehrie, C. (1982). The urban principal: Middle manager in the educational bureaucracy. *Phi Delta Kappan, 63,* 689–92.

Olivero, J. L. (1982). Principals and their in-service needs. *Educational Leadership, 39,* 340–44.

Peterson, K. (1985). The limits of on-the-job training. Paper presented at the annual meeting of the American Educational Research Association, Chicago.

Schön, D. A. (1983). *The reflective practitioner.* New York, N.Y.: Basic Books, Inc.

Wynne, E. A. (1981). Looking at good schools. *Phi Delta Kappan, 62,* 371–81.

15

The Challenge for School Leaders: Attracting and Retaining Good Teachers

DIANA G. POUNDER

INTRODUCTION

A fundamental challenge school leaders must address during the next five years is to attract and retain enough qualified teachers to staff our nation's schools. The objectives in this chapter are to outline briefly contributors to the growing shortage of teachers, to identify school-based reform targets addressing the work and the working conditions of teachers, and to discuss the implications of such strategies for instructional leaders, particularly school principals. The basic thesis in this chapter is that a primary responsibility of instructional leaders is to create school conditions that teachers will find attractive and that will enable teachers to do their jobs well.

Recent projections indicate that by 1988 there will be only enough teachers available to supply about 80 percent of the demand (Darling-Hammond, 1984). Strategies to meet the impending shortage fall into four basic categories: increasing the base pay for teachers, restructuring the career and the system of monetary incentives associated with performance, revising preparation program standards, improving working conditions, and redesigning the work of teachers (Cresap, McCormick, and Paget, 1984; Feistritzer 1983). Although the author agrees that much must and can be done to revitalize the teaching profession, many of the proposed reforms will cost money that taxpayers may be reluctant to provide. Restructuring the profession and making fundamental changes in teacher preparation programs will take time. Plans to link pay incentives to performance have met with resistance from teacher associations.

However, improving working conditions and redesigning the work of teachers, unlike the other strategies, can proceed immediately and do not necessarily require any major increases in direct expenditures for school personnel (Cresap, McCormick, and Paget, 1984; Lieberman and Miller, 1984). Additionally, these two strategies lend themselves to local initiative and are likely to receive strong support from teachers and their professional associations.

The intention is not to suggest that redesigning the work and improving the working conditions of teachers is an adequate substitute for increasing levels of teacher compensation, improving their preparation, or restructuring the career. Rather, enhancing working conditions and making the work itself more attractive represent relatively low-cost initiatives that can be undertaken immediately by school principals and teachers, with the support of the district superintendent and central office staff. Teachers *are* the key resource in schools, and their cultivation and development is a central responsibility of instructional leaders at every level.

THE IMPENDING SHORTAGE OF TEACHERS

During the past two decades teachers have expressed growing dissatisfaction with teaching as a career. In the early 1970s 10 percent of teachers stated that they wished they had chosen a different career, and by the early 1980s nearly 40 percent of all teachers expressed similar doubts (National Education Association, 1982). Further, Darling-Hammond (1984) reports that less than half of the teaching force sampled in 1980–81 intended to continue teaching until retirement, and that the best qualified teachers appear to be the most dissatisfied. Contributors to the growing shortage and threats to the overall quality of the teaching work force are summarized below:

- fewer persons are completing bachelor's degrees in education
- the academic ability of incoming teachers is declining
- the attrition rate is greatest during the early years and among the most highly qualified teachers
- education is steadily declining as the occupation of choice among women
- the base pay of teachers is lower than in other fields requiring a bachelor's degree, and the average pay of teachers declined 15 percent in real dollars during the 1971–81 period
- shortages already exist in mathematics, the sciences, and other specialty areas, and are expected to grow into a general shortage by the late 1980s

- a "mini baby-boom" will affect school enrollments in the mid–1980s and continue through the 1990s

(Darling-Hammond, 1984).

The statistics regarding the availability of new teacher candidates are discouraging. Since the early 1970s the percentage of graduates receiving bachelor's degrees in education dropped from over 32 percent to 14 percent of the total number of bachelor degrees awarded (National Education Association, 1981). Further, statistics indicate that as few as 50 to 70 percent of those completing teacher training programs actually enter the classroom (Feistritzer, 1983; National Center for Education Statistics, 1982b). During the same period the number of entering college freshmen expressing intent to become teachers dropped from nearly 20 percent to less than 5 percent (Feistritzer, 1983). Projections indicate that these trends will not change substantially, at least through the remainder of the 1980s.

These supply trends are further exacerbated by evidence suggesting that the more academically capable teacher candidates are not being placed in or remaining in the classroom (Schlechty and Vance, 1981). There has been a decline in the academic ability of students planning to become teachers, as measured by the Scholastic Aptitude Test (National Center for Education Statistics, 1982a), and it appears that the rate of attrition is highest among the most qualified (Vance and Schlechty, 1982). National teacher turnover rates average about 6 percent annually, but evidence suggests that as many as 50 to 60 percent of those entering the profession leave within the first four years (Schlechty and Vance, 1983).

Studies suggest also that the "best and brightest" are no longer being drawn to or remaining in the classroom (Boyer, 1983; National Center for Education Statistics, 1982a; National Commission on Excellence in Education, 1983). Though numerous reasons are offered to explain this change, the most compelling is the competition for competent professional women from other fields, such as business and science. Unlike previous times, teaching and nursing no longer have a "captive" labor market in terms of professionally oriented women.

Between 1970 and 1980 the number of women receiving bachelor's degrees in education dropped from 36 percent to 18 percent (National Center for Education Statistics, 1983). During the same period the proportion of degrees granted to women increased tenfold in the biological sciences, computer sciences, engineering, and law, with a parallel shift in the occupational choice of women from education, English, and the social sciences to business, commerce, and the health professions (Darling-Hammond, 1984: 8, 9; National Center for Education Statistics, 1983: 184, 188).

Other fields have not only provided more career alternatives for women, but also more attractive salaries. While the annual rate of increase in teachers' salaries nationwide is approximately 9 percent (Halstead, 1983), the beginning salaries for teachers are lower than in any other field requiring a bachelor's degree (Darling-Hammond, 1984; National Education Association, 1983). Further, despite increases in average levels of experience and education among teachers in the work force between 1971 and 1981, the average salaries of teachers declined almost 15 percent in real dollars (Darling-Hammond, 1984; National Center for Education Statistics, 1983: 102–3). Education has been steadily losing women (traditionally a majority of the work force in education) to fields offering greater career alternatives and higher salaries.

In contrast to the shrinking supply of highly qualified teachers is a changing demand pattern for teachers at all levels and in certain specializations. While declining student enrollments during the 1970s resulted in a large reduction in force among school employees, a "mini-baby boom" during the late 1970s has resulted in an increase in school enrollments that is expected to last through much of the 1990s (Darling-Hammond, 1984). The projected demand for preschool and elementary teachers is expected to increase by nearly 40 percent from the early 1980s to the middle 1990s. Although secondary schools will not experience this student population increase until the early 1990s, the eventual demand for secondary teachers is expected to increase by 13 percent (National Education Association, 1981).

Certain subject area specializations are already experiencing shortages. These shortages are greatest in mathematics and the sciences, but include many areas of vocational education, special education, industrial arts, bilingual education, and speech correction. Among the mathematics and science teachers hired in 1981, less than half were certified or eligible for certification in the areas they were assigned to teach, and less than 60 percent of newly hired secondary teachers in other subject areas met this criterion (Darling-Hammond, 1984: 4; National Center for Education Statistics, 1983). The shortage is most severe in the areas of math and science, and is expected to expand into a more general shortage by the late 1980s and early 1990s.

Compounding the more general national trends in teacher supply and demand are regional shifts in population. There is a general migration to the Sunbelt states, a proportionately greater increase in blacks (17 percent increase from 1970 to 1980) and Spanish-speaking persons (60 percent increase from 1970 to 1980), and an increase in the percent of minority persons living in large cities and certain states (U.S. Bureau of the Census, 1981). By the year 2000, fifty-three major U.S. cities and the state of California are expected to have a majority of "minority" residents (Futrell, 1983). As a result, certain cities and regions (e.g., the South, Southwest, and West) are expected to feel the pinch of a teacher shortage sooner and more dramatically than others.

These trends suggest a crisis of major proportions in education, and school principals can be expected to bear the major burden of these shortages. There are good teachers in our schools and they need to be retained. There are good recruits who do enter teaching, and they need to be encouraged to remain in education.

School principals cannot raise the base pay of teachers, restructure the teaching career, or directly influence the quality of teacher education programs. They can do much, however, to improve the work environment in schools, and they can do much to facilitate the redesign of the work of teachers to make it more attractive and satisfying. Teachers themselves are the key resource to more effective schools, and their observations and suggestions have much to offer instructional leaders at all levels, particularly school principals.

WORKING CONDITIONS AND THE "WORK" OF TEACHERS

Numerous factors have been identified as contributing to the unattractiveness of teaching as a career, including low salaries, low prestige, limited job options within the field of teaching itself, and unattractive working conditions (Boyer, 1983; Cresap, McCormick, and Paget, 1984; Feistritzer, 1983; Goodlad, 1984; Lortie, 1975; Rosenholtz and Smylie, 1983). The related problems of the occupational attractiveness of education and of the retention of qualified teachers are generally recognized as complex, and as requiring multiple solution strategies targeted at increasing basic compensation, improving teacher education, restructuring the teaching career itself, and improving the work and working conditions (Cresap, McCormick, and Paget, 1984; Darling-Hammond, 1984; Griffin, 1984; Lieberman and Miller, 1984).

The work of teachers, working conditions in schools, and organizational structures and processes represent one cluster of elements over which school administrators and teachers can exercise considerable control, and these are among the factors theoretically and empirically associated with employee motivation, involvement, and job satisfaction and dissatisfaction (Bridges, 1980; Duke, Showers, and Imker, 1980; Herzberg, Mausner, and Snyderman, 1959; Miskel, 1973; Miskel, 1982; Miskel, Feverly, and Stewart, 1979; Schwab and Iwanicki, 1982; Sergiovanni, 1967; Sterns and Porter, 1979). While competing theories and limited research on these matters in schools make it difficult for administrators to derive specific policy strategies, the available evidence does indicate that work itself, working conditions, and associated organizational structures and processes are related to productivity, turnover, morale, and associated variables (Bullock, 1984).

The work of teachers and the conditions that shape it have been

described in various studies, and "understandings" of the social realities of teaching provide a critical reference point for instructional
leadership and school improvement (Bidwell, 1965; Cusick, 1983;
Dreeben, 1970; Jackson, 1968; Lortie, 1975; Waller, 1952). These and
other studies underscore the essentially social character of teaching
and its complexity.

Central aspects of the work of teachers have been captured by
Lieberman and Miller (1978) and are summarized here to illustrate
aspects of teaching that frequently tend to be neglected by those who
formulate instructional improvement policies and school reform
strategies:

> The "style" of a teacher is developed through a trail and error process
> shaped by a confluence of contradictory forces—the necessity to teach
> children something, to keep them motivated to learn, and to keep the
> students under control. Teaching is learned in isolation from other adults,
> and the "rewards" that count most are intrinsic and come from their work
> with students. Most of the feedback for teachers comes from students,
> and there are few opportunities to work with peers on instructional mat-
> ters. Teachers work under conditions of uncertainty, never being sure that
> what they do will have the desired effect on children, and working under
> a cloud of expectations from others that often fail to consider the diffi-
> culties faced by teachers. The knowledge base available to teachers is
> relatively weak and not well codified, and teachers frequently look for
> better ways to be successful in reaching students. Teaching involves a lot
> of intangibles, and the connections between activities and outcomes are
> ambiguous and unpredictable; teaching is more like a craft than a science.
> Teachers work under a press for accountability, yet school goals are often
> unclear and even contradictory; translating goals into actions are an in-
> dividualized affair. Given the student subculture, teachers work hard to
> establish the control norms needed to move a class along and give it
> direction, and these often are influenced by school-wide norms regarding
> what it means to be a good teacher. And, teachers work in a setting that
> offers little support to their personal professional development; it's a sink
> or swim model where teachers generally work in isolation from one
> another.
>
> (condensed from Lieberman and Miller, 1978: 55–57)

Further, in describing the "dailiness" of teaching, Leiberman and Miller
(1978) note the "rhythms, rules, interactions, and feelings of teachers."
Some of their observations are summarized below:

> Teachers work in a highly regulated environment, rarely leaving it during
> the day, accommodating interruptions to their teaching, completing a
> variety of clerical duties, adjusting to the constant press of the class sched-
> ule in secondary schools, and trying to adapt activities in elementary

classes to the energy levels and moods of their students and themselves. They adopt a criterion of practicality in judging an idea's worth; solutions to problems are valued to the extent that they're concrete, immediate, and don't require too much work, and they tend not to share their experiences or their ideas with other teachers, students, administrators, or others outside the school. Their interactions with one another are not very open, tend to be limited to griping or jousting with each other, and generally aren't focused on substantive instructional matters. Relationships with students are primary and frequently go beyond teaching the subject to serving children as a role-model. They have comparatively few interactions with the principal, though the principal is viewed as having a great deal of power in influencing a teacher's work life. Teachers express ambivalence about the primacy of children in their daily work lives, are conflicted about how good they are as a teacher, and feel frustrated in trying to influence events outside their classrooms.

(condensed from Lieberman and Miller, 1978: 57–64)

These descriptions of the work of teachers provide hints to instructional leaders and educational policymakers about work and work-environment factors that may be associated with one's teaching effectiveness, with the attractiveness of schools as work settings, and with the satisfaction of teaching as "work." The number and types of factors that might be identified by teachers as sources of stress and frustration will vary across different school contexts and teaching circumstances. Conditions perceived as problematic could be quite extensive and might include elements such as:

- Excessive noninstructional duties and tasks
- Inaccessible media equipment and facilities
- A noise-polluted work-space
- Inadequate heating and cooling systems
- Lack of regular and systematic feedback on performance
- Paperwork overloads
- Inequitable scheduling and duty assignments
- Few or no opportunities to stop and relax during the school day
- Outdated equipment and instructional materials
- Poor lighting and lighting control
- Inadequate help with special students
- Overcrowded facilities
- An ineffective student discipline program
- Being isolated from others and feeling alone
- Too many subjects or students to teach adequately

(Swick and Hanley, 1985)

What is viewed as problematic and which action or policy initiatives are most appropriate will vary across school contexts and teaching circumstances. What serves to reduce dissatisfaction or increase job satisfaction and productivity in one setting or with one teacher may be inappropriate in different settings or for other teachers. Again, teachers are the key resource in both identifying problematic work and work-environment factors *and* in developing and implementing policies to address those issues.

The research on effective schools suggests numerous ideas aimed at improving classroom teaching practices and creating a school milieu that supports academic achievement by students, but relatively few of those strategies directly address the nature of the work of teachers or their immediate work environment. An exception is the broad admonition to create a safe and orderly environment for learning and teaching. The author supports this general advice and urges the reader to explore additional elements that might facilitate more effective teaching and learning and that might increase the attractiveness of working in schools.

It may be possible, through redesigning the work, to increase teachers' opportunities to gain intrinsic rewards and thereby to increase their job satisfaction and their motivation to teach well (Blase and Greenfield, 1981). For example, Lortie's study of teachers and their work concludes that intrinsic (psychic) rewards are teachers' major source of satisfaction, and that extrinsic rewards like pay and benefits are not a major source of satisfaction because they are derived primarily on the basis of seniority and advanced education, not on the basis of teacher effort and performance at work (Lortie, 1975). This relationship may change to the degree that compensation is linked directly to performance, as in the merit pay and career ladder proposals being debated and (in some states) implemented (Cresap, McCormick, and Paget, 1984). Nevertheless, it seems reasonable to conclude at this point that intrinsic rewards are still an important source of job satisfaction for teachers and that they are related to work efforts by teachers. Thus, to the extent that the work itself and conditions in the work environment can be made more attractive and intrinsically rewarding to teachers, motivation, work effort, job dissatisfaction, and productivity may be influenced in desirable directions.

The development and implementation of policies and practices aimed at accomplishing these broad objectives represent a potent but largely untested set of instructional improvement strategies available to school administrators. Some of these policies and the attendant strategies might be quite complex and aimed at changing the flow of work, the scope of responsibility, the school climate, some facet of the school culture, or perhaps the level of work interdependency among teachers (Bridges, 1980; Spady and Marx, 1984). Other strategies might be quite simple, taking less time and fewer resources; for example, reducing the number of intrusions in teachers' classrooms, painting corridors or rooms and otherwise "brightening-up" the physical environment, or perhaps making adequate instructional materials available and accessible to teachers.

In large measure, instructional leadership involves creating the conditions necessary for teachers to be effective and satisfied, and focusing teachers and instructional programs on the purposes and objectives to be achieved. The discussion thus far has suggested that the work of teachers and working conditions in schools can be influenced directly by school principals, and that redesigning the teacher's role and developing more favorable working conditions promises a twofold possibility: (1) increasing the attractiveness of teaching as "work," and of schools as work settings; and (2) increasing the likelihood that teachers will be effective and will find their work personally and professionally rewarding.

Because the work of teachers and the working conditions in schools have not been studied as extensively as other elements believed to be associated with effective schools, the suggestions offered in the next section are necessarily speculative and rather broad in scope. Nevertheless, school administrators and others concerned with leading and improving instruction are encouraged to embark on what might be called a school-based "study of practice" strategy for engaging teachers in a search for ways in which school working conditions and the work of teaching might be enhanced.

RECOMMENDATIONS FOR INSTRUCTIONAL LEADERS

The recommendations that follow seem simple and quite obvious, but the author suggests that they represent a much-neglected, yet promising set of strategies for improving schools. The goal of the strategies proposed below is twofold. The first objective is to identify and respond to matters of concern to teachers regarding their work and working conditions in their schools; the second is to cultivate a norm among teachers and administrators that places a positive value on the "study of practice" and "designing and experimenting" with strategies to improve practice.

School administrators cannot single-handedly make schools more effective. Teachers themselves are the key resource in schools, and the basic challenge for instructional leaders is to tap and cultivate teachers as vital sources of information regarding problems and strategies for enhancing their work and the general working conditions in their schools. The recommendations that follow are offered as a starting point for achieving these two objectives.

Listen

The first step for any instructional leader is to listen to the concerns of teachers. Some messages may be loud and direct, others more subdued and indirect. Frustrations may include everything from poor climate control in the building to inadequate resources to deal with problem students. Given the variety of school settings and work-environment factors, the potential list of teacher dissatisfactions and frustrations could be quite extensive.

In addition to listening to teachers' concerns about immediate work-environment factors, school leaders need to be attentive to the personal life dimensions and life-styles of faculty members. In order to attract and retain quality teachers, principals must begin to think in terms of the "whole person" when considering the work and working conditions of teachers. Schools are staffed by people who are multidimensional; work is only one component of their lives. The personal-life dimensions of employees are often overlooked or discounted in studying organizations and work improvement strategies. However, these personal-life factors may be central to teachers' employment decisions and work behavior. For example, the length of the school day and work year is viewed by many as an attractive feature of the occupation; some teachers, however, may prefer an eight-hour day and an eleven-month contract. For some teachers the typically short lunch period might be seen as a positive work feature (the price you pay for a shorter day), while those who value the opportunity to exercise or socialize with colleagues, as a way to relieve work stresses (or to meet adult affiliation needs at work), may prefer a longer lunch period. Attentive educational leaders need to consider how work factors might enhance or positively complement teachers' personal life priorities, as well as their professional life concerns.

The opportunities for gleaning information about faculty concerns are numerous. Principals will find that teachers may discuss certain kinds of issues in faculty meetings, but will share other frustrations only in a one-to-one exchange with the principal or a close colleague. Other "gripes" may be aired only in the faculty room or behind closed doors. No matter what the particular circumstance, be it through a formal or informal network, or in a group or individual setting, it is clear that the messages will be there for the principal who is attentive, "tuned-in," and listening.

Interpret

In addition to listening to teachers' messages, it will sometimes be necessary to interpret or "read between the lines" of a message. A teacher's verbal complaint of "too many children in the classroom" may really be intended to express any one of a variety of more specific concerns: "there isn't enough space for five small-group work situations"; "I can't manage, let alone *teach* this many students"; or "the teacher across the hall always seems to get fewer problem students than I do." The ability of a school principal to interpret accurately the concerns of teachers thus often requires "ferreting-out" the more covert information, and interpreting that information given his or her understanding of the individual and group dynamics of the faculty in that particular school.

Another function of interpreting teachers' concerns includes being able to see the "fit" between the type of employee and the nature of the work. While one cannot make sweeping generalizations about any occupational group, one might assume some global characteristics of individuals choosing to become teachers. For example, one could probably safely assume that persons in the teaching profession (as well as other human service occupations) typically prefer to work and be engaged with people (as opposed to machines or data only). If that assumption is correct, then one needs to consider which aspects of the work itself (i.e., teaching) may fail to meet the needs of that type of person. One of the most frequently identified characteristics of teaching as an occupational role is that most of the work is done in isolation from one's colleagues (Knoblock and Goldstein, 1971; Little, 1982; Lortie; 1975). There is very little structured time for engaging in meaningful work activities or instructional problem solving with other teachers or instructional personnel. This might be an example of the incompatibility of a feature of the structure of the work itself with the type of persons occupying or interested in entering the teaching profession.

Another example might follow from the assumption that teachers or potential teachers are individuals who want to help others or want to improve "the system" in some way. Aspects of the work of teaching that may frustrate or dishearten an altruistically oriented individual might include the complexity, uncertainty, or even contradiction of expectations felt from multiple others, as well as the "fuzziness" of the connection between multiple variables affecting student behavior and achievement (Lieberman and Miller, 1984). Initiatives by school leaders to reduce these frustrations might include simplifying and prioritizing school goals each year so that all faculty members understand and feel a shared sense of responsibility for the achievement of a few well-specified objectives. Evidence of their contribution to attained results might help teachers feel more intrinsic satisfaction from their work; that they are "making a difference" as teachers.

These are but several examples of the types of interpretation functions that might be required of instructional leaders in order for them to identify accurately problems associated with the work of teachers or with working conditions in schools. This interpretation step is critical because resolution of the "stated" problem may not adequately reduce dissatisfaction if the "true" problem goes unnoticed.

Respond

After having gathered and analyzed relevant data about teachers' concerns regarding their work or work environment, it is critical that school leaders respond appropriately, and in a timely fashion. The author's personal experience would suggest that nothing is likely to contribute to poor morale more quickly than a principal who solicits "input" and then shows no evidence of having done anything with it. Granted, no one can wave a magic wand and "make it all better." Many problems are too complex or complicated to be "fixed" easily. However, some sort of administrative response is required to keep employees from feeling a sense of hopelessness, from becoming apathetic or becoming increasingly frustrated.

While evidence of responsiveness to short-term, relatively simple and concrete problems may be visible immediately (e.g., "the page counter on the duplicating machine is working now"), evidence of responsiveness to more long-term, abstract, or complicated problems may not be so apparent. The principal may need to offer a periodic progress report to faculty concerning the resolution of more complex issues; if a problem cannot be addressed at the school level, by the principal, or if it is an issue that the principal feels must be addressed at a later date (or slowly, over a longer period), then the reasons for the delay (or perhaps a compromise decision) must be adequately explained to teachers. If this is done, it will be apparent to teachers that their voice has been heard and that the principal has made a reasonable effort to respond to their concerns.

CONCLUSIONS

Redesigning aspects of the work of teachers and the work environment in schools represent two important means by which school principals can enhance the attractiveness of choosing and remaining in education as a vocation. It was suggested that teachers themselves represent an untapped reservoir of ideas regarding ways in which the work and working conditions of teachers might be enhanced. Listening, interpreting, and responding to teachers' concerns were discussed as three key activities through which school principals could fulfill their responsibility to develop a productive and satisfied instructional staff. Schools will become more attractive and more effective as teachers begin to "study their practice" and to experiment with strategies to improve their practice.

Practices such as those discussed in this chapter represent a critical point of leverage for instructional leaders and hold much promise relative to improving school effectiveness and keeping good teachers. Teachers are the critical resource in schools, and a central dimension of the school principal's role is to attract and develop effective teachers and to provide them with the instructional materials and the work environment they need in order to perform their jobs well. While it is clearly appropriate to address some of the more specialized personnel management functions at the district level (e.g., salary and compensation policies, collective bargaining agreements, fringe benefit programs, and personnel records-keeping), managing and developing teachers is a central responsibility of the school principal. A productive and satisfied work force is the foundation for an effective school, and developing and focusing the energy and the skills of that work force are essential.

If schools cannot attract, retain, and develop enough well-qualified teachers, they are not likely to be instructionally effective. As the earlier review of teacher supply-and-demand statistics suggests, this is an immediate challenge confronting educators and policymakers at all levels. The failure to recognize and respond to the impending shortage will force administrators to hire marginally qualified instructional personnel, creating undesirable consequences for the instructional effectiveness of schools. Teachers are the key resource in schools, and by listening closely and responding to their ideas, it is suggested that school principals and superintendents can do much to make schools both more productive and more attractive places to work. Accomplishing these two goals can help school leaders meet the challenge of attracting good teachers and keeping them in the profession.

REFERENCES

Bidwell, C.E. (1965). The school as a formal organization. In *Handbook of Organizations*, edited by James G. March, pp. 972–1022. Chicago: Rand McNally.

Blase, J., and Greenfield, W.D. An interactive-cyclical theory of teacher performance. *Administrator's Notebook, 29* (5), 1981: 1–4.

Boyer, E.L. (1983). *High school: A report on secondary education in America.* New York: Harper & Row.

Bridges, E.M. (Spring, 1980). Job satisfaction and teacher absenteeism. *Educational Administration Quarterly, 16* (2), 41–56.

Bullock, R.J. (1984). *Improving job satisfaction: Highlights of the literature.* New York: Pergamon Press.

Cresap, McCormick, and Paget (1984). *Teacher incentives: A tool for effective management.* Reston, Va.: NAESP, AASA, NASSP.

Cusick, P.A. (1983). *The egalitarian ideal and the American high school: Studies of three schools.* New York: Longman.

Darling-Hammond, L. (1984). *Beyond the commission reports: The coming crisis in teaching.* Santa Monica, Calif. Rand Corporation.

Dreeben, R. (1970). *The nature of teaching: Schools and the work of teachers.* Glenview, Ill.: Scott, Foresman.

Duke, D.L.; Showers, B.K.; Imker, M. (Winter, 1980). "Teachers and shared decision-making: The costs and benefits of involvement." *Educational Administration Quarterly, 16* (1), 93–106.

Fiestritzer, C.E. (1983). *The condition of teaching: A state by state analysis.* Princeton, N.J.: Princeton University Press.

———. (1984). *The making of a teacher: A report on teacher education and certification.* Washington, D.C.: National Center for Education Information.

Futrell, M.H. (1983). Teacher excellence: An NEA perspective. In *School finance and school employment: Linkages for the 1980's,* edited by A. Odden and L.D. Webbe, Cambridge, Mass.: Ballinger.

Gallup, G.H. (1983). The fifteenth annual Gallup poll of the public's attitudes toward the public schools." *Phi Delta Kappan, 65.*

Goodlad, J.I. (1984). *A place called school: Prospects for the future.* New York: McGraw-Hill.

Griffin, G.A. (1984). The schools as a workplace and the master teacher concept." In *The master teacher concept: Five perspectives.* Austin, Tex.: Research and Development Center for Teacher Education, University of Texas, pp. 15–48.

Halstead, D.K. (1983). *Inflation measures for schools and colleges.* Washington, D.C.: U.S. Government Printing Office.

Herzberg, F.; Mausner, B.; Snyderman, B. (1959). *The motivation to work.* New York: Wiley.

Jackson, P.W. (1978). *Life in classrooms.* New York: Holt, Rinehart, & Winston.

Knoblock, P., and Goldstein, A.P. (1971). *The lonely teacher.* Boston: Allyn and Bacon.

Lieberman, A., and Miller, L. (1978). The social realities of teaching, *Teachers College Record, 80* (91), 54–68.

———. (1984). *Teachers, their world, and their work: Implications for school improvement.* Alexandria, Va.: ASCD.

Little, J.A. (1982). Norms of collegiality and experimentation: Workplace conditions of school success." *American Educational Research Journal, 19* (3), 325–40.

Lortie, D.C. (1975). *Schoolteacher: A sociological study.* Chicago: University of Chicago Press.

Miskel, C.G. (1973). The motivation of educators to work." *Educational Administration Quarterly, 9,* 42–53.

Miskel, C.G.; Feverly, R.; Stewart, J. (Fall, 1979). Organizational structures and processes, perceived school effectiveness, loyalty, and job satisfaction. *Educational Administration Quarterly, 15* (3), 97–118.

Miskel, C.G. (Summer, 1982). Motivation in educational organizations. *Educational Administration Quarterly, 18* (3), 65–88.

National Center for Education Statistics. (1982a). *The condition of education, 1982 edition.* Washington, D.C.: U.S. Department of Education.

———. (1982b). *Projections of education statistics to 1990–91, volume 1: Analytical report.* Washington, D.C.: U.S. Government Printing Office.

———. (1983). *The condition of education, 1983 edition.* Washington, D.C.: U.S. Department of Education.

National Commission on Excellence in Education. (1983). *A nation at risk: The imperative for educational reform.* Washington, D.C.: U.S. Government Printing Office.

National Education Association. (1981). *Teacher supply and demand in public schools 1980–81, with population trends and their implications for schools, 1981.* Washington, D.C.: NEA.

———. (1982). *Status of the American public schoolteacher.* Washington, D.C.: NEA.

———. (1983). *Prices, budgets, salaries, and income: 1983.* Washington, D.C.: NEA

Rosenholtz, S.J., and Smylie, M.A. (Dec., 1983). Teacher compensation and career ladders: Policy implications from research. Paper commissioned by the Tennessee General Assembly's Select Committee on Education.

Schlechty, P.C., and Vance, V.S. (Oct., 1981). Do academically able teachers leave education? *Phi Delta Kappan.*

———. (1983) Recruitment, selection, and retention: The shape of the teaching force. *Elementary School Journal, 83* (4), 469–87.

Schwab, R.L., and Iwanicki, E.G. (Winter, 1982). Perceived role conflict, role ambiguity, and teacher burnout. *Educational Administration Quarterly, 18* (1), 60–74.

Sergiovanni, T. (1967). Factors which affect satisfaction and dissatisfaction of teachers. *Journal of Educational Administration, 5,* 42–53.

Spady, W.G., and Marx, G. (1984). *Excellence in our schools: Making it happen.* Arlington, Va.: AASA and Far West Laboratories.

Sterns, R.M., and Porter, L.W. (1979). *Motivation and work behavior,* 2d. ed. New York: McGraw-Hill.

Swick, K.J., and Hanley, P.E. (1985). *Stress and the classroom teacher,* 2d. ed. Washington, D.C.: NEA.

Vance, V.S., and Schlechty, P.C. (Sept., 1982). The distribution of academic ability in the teaching force: Policy implications. *Phi Delta Kappan.*

Waller, W. (1952). *The sociology of teaching.* New York: Wiley.

U.S. Bureau of the Census, Current Population Reports. (1981). *Population profile of the United States: 1980.* Washington, D.C.: U.S. Government Printing Office.

16

Emerging Teacher Performance
Assessment Practices:
Implications for the Instructional
Supervision Role
of School Principals

CHAD D. ELLETT

INTRODUCTION

The widespread movement toward educational reform and improvement has been the predominant theme guiding American education in
the 1980s. A central focus of the reform effort has been the instructional
leadership role of building principals with a particular concern for more
direct supervision of teaching. This role definition for the school principal is certainly not new. In 1928, in his classic work on supervision,
Hubert Nutt described the function of the school principal as follows:

> The primary function of the school principal shall be to carry on an ef-
> fective program of instructional supervision in his building. He shall de-
> vote not less than two thirds of the regular school day to personal visitation
> and study of the work of the teachers in his building. . . . He shall select
> the number of teachers and the subjects which he will be able to work
> with intensively, and he shall visit each teacher not less than two full
> class periods in each subject selected during each week for a period of not
> less than four weeks. At the end of this period of intensive supervision,
> he shall select either a new group of subjects with the same teachers, or

a new group of teachers with the same subjects and continue as before. ... He shall continue this plan throughout the school year. (p. 524)

Nutt (1928) went on to describe how such a process was to be implemented and further detailed many of the elements that were later to emerge in various models of instructional supervision such as "clinical supervision" (Cogan, 1973).

Historically, those writing about the various roles, duties, and responsibilities of school principals have always placed a high degree of emphasis and importance on the instructional leadership function. A compilation and synthesis of over fifty separate descriptions of administrative responsibilities and duties of school principals by those writing on the principalship (Project Rome, 1974) identified instructional supervision and leadership as the most important responsibility. A perusal of popular texts on the principalship will also show the emphasis that writers place on the importance of instructional supervision. However, qualitative analyses of the principalship (Blumberg and Greenfield, 1986) and observation studies of principals at work (Kmetz and Willower, 1982; Martin and Willower, 1982; Peterson, 1977–78; Pool, and Hill, 1975) suggest that the modern principalship represents a myriad of complex roles and little time may actually be available for the direct supervision of instruction. The 1975 study by Ellett, et al., for example, showed that less than one half of one percent of the total work time available to seven school principals over six complete workdays was spent in curriculum and instruction activity. Thus, the professionally "preferred" role of the building principal as an instructional leader does not always match actual job performance.

While the finding that relatively little time was spent in the direct supervision of instruction by principals in the Ellett et al. study (1975) is probably as true today as a decade ago, instructional supervision on the part of school principals, nevertheless, seems to be reemerging as an important factor in facilitating positive school change. Recent syntheses of research and studies of effective schools (Block, 1983; Cawelti, 1980; Lipham, 1981; Shoemaker and Fraser, 1981; Sweeney, 1982) suggest that principals, through their instructional leadership roles, can and do make a difference in school productivity. A key assumption associated with carrying out the instructional leadership role in effective schools is that the amount of time spent in systematic observation and supervision of teaching is positively related to increased school productivity and achievement. Some reservations, however, have been expressed about the actual time available for such supervision given the complexities of the total instructional management function of the principalship (Bossert, Dwyer, Rowan, and Lee, 1982).

At the same time that research on effective schools and the instructional role of principals has begun to proliferate, a number of large-scale teacher performance assessment programs have emerged in response to public demands for increased educational accountability and reform. These programs have targeted a variety of decisions including initial and renewable teacher certification, career ladder promotions/endorsements, merit pay, employment screening, annual evaluations of teaching, and, most important, professional improvement. The states of Georgia, Florida, South Carolina, Tennessee, Kentucky, Virginia, North Carolina, Mississippi, Kansas, Connecticut, Arizona, and Texas, to name a few, have all mandated large-scale teacher performance assessment efforts which target one or more of the above decisions.

Typically, these programs require systematic collection of data about the quantity and quality of instruction through direct classroom observations of teaching. An "assessment teach" approach is usually implemented for data collection that, with few exceptions, involves the building principal from the school where a particular teacher to be assessed is employed. Each of the states mentioned above has developed, or is in the process of developing, large-scale performance assessment programs that possess the following important elements:

1. "state-of-the-art" observation instruments that measure teaching behaviors that are well documented as importantly related to school outcomes by results of process/product studies and research on effective teaching;
2. comprehensive (three- to five-day) training programs which include one or more "proficiency" tests to certify instrument users;
3. standardized assessment procedures to be followed by all data collectors;
4. on-going programs of research and development to support the technical and psychometric characteristics of the observation instruments and assessment procedures; and most important,
5. training in the use of the observation instruments and assessment data for ongoing supervision and professional development of teachers.

Literally thousands of hours (and millions of dollars) have been spent in developing these teacher assessment programs and in training observers in their use. These efforts, I believe, represent the largest investments resulting from the recent educational reform movement that have direct implications for the instructional supervision role of school principals.

The purpose of this chapter is to examine the emerging technology and measurement methodology of selected teacher performance assessment programs and practices in view of the instructional supervision role of the school principal. The content and structure of two widely used observation instruments will be explored relative to components of an expanded instructional supervision model. Findings from experiences in developing, implementing, and evaluating these large-scale assessment programs will be used to highlight important points. Issues pertinent to the impact of these newer performance assessment and supervision systems on the role of the principal will also be explored.

THE PRINCIPAL AS INSTRUCTIONAL LEADER: EVALUATOR, SUPERVISOR, OR BOTH?

One of the pervading issues in the extant writing in school administration and instructional supervision is whether the school principal, who is charged with the responsibility of evaluating building personnel, can function effectively as a supervisor of instruction. As the argument goes, the building principal is responsible for summative evaluations of teachers and should be as far removed as possible from the formative evaluation role. Most writers in supervision assume that instructional supervision is a "support" or "helping" activity designed as a service for teachers and that this role is incompatible with the school principal's (or other administrator's) responsibilities as a manager and evaluator of personnel. Oliva (1984) elucidates this conflict when he states:

> If we conceive of supervision as a service, it is difficult to see how supervisors can maintain rapport with teachers if teachers perceive them as people who control their destinies. For supervision to be successful teachers must want the services of the supervisor. They must feel that the supervisor is there to serve them and to help them become more effective teachers. (p. 43)

I suspect this issue is one that has its historical roots not only in the increasing complexities of schools as evolving organizations but in teachers' perceptions of the "credibility" of building principals to offer sound advice about improving classroom teaching performance. Certainly the role of the principal as "master teacher" has changed considerably since Nutt's (1928) description of what it ought to be. The credibility of principals as instructional supervisors and "helpers" may be, in part, a function of the quality of the evaluation instruments and procedures they are trained to use.

Recent case-study analyses of "exemplary" teacher evaluation programs administered at the local district level show that the development and use of teacher evaluation systems for both formative and summative purposes is indeed surrounded by many complex issues (Wise, Darling-Hammond, McLaughlin and Bernstein, 1984). A recent study of teacher evaluation instruments, procedures, and policies used by the one hundred largest school districts (Ellett and Garland, 1985) showed that: 1) few have comprehensive (three or more days) training programs for users; 2) most pay "lip service" to fulfilling instructional improvement purposes, but are deficient in the diagnostic structure and procedures necessary to accomplish this task; 3) few are content-valid relative to the research literature on teacher effectiveness; and 4) few had explicitly stated rules or procedures for combining formative and summative observation data.

The newest and most progressive teacher evaluation systems in use today can fulfill both formative and summative evaluation requirements and can assist building principals in meeting the demands of both sound evaluation and instructional supervision practices. A recent study of the implementation of a new teacher evaluation system designed to fulfill both purposes in a large urban school district corroborates this point of view (Performance Assessment Systems, 1983).

Recent developments in large-scale teacher performance assessment programs such as those in Georgia, Florida, and several other states have further explicated formative and summative teacher evaluation issues. These programs have also added much to the emerging measurement technology of teacher evaluation. When combined with the proliferating research on teacher and school effectiveness, these large-scale programs make timely a reexamination of the instructional supervision role of the principal. These teacher performance assessment systems more closely reflect and measure the work technology of teachers than those available as recently as ten years ago. Two factors seem to pervade this rapid change in quality. First, syntheses of research on effective teaching (e.g., Peterson and Walberg, 1979; Smith, 1983) have identified generic teaching skills that are applicable to, and can be measured in a variety of teaching contexts. The assessment of classroom management skills is a case in point. Second, our knowledge about how to establish technically and procedurally sound classroom observation systems that yield data for making both formative and summative decisions has greatly expanded in recent years. Translating these newer innovations into supervision skills for building administrators can, I believe, help change teachers' generally negative perceptions of principals' abilities as instructional supervisors. What are some of these newer teacher performance assessment systems? What are they designed to measure? How are they implemented? What are their implications for the instructional supervision role of building level administrators? These questions guide the discussion that follows.

GEORGIA'S *TEACHER PERFORMANCE ASSESSMENT INSTRUMENTS* (TPAI)

The state of Georgia has a long history of involvement in competency based education and performance evaluation. Georgia was the first state to implement a performance-based teacher certification model for beginning teachers. This model become fully operational in the fall of 1980. The implicit assumption of this model is that colleges and universities have the right to train teachers to meet institutional expectations, but the state has the right (and responsibility) to certify and license teachers.

In designing the performance-based certification model for beginning teachers, the Georgia Department of Education established three essential requirements that must be met to obtain a professional, renewable teaching certificate: 1) an appropriate degree from an approved college or university teacher preparation program; 2) a "passing" score on a criterion-referenced test of knowledge in the certification field; and, most uniquely, 3) acceptable, on-the-job demonstration of "generic" teaching skills. Thus, the ultimate concern in the Georgia model is whether a new teacher can demonstrate acceptable levels of teaching performance while teaching in a real classroom setting. Any new beginning teacher in Georgia must meet all three requirements to obtain the professional, renewable teaching certificate.

The *Teacher Performance Assessment Instruments* (TPAI) (Capie, Anderson, Johnson, and Ellett, 1980) were developed at the University of Georgia under contract with the Georgia Department of Education. Initial development of the TPAI began in 1976 with an extensive review of the literature on effective teaching, and a variety of content validation studies (Johnson, Capie, and Ellett, 1978; Johnson, Ellett, and Capie, 1981). The TPAI were subsequently field-tested and revised three times and a variety of research studies aimed at establishing validity and reliability characteristics of the instruments were completed (Capie and Ellett, 1982; Capie, Tobin, Ellett, and Johnson, 1980; Ellett, Capie, and Johnson, 1982a; Ellett, Capie, and Johnson, 1981b). The collective research base for the TPAI shows they are valid and reliable for the purposes for which they were originally designed (Capie, 1982).

Content and Structure of the TPAI

The TPAI are designed to assess fourteen generic teaching competencies. The competencies are considered "generic" since they apply to all teaching contexts. These competencies are classified within three assessment instruments: 1) *Teaching Plans and Materials* (TPM); 2)

Classroom Procedures (CP) and 3) *Interpersonal Skills* (IS). Each of the fourteen generic teaching competencies is further defined by a set of two to five performance indicators and each of these is quantified by a set of scoreable descriptors. The fourteen generic TPAI competencies used for the initial certification of teachers in Georgia are listed below. Competencies I - V comprise the TPM instrument; VI - XI the CP instrument; and XII - XIV the IS instrument.

The complete list of forty-five performance indicators that define the fourteen TPAI competencies will not be listed here. However, an example of a set of indicators for a competency and scoreable descriptors for two performance indicators are provided below.

TPAI COMPETENCY XIV: MANAGES CLASSROOM INTERACTIONS
PERFORMANCE INDICATORS

1. Provides feedback to learners about their behavior.
2. Promotes comfortable interpersonal relationships.
3. Maintains appropriate classroom behavior.
4. Manages disruptive behavior among learners.

Each of the forty-five performance indicators is scored from one to five with a set of scoreable descriptors which further operationalize each indicator statement. Sets of scoreable descriptors for two of the above performance indicators are shown below.

PERFORMANCE INDICATOR: PROVIDES FEEDBACK TO LEARNERS ABOUT THEIR BEHAVIOR.
SCOREABLE DESCRIPTORS

A. Makes expectations about behavior clear to learners.
B. Provides verbal feedback for acceptable or unacceptable behavior.
C. Provides nonverbal feedback (smiles, frowns, nods, moves closer to student, etc.) for acceptable or unacceptable behavior.
D. Uses language free of derogatory references when talking to or about learners.

PERFORMANCE INDICATOR: MAINTAINS APPROPRIATE CLASSROOM BEHAVIOR
SCOREABLE DESCRIPTORS

A. Uses techniques (e.g., social approval, contingent activities, punishment, keeps students on task, etc.) to maintain appropriate behavior.
B. Overlooks inconsequential behavior problems or none exist.
C. Reinforces appropriate behavior.

D. Maintains learner behavior that enhances the possibilities for learning for the group.

Administration of the TPAI in Georgia for Certification

The TPAI are administered by a team of trained observers. Each observer is certified as "proficient" in the use of the instruments by completing a comprehensive five-day training program and meeting a proficiency standard. The assessment team includes the building principal, a peer teacher (usually from the building in which the beginning teacher is initially employed), and a member of a regional assessment center who is not a district employee.

The teacher assessed develops a comprehensive (7–10 day) lesson plan portfolio which is independently scored by each member of the assessment team. Each assessor then conducts a full period of classroom observation of teaching relative to objectives/activities in the lesson plan portfolio. This relatively thorough assessment process is completed once in the Fall and again in the Spring until established performance standards have been met for each of the fourteen TPAI competencies. When standards have been met, the beginning teacher is issued a professional, renewable teaching certificate. Each beginning teacher has a maximum of three years to complete the process.

Implementation of the TPAI in Georgia (1980–1985): Some Observations and Findings

Georgia's performance-based certification (PBC) program was the first such program in the nation and has been used as a model for large-scale teacher assessment programs in many other states. Each year all building principals and selected assistant principals are either newly trained and certified, or "updated" in the use of the instruments. Approximately four thousand building-level administrators have been trained to complete TPAI assessments and to use the assessment data as a basis for supervision of instruction. More than twenty-five thousand assessments of teaching have occurred with the TPAI.

A number of informal and formal evaluation studies by the Georgia Department of Education and various regional assessment centers in Georgia suggest that Georgian educators believe the TPAI is an important means for improving instruction and for the professional development of beginning teachers during the initial years of employment. Thus, the PBC program and the TPAI are politically viable and practically implemented. Principals' evaluations of TPAI training sessions suggest that the TPAI are viewed quite positively as a means of reinforcing expectations for teacher performance in all contexts, for diagnosing teaching, communicating performance results to teachers, and for structuring professional improvement strategies.

In terms of actual teacher performance, approximately 65–70 percent of any cohort of beginning teachers meet the performance standards established for the TPAI during the first year of employment. Most of the "carryovers" either meet established standards during subsequent years, leave the state, or seek other employment. Analyses of statewide teacher performance data show some performance differences on the TPAI competencies when comparisons are made by college or university, school level, subject matter, and other demographic variables. The initial "pass rates" have gradually increased over the years as performance expectations have been raised.

The TPAI have also impacted the supervision of instruction for experienced teachers. Several school districts in Georgia have adopted the TPAI as a means of structuring professional improvement programs for experienced teachers based on principals' observations. Perhaps the strongest evidence of the credibility of the TPAI was the decision by the state of Mississippi in 1984 to adopt/adapt the TPAI and assessment process for implementing teacher assessment requirements of the Mississippi Education Reform Act of 1982.

Considered collectively, these findings suggest that the TPAI program has met with a high degree of success in Georgia and is a useful and widely adaptable means of assessing teacher performance and structuring professional improvement programs for teachers.

More recently, a comprehensive teacher evaluation program has been implemented in the Dade County Public Schools, Miami, Florida, which targets both formative (professional development) and summative (annual evaluation) decisions. The section that follows describes basic elements of this program and observations from initial program implementation.

DADE COUNTY, FLORIDA'S TEACHER ASSESSMENT AND DEVELOPMENT SYSTEM (TADS)

The *Teacher Assessment and Development System* (TADS) is a comprehensive program for assessing teacher performance, providing systematic feedback to teachers and structuring professional improvement activities. The TADS has been under development in the Dade County Public Schools (DCPS) since 1981. It has undergone extensive pilot and field testing and revision, and has been adapted to meet changing requirements for teacher observation/evaluation in the state of Florida. Though originally designed to improve procedures and criteria for making annual evaluations of teaching in DCPS, the TADS has also been adapted for use in DCPS to meet requirements of Florida's Beginning Teacher Program and State Master Teacher Program (merit pay).

A joint committee representing DCPS and The United Teachers of Dade (UTD) (American Federation of Teachers) worked with a variety of educators in DCPS and outside consultants to develop the TADS. The work of this committee was driven by several key concerns. Management concerns included: 1) developing greater instructional leadership skills and involvement in the direct supervision of instruction among building level administrators; 2) increasing performance requirements and expectations for all teachers; 3) providing greater diagnostic feedback for improvement in teaching; 4) consistency in teacher performance throughout the school year; and 5) more thorough and careful documentation of "unacceptable" teaching for possible personnel actions. For the teachers' union, key concerns were: 1) greater objectivity in interpretation of performance criteria and decision-making rules; 2) standardization of assessment procedures; 3) more thorough training of administrators; 4) fairness and equity in application of assessment instruments and procedures; and 5) stronger provisions for assuring due process.

The initial activity in the TADS program included developing an observation instrument to assess minimally essential, generic teaching skills applicable to all DCPS teachers in all instructional contexts. The primary summative decision was the annual evaluation of all DCPS teachers. The observation instrument was also designed to yield diagnostic information for formative evaluation purposes using data from the observation of TADS teaching behaviors and a series of supplemental "auxiliary teaching behaviors." The complete TADS program includes a comprehensive, four-day training program to certify administrators as proficient in administering the TADS and a comprehensive series of documents which specify: 1) standardized observation rules and procedures; 2) decision-making rules for combining data from multiple assessments to make annual evaluation decisions; 3) rules and procedures for placing deficient teachers on "prescription"; and 4) a prescription manual which contains suggested performance improvement activities for teachers identified as needing remediation.

The complete TADS program was pilot-tested in sixteen schools in DCPS in 1982–1983 and was expanded to a larger field test in 1983–1984. Full implementation of the assessment process with all thirteen thousand DCPS teachers began during the 1984–1985 school year. As the pilot and field test years occurred, all building-level administrators were trained to proficiency in the use of the TADS in a comprehensive, four-day program, and all received a one-day "update" training session before the 1984–1985 school year. In addition, all thirteen thousand teachers in DCPS received a standardized, multimedia orientation program to the TADS and three hundred UTD building stewards received a standardized, two-day TADS training program.

During the 1984–1985 school year an alternative, more rigorous version of the standard TADS *Classroom Assessment Instrument* (CAI) was developed to meet requirements of the Florida Associate Master Teacher Program. This program was the first among the states to use classroom observation data for the purpose of awarding merit pay increments to teachers. Thus, two versions of the TADS CAI exist. The first is designed to assess minimally essential, generic teaching skills to make formative and summative evaluation decisions and the second, the TADS-MPT (Meritorious Teacher Program) FORM, is designed to collect data for making merit pay decisions.

As the TADS and TADS-MTP FORM instruments were developed and field-tested, several research studies were undertaken to establish their reliability and validity characteristics (Performance Assessment Systems, 1984). These studies show reasonably strong support for the technical and psychometric properties of the TADS system when used for making annual evaluation decisions or when used in "merit" performance contexts (Capie, Ellett, and Cronin, 1985; Ellett and Capie, 1985a).

Content and Structure of the TADS-MTP FORM

The TADS-MTP FORM instrument was designed to assess nineteen performance indicators of teaching, reflecting four assessment categories: 1) Knowledge of Subject Matter; 2) Techniques of Instruction; 3) Classroom Management; and 4) Teacher-Student Relationships. These nineteen performance indicators are further defined by a total of eighty-two teaching behaviors. Sets of four to six teaching behaviors define each performance indicator. TADS-MTP FORM have been endorsed by educators in DCPS as important elements of teaching, observable in the classroom setting and appropriate for use in "merit" teaching contexts (Ellett and Capie, 1985b). The 19 TADS-MTP FORM performance indicators by each instrument category are listed below.

CATEGORY I: KNOWLEDGE OF SUBJECT MATTER

    A. Subject Matter Content
    B. Subject Matter Presentation

CATEGORY II: TECHNIQUES OF INSTRUCTION

    A. Matches Instruction to Learners
    B. Aids are Used to Facilitate Instruction
    C. Materials are Used to Facilitate Instruction

D. Instruction Follows an Appropriate Sequence
E. Clear Explanations and Directions are Provided
F. Directions and Explanations are Clarified When Necessary
G. Opportunities are Provided for Verbal Interaction
H. Makes Informal Assessments of Learner Performance and Progress during the Lesson
I. Information is Provided to Learners about Their Progress

CATEGORY III: CLASSROOM MANAGEMENT

A. Most of the Observation Period is Devoted to Some Form of Instruction Rather Than to Organizational Activities, i.e., Roll Taking, Distribution of Supplies/Materials, and Regrouping for Instruction
B. Attends to Routine Tasks Effectively
C. Maintains Learner Involvement Throughout the Instructional Period
D. The Teacher Uses Strategies to Prevent, Identify, and Redirect Off-Task Pupil Behavior
E. Pupil Behavior is Managed Appropriately

CATEGORY IV: TEACHER-STUDENT RELATIONSHIPS

A. Systematically Attempts to Involve All Learners in Class Activities
B. Promotes a Positive Interpersonal Environment
C. Demonstrates Warmth and Friendliness

The TADS-MTP instrument is scored by an observer checking "acceptable" or "unacceptable" for each sample teaching behavior (maximum score = 82). In arriving at these scores, observers are trained to consider how the lesson fits the larger unit of instruction, the specific lesson objectives, the sequence of lesson components/activities, contextual variables such as learner and learning environment characteristics, the number of opportunities in which a teaching behavior can be demonstrated, the effect of selected teaching behaviors on increasing student interest and involvement and on enhancing lesson objectives. If, for example, many learners who tried to contribute were ignored by the teacher, the teacher would not be scored as "acceptable" on teaching behavior number 1 for indicator G (Opportunities are Provided for Verbal Interaction) in Category II (TECHNIQUES OF INSTRUCTION).

The TADS-MTP form is a relatively thorough and elaborate teacher performance assessment system. Thus, use of the system for making important decisions such as merit pay assumes the development of an appropriate level of expertise and training so that dependable judgments can be made. When the instrument is used for supervision rather than merit pay decisions, the length of observer training can be somewhat shortened. Standard training in the TADS or TADS-MTP is from four to five full days and includes a "proficiency" check to be certified as able to make reasonably dependable judgements.

Administration of the TADS and TADS-MTP FORM in DCPS

Teacher observation/evaluation procedures in DCPS specify that observations may be announced or unannounced, depending upon the preference of the building administrator. On any observation, a teacher is required to possess a written lesson plan that meets minimal requirements (one or more objectives, one or more activities, and a way of monitoring pupil progress). After examining the lesson plan, the building administrator must observe for a minimum of thirty minutes, with the full period of a lesson being most typical.

The TADS-MTP FORM is administered in a manner similar to the basic TADS instrument. No written lesson plan is required, but a brief pre-observation interview must be held with the teacher to collect information about lesson objectives, activities, and context. Each teacher candidate is observed on two occasions: once by the building principal and once by the principal's designee. This second observer is usually an assistant principal or perhaps a principal from another building in the district. Observations of teaching are for a minimum of thirty minutes and an entire class period is typical.

Implementation of the TADS and TADS-MTP FORM instruments in DCPS (1982–1985): Some Observations and Findings

A comprehensive, four-day observer training program has been undertaken with all DCPS building administrators and selected area and district office administrators as well. Approximately twelve hundred administrators have been certified as "proficient" in the use of the basic TADS. A "turnkey" training model has also been developed and is implemented with new administrators in the district through the DCPS Management Academy. Many building principals and assistant principals have also been certified as TADS trainers and they assist the district in observer training and "update" activities. To date, more than thirty-five thousand assessments of teaching in DCPS have been made with the standard TADS and TADS-MTP FORM instruments.

During the 1982–83 pilot and 1983–84 field-test years, implementation of the TADS program was both formally and informally evaluated through: 1) meetings with administrators, teachers, and a joint DCPS/UTD TADS program committee; 2) structured interviews with teachers and administrators at the building level; 3) analyses of TADS performance data; and 4) formal surveys (Performance Assessment Systems, 1983). Results of these program evaluation efforts yielded several interesting findings. Among the most pertinent to this chapter are the following:

1. Sixty-five percent of teachers and 91 percent of administrators surveyed agreed that the TADS could improve the quality of instruction in DCPS if teachers and administrators worked cooperatively together toward this goal.
2. Almost without exception, both teachers and administrators believed the TADS to be much more comprehensive, objective, and fair than the previous evaluation instrument.
3. Ninety-one percent of teachers viewed TADS feedback during conferences as helpful; 78 percent reported that every item on the TADS was explained by administrators during formal conferences; 81 percent reported that administrators were willing to consider teacher input during conferences before making TADS decisions; and 93 percent viewed their administrators as "fair" in the use of TADS.
4. Sixty-three percent of administrators reported that they managed to hold formal conferences with teachers either the same day or the day after a TADS observation.
5. Ninety percent of administrators reported that they were willing to consider teacher input/explanation before scoring particular TADS items and 89 percent agreed that the TADS has helped teachers better understand what is expected in the classroom.
6. Eighty percent of administrators reported that the first TADS observation for teachers was "announced."
7. The number of teachers scored as "unacceptable" on the TADS at the beginning of the school year (compared to the previous teacher evaluation system) increased somewhat; but the number of teachers with unacceptable annual evaluations at year's end was similar to prior years.

These data seem to suggest that the TADS, as perceived by DCPS teachers and administrators is: 1) serving as the basis for effective supervision of instruction as carried out by building-level administrators; and 2) is viewed with a considerable degree of "credibility" by DCPS teachers. Additionally, self-reports from administrators about TADS suggest that DCPS administrators are scheduling the time to conduct relatively thorough supervision conferences with teachers based on the results of systematic assessments with the TADS. Thus, the TADS seems to be helping principals to fulfill successfully both the roles of instructional supervisor and evaluator of teaching in DCPS.

The TADS program has proven to be both practically viable and "do-able" given the professional concerns of management on the one hand, and labor on the other. Like the TPAI, administrators' and teachers' evaluations of the TADS program suggest that it is viewed quite positively as a means of reinforcing expectations for teacher performance, for diagnosing teaching strengths and weaknesses, and for structuring professional improvement activities (Performance Assessment Systems, 1984). Admittedly, the TADS program has made more demands on DCPS building administrators, some spending as much as two hundred more hours per year on instructional supervision activity than in prior years. However, administrators in DCPS have made the necessary work adjustments and are managing to implement the TADS with a great deal of integrity.

Analyses of actual TADS teacher performance data (Performance Assessment Systems, 1983) show that most teachers are managing to meet the "tougher" TADS performance standards. Interestingly, the number of teachers initially unacceptable on TADS (relative to prior years with the former evaluation system) has increased somewhat. However, the number of teachers who receive unacceptable annual evaluations is not appreciably above the number for prior years. This observation seems to suggest that the TADS is functioning as an effective supervision tool for teachers needing assistance during the school year.

IMPLICATIONS OF THE TPAI AND TADS
FOR THE INSTRUCTIONAL SUPERVISION
ROLE OF SCHOOL PRINCIPALS

Teacher performance assessment practices like the TPAI and the TADS are considerably different in complexity and quality from those that exist in most school districts today (Ellett and Garland, 1985; Wise et. al., 1984). These differences are evident in: 1) the number (and kinds) of teaching behaviors and classroom conditions measured; 2) the extensiveness of observer training required for effective use; 3) the attention given to establishing reliability and validity; 4) the widespread involvement of a variety of educators and constituencies in program development; 5) the care given to pilot testing and field trials; 6) the emphasis on using the resulting data as *the* primary basis for supervision; and 7) the extensiveness of orientation programs for teachers. These important differences and the extent to which the TPAI and TADS have been successfully used to assess and develop teaching skills, demonstrate that the technology for assisting principals in the supervision of instruction has changed in recent years.

Newer Technologies and Role Legitimacy

If "technology" can be considered a combination of the methods, processes, and materials that serve to solve particular problems, then comprehensive teacher performance assessment programs and practices like the TPAI and TADS represent technological advances applicable to the problems of instructional supervision. As newer, more innovative technologies are advanced, they usually become more "user friendly" and transportable (microcomputers are a case in point). Assessment manuals, training materials, trainers' guides, training activities, etc., for the TPAI and TADS represent highly developed, transportable technologies that can be effectively adapted/adopted to fit the instructional supervision needs of most school systems. This seems a timely development since recent evidence from studies of effective schools (Block, 1983) suggests that the instructional supervision role of the building principal is a key element of school productivity. Establishing direct links between instructional leadership skills and student achievement is admittedly difficult. However, recent research and development with these newer teacher performance assessment technologies has implications for reexamining the role of the principal as an instructional supervisor and expanding the supervision process. What has been learned? What are some of the implications of recent technological developments like those presented here?

A central issue pointed to at the beginning of this chapter was whether a school principal, charged with the responsibility of "evaluating" teachers (management function), can also fill the role of "helping" teachers (supervision function). Historically, I suspect this conflict has arisen, in part, because the available technologies for diagnosing important elements of teaching and communicating this information to teachers were sorely lacking. Principals have always been charged with responsibility for the quality of instruction; and most have held teachers accountable for the quality of instruction from the basis of "positional authority" rather than "supervisory expertise." Programs like the TPAI in Georgia and the TADS in DCPS may have changed teachers' perceptions of principals' "legitimacy" as instructional supervisors and principals' skills in supervision as well. As technologies have been developed and advanced in other professions, so has the legitimacy (and skill) of professionals utilizing them. The development and use of surgical technologies in medicine is a convenient example. Data from monitoring implementation of these two programs suggest that they can enhance the building principal's role as an instructional leader.

Both the legitimacy and effectiveness of principals as instructional supervisors in today's schools may depend upon the adaption/adoption of newer and more sophisticated technologies like the TPAI and the TADS. If the principal's functioning as an instructional leader is the key element of effective schools (Block, 1983), adopting newer technologies to effect changes in the principal's role may be one important and timely concern.

Applicability to Multiple Teaching Contexts

Performance assessment instruments like the TADS and the TPAI can be used by principals in almost all teaching contexts because they were designed to measure "generic" teaching skills. A teacher's classroom management skills, for example, are an important supervisory concern in basic skills instruction in elementary grades, middle-school physical education classes, or in the teaching of industrial arts in high school. In addition, these instruments focus on instructional "process" skills and deemphasize subject-matter knowledge. Thus, principals do not have to possess content knowledge in all areas to apply the instruments to supervision practices in their schools. Knowledge of subject matter may be helpful, but syntheses of research on effective teaching have shown process skills to have the strongest and most replicable relationships with student outcomes (Peterson and Walberg, 1979).

The TPAI and TADS were also designed to accommodate a variety of classroom context variables and to allow for some professional judgment in scoring on the part of the observer. In using these instruments, principals and other observers are trained to consider such factors as: 1) the nature of the learner (e.g., age, ability, developmental level, etc.; 2) the quantity and quality of available instructional aids and materials; 3) the specific objectives and sequence of activities in the lesson observed; 4) special classroom environment conditions that might enhance or impede the quality of instruction; 5) the frequency *and* effectiveness with which teacher performances occur; and 6) the number of opportunities a teacher has to demonstrate a particular performance.

Evidence exists (Capie, Ellett, and Cronin, 1985; Capie, Tobin, Ellett, and Johnson, 1980; Ellett and Capie, 1985) that assessments which use these instruments can be done with sufficient reliability and validity. A careful examination of individual items for the TPAI and TADS-MTP FORM instruments previously presented shows the flexibility that is desirable in using these instruments for supervision in a variety of contexts. For example, Sample Teaching Behavior 5, Indicator D, Category III (CLASSROOM MANAGEMENT) for the TADS-MTP FORM instrument states: "Efforts to redirect learners who are persistently off-task are successful ***or*** there is no persistent off-task behavior." In assessing this item, the observer must first examine what the teacher expects learner(s) to be doing, and then judge whether learner(s) are persistently off-task (momentary or inconsequential off-task behavior is of little concern). Second, the observer must examine whether the teacher attends to the behavior of off-task learners. And third, the observer must decide whether the teacher's attempts to get learner(s) back on task are successful. If no persistent off-task behavior occurs, then the teacher performance (by inference) is acceptable. This kind of methodology and scoring allows the TADS-MTP FORM and the TPAI to be applied to all teaching contexts.

Some put forth the view that the only legitimate means of reliably measuring teacher performance is through making tallies of the "frequency of occurrence" of specific teaching behaviors (Medley, Coker, and Soar, 1984). While possibly useful from a "pure" classroom research perspective, this argument does not hold well from the perspective of supervising instruction where flexibility in adjusting to classroom conditions and in making professional judgments about the quality of instruction are important concerns. Classroom conditions vary considerably within and among schools, within and among classrooms, and from one assessment/supervision occasion to the next. Thus, useful assessment systems must accommodate a variety of instructional contexts. The TPAI, TADS, and TADS-MTP instruments were developed with this goal in view.

Enhancing/Expanding the Clinical
Supervision Model: Lessons Learned

The development and implementation of large-scale assessment programs like the TPAI and the TADS have been based on the premise that assessment data should be used for the purposes of instructional improvement (formative evaluation) as well as for making summative evaluation decisions. Therefore, these programs include assessment process models in which the results of assessments are used to diagnose teaching strengths and weaknesses observed. If necessary, these data are then used to structure performance improvement programs for the teacher assessed. This assessment process is conceptually consistent with popular models of "clinical supervision." However, experience in implementing these newer technologies has implications for expanding/enhancing existing clinical supervision models.

A variety of models for the clinical supervision of teaching have been proposed (Goldhammer, 1969; Mosher and Purpel, 1972; Cogan, 1973; Acheson and Gall, 1980). Although these models differ somewhat, their basic components are the same: 1) communication with the teacher before an observation; 2) classroom observation of teaching; and 3) follow-up with the teacher after the observation. Thus, clinical supervision models reflect one-on-one approaches for working with teachers. Experiences with programs like the TPAI and TADS suggest that the clinical supervision model should be expanded to a "school-based" concept that emphasizes communicating similar performance expectations for all teachers. An expanded and enhanced model that accommodates experiences in using newer technologies like the TPAI and TADS is presented below. Each of the model components contains subelements that should be addressed when using the TPAI or TADS for supervision purposes.

The first component in this expanded model (ORIENTATION OF TEACHERS) emphasizes the importance of communicating perform-ance expectations to all teachers in a standardized manner. This can be done in many ways, but the most important element seems to be direct contact between the supervisor (in this case the building prin-cipal) and the teacher. Most clinical supervision models include a for-mal, pre-observation conference with the teacher before a classroom observation is undertaken. From a practical perspective, principals do not have time to conduct a lengthy, formal, pre-observation conference with each teacher before every observation, nor is this needed. A stand-ardized orientation program for all teachers before the supervision pro-gram is implemented is sufficient. The important elements to be addressed in the orientation program are listed above. The emphasis is on establishing clear performance expectations for all teachers in a manner that is perceived as equitable and fair. Establishing such ex-pectations and reinforcing them during the school year are important elements of administrative leadership in effective schools (Block, 1983).

The second model component (PRE-OBSERVATION INTERVIEW) is *essential* to the use of technologies like the TPAI and TADS. The purpose of this component is to assess how the lesson will be imple-mented and to establish context characteristics for the ensuing obser-vation of teaching. This component is implemented immediately prior to an observation and usually requires only a minute or two of the teacher's time. An important issue pertains to the form and thorough-ness of lesson plans. Lesson planning is perhaps the "stickiest wicket" in teacher assessment. Most schools require that teachers have plans for each lesson taught. However, the format and structure of written lesson plans varies widely. The important point for the principal as supervisor is to use the pre-observation interview to understand what the teacher plans to do during the lesson observed. Essential interview information to be collected from the teacher includes: 1) lesson objec-tives (statements from which learner outcomes can be inferred); 2) a description of teacher-centered and/or learner-centered activities and their sequence; and 3) a description of the manner in which the teacher is going to monitor learner progress during the lesson. An observer who has not first determined the "what" and the "how" of a lesson can not make reliable (or fair) assessments of teaching performance.

The observation context also needs to be established through direct communications with the teacher. Characteristics of learners, other factors that might impede the quality of teaching or pupil learning, where the lesson fits in the larger instructional unit, and explanations of unusual or unique teaching strategies or techniques are examples of information important to understanding the observation context.

The third model component (SYSTEMATIC OBSERVATION OF TEACHING) refers to the actual observation of the lesson defined through the pre-observation interview. The purpose of the observation is to make a continuous record of teacher behavior and associated classroom events. Some TPAI and TADS observers use classroom observation worksheets which contain brief "keys" to assessment items. However, the great majority simply learn to use a blank note pad.

A key issue in conducting the actual observation of teaching is the length of the observation. Experience with the TPAI and TADS shows that a minimum of thirty minutes of continuous observation is needed, with the full period of a lesson (e.g., fifty-five minutes) recommended. Three concerns are reflected here: 1) the longer the observation, the greater the sample of teaching behavior and class-room events obtained and the more reliable (and defensible) the score on the instrument; 2) some instrument items require data from events that may occur late in the lesson, for example, lesson closure and perhaps changing group size for instruction; 3) estimates of learner on-task behavior should be made throughout the entire lesson.

The observer should remain as unobtrusive as possible and should not interfere in any way with the lesson. It is important for the observer to be positioned so that estimates of learner on-task behavior, or "academic engagement," can be made by systematically scanning learners throughout the lesson. Whole class scans have been shown to be the most efficient procedure. Using a predetermined schedule (perhaps once every two or three minutes), the observer should scan the entire class and count the number of learners who appear to be off-task. This procedure is repeated throughout the lesson and a percentage of on-task behavior is then computed for the lesson. Observers will make both errors of omission and commission in assessing whether or not a particular learner is academically "engaged." However, these kinds of errors tend to balance each other in the on-task percentage estimates if a sufficient number of scans are made.

The fourth model component (POST-OBSERVATION INTERVIEW) is a short period of time (usually one or two minutes) that the observer should use to clarify observation data as needed and provide the teacher with brief, summary feedback about the lesson. Most teachers are somewhat anxious after an observation and desire immediate feedback. Very few lessons are totally negative and the observer should emphasize positive elements when providing immediate feedback. A more formal, lengthy conference to discuss the lesson in greater detail will occur later if needed.

Sometimes events occur during a lesson that are difficult to interpret, and questioning the teacher immediately after the lesson can be helpful. For example, one or more learners may have persistently raised their hands during the lesson and the teacher may have failed to recognize them. Several interpretations of this observation might be made. The teacher may have simply ignored these learners (perhaps in an attempt to modify their behavior), or the teacher may not have noticed these learners (possibly a lack of skill in monitoring learner behavior throughout the lesson). Open-ended questions during the post-observation interview have proven to be helpful in clarifying these kinds of observation data. They are also an important source of information about the teacher's awareness of learner behavior and selection of appropriate teaching strategies.

The fifth model component (INSTRUMENT SCORING/SUMMARIZING DATA) should occur as soon as possible after the observation to reduce forgetting which will naturally occur. Thus, the preferred strategy is to score an observation instrument like the TPAI or the TADS for one teacher before observing the next teacher. The TPAI and the TADS both have a response form that the observer uses to record scores for each instrument item. The observer should also make summaries of particular events from the lesson using notes taken during the observation. These summaries should reflect particular teaching strengths, weaknesses (if observed), and points of concern. It has been my experience that the more notes taken during the lesson and the more carefully summaries are prepared, the greater the legitimacy of the formal conference with the teacher that follows.

A FORMAL POST-OBSERVATION CONFERENCE to discuss the results of the observation in detail should be held with the teacher as soon as possible. Sufficient time should be planned to discuss the observation results and points of concern, and to solicit teacher input about these data. Any questionable observation data should, again, be clarified through the use of open-ended questions. When supervisory conferences are hurried, teachers usually feel the supervision process is superficial and the supervisor usually loses a great deal of legitimacy. Studies of the quality with which this important component of supervision is implemented with the TADS in DCPS shows this to be the case (Performance Assessment Systems, 1983). The post-observation conference should also be used to set performance improvement goals as needed, to establish appropriate resources and time lines for assistance, and to arrange for subsequent observation(s).

INFORMATION OBSERVATION (S)/FOLLOW-UP activities with the teacher is the final component in this expanded supervision model. Depending upon the nature of prior observation data and agreements with the teacher supervised, follow-up visits to the classroom might be announced or unannounced. Announced visits are probably preferred; however, the nature of a particular supervision problem may make unannounced visits more beneficial. Whichever procedure is used, the assessment and supervision process should not be viewed by the teacher as a "gotcha" system! Subsequent observations are considered "informal" because the supervisor may focus on only selected aspects of teaching that are problematic. Variation in the amount of time that needs to be spent in the classroom can be expected from one teacher to the next. Ideally, complete assessments with instruments like the TPAI and TADS should occur on each visit to the classroom. However, the practicalities of this procedure may vitiate complete assessments when the teacher/principal ratio is high. The number of follow-up observations and their length should, of course, be determined by the nature of the teaching deficiencies observed. Informal observations to reinforce strong teaching performances should also occur.

In comparing the TPAI and the TADS-MTP FORM for supervision purposes, it should be remembered that the TPAI was originally designed to assess a set of generic teaching competencies for the purposes of initial certification of beginning teachers. Thus, the lesson planning requirements are far more comprehensive than those required of teachers from day to day. Preparation of a comprehensive portfolio, and teaching lessons pertinent to it, may be of particular value to new beginning teachers in any school. The MTP-TADS instrument was designed to award merit pay in DCPS as part of the Florida merit teacher program. It has no formal lesson plan requirement, but users must hold a pre-observation interview with the teachers assessed to determine lesson objectives and activities that will be observed. The criterion of "effectiveness" invoked for scoring selected TADS-MTP FORM items makes this instrument somewhat more difficult than the TPAI. Both instruments, however, strongly focus on the assessment of generic teaching process skills and both were designed, along with their training programs, to be used in all teaching contexts.

SUMMARY AND CONCLUSIONS

The purpose of this chapter was to examine two emerging teacher performance assessment programs and practices in view of the instructional supervision role of the school principal. These newer, more innovative technologies have evolved from large-scale assessment programs targeting summative evaluation decisions such as certification and annual evaluation of teachers. However, these systems represent far more comprehensive diagnostic tools for the supervision of instruction by school principals than those currently used in most school districts (Ellett and Garland, 1986). Since recent research on effective schools identifies the instructional leadership role of the school principal as a key factor in school productivity (Block, 1983), use of these newer technologies can seemingly facilitate implementation of this role. Admittedly, there is some controversy over the specific nature of instructional leadership, management, and school productivity (Bossert et. al, 1982) and potential for school change (Cuban, 1984). However, benefits of using these newer teacher performance assessment systems may eventuate since they were designed to measure elements of teaching documented through syntheses of research on teacher effectiveness.

Two teacher performance assessment systems were described in detail. The *Teacher Performance Assessment Instruments* (TPAI) have been used in Georgia beginning teacher certification since 1980. The *Teacher Assessment and Development System* (TADS) has been used in the Dade County Florida school system for the annual evaluation of all teachers since the 1984–1985 school year. A variation in the standard TADS instrument, the TADS-MTP FORM, which was designed to meet requirements of Florida's Associate Master Teacher Program (merit pay), was presented. Both of these assessment systems have been used exclusively by school principals for supervision purposes and have served to increase principals' professional legitimacy as supervisors of instruction.

An expanded and enhanced clinical supervision model derived from experience with these newer technologies was described. The model was designed to accommodate several issues and concerns relative to the principal's role as an instructional supervisor at the building level. First, when comprehensive assessment systems like the TPAI and the TADS are used for supervision, teachers should be thoroughly oriented to these instruments to reinforce performance expectations. Establishing and reinforcing high expectations for performance is a key element in school productivity (Block, 1983). Second, a key element in the principal's role as a supervisor of instruction is perceived legitimacy and credibility on the part of teachers. The breadth and content focus of the TPAI and the TADS (process skills) make these instruments applicable to all teaching contexts, and the standardization of the accompanying assessment/supervision procedures increases the legitimacy of the principal as an instructional leader (Performance Assessment Systems, 1983). Third, experience with the TPAI and the TADS has shown that pre- and post-observation interviews with the teacher are important elements for making valid and reliable judgments about the quality of teacher performance and the interpretation of classroom events.

Considered collectively, the emerging technology in teacher assessment practices, research on effective schools, results of teacher effectiveness studies, and the use of these technologies in an expanded supervision model can positively impact the role of the principal as an instructional supervisor at the building level. In more simple times, the principal's primary function was instructional supervision (Nutt, 1928). These emerging technologies can, I believe, help regain that focus... a focus many see as the key to enhancing instructional quality, school productivity, and pupil learning.

REFERENCES

Acheson, K.A., and Gall, M.D. (1980). *Techniques in the clinical supervision of teachers: Preservice and in-service applications.* New York: Longman.
Block, A.W., ed. (1983). *Effective schools: A summary of research.* Arlington, Va.: Educational Research Service.
Blumberg, A., and Greenfield, W. (1986). *The effective principal.* 2nd ed. Boston: Allyn and Bacon.
Bossert, S.T.; Dwyer, D.C.; Rowan, B.; Lee, G.V. (1982). The instructional management role of the principal. *Educational Administration Quarterly, 18* (3), 34–64.
Capie, W. (1982). *Technical manual for the Teacher Performance Assessment Instruments.* Athens, Ga.: Teacher Assessment Project, College of Education, University of Georgia.
Capie, W.; Anderson, S.J.; Johnson, C.E.; Ellett, C. D. (1980). *Teacher Performance Assessment Instruments: Teaching plans and materials, interpersonal skills, professional standards, student perceptions.* Assessment manual. Athens, Ga.: Teacher Assessment Project, College of Education, University of Georgia.
Capie, W., and Ellett, C.D. (1982). Issues in the measurement of teacher competencies: Validity, reliability and practicality of Georgia's assessment program. Paper presented at the annual meeting of the American Educational Research Association, New York, N.Y.
Capie, W.; Ellett, C.D.; and Cronin, L. (1985). Assessing meritorious teacher performance: Reliability, decision-making and standards setting procedures. Paper presented at the annual meeting of the American Educational Research Association, Chicago, Ill.
Capie, W.; Tobin, K.; Ellett, C.D.; Johnson, C.E. (1980). *The application of generalizability theory to assessing the probability of misclassification with the Teacher Performance Assessment Instrument measures.* Research report. Athens, Ga.: Teacher Assessment Project, College of Education, University of Georgia.
Cawelti, G. (1980). Effective instructional leadership produces greater learning. *Thrust for Educational Leadership,* Association for California School Administrators, *9,* (3), 8–9.
Cogan, M.L. (1973). *Clinical supervision.* Boston: Houghton Mifflin.
Cuban, L. (1984). Transforming the frog into a prince: Effective school research, policy and practice at the district level. *Harvard Educational Review, 54,* no. 2, 129–51.
Ellett, C.D., and Capie, W. (1985a). Assessing meritorious teacher performance: A differential validity study. Paper presented at the annual meeting of the American Educational Research Association, Chicago, Ill.
———. (1985b). The Teacher Assessment and Development System (MTP

FORM): Instrument structure, observation procedures and content validation. Paper presented at the annual meeting of the American Educational Research Association, Chicago, Ill.

Ellett, C.D.; Capie, W.; and Johnson, C.E. (1981a). *Criterion-related validity of the TPAI: Analyses of teacher performance and pupil achievement on teacher-made tests.* Research report. Athens, Ga.: Teacher Assessment Project, College of Education, University of Georgia.

————. (1981b). *Teacher performance and elementary pupil achievement on the Georgia criterion-referenced tests.* Research report. Athens, Ga.: Teacher Assessment Project, College of Education, University of Georgia.

Ellett, C.D., and Garland, J. (1986). Examining teacher evaluation practices and policies: Results from a national survey of the one hundred largest school districts. Paper presented at the annual meeting of the American Educational Research Association, San Francisco, Calif. (In review)

Ellett, C.D.; Pool, J.E.; and Hill, A.S. (1975). A time-motion study of principals in Thomas County, Georgia. *CCBC Notebook,* 4, no. 1, 4–6.

Goldhammer, R. (1969). *Special methods for the supervision of teachers.* New York: Holt, Rinehart & Winston.

Johnson, C.E.; Capie, W.; and Ellett, C.D. (1978). *Reviews of the references relating to the content of the Teacher Performance Assessment Instruments.* Research report. Athens, Ga.: Teacher Assessment Project, College of Education, University of Georgia.

Johnson, C.E.; Ellett, C.D.; and Capie, W. (1981). *Experts' opinions studies of the Teacher Performance Assessment Instruments Report VI: Study of the revised 1979 edition of the TPAI.* Research report. Athens, Ga.: Teacher Assessment Project, College of Education, University of Georgia.

Kmetz, J. T., and Willower, D. J. (1982). Elementary school principals' work behavior. Paper presented at the annual meeting of the American Educational Research Association, New York, N.Y.

Lipham, J.A. (1981). *Effective principal, effective school.* Reston, Va.: National Association of Secondary School Principals, 1–18.

Martin, W., and Willower, D. (Winter, 1981). The managerial behavior of high school principals. *Educational Administration Quarterly,* 17, 69–90.

Medley, D.M.; Coker, H.; and Soar, R.S. (1984). *Measurement-based evaluation of teacher performance: An empirical approach.* New York: Longman.

Mosher, R.L., and Purpel, D.E. (1972). *Supervision: The reluctant profession.* Boston: Houghton Mifflin.

Nutt, H.W. (1928). *Current problems in the supervision of instruction.* New York: Johnson Publishing Co.

Oliva, P.F. (1984). *Supervision for today's schools.* New York: Longman, 2d ed.

Performance Assessment Systems (1983). *Implementation of the Teacher Assessment and Development System (TADS) in 16 pilot and selected non-pilot schools: Final program monitoring report.* Miami, Fla.: Dade County Public Schools.

————. (1984). *Development, implementation and evaluation of the Teacher Assessment and Development System (TADS) for use in the Florida meritorious instructional personnel program.* Research report. Miami, Fla.: Dade County Public Schools.

Peterson, K. (1977–78). The principals' tasks. *Administrator's Notebook,* 26(8), 1–4.

Peterson, P., and Walberg, H.J. (1979). *Research on teaching: Concepts, findings and implications.* Berkeley, Calif.: McCutchan.

Project Rome. (1974). *Competencies for building level administrators: A re-*

view of the literature in educational administration. Athens, Ga.: College of Education, University of Georgia.

Shoemaker, J., and Fraser, H.W. (1981). What principals can do: Some implications from studies on effective schooling. *Phi Delta Kappan, 63* (4), 263–67.

Smith, David C., ed. (1983). *Essential knowledge for beginning educators.* Washington, D.C.: American Association of Colleges of Teacher Education/ERIC Clearinghouse on Teacher Education, No. SP022600.

Sweeney, J. (1982). Research synthesis on effective school leadership. *Educational Leadership, 39* (5), 346–52.

Wise, A.; Darling-Hammond, L.; McLaughlin, M.W.; Bernstein, H.T. (1984). *Teacher evaluation: A study of effective practices.* Report to the National Institute of Education (R–3139-NIE). Santa Monica, Calif.: Rand Corporation.

17

Administrator In-Service: A Route to Continuous Learning and Growing

JOHN C. DARESH

There appears to be general agreement in the private sector that the world today is sufficiently complex that in-service training is not only a good idea for corporate employees, it is an essential ingredient for companies that want to remain on the "cutting edge" of their business. In fact, the predominant view is that the higher an individual goes in an organization the more valuable he or she becomes, and the more likely it is that the individual will be worth the cost of additional training to acquire new skills or sharpen old ones. In-service is seen as a wise investment, particularly in the corporate world.

This view is in direct contrast with what seems to be the rule in professional education. In schools, in-service training and professional development activities are often perceived as a "necessary evil" that is "done to" people once in a while, in much the same way that the oil in the family car must be changed every few thousand miles. In-service education is not generally viewed by teachers and school administrators as a valued and needed activity.

This state of affairs does not need to be an enduring reality of schools. There are ways of improving the overall quality of professional development for educators. The chapter begins with a brief examination of effective practices for the design and implementation of in-service training and professional development programs. Next the ways in which these ideas are reflected in current practices is summarized. Implications and recommendations for the improvement of in-service education for school administrators conclude the chapter.

CHARACTERISTICS OF EFFECTIVE IN-SERVICE
PRACTICES

In the past decade dozens of journals have published hundreds of articles on the subject of in-service education. The problem is that the majority of these reports are not based on any sound research foundation. The research that has been conducted in this area tends to be found mostly in doctoral dissertations (Daresh, 1985). Thus, we are faced with a situation described by Hutson (1981) as "deplorable," wherein hard research is meager and broad-based conceptualizations are lacking. Despite this circumstance, enough data are available to enable a number of reviewers (Lawrence, 1974; Nicholson et al., 1976; Paul, 1977; McLaughlin and Marsh, 1978; Hutson, 1981) to offer guidelines regarding the design of effective in-service education:

1. Effective in-service is directed toward local school needs.
2. In-service participants are actively involved in the planning, implementation, and evaluation of programs.
3. Effective in-service is based on participant needs.
4. Active learning processes, rather than passive techniques such as lectures, characterize effective in-service instruction.
5. In-service that is part of a long-term systematic staff development plan is more effective than a "one-shot," short-term program.
6. Effective local school in-service is supported by a commitment of resources from the central office.
7. Effective in-service provides evidence of quality control and is delivered by competent presenters.
8. Programs that enable participants to share ideas and provide assistance to one another are viewed as successful.
9. In-service programs are effective when they are designed so that individual participant needs, interests, and concerns are addressed.
10. Rewards and incentives, both intrinsic and extrinsic, are evident to program participants.
11. In-service activities are provided during school time.
12. Effective in-service is accompanied by ongoing evaluation.
(Daresh and LaPlant, 1984)

The assertions noted above are rather general, but nevertheless serve as a useful set of guidelines to be considered in designing, developing, and implementing an effective in-service program. Other elements related to effective in-service have been identified by Sprinthall and Thies-Sprinthall (1983), and O'Neal, Estes, and Castleberry (1983), and much can be gleaned from a growing knowledge-base regarding adult learning (Zemke and Zemke, 1981). Rossmiller (1984) describes a number of these and related elements associated with efforts to use continuing professional development programs to improve educational practice:

Collaboration between participants and program sponsors— Building or district-wide professional development councils can foster collaboration and cooperatio: in planning effective in-service programs.

Learning needs are identified by participants—Professional development programs responsive to the needs of participants will maximize the probability of success. A comprehensive assessment of needs should be undertaken before planning specific programs.

Programs are offered at convenient locations—Sites are easy to get to.

Intrinsic and extrinsic rewards are provided—Extrinsic rewards could include certificates, enhanced promotional opportunities, or increments in pay. Intrinsic rewards are derived by gaining competence (self-esteem) or success (self-actualization).

Modeling by experts of skills and concepts—Demonstrations by skillful practitioners should be an integral part of professional development programs.

Utilization of participants' talents and abilities—Independent study, role-play exercises or presentations by participants can be used to draw upon their talents and abilities.

Synthesis of content and adaptation to diverse situations—Case analyses, site visits, or guided group discussions may be employed to achieve synthesis of content and to explore its adaptation to diverse situations.

Learning activities should be individualized—Small group discussions, private counseling, or case studies written and analyzed by participants may be useful.

Significant and challenging role-taking experiences—Role-play can be an integral part of many professional development programs, particularly those dealing with interpersonal relationships or instructional procedures.

Opportunities for reflection—Time for reading and reflection is essential; programming must provide time for this to occur.

Continuity and logical sequencing of activities—All presentations and activities should be carefully planned and coordinated to build on previous learning.

Both personal support and personal challenge—Participants grow through confrontation with challenges; they must have freedom to try, to fail, and to try again without penalty.

Assessment of results—The program should be evaluated in terms of its objectives which might be cognitive, affective, or psychomotor development, or a combination thereof.

(Rossmiller, 1984)

It is clear that a knowledge of useful and effective practices regarding in-service education and professional development is available. However, school districts and other agencies engaged in those activities too often tend not to be responsive to the practices and guidelines noted here. As a consequence, in-service training efforts are not as effective as they might be, and the attitudes of teachers and school administrators toward the whole issue of continuing learning and professional development frequently are negative. The writer believes that part of the reason for the rather sad state of affairs regarding in-service training of professional educators can be attributed to the nature of the in-service and professional development models that have traditionally served the field. These are discussed briefly in the next section.

CURRENT IN-SERVICE PRACTICES

A review of the literature suggests that there are discernible categories of in-service programs or activities (Daresh and LaPlant, 1984). Brief descriptions of these models and several of their respective strengths and weaknesses are discussed next. The five models noted here are not the only alternatives in use, but they appear to be those used most extensively, and because they are embedded in and supported by a variety of suprastructures (professional associations, state education agencies, and universities in particular), it is likely that these models will dominate the administrator in-service scene for the foreseeable future. This trend may change as local school boards and superintendents raise their expectations for school leaders and as they place a greater value on the importance of professional development as an antidote to administrator obsolescence.

Traditional Model

The traditional model is represented by administrators enrolling in credit courses at colleges and universities, and is the most frequently employed strategy for professional development. This model represents an efficient way to provide information to practitioners in areas of particular professional interest, to obtain advanced degrees, and to renew or upgrade administrative certificates.

A major strength is that the content of university courses is generally the product of advanced planning by a qualified educator. A drawback, however, is that such courses rarely reflect participant involvement in selecting objectives, designing course formats, or selecting learning activities. Meeting the specific in-service and professional development needs of participants is not, after all, the major goal or focus of graduate study. University courses tend to be excellent ways for participants to earn graduate degrees, to satisfy scholarly curiosity, or to meet state certification standards. However, as long-term solutions to the need for effective administrator in-service, they present definite problems and limitations.

Institutes

Another popular model is the institute; a short-term topic-specific learning experience. Institutes—or workshops and seminars are they are frequently called—have a number of commendable features. They tend to address the real and immediate concerns of most practitioners, even though participants are not usually involved directly with the design of the institutes. An enormous variety of such short-term training programs are available to administrators. Professional associations, state departments of education, and numerous other agencies tend to bombard the field with offers of programs; just about any administrator will be able to find something of interest. However, the short duration of most institutes is disadvantageous in that institute participants receive only limited treatment of important issues. Short-term training events such as institutes too often are viewed as "quick-fix" solutions to individual developmental needs or school improvement goals that require in-depth training and more long-term commitment by participants.

Competency-Based Training

In its broadest sense, competency-based administrator training can provide a useful framework of knowledge, attitudes, and skills toward which an effective school leader may strive. There are currently some competency-based programs with great potential for use as an administrator in-service strategy. One good example is the Assessment Center of the National Association of Secondary School Principals (Scmitt, 1980). Competency-based programs assume that when skills are identified, in-service can be directed toward the attainment of those skills. Competency-based programs offer administrators the chance to work toward professional development in a more focused way than the sporadic efforts associated with institutes and university courses. Also, because of the heavy involvement of the administrators' professional associations, motivation to participate comes from colleagues and not external agencies.

However, competency-based programs have some drawbacks. Competency frameworks have the tendency to foster "recipes for effectiveness," i.e., if an administrator successfully completes a series of prescribed learning tasks, he or she will be an "effective" school leader. Another limitation is the availability of appropriate training processes and expertise to deliver the targeted competencies. It is not clear who would lead administrators toward increasing their decisiveness, stress tolerance, sensitivity, or any other skill. Questions such as these need to be answered before competency-based approaches will be able to achieve their full potential.

The Academy

Another approach to professional development is found in the relatively recent emergence of the in-service academy, an arrangement wherein a school district or state education agency provides structured learning experiences to administrators on an ongoing basis. The classes and courses that are offered are changed periodically to reflect different needs and interests of probable participants; content is based on needs-assessments conducted at the local or state level. A major advantage of the academy is that it is a stable and structured strategy that tends to be based very directly on the specified needs and interests of participants. However, an important disadvantage to this model is that most of the instruction is based on one-way communication. Another disadvantage is that in the effort to ensure that academy course offerings are relevant to participants, the focus of the curriculum tends to emphasize the "here and now." Thus the basic limitation is that they may ultimately represent little more than a protracted institute.

Networking

Networking refers to formal and informal associations of individuals in different schools or districts for the purpose of sharing concerns and effective practices on an ongoing basis. In networking, the primary responsibility for controlling learning experiences resides with participants themselves, not with universities, professional associations, or state education agencies. Individuals who share common problems are able to come together periodically to gain support from colleagues and also to gain additional insights from others who face similar problems. However, it is not unusual for a network originally established to deal with school-related concerns to shift its focus and to become a social rather than a professional gathering. There also is a tendency for networks to become so informal and so loose-knit that members drop in and drop out of the group. Too often there is not long-term commitment by participants to the network as an instrument of continuing professional development.

IMPLICATIONS

Bluntly stated, teachers, administrators, and other educational personnel will probably not engage in professional development activities,
regardless of their quality, if there are not clear signals within the local
school district to the effect that it is an expectation in that system
that in-service education be undertaken. Superintendents will not feel
at ease in pursuing ongoing learning activities if the board of education
does not indicate its pleasure in seeing such behavior. In similar fashion, principals will not take in-service seriously if superintendents do
not visibly promote that activity.

In recent years it has become a widely accepted "good" idea for
the superintendent to participate in in-service training sessions for
district principals. Such an approach provides the type of implicit endorsement of professional growth what will encourage people to engage
in such learning activities. In short, while one can argue long and loud
about intrinsic values that may be gained through participation in
professional development programs, no words will speak as loudly as
those that are spoken or demonstrated by "the boss."

Even in situations where there are few resources available to support in-service directly, when administrators are made aware that
growth and continued learning are viewed in their district as expectations of normal performance, involvement in professional development will likely occur. Several implications regarding organizational
supports and policies on in-service education are discussed next.

Organizational Support

It is tempting to reduce the whole argument regarding the importance
of organizational support to the demand for more dollars. Unquestion-
ably, there is some validity to the idea that, when it comes to in-service
education, "You only get what you pay for." Realistically, it is not
likely that school districts will be able to afford spending huge sums
of money for the purpose of providing continuing education for school
principals, particularly when there is frequently a shortage of funds for
basic salary adjustments. It is too simplistic to suggest that more
money pumped into in-service programs will be enough to guarantee
their success.

Financial support for professional development is as much a values
commitment and orientation by the organization as it is an actual case
of spending money per se. What is needed is the regular commitment
of dollars in a predictable way to ensure that principal in-service is a
normal part of what goes on in a school system. It may not mean a
large amount of dollars, but it is important that support for professional
development become a continuing priority, much like the practice of

allocating a regular part of the general fund for the replacement of instructional materials or repair of furniture. This type of *normalization of support for in-service* should have the eventual effect of reducing the complaint that helping principals is "stealing money from students." When any practice becomes part of standard operating procedures it tends to be much more acceptable.

A second type of organizational support needed to establish a facilitative environment for principal in-service is intellectual, or conceptual, support. Individuals must be *aware of the value and need for principal in-service* and, moreover, must be alert to ways in which it can be improved. School districts cannot treat administrator in-service as a peripheral activity that is carried out sporadically to meet momentary problems faced by the organizations. Allocating continuous intellectual and conceptual talent toward monitoring in-service programs lowers the chances that such training is reduced to something that is casually tossed together to help principals deal with immediate crises. Someone must be in a position to oversee a long-term developmental agenda that will serve as an organizing framework. Time and talent in the school system must be devoted to thinking about and working toward a vision of desirable principal performance. In addition, the in-service process must be monitored to determine if progress is truly being made toward improvement. If in-service is consistently relegated to external consultants or left solely in the hands of principals, organizational commitment and support are lacking.

A third form of organizational support is *the provision of adequate time* for administrators to engage in in-service activities. Is the improvement of executive skills of sufficient value to the school district that time is regularly allocated to in-service activities? Is time provided during the normal workday? It is one thing to tell principals to go out after the workday or during the summer to take courses or attend workshops on their own. Quite a different commitment is implied when the superintendent indicates to his or her principals that they are not expected to be in their buildings on one day each month so that they may engage in professional growth activities. In this latter instance, the district is making a very strong statement as to the importance of in-service. Such practices can lead to the creation of new operational values and norms that suggest that it is good to engage in professional development, and that a person will be commended when he or she participates in in-service and takes responsibility for personal growth and learning.

Modification of Policies

Policy-makers at every level need to find ways of supporting and promoting professional development. Consider, for example, the ways in which state education agencies, local school districts, and universities—three groups with a direct stake in the training of school administrators—might change in order to encourage more effective in-service.

Most states have a practice of requiring administrators to validate and upgrade their licenses from time to time. For the most part, such requirements may be satisfied through the completion of university credit courses or selected workshops which grant continuing education units (CEU). There is nothing wrong with this basic approach, even though it does tend to assume that learning is best achieved through only two of the generic models—the traditional model and institutes. Collecting an additional six, nine, or twelve CEU or semester hours of university credit during a fixed period of time is an easy way to keep track of people on paper, but such a strategy encourages a disconnected approach to administrator in-service.

Professors who field questions such as "What courses are offered next semester that I haven't already taken?" are well aware that many practitioners give little serious thought to the nature of their professional development. A more enlightened practice might be for administrators who need additional in-service to specify their long and short-range career and professional goals and describe how those objectives can be met. The function of the state agency might then be to review that plan to determine the extent to which recertification objectives can be met as a result of the individual's proposed professional development plan. A *strong commitment to improving the quality of educational leadership* in a state might justify the shifts in intraorganizational policies and priorities that would be necessary to support more individualized treatment of principals and other administrators.

Local school districts have the opportunity to examine and perhaps modify existing policies as a way to promote more effective and positive in-service for administrators. If there is no *deliberate value expressed for continuing growth and learning* in the established job descriptions or role expectations for administrators, it should not be surprising when they express little or no interest in professional development. Another shift in local school district policy could occur at the point of initial screening and hiring of principals. Rarely is there a strong selection criterion addressing a candidate's prospects for continuing to learn while on the job. Given the technological advances and information explosion that have occurred this past century, and that are expected to continue at an ever-increasing pace, such a criterion seems especially warranted. School administrators need to keep pace with such changes, and will need to engage in continuous learning of new knowledge and skills if they expect to avoid obsolescence.

Historically, departments of educational administration have defined their teaching function almost exclusively in terms of preservice preparation. Except through the use of conventional courses for credit, universities have generally not done much to promote in-service education. With the exception of a few cases, in-service support by colleges of education has largely been confined to individual faculty occasionally serving local administrator groups on a consultative basis. Few colleges or departments have deliberately and consciously defined in-service support to the field as part of their mission. Notable exceptions are the emergence of summer institutes and principal "centers" such as those at Harvard University, Vanderbilt University, and the "LSU Advance" program at Louisiana State University. These are promising developments and provide good examples of the ways in which universities can be responsive to the training and development needs of school administrators.

Principal in-service, no matter how valuable it may seem to participants or how effective it might be in promoting more effective practice, will never succeed for very long without a *serious commitment of support* from the organizations with a vested interest in the professional development of principals. These organizations would certainly include local schools, universities, and school districts, and perhaps other organizations in the surrounding community, such as banks and business corporations. These organizations need to work together to create a facilitative environment that would ensure not only that effective in-service is started, but that such efforts are *sustained*. There is nothing so frustrating as having a good idea get off the ground, only to crash shortly thereafter because it did not receive the type of support that could have kept it alive. An environment created to support continuing professional development for administrators is possible; discovering ways of providing the financial, intellectual, and other material resources needed to increase the probability that effective in-service will occur is an important responsibility of school superintendents and Boards of Education.

RECOMMENDATIONS

Assuming a greater commitment by school districts regarding the value of administrator in-service, and that policies can be changed to promote a more facilitative environment for continuous learning and professional development, what are some of the alternative practices that might be tried? A few proposals for new directions in administrator in-service are offered in this concluding discussion.

One thing that needs to be done is to develop and experiment with new models for delivering in-service support. Better alternatives are undoubtedly possible. For example, little has been done to examine how administrator continuing education has been carried out in other settings. How are managers in private industry kept alive and active in their jobs? Periodic job exchanges where school administrators spend a day or two each month in private industry, and thus learn about new and different approaches to management, is an alternative that seems promising.

Another idea that holds promise is the sharing and analysis of professional case histories, an approach currently being utilized in the Apex Principals' Center at the University of Illinois (Silver, 1986). Principals and other administrators write short reports that identify and diagnose actual problems, including descriptions of how they responded to the problem and the effectiveness of their response. These reports are collected and made available to other participants.

A fourth practice is to make participation in professional development a more valued activity in school districts by linking it more directly to district priorities. One way that this might be accomplished is for administrators, as part of their normal annual goal and work statements, to negotiate with the district for in-service arrangements, released time, and financial support that might be based on the attainment of specific job targets and productivity goals. The aim of such a practice is to make the connection between effectiveness and continuous professional development explicit, and to provide administrators with incentives to engage in such activities as a regular part of one's work.

Districts might also encourage more focused approaches to administrator and school evaluation. In-service programs could be based on specific goals and objectives for improvement derived from assessments of administrator performance and evaluation of school programs. Another activity could be the creation of programs to counsel administrators at critical points in their careers. A major problem which now exists is that it is virtually impossible to know what administrative work is like before one actually enters such a role; individuals assuming such positions may find that they are unhappy or unsuited for the role, but stay on because they feel there is no way out. It is difficult to "admit defeat" and move back to the classroom—both in terms of financial considerations, and also because of personal pride.

Developing a system wherein consultative help is available to administrators, particularly those first entering the field, may be one way to reduce this problem. Another advantage of such career counseling services is that they would permit more individualized treatment of administrator training and development needs on an ongoing basis. A finding of nearly every study of effective in-service processes is that in-service works best when it takes into account the individual differences among learners—beginners have different needs than do those approaching retirement. Unfortunately, the majority of programs now available still treat educators as if they all had the same kinds of training needs. Individual counseling for professional development can greatly increase the likelihood that administrators' needs will be diagnosed in a timely and appropriate fashion.

The recent emergence of state-sponsored administrator academies in at least seventeen states is a strong indication that professional development for school leaders is gaining recognition as an important responsibility of state education agencies. More can be done in this area. One of the most important things that state departments can do is to provide sufficient financial resources to enable local school systems to engage in development activities. It is commendable, for example, that state departments are investing dollars for centralized in-service academies for all administrators in the state. However, this support must be extended to provide local school districts with the resources needed to conduct activities that are designed to support local priorities.

Different forms of state support might include block grants to local districts to encourage in-service activities, or stipends to districts to cover all or part of administrators' salaries so that they could engage in periodic short- or long-term professional leaves. At present, such opportunities are available occasionally to administrators in only a few districts, but usually only to support formal graduate studies. There is something quite valuable in the practice of letting executives get away from their desks from time to time, regardless of whether a graduate degree is to be earned or not.

One area where the research skills of university professors are now being utilized with greater frequency is in the ongoing analysis of the real world of work of school administrators (Peterson, 1986). There is a logic to the notion that the first step to providing better in-service is to understand more about the work of school administrators. Research conducted by school personnel and university professors can be helpful in identifying problems of practice that administrator in-service programs might address. Another way in which universities can engage more actively and effectively in the administrator in-service arena is to cooperate more frequently with other actors in the in-service process: state education agencies, local districts, and professional associations. The key is to build upon the mutual self-interests of individuals and groups to form alliances and partnerships capable of addressing the larger issues. Is the goal of university preparation programs to "get students into classes," or is it to improve administrative practice?

CONCLUSION

The basic theme in this chapter is that, despite the field's attempts to provide effective administrator in-service, most efforts have not been terribly successful. This is a bit puzzling because we have a reasonably useful knowledge base in the areas of in-service education and adult learning. Unfortunately, we are not using much of that knowledge. Furthermore, it was suggested that attention needs to be given to developing a real commitment from local districts and other agencies regarding the value of in-service education for educational administrators. Organizational supports for in-service education need to be cultivated, and local and state policies need to be examined to determine where modifications may facilitate more effective in-service practices. Administrators are important people in terms of supporting quality educational programs. Because of that importance, ways to keep them alive, learning, and growing as professional educators are needed. If schools are not alive at the leadership level, it is likely that little growth will take place at any point in the organization.

REFERENCES

Daresh, J. C. (1985). Status of research on administrator in-service. *National Form of Educational Administration and Supervision. 3*, 23–31.

Daresh, J. C., and LaPlant, J. C. (1983). In-service for school principals: A status report. *Executive Review. 3.* 1–8.

———. (1984). The status of research on administrative inservice. Paper presented at the meeting of the American Educational Research Association. New Orleans.

Donaldson, G. A. (1982). Rx for school leadership: The Maine Principals' Academy. *Phi Delta Kappan, 63*, 402.

Hoyle, J. R. (1983). *Guidelines for the preparation of school administrators.* Arlington, Va: American Association of School Administrators.

Huddle, E. W. (1982). A Maryland program for the professional development of school principals. *Phi Delta Kappan, 63*, 400.

Hutson, H. M. (1981). Inservice best practices: The learnings of general education. *Journal of Research and Development in Education, 14*, 1–10.

Knowles, M. S. (1970). *The modern practice of adult education.* New York: Association Press.

LaPlant, J. C. (1979). *Inservice education for principals.* Dayton, Ohio: Charles F. Kettering Foundation.

Lawrence, G. (1974). *Patterns of effective inservice education.* Tallahassee, Fla.: Florida Department of Education.

McLaughlin, M. P., and Marsh, D. D. (1978). Staff development and school change.*Teachers College Record, 80*, 69–94.

Nicholson, A. M.; Joyce, B. R.; Parker, D. W.; Waterman, F. T. (1976). *The literature on inservice teacher education: An analytic review* (ISTE Report III). Washington, DC: U. S. Office of Education.

Paul, D. A. (1977). Change processors at the elementary, secondary, and post-secondary levels of education. In *Linking processes in educational improvement*, edited by J. Culbertson and N. Nash. Columbus, Ohio: University Council for Educational Administration.

Peterson, K. D. (1986, Summer). Principals' work, socializing and training: Developing more effective leaders. *Theory Into Practice, 25*, 3.

Silver, P. A. (1986, Summer). Continuing professional development for administrators: A reflexive practice approach. *Theory Into Practice, 25* (3).

Epilogue

With reluctance, I finish reading this book. Contrasting images remain in my mind. The story of the successful high school principal who spends three hundred hours a year in observations of teachers can be contrasted to the story of another principal who spends little time in the classroom and instead attends mostly to the broader affairs of school and community. The image that effective schools have "great" leaders can be contrasted with the story of the school where innovative leadership is viewed as historically tied to social and political forces outside the school. Accounts of the critical role of the principal in school change contrast with an account of the potential role of central office personnel in school change, and a compelling view of the role of teachers as important decision makers in contributing to the school improvement process. Descriptions of how working with teachers in collegial and facilitating ways can improve schools stand in stark contrast to the view that teachers need to be objectively and systematically controlled and evaluated in order for schools to be become better.

It is easy to discount the lessons embedded in these contrasting images with statements like "one image is true and the other is false" or "there is some truth in of all these images." Such views avoid the tough questions: Can research provide evidence that instructional leadership consists of discrete skills, particular practices, or certain forms of knowledge? Can different skills, practices, and knowledge be equally successful? To answer such questions with a simple yes or no or to suggest there is a place for all types of endeavors belies the complexity of schools and the nature of leadership in schools.

In the world of social interactions with people, we know from our experiences that behaving similarly with different persons often results in varied reactions on the part of those individuals. We know, again from our experiences, of leaders who were successful in one school and were literally destroyed in another school. Experientially then, we know that uniform and consistent actions across different situations and people are not always effective. Those who aspire to lead schools may be frustrated by research findings that suggest there is not a single best way of leading.

There are multiple ways of leading schools well, and that which is most effective in one circumstance, or for one leader, may be ineffective, perhaps inappropriate, in a different school. While such an answer unhooks us from being technicians to someone else's prescriptions, it also leaves us without much of a guide to action. As a school principal, I truly wanted to know what to do, and for some "expert" to tell me that there was no sure answer created contempt in my eyes for their practical value to me. Without this hoped-for guidance on "correct" ways of proceeding, I was left only with my belief that somehow, someway, I could be successful as a school leader.

How do we resolve the dilemma that while there are no fixed answers, there are ways of leadership that are better than others? Lewin (1935) helped with this dilemma years ago by explaining that behavior, or how we choose to act, is a function of the person's interaction with the environment. The school environment in which we work is shaped by many factors, including individual teachers, groups of teachers, physical space, history, norms and values of the work place, community demographics, system-wide policies, superior's priorities, school board sanctions, and political influences of the community and larger society. The organizational culture and other features of schools, school systems, and aspects of the school community can enhance or restrict leader behavior and can explain why some leaders are more successful than others.

The situation can indeed help to determine the success of leadership. However, contingency and situational theories of leadership are not by themselves an adequate explanation of how we choose to act. They provide no guidance regarding the moral question of what a leader should do, nor do they help us explain the meaning of leadership in schools.

The individual who wants to know what to do must build his/her own theory of action in a particular situation. The situation does not dictate the theory but instead, the individual's own values and goals become the criteria for responding to the situation. What we believe about the aims of education, what we believe about teachers, and what we believe about our own mission becomes the filter by which we judge leadership practices. The contents of this book thus help us with the question of whether certain ways of operationalizing leadership help us to accomplish our goals. Yet, while research and experience help us see the connections between actions and outcomes, they cannot select our goals for us. In this regard, values and beliefs become central.

The contrasts of leadership as described in research and practice in this book are ultimately contrasts in desired goals and values of leadership and aims of education. Doing frequent observations can be a successful practice when a leader views his/her mission as actively promoting a dialogue of instruction in his/her school. Concentrating one's time in the community can be a successful leadership practice when a leader sees education as primarily the linkage of learning between school, home, and community. The leader who believes in the importance of uniform and consistent teaching will find that shaping staff inservice, developing prescriptive curriculum, and evaluating teachers can be successful practices. The leader who believes in the collective wisdom of others will find that practices of action research and teacher leadership teams can be effective strategies. Effective leadership involves purposeful action shaped by the constraints and opportunities at hand in a given situation and, as importantly, shaped by one's beliefs, values, knowledge, and skills.

This book drives home the point that every person can be his/her own theorist, that one can consider, select, and screen research and advice, and that one can accomplish his/her own goals. In this sense, leadership can be likened to a craft where knowledge, skills, and practices are of little use unless there is a functional purpose to one's work. However, one who aspires to craft or to lead is at a loss if he/she has a functional purpose but lacks the knowledge, skills, or practices to work toward or to achieve that end. Therein lies the value of research and experience.

As the cognitive psychologist Sternberg (1985) has noted, in the real world of decision making we often deal with problems that are unclear, messy, create unanticipated consequences, and do not have a single answer. It is when we realize that most problems of school leadership are that way that we open our minds to looking for our own answers rather than someone else's. This book has helped to open our minds to the complexity and beauty of working with people in school settings. Sternberg further noted that decisions made in the real world are often made without full information about the problem or the actions that could be taken. We will never have all the information about leadership needed for every decision, but this book has provided more of it and, as a result, our future decisions should be more intelligent.

My friend tells me the story of when he asked a small child to describe the world. The child looked up at him and said, "Well, the world has grass, trees, and clouds." The child paused for a second and then said "Uh, I think I left something out." Well, after reading this book, we know that the world of instructional leadership has more than grass, trees, and clouds. It has individual blades of grass, forests of vegetation, and restless seas; a core of soil, sediments, and gases to undergird it; and a vast sky of hemispheric layers that reach out into an awesome universe. We still have left something out, but we now know more about our world.

Carl D. Glickman

REFERENCES

Lewin, K. (1935). *A Dynamic Theory of Personality*. New York: McGraw- Hill.
Sternberg, R. J. (1985). Teaching critical thinking, Part 1: Are we making critical mistakes? *Phi Delta Kappan, 67*(3), 194–198.

DATE DUE